Debating
Women

RHETORIC AND PUBLIC AFFAIRS SERIES

DEBATING WOMEN

GENDER, EDUCATION, AND
SPACES FOR ARGUMENT, 1835–1945

Carly S. Woods

MICHIGAN STATE UNIVERSITY PRESS • *East Lansing*

Michigan State University Press
East Lansing, Michigan 48823–5245

Printed and bound in the United States of America.

27 26 25 24 23 22 21 20 19 18   1 2 3 4 5 6 7 8 9 10

LIBRARY OF CONGRESS CATALOGING-IN-PUBLICATION DATA
Names: Woods, Carly S. author.
Title: Debating women : gender, education, and spaces for argument, 1835–1945 / Carly S. Woods.
Description: East Lansing : Michigan State University Press, 2018. | Series: Rhetoric and public affairs series
| Includes bibliographical references and index.
Identifiers: LCCN 2017055642 | ISBN 9781611862959 (pbk. : alk. paper) | ISBN 9781609175757 (pdf)
| ISBN 9781628953381 (epub) | ISBN 9781628963380 (kindle)
Subjects: LCSH: Public speaking for women—History—19th century.
| Publicspeaking for women—History—20th century. | Debates and debating—United
States—History. | Debates and debating—Great Britain—History.
Classification: LCC PN4192.W65 W66 2018 | DDC 808.5/1802—dc23
LC record available at https://lccn.loc.gov/2017055642

Book design by Charlie Sharp, Sharp Des!gns, East Lansing, MI
Cover design by Erin Kirk New
Cover image of the Penn State Debaters, Winners of the Delta Sigma Rho Tourney, Pittsburgh 1935 is from
"Debate Scrapbook, 1935–1957," Pennsylvania State University Department of Speech records, 1925–2007 (1359);
and is used with permission from the Eberly Family Special Collections Library, Penn State University Libraries.

Visit Michigan State University Press at *www.msupress.org*

To Alexandra and Damien

Contents

———•◆•———

Preface

—·◆·—

In 1861, a degree-granting women's college was founded in New York's Hudson Valley. From its inception, the Vassar Female College sought to create an educational environment for women that would parallel what was available for men in the 1860s.[1] However, it also had to carefully navigate gendered expectations of the period. A prospectus for the institution, intended to guide the all-men board of trustees, asserts that women should strive to be "as intelligent as a man, as broad in the range of her information, as alert and facile (if less robust) in her use of her faculties . . . but her *methods* should be all her own, always and only *womanly*."[2] In other words, women's "special place" in society ought not be obscured by higher education. What were these womanly methods? At Vassar, students would learn the arts of conversation, letter writing, and recitation, for these activities were ones that could be undertaken in a suitably feminine manner. Debating, however, could not.[3] The students would be encouraged to express their convictions in conversation at social gatherings and in voluntary societies, yet debating societies, "so appropriate and useful in a school for young men," were to be considered "utterly incongruous" and "out of taste in one for young ladies."[4] To label something "incongruous" is to point out an improper or inharmonious pairing, where one element simply does not belong. It is literally "out of place."[5] Although it was expressed here with particular panache, this declaration was far from idiosyncratic. The Vassar prospectus simply articulated a sentiment that has long haunted debating women: whether justified through the argument that they were not suited to activity or that the activity was not suitable for them, women have been consistently told they are "out of place" and "out of taste" in debate.[6]

The implications of this gendered anxiety are far-reaching, for debate is a symbolic enactment of the greatest dreams and the greatest fears of public life. The decision to debate is one imbued with optimism about the potential to hear the voices of others and to have one's voice heard. It plays a hallowed role as a performance of democratic participation for elected officials and citizens.[7] Debate is built into the structure of governance in both houses of the British parliament. A commitment to debating was integrated into the American colonies, and sown into the fabric of the early republic.[8] In the United States and the United Kingdom, citizen-organized debating clubs flourished as forums for education, entertainment, and self-improvement. Student-led debating societies developed as significant extracurricular undertakings in institutions of higher learning during the nineteenth and twentieth centuries. From political debates to deliberation at town hall meetings, democratic societies continue to value the ability to come into communicative contact with others, exchanging ideas, refining opinions, and expressing citizenship through the process of argumentation. At its best, debating allows individuals to gain and express knowledge, to acquire portable skills, and to share in decision-making on civic matters.

At its worst, however, debate is not about quality argumentation at all. It functions as a practice for those with power to further exercise their power. Adversaries meet to air their opinions in zero-sum competition with little regard for advancing collective knowledge or shared decision-making. We groan at electoral debates that seem to succeed only in giving candidates additional opportunities to grandstand. We bemoan what *[margin note: One of my common sources! :)]*

linguist Deborah Tannen calls "the argument culture": an "atmosphere of animosity [that] precludes respect and poisons our relations with one another."[9] These exclusionary displays are enough to cause some to reject debate altogether in favor of less antagonistic practices. Yet should we really throw the proverbial baby out with the bathwater when critical thinking, deliberation, and argumentation are so foundational to democratic culture? I view this tension as reason enough to redouble efforts to pursue a model of debate that can enact a more inclusive public discourse. This requires studying historical debating practices in context and becoming attuned to our assumptions about who belongs in debate. Who deserves a spot at the podium, or even a seat in the audience, and how do the answers to these questions bear on civic participation?

[margin note: Encourage inclusive public discourse.]

Akin to the eighteenth-century coffeehouses, salons, and table societies (*Tischgesellschaften*) that inspired Jürgen Habermas's theory of the public sphere, nineteenth- and twentieth-century debating societies "organized discussion among private people that tended to be ongoing."[10] In the United States and the United Kingdom, these organizations were primarily sites of argumentative engagement and rhetorical education. Rhetoric, broadly conceived, is the art of using symbols to create change on issues of common concern. Rhetorical education, as defined by Jessica Enoch, is an "educational program that *develops* in students a communal and civic identity and *articulates* for them the rhetorical strategies, language practices, and bodily and social behaviors that make possible their participation in communal and civic affairs."[11] More specifically, speech and debate education can be traced back to the ancient world and is perennially reinvented as a part of civic practice.[12] Knowledge gleaned from participation in debating clubs and societies has long been seen as preparatory for robust participation in public life. In examining the quotidian activities of debating organizations in and around institutions of higher learning, we gain considerable insight into the performance and critique of oral argument beyond formal classroom instruction.

[margin note: def.]

Yet according to many historical accounts, debate was an educational game dominated by white men. When women are mentioned in this narrative, it is often only apologetically or in passing, suggesting that they were absent or peripheral players.[13] For example, Jarrod Atchison and Edward Panetta note that in the United States, "the exclusive nature of higher education throughout the 19th and early 20th centuries did not create a diverse set of participants in intercollegiate debate."[14] So marginalized are women and racial minorities in forensics that Michael D. Bartanen and Robert S. Littlefield deem "white male hegemony" the dominant paradigm of the twentieth century. Quite simply, they say: "men founded forensics."[15] If one's purpose is to trace formal debating networks and organizations, it is difficult to quibble with these claims.[16] White men were, by far, the most visible participants in intramural and intercollegiate debates in the United States and the United Kingdom. Others who wished to debate faced myriad challenges, including struggles with access, resources, and a rigid sense of propriety predicated on gender, race, and class status. But like so many other histories that appear dominated by a narrow demographic, it is necessary to put pressure on this narrative.

Debating Women offers a history of debate with women at its center.[17] It pushes back against the idea that they were "out of place" and "out of taste" in debate by demonstrating how women enthusiastically made space for themselves in intramural and intercollegiate debate organizations between 1835 and 1945. This is a pivotal period in which many universities in the United States and the United Kingdom transitioned to coeducation, yet most debating societies and teams remained segregated by gender. Tracing a historical arc that spans women's formal exclusion from some nineteenth-century intramural societies through their fuller inclusion in mixed-gender twentieth-century intercollegiate competitions, I demonstrate the importance of debate participation as women sought fuller access to the fruits of higher education.

This book strengthens a diverse and burgeoning store of evidence that women were actively engaged in nineteenth- and twentieth-century civic life, including in those activities that are typically coded as public and masculine. Here, I join a dynamic cadre of feminist rhetorical historians who argue that if we do not see women in the histories of rhetoric and education, we are simply not looking hard enough or in the right spaces. Because of this work, it is now abundantly clear that women actively participated in writing, teaching, platform speaking, lyceum lecturing, parlor performances, reading circles, and acts of social protest.[18] Debating societies, I argue, represent another consequential, yet understudied, path for women into public culture. Despite various obstacles, women debaters transformed forests, parlors, dining rooms, ocean liners, class-rooms, auditoriums, and prisons into vibrant spaces for argument. There, they accessed a skill set usually afforded to men: they learned to listen carefully, think critically, speak eloquently, and craft strategies for other forums of public address. *what Pub. Speak. teaches*

Debating Women also reveals how debaters enacted a vision of argu-mentation in which women were able to flourish—even under conditions of exclusion and marginalization. To be clear, my claim here is not that debating women deployed a particular communicative style in these con-texts, but rather that they used their involvement in debate for different, underappreciated purposes because of their unique gendered circum-stances.[19] Namely, in addition to the skill set just described, they debated to create a legacy within coeducational institutions of higher learning, to negotiate intergenerational differences, to foster intercultural under-standing, and to articulate themselves as citizens. Moreover, the study of debating organizations provides a greater appreciation of the social, political, and cultural milieu as filtered through the eyes of women as they engaged the topics of the day.[20] *Debating Women* thus makes space for women in histories of rhetoric and education, complicating existing accounts of intramural and intercollegiate debating, and tracing the im-portance of their involvement in an activity at the heart of civic culture.

what I hoped to demon-strate.

why p debated

• • •

The book begins with an introductory chapter that takes on the admit-tedly ambitious task of synthesizing extant accounts of debating organiza-tions in the United States and United Kingdom with particular attention to their gendered dynamics. It also provides an orientation to "argument cultures" and "spaces for argument," two concepts that animate this book. In the tradition of feminist rhetorical and public address scholar-ship, rhetoric and history are viewed here as social processes that must be evaluated and interpreted in context.[21] Accordingly, each of the four case study chapters draws upon a range of rich historical and archival texts to understand both the private and the more public operations of women's debating organizations.[22] The surviving traces of past debating women take many forms, including minute books, scrapbooks, photographs, speech texts, letters, pamphlets, and flyers. In order to understand public representations and perceptions of the debaters, I also sought published accounts where they existed in journals, newspapers, yearbooks, university histories, alumni newsletters, biographies and other secondary source materials. In each chapter, I provide a thick description and perform a close reading of artifacts that are not in wide circulation. I supplement this focus on lesser-known primary texts with discussions of major historical developments, events of national and international import, and attitudes toward women's education and roles in public life.[23] This approach is intended not only to enrich the history of debate beyond prevailing accounts that exclude women, but also to see how argument cultures may be contextualized within larger cultural currents. In my analysis, I pay particular attention to physical descriptions and metaphors of space and travel as debating women described their experiences. Where did women make space for argument from 1835 to 1945? Where must we travel to understand these historical argument cultures?

Our journey begins with the origin story of the first college women's debating club in the United States at Oberlin College. The institution is a celebrated pioneer in coeducational and interracial higher education, and many of its alumni are well known for their later social activism. Yet there is still much to explore in navigating the layers of memory that animate narratives about this early college debating society. Drawing primarily from minute books and stories passed down among cohorts of debaters and alumnae, I explore the relationship between gender ideology and civic participation as it manifested in two versions of women's debating at Oberlin: in a secret debating society in the woods behind the campus and the parlor of an African American woman in the village, and in an institutionally sanctioned society that met in campus buildings. Under the scrutiny of the college's administration, Oberlin women teach us about the importance of securing spaces for argument as part and parcel of creating a legacy for debating women at the nation's first coeducational institution between 1835 and 1935.

Another case study is set in the United Kingdom, exploring the seventy-year history of a single community-based debating society. Founded in 1865 when women were not yet permitted to attend universities in Scotland, the Ladies' Edinburgh Debating Society was a steadfast and vital center of rhetorical education. The society, which met monthly in the dining room of Sarah Elizabeth Siddons Mair, featured a wide variety of members. Some joined for relatively short periods of time; others remained for decades. Some used the society as a private outlet for voicing their perspectives on public issues; others were vocal advocates in movements for women's education and suffrage. When the society dissolved in 1935, the former debaters took it upon themselves to publish a retrospective book and to donate their books of meeting minutes to the National Library of Scotland—providing a unique opportunity to explore recurrent topics, themes, and practices of this remarkable intergenerational argument culture.

While the first two case studies involve women debating in gender-segregated space, the next exploration is of the world of mixed-gender, intercollegiate debate competitions in the 1920s. The third case study provides a bridge between debating practices in the United Kingdom and United States, pivoting away from argument cultures forged in particular locales to examine three debating women on the move. In 1928, Leonora Lockhart, Nancy Samuel, and Margery Sharp were selected to represent the United Kingdom on a debating tour of the United States. The debaters were treated as cultural ambassadors and received extensive media attention because they were British women debaters who competed against U.S. men and women students in public debates. In examining the media coverage, and doing a close read of a full transcript of one of their debates, I show how the debaters engaged in important moments of intercultural public address and cultural criticism. This debating tour yields insight into gender and national identity when international argument cultures intermingled.

The final case study examines debate from 1928 to 1945, at a time when women's intercollegiate debating was more accepted in institutionalized educational spaces. Yet students were profoundly impacted by economic recession, war, and evolving attitudes about women's education and employment. During this period, large numbers of women sought to participate in the activity, yet most intercollegiate debate teams remained sex-segregated. I consulted a wide range of materials—newspapers, yearbooks, scrapbooks, and public and internal team documents—to understand the argument cultures created by women students at the University of Pittsburgh and Pennsylvania State College. I also trace how debaters and faculty coaches (including renowned rhetorical critic Marie Hochmuth Nichols) had to argue vigorously for an image of debate that comported with prevalent ideals of femininity as they participated in intercollegiate competitions and public events for the community. In doing so, we can explore how the category of "debating women" was recast as one that allowed them to hone conviction and poise. Their argument cultures were then reoriented around the goal of cultivating proper women citizens who were prepared to participate in their communities without sacrificing their social graces.

Together, these chapters demonstrate the historical richness and diversity of debating women in the United States and United Kingdom between 1835 and 1945. They illustrate the importance of space and mobility in the creation and sustenance of argument cultures. The conclusion of *Debating Women* revisits the implications of this alternative narrative, suggests possibilities for future work, and unpacks its significance for contemporary debate practice.

Acknowledgments

———•◆•———

D*ebating Women* has been a labor of love from start to finish, even on those days when I felt that I might not finish. My ability to write this book was dependent upon many people who provided professional, intellectual, and personal support, and I am happy for the opportunity to acknowledge them here.

Perhaps it will come as no surprise to hear that I was (am!) a debating woman. My life was transformed in no small way through my involvement in debate teams at Oak Harbor High School, the University of Mary Washington, and the University of Pittsburgh, and on the National Communication Association's Committee on International Discussion and Debate tour of Japan and South Korea. I am especially grateful to Timothy O'Donnell, P. Anand Rao, Gordon Mitchell, and members of the Schenley Park Debate Authors Working Group (including Gordon Mitchell, Matt Brigham, Eric English, Brent Heavner, Takuzo Konishi, Stephen Llano, Cate Morrison, Joe Packer, Damien Pfister, Shanara

Reid-Brinkley, John Rief, and Brent Saindon) for important lessons about translating the debate skill set to research publications. Although I transitioned out of the competitive circuit long ago, those experiences inspired this project, and I am so very glad that I was able to learn from many debaters, coaches, and judges across the country and the globe. One of the true delights of this project was connecting with former debaters who were able to help me better understand this history. I thank Jane Blankenship, Mimi Barash Coppersmith, Joan Huber, and Thomas Kane for making the time to share their stories.

Without generous financial assistance to support research visits, *Debating Women* would not have been possible. This project was funded by the Frederick B. Artz Summer Research Grant (Oberlin College Archives), the Helen F. Faust Women Writers Research Travel Award (Penn State University Eberly Family Special Collections Library), the Carrie Chapman Catt Prize for Research on Women and Politics (honorable mention from the Iowa State University Carrie Chapman Catt Center), the Frank and Vilma Slater/Scottish Nationality Room Scholarship (University of Pittsburgh Nationality Rooms), and the Student Research Fund Award (University of Pittsburgh Gender, Sexuality, and Women's Studies Program).

Archivists and library staff provided expert assistance and demonstrated incredible hospitality throughout this process. They include Ken Grossi, Louisa Hoffman, and Roland Baumann at Oberlin College; Olive Geddes at the National Library of Scotland; Mandy Wise at the University College London; Nigel Shepley and Margaret Imlah at the St. George's School for Girls; Lisa Renee Kemper and William J. Maher at the University of Illinois at Urbana-Champaign; Grace Young at Carlow University; Elaine Ardia at Bates College; Marianne Kasica and Miriam Meislik at the University of Pittsburgh; Paul Royster and William Dooling at the University of Nebraska–Lincoln; and Jacqueline Esposito, Rachael Dreyer, Alex Arginteanu, Doris Malkmus, and Eric Novotny at Penn State University. Thanks, too, to the many staff members who fielded email questions, scanned documents, and attended to a seemingly endless stream of interlibrary loan requests.

The publication process with Michigan State University Press's Rhetoric and Public Affairs series has been wonderful. I am very fortunate that

Martin J. Medhurst saw the potential in this project and allowed me the time to make it better. This book has been undoubtedly improved due to Marty's skilled editorial guidance as well as the wise and generative feedback of Angela G. Ray, Paul Stob, and the anonymous reviewers. It has been a pleasure to work with the Michigan State University Press staff. Thank you to Kristine Blakeslee, Elise Jajuga, Beth Kanell, Julie Loehr, Julie Reaume, Annette Tanner, Lauren Spitzley, and Ana Wraight for all you have done to shepherd this project through to publication.

Portions of chapter 5 were reproduced from my chapter, "Taking Women Seriously: Debaters, Faculty Allies, and the Feminist Work of Debating in the 1930s and 1940s," originally published in J. Michael Hogan, Jessica A. Kurr, Michael J. Bergmaier, and Jeremy D. Johnson, eds., *Speech and Debate as Civic Education* (University Park: Penn State University Press, 2017). Thank you to Sheila Sager Reyes and Penn State University Press for permission to do so.

I thank my outstanding mentors at the University of Pittsburgh— Gordon Mitchell, Jessica Enoch, Kathryn Thoms Flannery, John Lyne, and Ronald Zboray—for helping to shape these ideas in their earliest stages and continuing to lend their knowledge over the years. Gordon Mitchell was a champion of this project from beginning, kept the conversation going as it developed into a book, and has been dedicated to making sure that new generations of students know this history. I value his enthusiasm and guidance. As a faculty member in the Department of Communication Studies and the Women's and Gender Studies Program at the University of Nebraska–Lincoln and now in my new position in the Department of Communication at the University of Maryland in College Park, I have had the privilege of working with exceptional colleagues and have benefited from various forms of institutional support. My department and program chairs—Dawn Braithwaite, Marie-Chantal Kalisa, Shawn Parry-Giles, and Shari Stenberg—deserve special praise for their support and guidance of junior faculty. T. C. Anthony, Christina Castle, Paige Glasshoff, Betty Jacobs, Renee McDuffie, Glenda Moore, Donelle Moormeier, Lillie Sullivan, and Kathy Thorne did the important work of helping to sort out administrative, travel, and grant arrangements. Thank you to my students, especially my advisees, Amy Arellano, Chase Aunspach, Joshua Ewalt, Christina Ivey, and Kyle Stephan. My sincere appreciation goes to Joshua Ewalt, Jonathan Carter, and Randall Fowler for their excellent research assistance.

Research talks at several National Communication Association conventions; the Popular Knowledge, Public Stage conference at the Alexandria Lyceum; the Eberly Family Special Collections Library at Penn State; and the Department of Communication's colloquium series at the University of Kansas allowed me to test and hone the ideas in the book. I am thankful to Johanna Hartelius, Bill Keith, and Alyssa Samek, for reading various portions of this manuscript and providing vital feedback as it developed. Numerous other scholars and friends also left their imprints through their interest, suggestions, and encouragement: Jean Ferguson Carr, Karma Chávez, Carrie Crenshaw, John Davis, Aaron Duncan, Jessica Enoch, Michelle Gibbons, G. Thomas Goodnight, Dale Hample, Debra Hawhee, Rose Holz, Margaret Jacobs, Robin Jensen, Emily Kazyak, Jody Kellas, Jim Klumpp, Takuzo Konishi, Kathy Krone, Brian Lain, Carol Lasser, Karen Lee, Ron Lee, Allan Louden, Kristen Lucas, Kristy Maddux, Junya Morooka, Jessy Ohl, Lester Olson, Cate Palczewski, Trevor Parry-Giles, Shanara Reid-Brinkley, Jen Rome, Bill Seiler, Peter Simonson, Jordan Soliz, Belinda Stillion Southard, Bjorn Stillion Southard, Leah Sprain, Catherine Knight Steele, Paul Stob, Scott Stroud, Dave Tell, Michelle Murray Yang, David Zarefsky, and Mary Zboray. Special thanks to Michele Kennerly for being a treasured confidant and for infusing wit, humor, and perspective into every conversation.

The profound influence of Angela G. Ray's scholarship should be clear to anyone who reads this book. Yet I am also deeply indebted to Angela for her kind and sustained interest in this project, her detailed and incisive feedback on multiple full drafts, and her suggestions for how to reach broader audiences. Thank you so much, Angela, for going above and beyond.

My family and extended family have always encouraged my academic endeavors, and I truly value their ongoing support and understanding. In particular, I want to express my heartfelt gratitude to my parents, Dave and Debbie Woods, and my mother-in-law, Darlene Smith, for allowing me the time and space to work.

Finally, to the darlings who make my house a home. Thank you to my canine companions, Thora and Loki, the finest pups to ever emerge from

Wahoo, Nebraska. Thank you to my child, my own "Historical Woman," who brings love and laughter into my life every single day. She arrived midway through this process and has given my work renewed purpose. And thank you to Damien Smith Pfister, partner of the year for fourteen years and counting. He has truly been there with me every step of the way with this project, reading every page with his signature curiosity and generosity. For the conversations, the feedback, the proofreading, the comic frame reminders, the pep talks, the travels, the nook chats, the infinite understanding, and the extraordinary life we have cultivated together, I am forever grateful.

Introduction

———•◆•———

D ebating is an ancient practice that has flourished across historical periods and cultures around the globe.[1] The English word *debate* comes from the fourteenth-century Old French *debatre*, meaning "to quarrel, to dispute" or "a quarrel, a dispute."[2] As these definitions suggest, the word can be treated as a verb (the practice of debating) and a noun (a debate event).[3] Indeed, if defined broadly as the process by which arguments are "advanced, supported, disputed, and defended," debating is difficult to avoid.[4] Anyone who takes part in a reasoned exchange of ideas—a squabble over politics at the bar, a spat at home over who does the dishes—may casually claim that they debated.[5] G. Thomas Goodnight usefully distinguishes between informal argument, which is "typically fluid, ephemeral, private, and more loosely bound," and debate, which is "more formal, enduring, public, and governed by expectations stated in the codes of the forum and historically embodied by precedents set by the audience."[6] For the purposes of this book, debate is defined as a structured activity that brings individuals together to collectively engage in the ritual practice of argumentation. Attempting to document a comprehensive history of the activity is complicated because the language of debate is often used to describe other genres of rhetorical activity such as oral competition, declamation, and discussion.[7] Throughout this study, I focus on debating organizations in and around educational institutions, making a specific effort to highlight historical moments in which women deliberately used the term "debate" to refer to their activities. This includes bringing forward extant evidence as to the specific debate format and rules of their specific organizations. Three types of debate can be delineated: public debating, intramural debating, and intercollegiate debating. Though they often overlap, these distinctions highlight important structural changes that impacted the possibilities for debating women in the nineteenth and twentieth centuries.

Public Debating

Public debating can be defined broadly as "argumentative interaction between individuals and/or groups with different positions on the issue in question."[8] *Public debating events* are likely what most readers would envision when they hear the word "debate": debaters standing behind podiums on a stage, engaging each other and addressing an audience through a presentation of oral arguments. Throughout history, women engaged in print or epistolary debates that were, in fact, acting in a profoundly public way, as with Catharine Beecher and Angelina Grimké's 1837 exchange over abolition.[9] However, if we narrow our focus to events in which oral arguments were exchanged in a structured public debate event, women are harder—though not impossible—to find. Public debates are of great historical interest, and rhetoricians have demonstrated how such performances function as consequential moments of public address.[10] Nineteenth-century lyceum circuit debates, debates at social or political conventions, and electoral debates can all be placed under the umbrella of public debating events. Most exemplary in this tradition are the Lincoln–Douglas debates of 1858, which, as David Zarefsky contends, were not solely oratorical performances, but interacting argument narratives that evolved and unfolded over time."[11] Public debate events often bring people with particular claims to celebrity, power, or expertise together. It is advocacy for a specific cause (i.e., a suffrage advocate participating in a public debate about suffrage) or an occasion (i.e., an upcoming election) that forms the basis of their engagement. In this way, public debating can be contrasted with intramural and intercollegiate debating, which brings debaters together for the purposes of ritual argumentation in organizations unlinked to any particular cause or occasion.[12]

Intramural Debating

For members of intramural debating clubs, "debate" takes on a specialized meaning that is determined by rules and expectations generated by their organizations over time. Intramural debating societies were spatially determined and required physical co-presence. Their meetings and events took place within the walls of a building in a particular city or on a college campus, and their membership was derived from that same community. Sharp distinctions between literary and debating societies are sometimes difficult to discern, because the main activity of nineteenth-century literary societies was debating.[13] Literary society programs often included musical performances, skits, papers on current events and topics, and debates that "concluded with a critic's report, which was generally entertaining and always frank."[14] Intramural society debates involved a shared proposition or question that limited the scope of the debate. Debaters were selected in advance so that they could research and prepare for the event. A typical format included initial speeches establishing each side's major arguments, the opportunity for refutation, and cross-examination by an opposing debater or audience members. This framework is designed to facilitate argumentative clash—the interactions of competing ideas—as it allows informed participants to test an argument before a third party (audience members, a panel of judges, or a critic) who provides feedback on the exchange. Although they sometimes opened the doors to larger audiences of community members, the primary audience for many nineteenth-century intramural debating societies was their own membership.

As the Vassar example mentioned in the preface illustrates, gendered decorum dictated that the presumed membership of such debating clubs were men. Though debating clubs are often seen as serving only the privileged and educated few, some firsthand accounts complicate that view. For example, the Franklin Debating Society, an antebellum community-based club in New York City, is described as a gathering of "some twenty-five young men; all of the[m] middle class; all earning their bread in useful occupations, and all striving to gain an education and a development of their powers such as would enable them to do good work in the world."[15] Community-based U.S. debating societies could be aspirational, focused on efforts to model elite citizenship for young, white men of the lower and middle classes.[16] In her study of antebellum white men's debating clubs, Angela G. Ray observes that such organizations functioned as "emergent publics" where participants "discursively constructed an imagined national public."[17] Perhaps unsurprisingly, these rhetorical exercises functioned within an exclusionary model of citizenship, where "masculine gender customarily was articulated as an inflexible, defining feature of the citizen" and women typically participated only as audience members. Despite these rigid notions of citizenship, the men debaters sometimes debated about issues concerning women, Native Americans, and African Americans.[18]

Yet disenfranchised groups were not solely the subjects of debate; at times, they were the debaters. We can answer the call to study these understudied publics by paying attention to the gaps and silences in historical accounts, thinking critically about how perceived differences may limit or open up an individual's ability to engage in meaning-making, and refiguring dominant notions of what constitutes participation and influence in associational cultures.[19] For example, women who could afford the admission fee participated in some public debating societies and even formed their own societies in late-eighteenth-century London.[20] Some girls and young women in the United States learned about speech and argumentation through school-based literary societies in the early republic and throughout the nineteenth century.[21] A growing literature demonstrates that African American men and women enthusiastically formed community-based literary and debating societies in the antebellum and post-Civil War periods.[22]

At the end of the nineteenth century, and into the twentieth, a wave of women's organizations provided fresh opportunities for self-improvement, education, and volunteerism.[23] In this way, women's literary and debating societies can be considered in the context of a broader club culture. The "women's club movement" is often characterized as a movement for older white women of the middle and upper classes. However, there is evidence that women from a variety of backgrounds formed clubs across the United States. Anne Ruggles Gere's careful research sheds light on how diverse clubwomen—"Mormon, Jewish, working-class, African American and white Protestant"—were active between 1880 and 1920.[24] These clubs empowered women to realize their potential to collectively organize, "making their own history and defining their own cultural identity."[25] Peter Gordon and David Doughan detail the emergence of women's clubs in the United Kingdom as they followed a similar course, focusing first on reform and mutual improvement and then developing with more specific activist aims in mind.[26] Perhaps it is not surprising, then, that many of the debaters featured in this book were also active in other women's clubs and movements for education, abolition, suffrage, and temperance. Debating societies provided a structure where they could learn, advocate, and organize in communities and on university campuses.

However, the development of debate as an intramural campus activity looked very different in the United Kingdom than it did in the United States, especially for women students. This is largely due to their distinct trajectories toward coeducation.[27] Men's debating unions were established at Cambridge University and Oxford University in 1815 and 1823, respectively. Meanwhile, access to university education was a painfully slow process for U.K. women. Separate women's colleges were not established at Cambridge and Oxford until the 1860s and 1870s, and women began forming their own intramural debating unions shortly thereafter.[28] Women were not granted full university membership status at Oxford until 1920; Cambridge followed suit twenty-eight years later.

Throughout the twentieth century, too, university debating in England and Scotland remained student run and gender segregated. There were moments when men-dominated unions temporarily permitted women's participation, as when suffragist Millicent Garrett Fawcett famously stood and spoke in the debating hall of the Oxford Union in favor of the proposition that "in the opinion of this House the time has come when the government should be urged to remove the disabilities of Women" in 1908.[29] However, women would not be permitted to directly debate against men at Oxford Union for eighteen more years and were not admitted with full membership in the Cambridge Union until fifty-five years later.[30] Similarly, the University of Edinburgh Union was chartered in 1889 with a specific provision in the constitution that prohibited women from joining (women could not matriculate to any Scottish university until 1892). Edinburgh's women students founded their own union in 1905 and conducted intercollegiate debates with women at the University of Glasgow. The University of Edinburgh Union did not become officially coeducational until 1971.[31]

This can be contrasted with the United States, where the Oberlin Collegiate Institute in Oberlin, Ohio, was coeducational upon its founding in 1833. By 1870, twenty-nine percent of the nation's colleges were open to both men and women; that number rose to sixty-nine percent in 1930.[32] There is evidence of a men's debating club dating back to 1719 at Harvard University, but student-led intramural debating societies flourished as an extracurricular activity at U.S. institutions of higher learning throughout the nineteenth century.[33] James Gordon Emerson explains that these societies were a centerpiece of nineteenth-century campus life: "the end-of-the-week diversion of hosts of young men and women looked forward to through the humdrum of study and recitation, the dessert to the intellectual meal, the frosting on the delectable cake of sociability."[34] By the 1880s, U.S. women's literary and debating societies were active at many colleges, including all-women institutions like Vassar College, Wellesley College, and Mount Holyoke College and coeducational institutions such as Bates College and Northwestern University.[35]

It is fair to say that women participated in intramural debating activities throughout the Progressive Era, but the status of such clubs differed by institution and region. For example, as institutions of higher education spread toward the Pacific, literary and debating societies waxed in the western United States while northern and southern societies waned.[36] Some land-grant institutions and normal schools, especially those in the Midwest and West, permitted coeducational societies and mixed-gender debates.[37] Andrea G. Radke-Moss provocatively argues that "perhaps at no other level in American society in the 1870s and 1880s were men and women publicly discussing current social and political issues in open, organized meetings."[38] However, where mixed-gender debates took place, they often operated under a "type of ideological separation" that deemed some topics off-limits. Some women embraced the opportunity to debate men, while others retreated from such encounters, finding the men's styles too aggressive or questioning their own sense of gendered decorum.[39]

One issue grappled with throughout this book is the way that women participants blurred distinctions that might otherwise apply in intramural forums—writing/reading versus speaking/debating, the private literary society versus the public debating society—even while they were sometimes formally prohibited from occupying the latter categories. This insight is particularly important for rhetorical scholars because such distinctions have defined and ushered in new lines of inquiry on the basis of disciplinary self-identity. Rhetoric and composition scholar Robert J. Connors controversially claims that rhetoric was primarily oral, civic, and argumentative at the beginning of the nineteenth century, but "exited the nineteenth century as composition, a multimodal discipline, primarily written and with a personal, privatized nexus."[40] This argument hinges on the idea that the decline of ritualized agonism had much to do with the entrance of women into higher education. He traces (at least part of) the decline of interest in college debate clubs after 1870 to the idea that debating against women was "unnatural, demoralizing, demeaning the men."[41] I side with scholars who have pointed out that this claim about the "feminization of rhetoric" overlooks many examples of women's involvement in public and oral rhetorical activities in the 1870s and beyond.[42] To those arguments, I add two. First, some intramural societies, such as the Oberlin Ladies' Literary Society, continued well into the twentieth century. Second, many debating societies did not fade away; they were reinvented in the twentieth century as competitive intercollegiate debate teams. This is the historical narrative that emerges in histories of speech communication. Literary societies may have served different purposes, but as William Keith notes, they functioned as "forerunners of contest debate."[43]

Intercollegiate Debating

U.S. university debating was transformed by the introduction of intercollegiate debating at the turn of the century.[44] Intercollegiate contests were initially arranged between two colleges that negotiated the rules of the competition and even signed contracts to codify their agreements.[45] A Harvard–Yale debate in 1892 is often credited with igniting a flurry of intercollegiate competitions across the United States, although there is evidence of intercollegiate debating events before that.[46] Early observers of this structural change in debating attribute the shift from intramural to intercollegiate debating to a desire for rigorous competition and more formalized logistical, evidentiary, and logical norms for debate.[47] Debaters prepared for months before competitions, reading available books on the topic in the library and writing, revising, and practicing material for opening speeches and rebuttals. Intercollegiate debating made travel routine, thus increasing the need for financial and institutional support.[48] As with athletic events, many debating competitions were infused with school spirit. Campus and surrounding communities held pep rallies and parades in honor of the debaters who participated in this "intellectual sport."[49] It was not uncommon for debaters to be met by cheering crowds at the train depot upon their return from a successful competition with a rival university.

Debate matches between just two schools evolved into triangular and quadrangular league debate competitions in the first decade of the twentieth century. These contests were organized based on preexisting rivalries, geographical proximity within a state, or shared religious denominations.[50] The inclusion of three or more schools meant that the teams could not simply decide on sides on a contract basis, as they had previously. Each university prepared arguments on both sides of a question, or proposition, for debate.[51] Propositions were carefully crafted in order to delineate argumentative ground for the teams representing the affirmative and negative sides. Though triangular and quadrangular leagues allowed more debating to take place, they also introduced the ethical question of whether students should be asked to debate against their personal convictions by preparing cases on both sides of a proposition (commonly referred to as "switch sides debating"). This ethical dilemma would become a perennial concern for twentieth-century debate theorists and practitioners.[52]

Other controversies in intercollegiate debate during this period centered on the role of the judge, whether speeches should be written or extemporaneous, and the influence of the debate coach.[53] The debate coach, or faculty advisor, was a development unique to the United States, one that that accompanied the creation of speech communication as a distinct field of university study. Professors of public speaking, previously housed in departments of English, came together as the Eastern Public Speaking Conference in 1910 and then as the National Association of Academic Teachers of Public Speaking in 1914.[54] Before this shift, professors of English, history, or economics lent their expertise to help prepare debaters.[55] As Egbert Ray Nichols describes, departments of speech "entered the college through the debate interest and the coaching door" because higher education administrators saw debate victories as a sign of their institution's academic excellence.[56] The first issues of the *Quarterly Journal of Public Speaking* from 1915 to 1917 showcase the extent to which the early speech field was entwined with formal debate activities. Because many speech professors were also debate coaches or faculty advisors, critical issues in intercollegiate debate practice appeared as scholarly articles in the field's flagship journal.[57] These discussions continued in the journal's later iterations as the *Quarterly Journal of Speech Education* and the *Quarterly Journal of Speech.*

A transition from league debating to tournament debating also began in the 1920s. Instead of three or four universities assembled in triangular and quadrangular leagues, tournaments enabled many universities to come together at a common campus. The league debates were conceptualized as improving the quality of civic discussion for wider publics, whereas tournament debating increased the competitive stakes by creating a format that crowned a single winning team at the end. Students could expect to travel to a tournament and debate many rounds against different opponents on both sides of the proposition, with the top teams from the preliminary rounds of competition moving on to elimination rounds that would produce a single winner. This system provided "opportunities for increased numbers of intercollegiate debates at minimum expense" but necessitated "significant changes in debating methods and techniques."[58] Two-person teams were preferred to debating formats that featured larger teams of three, four, or five people, and speech times were reduced in order to maximize the number of debates that could be held in a weekend. Rather than having to convince auditoriums filled with public audiences, tournament debating focused on persuading a single judge or a small panel of judges.[59] The tournament setting allowed debating practices to become more specialized. However, this specialization was accompanied by the gradual exclusion or regulation of debaters who did not adhere to highly developed norms. Over time, this change increased entry barriers to debate through the creation of intricate, complex argumentation jargon. The question of whether debate should be viewed as an insular game played by only a few or as preparation for public life for the many thus came under consideration.[60]

Most accounts indicate that women students did not participate in intercollegiate debating in large numbers until the 1920s because, according to L. Leroy Cowperthwaite and A. Craig Baird, "throughout the early years of intercollegiate forensic competition the appearance of women upon the public platform continued to be viewed with disfavor."[61] The increase in "co-eds" on campus in the early twentieth century was not welcomed by all. They were often the targets of humor, some vicious and some lighthearted. For example, an anonymous writer in the University of Pittsburgh's 1914 yearbook proclaimed that "the word 'co-ed' comes from the Greek, 'dough-head' meaning 'low-head' or 'low-brow' . . . she is a distraction in the classroom, an attraction on the campus, which is to her delight."[62] Likewise, women debaters were caricatured in several comic outlets. For example, this joke circulated in newspapers in the U.S. and New Zealand as early as 1904 and as late as 1922:

> "What broke up the ladies' debating society?"
>
> "The leading member was told to prepare an essay on the Yellow Peril. She did so, and the opening sentence read: 'Yellow apparel is very trying to most complexions.'"[63]

At first glance, the humor of this joke seems to rely on a simple word play. But, more perniciously, the joke illustrates dominant assumptions at the time: that women could not handle the "manly self-confidence" provided by a debating society; that they would only be interested in frivolous topics rather than political topics of international concern.[64] This was especially true of intercollegiate competitors, who would serve as representatives of their universities. There were notable exceptions, some of which are discussed in the course of this book, but controversy tended to ensue when those who fell outside of the white male norm attempted to participate.[65]

Men's intercollegiate debating, as with most extracurricular activities, was drastically reduced during the First World War. Women students maintained intramural societies during that time.[66] By the 1920s, women were finally able to participate in intercollegiate competitions in larger numbers, but typically participated in gender-segregated teams.[67] This upsurge in women's debating teams—which continued to gain steam between the 1920s and the 1940s—led to the appointment of new faculty advisors. These figures were in the inimitable position of advocating for debating women at their institutions, competing for resources, and achieving competitive success without violating gender norms.[68]

It was not until the formalization of transatlantic international debating exchanges in the 1920s—when delegations of debaters were sent to represent their nation as they toured foreign universities—that the distinct debating cultures formed in the United States and the United Kingdom came into direct contact. These tours were dominated by men until 1928, when Britain sent its first delegation of women students to debate men and women in the United States. As discussed later, the tour allowed questions about gendered decorum to bubble up to the surface. How should women and men conduct themselves stylistically in debates? Should they debate the same topics? Debating women on both sides of the Atlantic contended with these questions throughout the interwar period. In short order, the Second World War would present yet another opportunity for women debaters to expand their influence on university campuses and in their communities.

As this necessarily sweeping historical account shows, women's debate developed alongside the desire for and actualization of coeducation in nineteenth- and twentieth-century universities. The three types of debate—public, intramural, and intercollegiate—offer a flexible typology to clarify the scope of this study. *Debating Women* focuses on the latter

two categories—intramural debating and intercollegiate debating. It was
in these categories that women nourished and cultivated a love for argument on their own terms.

Argument Cultures

For many, the promise of a vibrant public sphere is rooted in civic activities beyond the penumbra of the state. In the wake of the English
translation of *The Structural Transformation of the Public Sphere*, scholars from varied intellectual traditions have found the idea of the public
sphere generative, but also critique Habermas's account as universalizing,
abstract, and exclusionary.[69] Scholars of rhetoric and argumentation are
particularly adept at studying "actually existing" public sphere activity
because of their commitment to close analyses of situated discourse and
nuanced understandings of the role of argument in sustaining publicity.[70]
Goodnight's theory of argument spheres, developed in the early 1980s,
contends that "more than the content of issues, what is put at stake by
contention and disagreement are the communicative practices invoked
to articulate and enact a public sphere."[71] This approach foregrounds the
practice of debate while recognizing the importance of particular contexts
for argument. When "implicit norms, conventions of propriety, or explicit
rules" assumed to characterize the spheres are themselves enrolled as
"part of the debate," social change is possible—as when historical wom-
en's movements contested presumed boundaries between the public and
the private.[72]

Nested within these larger scholarly conversations, case studies of
women's debating societies provide a particularly illuminating way to
examine argument-oriented collectives that coalesced within and beyond
a dominant public sphere.[73] Many studies have examined how subaltern
publics employ diverse modalities of communication, noting that the
norm of rational-critical debate was at least partially responsible for their
conditions of exclusion from the bourgeois public sphere.[74] However,
there is considerable insight yet to garner when we delve into the details
of how women utilized and organized around even that most traditional
of rhetorical practices: debating. Unlike voluntary societies, religious

associations, or other groups organized around a shared interest in a social or political cause, debating societies foreground a commitment to ritual argumentation on a range of issues.[75] Ritual argumentation may have a negative connotation if reduced to agonistic argument for argument's sake. Yet defenses of argument point to its social dimensions: that "arguments are not in statements, but in people," and those people are embedded in fields, spheres, or communities of discourse.[76] That is, arguments are crafted by particular people, within particular contexts, and with particular audiences in mind.

In this spirit, David Zarefsky suggests that we move from broad-based declarations about the harms of *the* argument culture to instead consider the potential of *argument cultures*.[77] Argument cultures coalesce when they collectively recognize the importance of audience, embrace uncertainty, value conviction, focus on justifying one's claims, emphasize cooperation, and involve self-risk on the part of the participants.[78] Throughout this book, I view historical debating societies and teams as argument cultures, aiming to contribute to studies of the public sphere by exploring actual collectives of women brought together through a commitment to debate. I follow these argument cultures within and around scholastic institutions, and within and across national borders. "Argument culture" is preferable to other possibilities (publics, counterpublics, discourse communities, etc.) because it is a flexible term that allows us to attend to the spatio-temporal dynamics of debating collectives. Culture has varied meanings, but it generally "designates a body of norms and practices, and the people that engage in them, that are sustained across time."[79] The term also foregrounds the import of collective human achievement through education. Debating societies and teams provided a nexus of deliberative activity where ideas could be exchanged and refined, and at least hypothetically, taken up in other spaces. Historical argument cultures materialized, blossomed, and dissolved over time and in particular spaces as debaters moved in, moved out, and moved on.

Predictably, gender loomed large as a primary, organizing axis of difference in women's debating organizations. Participants connected by their identification with a historical category of "women" or "ladies" often chose to explicitly thematize gender issues in their debate propositions. "Debating women" was thus a social identity that invited reflection, negotiation, contestation, and revision of gender norms.[80] Their presence provides evidence that debate was more diverse than previously thought when it comes to gender. Yet we need not labor under the illusion that other markers of social status were bracketed or transcended in the argument cultures that are the subject of this book. Participants in debating societies and teams were bound by decorum, which manifests in localized rules and expectations for argument and reflect and reinforce gendered, raced, and classed attitudes of a dominant culture. A debating society is no guarantee of progressive public argument, and critical self-reflexivity was not the motivation of all participants. Identities and identifications may be solidified in pursuit of competitive success in debate. However, the emancipatory potential of such groups is that they thrive on argumentative engagement, which, when done well, requires imagination and the intellectual acuity to see beyond one's own social location. Ideally, the pursuit of knowledge invites debaters to interface not only with gender, but also with race, class, and nation in argument cultures over time. Moreover, because they often had to generate topics for debate, debaters could question, validate, or contest the limits of public issues as demarcated by the prevailing media of the time. The records of debating societies and teams reveal moments when dominant ideas about social values were, by definition, "up for debate." These organizations thus became spaces for argument, fostering rhetorical practices that had the potential to "alte[r] ongoing social conversation."[81]

Spaces for Argument

Before it came to signify collective achievement of a particular group, and before it was associated with arts and civilization in a grander sense, "culture" was about nurturing the development of living things.[82] Farmers (agriculturalists) cultivate the land so plants can thrive. Biologists create cultures so bacteria can thrive. In both of these senses, we are drawn to think of the creation and tending of an environment. We may also think of argument cultures as material and symbolic environments where arguments, ideas, and people can thrive together. What are the conditions that make this possible?

This work is intended to make space for women in dominant narratives about debate. I also mean to tell the story of women who made space for themselves to debate by claiming, cultivating, and sustaining spaces for argument. To be sure, space is likely of importance to all kinds of debaters, as it confers a sense of legitimacy upon the activity and its practitioners. However, the importance of securing spaces for argument is especially pronounced within the discourses of women's debating clubs. It is easy to take for granted the contemporary built environments that lend themselves to debate—classrooms, conference rooms, auditoriums, even virtual forums—but historical limitations on the movement of women in cities, on campuses, and in classrooms meant that space was a more complex consideration. As urban planning and environmental studies scholar Daphne Spain explains,

> Both geographic and architectural separation have played a role in segregating women and men in formal education. Initially, women were denied admission to schools, creating geographic distance between them and sources of knowledge. When schools eventually opened their doors to women, many placed them in separate classrooms that substituted architectural for geographic segregation. Both types of segregation were justified by the prevailing ideology of separate spheres for women and men.[83]

Spatial differentiation is a historically powerful way to prevent people from accessing knowledge. The creation of distinct women's argument cultures combatted this problem in the context of speech and debate education. Women participants could claim that they were neither "out of taste" nor "out of place" if they created their own spaces for debate or integrated existing ones.[84] This is the story of the movement of arguments, ideas, and bodies, of women pushing debating into new spaces and experiencing attendant pushback.

This move—to think critically about gender, communication, and space—is made in light of a larger spatial turn in the humanities and social sciences. It is supported by a robust transdisciplinary literature, which highlights the construction and contingencies of spatial divisions including borders, regions, spheres, and other boundaries. An important part of the spatial turn is its tracing of what has been termed the "geography of knowledge." Here, scholars connect the movements of ideas as they flow across borders real and imagined.[85] Attention to "spaces of knowledge" has been particularly useful in thinking about shifting senses of knowledge and expertise as intellectuals engage in boundary work in academic disciplines and in communication with wider publics.[86]

If space is bound up in power relations, it can also structure dominant beliefs about who has the right and ability to know and to express oneself about that knowledge. Geographical thinking itself has a universalizing tendency in scope and in style, which "tends to exclude women as producers of knowledge, as well as what are seen as women's issues as objects of knowledge," according to feminist geographer Gillian Rose.[87] That is, to understand spaces of knowledge, we acknowledge that particular ideas and particular bodies may be corralled according to these imagined boundaries. Binary spatial divisions delineating the inside from the outside and the public from the private often also structure gender relations between the masculine and the feminine.[88] Expectations of bodies, who they are, where they belong, what they can do there, how long they will stay—these are all issues of space that are routinely, and sometimes mundanely, disciplined and negotiated.[89]

In this vein, philosopher Lorraine Code argues that examining spatial metaphors in concert with material spaces can help to understand how hierarchies of power and privilege shape discursive possibilities. For Code, the language of "rhetorical space" emphasizes the situatedness of any given speech act, to "move it into textured locations where it matters who is speaking and where and why, and where such mattering bears directly upon the possibility of knowledge claims, moral pronouncements, descriptions of 'reality' achieving acknowledgment."[90] This approach resonates with feminist and critical race scholars who foreground space as a necessity for understanding the contours of these exclusive relationships and for revaluing previously overlooked localities.[91]

Where could individuals marginalized by gender, race, and class status gain access to literacy, rhetorical education, and other forms of knowledge in the nineteenth and twentieth centuries? Where could they interact, argue, and express themselves? Following Code, rhetorician Roxanne Mountford urges us to study "the geography of a communicative event, [which,] like all landscapes, may include both the cultural and material arrangement, whether intended or fortuitous, of space."[92] We must pay attention to symbolic and physical spaces, how they are valued and interpreted, and how particular bodies imbue them with meaning. In varied studies, classrooms, churches, beauty parlors, and private residences have emerged as important locations in which the dynamics of "rhetorical space" could be understood, critiqued, and reformed.[93] The challenge for rhetorical scholars, then, is to "rema[p] rhetorical territory" to include marginalized rhetors, while simultaneously resisting the impulse to present those rhetorics and the spaces they occupied as fixed, static, or settled.[94]

In order to avoid reading these relationships as inert, this study treats movement and mobility as part of a critical vocabulary for analyzing rhetorical history.[95] Movement and mobility have long been captured in the language of argument and debate, but in a way that conceives of debate as a battle waged by moving arguments around a competitive field for glory. Many critiques of argument fault this kind of zero-sum, militaristic thinking. For example, Deborah Tannen's critique of the argument culture points to the fact that debate over public issues is often expressed in the language of agonism and combat ("the war on drugs, the war on cancer, the battle of the sexes, politicians' turf battles").[96] Feminist critiques of argumentation point to the ways in which "argument as a process has been steeped in adversarial assumptions and gendered expectations."[97] This perspective does not suggest that women are inferior or incapable of deft argumentation, but rather points to the ways that the very confrontational frameworks and styles implied by debate do not serve anyone well. Drawing upon the language that historical debating women used in documenting and remembering their argument cultures, this book proposes adopting the conceptual metaphor of "argument as travel."[98] The travel metaphor is powerful because it builds on the history of geographical metaphors that have dominated the intellectual landscape of feminist and rhetorical history.[99] Thinking in terms of travel emphasizes an aspect of that language that acknowledges the importance of movement—specifically, movement across and between spaces for argument. Whether literal or figurative, women's mobility is often perceived as radical because it has the potential to unsettle gender hierarchies. As Doreen Massey advises, "one gender-disturbing message might be—in terms of both identity and space—keep moving! The challenge is to achieve this whilst at the same time recognizing one's necessary locatedness and embeddedness/embodiedness, and taking responsibility for it."[100] Viewing argument as travel orients our attention to the ways that the vehicle of debate offered ideas, arguments, and people a way to move.

Debating Women explores women's debating organizations in a variety of spatial configurations. The women who populate this book were not all extraordinary in terms of how history remembers them, but all had the extraordinary experience of participating in an argument culture.[101] Some debaters stayed physically stationary while their ideas moved through exposure to new perspectives; others used their involvement in debate as a reason to move—across towns, states, and even national borders—for the purpose of intercollegiate competitions. Whether in the enclaved intramural societies that met in private residences or in the institutionalized teams that met in university classrooms and auditoriums, debating women demand our attention.

CHAPTER 1

"The First Girls' Debating Club": Creating a Legacy at Oberlin College, 1835–1935

———•◆•———

The first college women's debating society in the United States developed in the context of a grand nineteenth-century experiment. In 1833, it was "generally frowned upon" for institutions of higher learning to admit students of color, and a "somewhat shocking departure" to admit women students, yet in Oberlin, Ohio, the founders of the Oberlin Collegiate Institute did both.[1] Oberlin's women students then set themselves apart by pursuing spaces for the sustained practice of argumentation and debate. Brief accounts of Oberlin's pioneer debating society circulate in a variety of academic texts, including feminist anthologies,[2] public address textbooks,[3] rhetoric and composition histories,[4] and feminist rhetorical scholarship,[5] as well as in books aimed at a more popular readership, such as biographies,[6] twentieth-century power feminist bestsellers,[7] and historical romance novels.[8] Each iteration of the Oberlin case provides a tantalizing tidbit that anchors broader discussions about nineteenth-century gender politics, especially prohibitions against women's speech.

The honor of the first women's debating society is at times bestowed upon Oberlin's Young Ladies' Association, an institutionally authorized organization founded in 1835.[9] Open to all of Oberlin's women students, the Young Ladies' Association formed to aid the intellectual growth of its students beyond the classroom, primarily in matters of literature and religion. The group later changed its name to the Young Ladies' Literary Society, and then to the Ladies' Literary Society. The term "ladies" gradually fell out of fashion for Oberlin students, as it did with many U.S. women's clubs.[10] Postbellum debaters reportedly wanted this change because they saw "ladies" as antiquated and thus more accurate for the generations that had come before than for the new woman of the late nineteenth century. In 1878, they agreed to change the name again to become known as the LLS: an acronym standing not for Ladies' Literary Society, as one might presume, but for an adopted motto, *Litterae Laborum Solomen* (translated as "literature is comfort from troubles").[11] As members graduated and moved on, the LLS became a storied institution in its own right. At various points, members, alumnae, and admirers repeated with pride the tenuous claim that the LLS was the first ever women's society, full stop. They gradually revised that claim to call it either the first *college* women's society or the "first women's debate society in the country."[12] Celebration of the society reached its pinnacle in 1935, when generations of LLS members returned to Oberlin's campus for the club's centennial jubilee.

However, this is just one version of the origin story. A more popular rendering focuses on a different debating club—one in which brave and persistent women traveled to new, precarious spaces for argument. In this version of the story, Oberlin's women students were told that they could be audience members but could not take part as speakers in classroom debates. Frustrated with this injustice in coeducation, Lucy Stone and Antoinette Brown (later known as Antoinette Brown Blackwell) pushed beyond authorized spaces, risking discipline and impropriety to form a secret debating society in the woods behind the college.[13] More detailed accounts of this story report that in the colder months, Stone and Brown's debating club met in the house of a black woman who lived in the town. The secret debating society was called "the first debating club ever formed among college girls."[14] Thus, the LLS and the secret debating society in the woods have been fused and confused in scholarly and popular memory. This is done in error, for among other inconsistencies, Lucy Stone and Antoinette Brown did not come to Oberlin until 1843 and 1846, respectively. This would have been eight and eleven years after the first meeting of the Young Ladies' Association (Brown would have been ten years old at that time).[15]

There are several reasons why this conflation may have happened. First, Stone and Brown were both members of the LLS when their secret debating society in the woods was founded. Second, though the LLS is often called a debating society, it is a matter of dispute as to whether the activities of the society required women to participate in written or oral argumentation. The very idea that Stone, Brown, and others would seek refuge in their secret debating society suggests that the LLS was not providing the training in oratory that they desired for their post-Oberlin careers.[16] Stone and Brown kindled a lifelong friendship during their time at Oberlin but are better known for their later careers: Stone became a renowned lecturer, abolitionist, and suffragist, and Brown was a pioneering woman minister, reformer, and author.

Though the story of this early debating society is in wide circulation, previous accounts do not attempt to reconcile the competing versions of the origin story, nor do they account for how Oberlin's women debaters have been remembered beyond that initial period of clandestine debating.[17] Rather than focusing on one club or the other, we must widen our scope to understand debating women at Oberlin over the 100-year period between 1835 (the year the Young Ladies' Association was created) and 1935 (the year the centennial jubilee was held). I do this by offering a close reading of archival materials, including society minutes, correspondence, and various published narratives from members, alumnae, and scholars. I begin with the story of the sanctioned and secret societies, exploring details generally omitted in the more widely circulated anecdotes, and then move beyond these origin stories to examine the interplay of history and memory in the activities of subsequent generations of LLS members. Crucial to Oberlin's argument culture, I argue, were two prevailing themes: the importance of securing spaces for argument, and the sense of belonging fostered when debating women reflected on their legacies as members of the society by imagining the debaters who had come before and would come after them.

Gender, Race, and Degrees of Publicity

Oberlin was established as a colony and a college imbued with Christian principles. The Oberlin Collegiate Institute differed from other institutions of higher learning in the 1830s due to its unique admission policies, dedication to manual labor, rootedness in the religious reform tradition, and moral stance on slavery. It was not a school for the elite. Faculty and students alike lived and ate simply. Their daily routines included studying, praying, and working. Meals in the boarding hall consisted of Graham brown bread, milk, and vegetables such as the shelled corn grown on the campus.[18] The majority of early attendees were the children of poor farmers from New England and Ohio who were galvanized by the knowledge that Oberlin's motto of "learning and labor" meant that they could pay their educational expenses by completing a daily schedule of farm and domestic tasks.[19]

Oberlin students had to possess good moral and intellectual character, be willing to perform manual labor, and abide by the rules of the university, which included regular public prayer and the complete avoidance of alcohol and gambling. There was no formal admissions process; potential students sent letters making the case for their eligibility or had friends and family members testify on their behalf. For example, when Silas R. Badeau wrote to Oberlin requesting admission for his daughter, he marshaled many of the themes that defined the College at the time, explaining: "we are unable to sustain her at any but a Manual Labour Institution. And though away from Parents, she will be surrounded by religious influence instead of worldly. And again we sympathize with the Oppressed and those who have no comforter, and we wish our Child to be with those who do so preeminently, manifesting it by their works."[20] This final comment was a reference to Oberlin's commitment to abolitionism. The institution is rightly revered as a leader in nineteenth-century interracial education, although the decision to play that role was not as unanimous or straightforward as it may seem. According to former Oberlin archivist Roland Baumann, it was a "combination of financial need, chance opportunity, and the colonists' religious sense of obligation" that ultimately propelled Oberlin toward admitting people of color.[21] After much contentious debate, in 1835 the Oberlin trustees approved a resolution that "the education of people of color is a matter of great interest and should be encouraged & sustained in this Institution."[22] Thereafter, black men were admitted, and black women were admitted in the 1840s.[23] Oberlin received many inquiries as word about their fair treatment at the college spread.[24] Though African American students made up only a small percentage of the total student body during the antebellum period, Oberlin's admissions policy was progressive compared to other U.S. colleges at the time.[25]

Progressive gender ideology, however, was not the primary inspiration for the admission of women students. Although the college professed a desire to "brin[g] within the reach of the misjudged and neglected sex, all the instructive privileges which hitherto have unreasonably distinguished the leading sex from theirs," those expecting gender equality would have been sorely disappointed.[26] As Lori D. Ginzburg reminds us, Oberlin's dedication to coeducation was motivated out of an evangelical reform ideology that connected feminine virtues and Christian virtues. As such, the goal was never equality of the sexes; it was to enable the piety, submission, and quiet grace attributed to women to remedy the excesses of a "male sphere" gone awry.[27] Women students at the college could anticipate "washing the men's clothing, caring for their rooms, serving them at table, listening to their orations, but themselves remaining respectfully silent in public assemblages."[28] If they listed goals beyond the roles of wife and mother, Oberlin's women students typically aimed to go into teaching or missionary work.[29]

Designed to provide an education that surpassed the best seminaries and academies of the time, the Ladies' Course (also called the "Literary Course") was a four-year curriculum that allowed women and men to be in the classroom together. However, it "omitted the more rigorous subjects" such as advanced mathematics in favor of more coursework in poetry and history.[30] The 1838 catalogue for the Ladies' Course reveals that students were taught "Whately's Logic and Rhetoric" in their second year of study, though their coursework encouraged them to write and not speak their arguments.[31] Graduates of the Ladies' Course earned diplomas, not degrees. Not until 1837 did three women students matriculate to the baccalaureate program. Each of these students—Mary Caroline Rudd, Elizabeth Prall, and Mary Hosford—was also a member of the

Young Ladies' Association. However, even enrollment in the degree-granting program (which had been called the "Gentlemen's" or "Classical Course") did not afford women students the opportunity to perform public orations.

This regulation of women's speech exemplifies feminist rhetorician Karlyn Kohrs Campbell's observation that "quite simply, in nineteenth-century America, femininity and rhetorical action were seen as mutually exclusive. No 'true woman' could be a public persuader."[32] Of course, some U.S. girls and women had actually enjoyed considerably more freedom to learn and perform oratory in the late eighteenth and early nineteenth century.[33] Yet the cult of true womanhood, an ideology associated with white, upper and middle class femininity, took hold in the 1820s and was very much alive in the early years of coeducation at Oberlin.[34]

Navigating public activities was particularly vexing for women students at a coeducational religious institution. Oberlin historian and LLS alumna Frances Hosford observes that under this ideology of separate spheres, women who wanted to partake in the benefits of public speech would face opposition on multiple fronts: "the religious called it unscriptural for a woman, the cultured thought it unseemly, the cynical found in it material for their bitter sneers, the evil-minded felt free to make a woman orator the target of vulgarity."[35] Oberlin's women students were, in theory, forbidden from speaking in front of mixed-gender audiences and from speaking in church. In practice, this was difficult to negotiate and enforce.[36] Oberlin's early graduates were therefore governed by access to different degrees of publicity, enforced by subtle and somewhat arbitrary directives on the basis of gender and sex.

Oberlin's commencement ceremony displayed the institution's divided commitments to women's education and feminine propriety. Graduates of the non-degree-granting Literary Course were invited to read their graduation essays aloud, because their ceremony involved, in theory, an audience of other women students. Women graduates of the Classical Course were prohibited from reading their essays because that degree was coeducational, and they would share the stage with men graduates (who were, of course, permitted not only to read their essays, but to give orations). A professor of rhetoric (a man) read the women's essays at the ceremony. In practice, men friends and family members were in the audiences at both commencement exercises, making the strict regulation of women's public speech before mixed audiences difficult and discretionary. For example, this distinction was in place in 1847, when Antoinette Brown was permitted to read her essay, "Original Investigation Necessary to the Right Development of Mind," because she received a diploma from the Literary Course. That same year, her beloved friend Lucy Stone, a graduate of the Classical Course, was asked to hand her essay over to James A. Thome, Professor of Rhetoric and Belles Lettres. Stone refused to write the essay in protest.[37]

Thirty-six years later, Stone finally appeared upon her alma mater's stage as the sole woman invited to give a keynote address at Oberlin College's fiftieth anniversary celebration. By that time, she was an illustrious orator and a distinguished alumna who relished the opportunity to speak publicly in front of a mixed audience at Oberlin. In her speech, "Oberlin and Woman," she praised the institution for its many progressive achievements, claiming that the "highest glory" was in establishing coeducation. However, she made certain to note that Oberlin had done her no favors when it came to cultivating her oratorical skills. Doing some rhetorical finger-wagging of her own, Stone recalled the rigid rules that defined her time at the college, stating, "custom, which held women to silence in public places, sat with the Faculty and with the Ladies' Board, and shook its minatory finger at the daring girls who wanted the discipline of rhetorical exercises and discussions, and to read their own essays at Commencement."[38] During her tenure at the school, Oberlin's debating societies afforded opportunities for the kinds of rhetorical education that Stone desired.

The First Literary Society for U.S. College Women

On July 21, 1835, approximately ten women met in the lower hall of the campus seminary to create a society aimed at the intellectual and moral improvement of its members.[39] Men had organized the Oberlin Lyceum in 1834, though it was active for only two years before participation waned.[40] By contrast, the women's group had a presence on Oberlin's campus from

1835 to 1952. In the autumn of 1835 and beyond, meetings for both men's and women's clubs took place in different areas of the newly constructed Ladies' Hall. The men's lyceum occupied an assembly room on the second floor of the building, while the women occupied the attic. The women members scaled several flights of stairs in order to gather in a dark space memorable only for its austerity. The room was long and narrow with a "bare unfinished floor, backless oaken benches, and a lighting system composed of candles."[41] Though they had to converse by the flickering of candlelight, the students did not want for heat in their meeting space. Oberlin's men gifted them a stove, perhaps due to some residual guilt that their fellow students had to climb those extra stairs to gather in a less-than-welcoming (yet undoubtedly treasured) space.[42] With the stove came the need for cleaning up, and the club's vice president was reportedly tasked with maintaining the tidiness of their tiny room.[43]

It is in this space that the Young Ladies' Association (hereafter referenced by its later name, the LLS) began as a forum to discuss literature and religion, and its focus on individual improvement in these areas distinguished the group from other reform societies on campus at the time. Records of the earliest activities of the society are no longer available (perhaps they were lost in a fire, if they were indeed kept at all), so information about the LLS in the 1830s is drawn from stories passed down through generations of alumnae and references to the club in college documents. For example, when trustees John Keep and William Dawes left for the United Kingdom in 1839 to pursue financial support for the college from British philanthropists, the students prepared a formal description of their organization. The document lends insight into the activities of the society, revealing that each member of the organization "writes and communicates to us her thoughts on some important and interesting subject. We hold correspondence with many distinguished & pious ladies of our own and other lands and with some who have left for pagan shores, by this means we collect much valuable information and often have our spirits refreshed."[44] Note that the description is written as modestly as can be, with an emphasis on the group's piety. In this carefully crafted public document, the focus is on written communication instead of oral argumentation (the extent to which they actually participated in oral argumentation in their meetings is discussed later).

A crucial distinction between the LLS and the secret debating society is that the former operated as a non-exclusive, non-secret organization from its inception. In fact, the openness of Oberlin's literary societies was a source of general pride on campus, as heralded by this 1858 *Oberlin Evangelist* article: "the literary Societies (of Oberlin) move on harmoniously, are not secret, and neither now nor ever, have they been, as too often in some other Colleges, prolific centres of jealousies and plots against the government of the College."[45] The LLS operated in full view of the Ladies' Board of Managers, a regulatory body that oversaw the activities of all women students on campus. The board was composed of the women spouses of Oberlin's men faculty and trustees (there were no women faculty or trustees at the time), who "had the narrow horizon of home women who have never known enlarging studies or experience in the outside world."[46] Marianne Parker Dascomb, member of the Ladies' Board of Managers and first Principal of the Female Department, was listed as an honorary member of the LLS when it was founded. Over the years, the Ladies' Board maintained strict supervision of the group. Dascomb and other members of the board visited meetings periodically, and faculty were invited to read prayers or lecture to the group. Gendered decorum was a consideration at every step, and the Ladies' Board readily intervened whenever the group was seen as pushing the boundaries of femininity too far. For example, a frenzy of interest coalesced around the idea that the society should publish a newspaper. Members contacted an editor, had a publishing contract drawn up, and even decided that the new publication would be called the "Oberlin Ladies' Banner." When the Ladies' Board heard of the plan, its members expressed that they "totally disapproved," and the idea was swiftly squelched.[47]

Records of LLS meetings were preserved beginning in 1846, and the minute books provide a sense of the society's constitution, business, and agenda.[48] On May 6, 1846, the group adopted a constitution stipulating that membership was open to any "young lady" willing to abide by the rules of the society.[49] Moreover, all members were required to attend the society's weekly meetings. Those who were tardy or absent without a good excuse were subject to the hardly insignificant fine of 6¼ cents. New officers were elected each month to the roles of president, vice president, recording secretary, corresponding secretary, treasurer, and critic.

Committees were devised with specific tasks to research in order to guide discussion and collective decision-making.

But did members actually debate at LLS meetings, such that the society deserves the title of first college women's debating club? According to the minutes, meetings often included collective singing, the reading of essays, and discussion of a controversial question or resolution. This final task generally involved two participants (called "disputants"), who were assigned to the affirmative and negative side of the question. It also included "remarks from a critic"—one of the students who provided feedback—or was opened up for commentary from anyone in the society. A meeting held on June 5, 1846, is typical of the period. It began with a roll call, followed by singing, prayer, and then more singing. Louisa Lovell read an essay, "A Glance at the Present State of the World." A "discussion" then ensued on the question, "is it the duty of Christians in the USA to go on foreign missions while there are three million heathens in our own country?" Elizabeth Wakely argued in favor of the affirmative side, while Lucy Stone took the negative. Other propositions featured at meetings during this period similarly highlight the conservative and religious focus of the society: "Ought this institution to be devoted exclusively to the education of pious young persons?,"[50] "Would it be for the advantage of the country to have a national costume established by law?,"[51] and "Resolved, that it was expedient to form a new missionary society."[52] While these topics certainly seem to lend themselves to oral argumentation, LLS minutes of this period do not provide information about the content of their exchanges, nor was a vote recorded (if the society put it to a vote at all). One account suggests that while discussions were plentiful during the early years of the LLS, the first oration was not performed until 1874.[53] However, another club publication maintains, "orations and debates had long prevailed in the private meetings of the societies."[54]

Early LLS discussions seem to be based upon the oral presentation of two competing perspectives that members prepared in advance and in writing. In so doing, Oberlin women were likely attempting to maintain a distinction that may appear arbitrary to the contemporary reader.[55] However, their meetings would certainly have allowed for some experimentation before that time. Frances J. Hosford speculates that the meetings must have entailed "a written discussion and not a free debate" but can't help but wonder whether the line was ever crossed. Especially in the case of the defiant Lucy Stone, Hosford queries, "did she follow her text always, or did her facile thought and speech sometimes leap unbidden into the thick of the fight?"[56] I surmise the LLS chose to call their activities "discussions" instead of "orations" or "debates" in their records in order to avoid rousing the suspicions of the Ladies' Board. As detailed in the next section, Stone, Brown, and others decided to move beyond the surveilled space of the LLS in order to create their own opportunity to engage in unbridled oral argumentation.

The First Debating Society for U.S. College Women

The first rule of the secret debating club was, apparently, "you do not talk about the secret debating club." How else can we account for the fact that many of the details surrounding the story of Lucy Stone and Antoinette Brown's society remain elusive? Its clandestine nature meant that there are no grand accounts of its activities. The group lacked the formality and institutional oversight that characterized the LLS. There are no meeting minutes. In fact, the first public mention of the secret club came more than forty-five years later, in 1892, when the nationwide U.S. women's club movement had gained considerable momentum. Around that time, Stone and Brown sought to remember the details of the club in order to promote the claim that they founded the first women's debating society.

Lucy Stone first came to Oberlin from her home in West Brookfield, Massachusetts, in 1843. Her father disapproved of Stone's plan to go to college and initially refused to support her financially. As a result, she was not able to enroll at Oberlin until she was twenty-five years old, having saved up years of teaching wages to support her studies. Stone also took advantage of Oberlin's commitment to learning and labor. She paid her expenses during her first year by teaching in Oberlin's Preparatory Department for 12½ cents per day and cleaning the boarding halls for 3 cents per hour (she reportedly propped up her Greek book so she could study while washing the dishes).[57]

Stone also found employment working in the village of Oberlin. The abolitionist view of the college prevailed among the villagers, and many people of color found a welcoming home in Oberlin in the 1840s. Oberlin's schools, and some churches, were integrated, and people of color made up a significant portion of the overall population.[58] Historian J. Brent Morris argues that the village was "one of the most important communities in the abolitionist movement . . . because of the unique circumstances in its early years that gathered an unprecedented multiracial and cohesive abolitionist population in the Ohio wilderness that maintained a fever pitch of reform agitation throughout the antebellum period."[59] Moreover, it was a crucial stop on the Underground Railroad—the last before reaching Canada. Stone earned money by teaching African American adults, many of them formerly enslaved, at the Liberty School.[60] By day, the space served as a school where students learned literacy skills; by night, it was a meeting place for people to share stories and testify about the horrors of slavery.[61]

On campus and in the wider community, abolitionism was rooted in the Church and the Constitution, which made Lucy Stone's identification as a radical Garrisonian a liability.[62] She regularly felt the watchful eye of the Ladies' Board upon her. As she pushed gendered boundaries ranging from speaking in public to refusing to wear a bonnet in church (due to headaches), Stone ironically acquired some rhetorical practice in pleading her case before the board. Luckily, in Antoinette Brown, Stone found a kindred spirit who was also dedicated to a career in public life. Brown sought to become a minister at a time when it was unheard-of for women to do so. She arrived on campus in 1846, and was able to complete Oberlin's Literary Course at an accelerated pace due to her prior schooling. Both friends graduated in 1847.[63] Stone and Brown had an intimate friendship that began at Oberlin and thrived throughout their lifetimes. They referred to each other as "sisters" and, fittingly, became sisters-in-law when they later married the Blackwell brothers, Henry and Samuel.[64]

The secret debating society was likely founded in 1846 or 1847, when both Stone and Brown were in residence at Oberlin and thinking ahead about their future paths.[65] It is around this time that both students also found the activities of the LLS lacking, as Stone's prospective career as anti-slavery lecturer and Brown's as a preacher came into focus.[66] In particular, Stone's resolve to gain rhetorical skills at Oberlin redoubled.

In 1846 alone, she checked out Hugh Blair's *Lectures on Rhetoric and Belles-Lettres* from the Oberlin College Library,[67] delivered her first public speech, "Why Do We Rejoice Today?," to the "Disenfranchised Americans of Oberlin, Ohio" as they celebrated West Indian Independence Day,[68] and was deeply inspired by the passionate lectures and debates of Abby Kelley Foster and Stephen Foster, who visited Oberlin twice that year.[69]

The fullest account of the secret debating society deserves lengthy quotation, as it details the events that led to the creation of the group:

> The young men had to hold debates as part of their work in rhetoric, and the young women were required to be present, for an hour and a half every week, in order to help form an audience for the boys, but were not allowed to take part. Lucy was intending to lecture and Antoinette to preach. Both wished for practice in public speaking. They asked Professor Thome, the head of that department, to let them debate. He was a man of liberal views—a Southerner who had freed his slaves—and he consented. Tradition says that the debate was exceptionally brilliant. More persons than usual came in to listen, attracted by curiosity. But the Ladies' Board immediately got busy, St. Paul was invoked, and the college authorities forbade any repetition of the experiment. A few of the young women, led by Lucy, organized the first debating society ever formed among college girls. At first they held their meetings secretly in the woods, with sentinels on the watch to give warning of intruders. When the weather grew colder, Lucy asked an old colored woman who owned a small house, the mother of one of her colored pupils, to let them have the use of her parlor. At first she was doubtful, fearing that the meetings might be a cover for flirtation; but when she found that the debating society was made up of girls only, she decided that it must be an innocent affair, and gave her consent. Her house was on the outskirts of the town, and the girls came one or two at a time, so as not to attract attention. Lucy opened the first formal meeting with the following statement: 'We shall leave this college with the reputation of a thorough collegiate course, yet not one of us has received any rhetorical or elocutionary training. Not one of us could state a question or argue it in successful debate. For this reason I have proposed the formation of this association.'[70]

This passage appears in a biography of Lucy Stone authored by her daughter, Alice Stone Blackwell, who pieced together this account based on the recollections of her mother and her aunt, Antoinette Brown.

It is necessary to take this story with a grain of salt. Refracted through a fusion of cognitive, linguistic, and affective experience, stores of auto-biographical memory can be activated in narrative form at various points in one's life.[71] Memory, of course, is often fragmentary.[72] A later episode illustrates the complexities of memory as Stone and Brown attempted to note the importance of the debating society in their later lives. In 1892, forty-five years after their graduation from Oberlin, Brown was invited to give a speech to the General Federation of Women's Clubs meeting in Chicago.[73] The number of women's clubs had grown enormously by the last decade of the nineteenth century, and Brown was intent on securing the legacy of their early debating society. She wrote to Stone, imploring her to recall whatever she could about their secret club. Brown's letter reveals that she was quite fuzzy on the details ("Just *who* besides ourselves took part, at least now and then?," "Please think of *every thing* and remind me. We discussed ways & means of work what else?"), but did remember that the club was informal, without a constitution or officers, and met at a house on the outskirts of Oberlin.[74] That they did not have a constitution or officers is yet another piece of evidence distinguishing the secret society from the LLS. Emphatic that the society be recognized as the first in the history of women's clubs, Brown's purpose was clear: "I go to Chicago on *purpose to immortalize* that primary women's Club."[75]

After ostensibly sending a reply that was lost in the mail, Stone wrote again on May 5, 1892, just days before Brown's speech, with her recollection:

> It was at the house of a colored woman whom I was teaching to read. I think she was the mother of Langston. His father was a white man who brought her with her children there to education. But this is nothing. I asked her to return the favor of my teaching by letting me have the use of her parlor one P.M. a week. She asked if there would be any boys, and I said no, and then she let us have her little parlor. You and I and Lettice Smith, and Helen Cooke and I think Elizabeth Wakely and perhaps Emmeline French. We discussed educational, political, moral

& religious questions, and especially we learned to stand and speak, to put motions, how to treat amendments &c.[76]

This letter, which captures Stone's reminiscences about the parlor debates and the students who took part, contains the extent of the additional details to be gleaned about the clandestine debating society. Writing just five months before her death, Stone recalls some details, but her memory is foggy. There is no mention of debating in the woods behind the college. "Langston" likely refers to John Mercer Langston, who graduated from Oberlin in 1849 and went on to become a U.S. congressperson. However, his mother died in 1834 and never took up residence in Oberlin (Langston boarded with white families).[77] Thus, the identity of the woman who hosted the debates is, regrettably, unknown. Stone does supply details about the students who may have been present in the secret meetings, and gives a broad sense of the topics they pursued. Most significantly, she highlights that the society asked its members to "stand and speak" on a wide range of issues—phrasing that suggests that they did indeed focus on oratorical performance instead of reading essays or prepared written arguments.

When Brown ultimately delivered her speech to the gathering of ardent clubwomen, she repeated many of these details, emphasizing the freedom they felt because their club met off campus. She credits her friend with primary leadership of the club: "Lucy Stone was the Leif Ericsson of our venture, when this band of now almost traditional Norsewomen put forth upon the unknown sea."[78] Comparison to the Icelandic explorer is odd but apt if we consider that the established rhetorical activities on Oberlin's campus were familiar, tame, and carried out under the authority of college faculty and administrators. The secret debating society was an adventure into new and uncultivated spaces. Hazardous as it was, those choppy waters provided the opportunity to experiment. Stone passed away in October 1893 at age seventy-five. Brown, seven years her junior, lived to see ninety-six. Even in her twilight years, she continued to tell the story of the "first girls' debating club." At times, she emphasized their meeting place in the village house, and at others, described how the women enjoyed their "debating class in the woods." This memory became incredibly important to Brown's understanding of herself, her friendship with Stone, and their collective legacy. Upon her death in 1921, Brown's obituary even noted her involvement in the first debating society for "college girls."[79]

Why does this story continue to resonate as a historical narrative? Contained in the vignette of the secret debating club are all of the elements of a riveting feminist tale: it has a hook, a dash of intrigue, and it places two well-known figures, Stone and Brown, at its center. Historian Joan Wallach Scott suggests that history itself is "a fantasized narrative that imposes sequential order on otherwise chaotic and contingent occurrences."[80] As stories are repeated and passed down over time, they are necessarily distorted, in that a reproduction is always partial and altered from the original.[81] Yet as they reverberate through different historical contexts, feminist narratives are familiar enough to suggest continuities between past and present subjects.[82] I contend that the story of Stone and Brown's club is told so often because it activates a particularly dramatic element of feminist historical imagination: the right to speak and be heard. It has come to function as a representative anecdote for larger struggles for inclusion in the history of public address and education. Filtered through layers of history and memory, the story pivots on spatial politics in their gendered and raced specificities, commandeering our attention because of the perils and pleasures involved in creating and traveling to spaces for argument.

The institutional regulation of space in nineteenth-century Oberlin was a manifestation of tensions between the college's inclusionary ideal and the realities of its execution—and with good reason. The layout of many nineteenth-century women's colleges differed greatly from that of men's colleges. Men college students could expect to move freely between buildings across the campus and stayed in dormitories with multiple entrances; women's colleges such as Mount Holyoke, Vassar, and Wellesley consolidated classrooms, chapels, libraries, and even housing in a single building where students could be constantly overseen.[83] As more institutions turned to coeducation at the turn of the nineteenth century, they often maintained spatial segregation through separate classes or through the creation of geographically distinct "junior colleges" or "sister colleges" for women.[84] Oberlin's much earlier experiment in coeducation meant that students were under internal and external scrutiny. In order to guard against fears of coeducation gone amiss (the masculinizing of women students, the feminizing of men students), Oberlin's administrators maintained rules regarding proper and respectable uses of the space on and around the campus. There were strict regulations governing when students had to be in the boarding halls, although visitors were allowed during designated hours. Romantic relationships among students were discouraged (although they did occur). Women students could walk together, enjoying a "good deal of liberty in a sensible way," but could not walk with men for leisure without permission.[85] The Ladies' Board even admonished women students for "engaging promiscuously in playing in the yards of their boarding house" in 1854.[86] Although all students could occupy the same classrooms, gendered expectations structured the possibilities of what could be allowed to occur there.

The rhetoric classroom itself became another space to enact symbolic power. Women students could be there, but they could not share in the benefits that embodied, oral argumentation provided. Pierre Bourdieu argues that the symbolic power of social position manifests through extra-linguistic phenomena such as clothing choice or an orator's proximity to a podium, "all of which place the legitimate speaker in a pre-eminent position and structure the interaction through the spatial structure which they impose on it."[87] Rituals of exclusion regulate the gendered space of a formal university debate. Oberlin's women were required to sit in the audience, physically separated from the stage and podium where the authorized speakers (men) practiced and refined their rhetorical skills. Active complicity may have characterized the relationship between the women students and the dominant group when they obeyed college policy and remained audience members for the debates. However, Stone and Brown subverted this power when they asked Thome for the opportunity to debate. The institution then flexed its metaphorical muscle and demanded that they be silenced for not performing proper gender roles. The act of going beyond the institution to create a secret debating society in the woods and in a private residence in the village can be understood as a move to seize symbolic power again by cultivating new spaces for argument.[88]

Studying these unexpected spaces for argument is crucial to understanding the varied ways that women have historically participated in civic life. For example, Nan Johnson argues that we must look we look for women not only in the "powerful public rhetorical space of the podium and pulpit," but also in the parlor.[89] The Oberlin case shows us that we may indeed find debating women in the parlor or in the shadows of a wooded area. The desire to debate took Oberlin women traveling, across the campus and into the village. By design, we cannot know the details of what happened in those sacred spaces. Stone and Brown could not even fully remember them when they tried later in life. Yet this early debating club demonstrates the porousness of public and private spaces, where a stealth debating society incubated skills that would later be utilized in more conventional spaces, including the public stage and the pulpit.

Imagine the exhilaration the debaters must have felt as they snuck out to assemble in secret at their arboreal meeting place. Oberlin itself was a community "carved out of the wilderness," and a departure from the highly regulated, built environment of the campus and into the untamed woods must have been both frightening and liberating.[90] The words they spoke during these gatherings were evanescent, lost among the other secrets of the forest. Yet we do know that this deliberate movement to new spaces made them agents of rhetorical action. These women traveled, and they debated—they made noise, they tested ideas, they were temporarily unhampered by the scrutiny of the Ladies' Board—as lookouts stood watch, ready to alert the group of those who would puncture the treasured space they created.

Their story is one that galvanizes familiar tropes in feminist history. Joan Wallach Scott argues that one of the most prevalent scenes in Western feminist memory is that of the great woman orator. Stories of iconic women taking the podium—despite all odds—provide successive generations of feminists with fodder for their own time. Such fantasies "function as resources to be invoked," where the details do not matter as much as the "shared jouissance" in finding commonality with other women.[91] Though in this case there was no podium to seize, the narrative of the stealthy debaters is alluring because it involves orating women, transgressing traditional boundaries.[92] Add that this band of orating women moved, literally and symbolically, into unauthorized spaces and places. In patriarchal cultures, gatherings of women in the woods are often mythologized as a threatening force. Emboldened by lunacy and witchcraft, and set against the backdrop of the dark forest, such assemblies are to be feared. Even years later, the woods behind the college presented a worrisome problem for the Ladies' Board. In an attempt to corral other adventurous young women who favored uncharted treks into the woods, they created the "Ladies' Grove," a designated and approved space in which they might perambulate. The Female Department revised its regulations in 1859 to say "Young ladies, who do not reside with their parents, are not allowed to walk in the fields or woods, excepting the grove assigned for this purpose."[93] Thus, a space of intrigue that once hosted covert rhetorical activity was later brought within the purview of the institution, colonized and manicured for approved gendered behavior.

The Oberlin debaters, as far as we know, escaped into the woods for fairly conventional reasons. Yet this version of the origin story is certainly made more intriguing by the sense of risk that characterizes it. In seizing a rhetorical education denied them by their institution, these Oberlin students participated in debate under duress. What kind of punishment would have awaited Stone, Brown, and the other debaters if they had been caught? The narrative is animated by the very idea that they would have faced the wrath of the disapproving Ladies' Board and perhaps even broader punishment, given their violation of rules regulating gendered space.

They thus engaged in risk-taking in a very real and material sense, but theorists of argumentation will note that the very act of debating is a self-risking enterprise. Ideally, interlocutors will envision debates as spaces of mutual respect, acknowledging and remaining open to the possibility that their perspectives may be transformed as a result of their encounter.[94] As Douglas Ehninger explains, argument itself is "person-risking" and "person-making," through an acknowledgment of shared humanity. For argument to succeed, interlocutors commit to a "restrained partisanship," which confers personhood upon their opponents and allows them to gain personhood for themselves.[95] The formation of the secret debating society can be seen as a deliberate cultivation of space that created the possibility of such person-risking and person-making for its participants. As Stone made clear in her remarks—"we shall leave this college with the reputation of a thorough collegiate course, yet not one of us has received any rhetorical or elocutionary training"—they were being treated as less than full persons, kept from accessing the full bounty of higher education.[96] To engage, finally and freely, in the rhetorical exercises they wished to must have made the women debaters experience the force of their acquired "personhood" rather acutely.

As the story goes, the debaters sought refuge in a parlor in the village during the frigid winter months. Jasmine Nichole Cobb argues that the early nineteenth-century parlor was largely seen as a protected domestic space for privileged white women; "no matter her civil status, occupation, or wealth, a woman of African descent did not belong within the conceptual space of the parlor or its indispensable notions of domesticity."[97] Still, some African American families maintained parlors during the antebellum period, and the very idea of a parlor became a "place where White and Blacks collectively experimented with the free Black body and visions of national inclusion."[98] Oberlin—an "antebellum interracial utopia"—was a unique place for the story of the secret women's debating society to unfold.[99]

Details about the woman who hosted the debaters are not available, but it is possible to narrow down the possible location of the hibernal meeting place. Housing in the village of Oberlin was racially integrated during this period, and wealth often determined where people lived. The poorest people of color clustered in the southeast portion of the town while wealthier families tended to live in the northeast near the Liberty School House (where Stone taught to earn extra money).[100] Alice Stone Blackwell's account tells us that the meeting place was in a small house on the "outskirts" of town. Stone's 1892 recollection framed the interaction as a favor between herself and the woman who lived there: Stone taught the woman to read, and in exchange, called upon her to allow the debaters to congregate in her home.

Part of the story's appeal is that it evokes fantasies of (and perhaps genuine longing for) gender and race diversity in the history of debate. It is refreshing to hear that the first college women's debating society in the United States took place, in part, in the home of an African American ally. One can imagine the parlor a potential as a contact space, a site for women of different races to "stag[e] public displays for private audiences."[101] There is ample evidence that African Americans were actively participating in community-based literary and debating societies around the country at this time; in the 1830s and 1840s, they were especially prevalent in urban neighborhoods of Philadelphia and Pittsburgh.[102] However, there is no evidence that women of color participated as debaters in the secret club in Oberlin. According to Oberlin's student records, eight students were recorded in the catalogue under the labels of both "female" and "colored students" between 1846 and 1847.[103] While at least one of these students appears in the minutes of the LLS, none were included in Stone's memory of the parlor debate participants. Thus, the more precise story of the clandestine society is that it is one about white women debaters in the home of an African American woman. Still, she plays an important role in opening her parlor to the Oberlin debaters. Though her initial impulse was to worry about decorum, fear of the immodesty of a mixed-gender debate gives way to relief when she realizes it was composed of women participants.

In sum, the Oberlin story is one of famous orators who got their start by negotiating the bounds of propriety and ultimately triumphing over various prohibitions of the time period, but we ought not paint too rosy a picture about what it meant for gender or race emancipation. After Stone and Brown graduated in 1847, the locus of rhetorical education for Oberlin women was again concentrated in the LLS, and later, in the Aeolioian Society. These societies included a more racially and ideologically diverse set of debaters who were similarly concerned with securing spaces for argumentation and creating a legacy for their argument culture.

The LLS and Aeolioian Society

Every year, new cohorts of students cycled through Oberlin's authorized literary society for women, the LLS. The minutes reveal that there was continued concern about the proper behavior of women as they engaged in rhetorical education and performance. On August 8, 1849, a meeting centered on the issue of whether their anniversary showcase event (held the week before the commencement ceremony) could take place in the evening. Members were alarmed that an evening event might be perceived as indecorous, noting, "there is romance in the night, its soft and dusty light." Instead of sneaking off into the woods at night as the secret debating society had, the LLS self-regulated when it came to the possibility of nocturnal impropriety. The Ladies' Board also continued to have a heavy hand in the activities of the society. In September of the same year, two members of the Ladies' Board attended a meeting to advise the club that they ought to meet less frequently, as the board feared that their activities were interfering with the regular course of study.[104] Meanwhile, the society's regular exercises included fewer discussions in favor of more compositions and declamations.

During this period, the LLS benefited from the leadership of another notable Lucy: Lucy Stanton (later Lucy Stanton Day Sessions).[105] Stanton was an African American woman who grew up in Cleveland. Her stepfather, John Brown, was a barber—a successful businessperson who was also a major figure in the Underground Railroad. The family housed fugitive slaves in their home and in Brown's barber shop. They were active in the social life of the city, and Brown became "Cleveland's wealthiest African American citizen" after he invested his barbershop earnings in real estate. He later joined a group to organize a school for African American children.[106] Stanton enrolled as a student at Oberlin in 1846. While she is not among those who participated in the secret debating society according to Stone's recollection, she was active in the LLS, regularly reading essays on topics like "Scenes of the South" and "The Female Missionary" and contributing critic's remarks.[107] Fellow member and anti-slavery activist Sallie Holley nominated Stanton for the position of LLS president in August 1850. Though Holley argued that Stanton earned it as the result of her "dignity, ability, and faithful service," other members worried that having an African American president would make Oberlin "more notorious and hated than ever."[108] Despite their reservations, Stanton was elected to a one-month term. The duties of the president included leading the meetings, enforcing the constitution and bylaws, and delivering a farewell address when the term came to an end.[109] Because of the month of her election, Stanton also presided over the LLS anniversary exercises.

As a graduate of the Literary Course, Stanton was invited to read her essay at Oberlin's commencement ceremony. While her classmates spoke on subjects such as "The Sublimity of Life" and "The Charm of Science," Stanton's impassioned speech was entitled "A Plea for the Oppressed."[110] She called upon her audience as statespeople, women, reformers, and

Figure 1. Lucy Stanton
Day Sessions. Photo
courtesy of the Oberlin
College Archives.

Christians to acknowledge that slavery is the highest crime."[111] Delivered just weeks before the enactment of the Fugitive Slave Act of 1850, Stanton's speech made an impact. One observer reported in the *Oberlin Evangelist* that Stanton's performance met every expectation: "her charming voice, modest demeanor, appropriate pronunciation and graceful cadences, riveted attention, while the truthfulness of her pictures controlled the emotions of her hearers."[112] So emotionally captivated were they that one audience member and trustee, the Reverend John Keep, stood up and declared that Stanton's piece disproved all of the naysayers who predicted that the admission of people of color would ruin the institution back in the 1830s. The rest of the audience momentarily violated a rule of the ceremony by bursting into applause.[113] Stanton is recognized as the first African American woman to complete a college course, but it was Oberlin's non-degree-granting Literary Course, so she is not usually credited with being the first African American woman graduate (that honor goes to Mary Jane Patterson, who graduated from Oberlin with a bachelor's degree in 1862). Stanton went on to marry Oberlin alumni William H. Day and later lived in Cleveland. She was a writer and librarian, and worked with Day on editorial tasks for *The Aliened American*, an African American newspaper. Later, an estrangement and divorce from Day made it extremely difficult for Stanton to gain employment, but she ultimately did teach at schools in Ohio, Mississippi, Georgia, Alabama, and Tennessee. She was also an advocate for abolition and temperance, a lifelong clubwoman, and an active member of the AME Church.[114]

Though it had certainly served Stanton well, the LLS struggled with discussions during this period. The society's newly revamped constitution, adopted on April 10, 1850, specified that the club was dedicated to "writing, speaking and discussion" and levied a hefty 10-cent fine for neglecting to perform assigned duties. When the discussions were successful, they engaged topics such as "Resolved, that the Indian has greater claims upon the American people, for their labors and missionary efforts than the African race, in Africa" (October 13, 1852) and "Resolved, that the medical profession is a sphere for which woman is well adapted and that the elevation of the sex requires that she should understand the theory and practice" (May 25, 1853). Still, many discussions failed due to an absent or unprepared disputant. Though the constitution placed considerable importance on the discussions, LLS members appear to have been split on their utility. On April 24, 1850, Sallie Holley and Sarah Pellet debated the resolution "resolved, that discussions and declamations should not be sustained in a young ladies' literary society." One of the disputants failed to show at the very next meeting, so Pellet "occupied the floor [with] eight minutes on the subject, [that] we want no inefficient members in the society."[115] The topic of whether they should participate in discussions at all continued to be a theme at LLS meetings throughout the 1850s, and there were various attempts to improve them. In March 1852, a member proposed that that they change the number of disputants from two to four. The society voted to approve this measure, but the discussion failed at the next two meetings due to unprepared members.[116] In April 1853, members again deliberated over whether discussions should be eliminated. The somewhat bewildering outcome of that deliberation was to make disputants do more work earlier, by requiring that they present their question to the president one week before it was performed. In what was perhaps a show of defiance, discussions at the next three meetings failed due to lack of preparation on the part of the disputants.

Disgruntled with the lack of debate and oration in the LLS, Catherine Von Volkenburg convinced a small group of members to peel off in 1852. They founded the Young Ladies' Lyceum (known after 1862 as the Aeolioian Society, a name meaning "light bearers"), which was variously considered a "daughter" society or a "rival" society to the LLS. Aeolioian members were indeed more daring in their approach, and their meetings were likely studded with spirited barbs as they debated topics like foreign emigration, the value of large bonnets, and the relative benefit of the Crusades to humankind.[17] In the privacy of their meeting space, Aeolioian members could practice those rhetorical skills that their predecessors in the earlier secret society craved.

Still, the LLS and Aeolioian were never entirely different. They had a similar organizational structure, and worked together to establish a library.[18] Attendance problems seem endemic to the activity, as the Aeolioian minutes also reported periodic discussion failures. In the 1860s and 1870s, the LLS regained much of its vitality. Almost every major issue in public culture was reflected in LLS meetings. On May 10, 1865, the group decided to forgo normal business in order to pass a number of statement honoring President Abraham Lincoln. Included among them was this solemn resolution: "Resolved, that since the death of our President we cherish if possible our intenser hatred toward Slavery which has generated in our Republic this foul Rebellion, and which has dared to lay its murderous hands upon the noblest ruler the world has ever seen." Discussions of this period included probes into suffrage (July 12, 1866), the annexation of San Domingo (March 29, 1871), and the expedience of the Civil Rights Act of 1875 (April 7, 1875). Members also debated about the mechanics of their rhetorical activities: should they stand while speaking? They resolved they should not. Does the speaker or the writer exert more eloquence? No vote was recorded. Should they merge with the Aeolioian? They did not at that time.[19]

Attitudes about the suitability of women orators gradually changed on campus. Bold students consistently challenged the rule prohibiting women graduates of the Classical Course from reading their commencement essays. In 1858, a demure Quaker student made the request, and the administration reportedly relented, faced with the absurdity of the notion that she could pose a threat to their ideas about proper feminine behavior.

After that, women graduates of the Classical Course were permitted to read (but not extemporaneously deliver) their essays.[120] That final prohibition finally gave way in 1870, when graduate Harriet Keeler rebelled and launched into extemporaneous delivery (making eye contact with the audience and abandoning a prescripted message), rather than reading her essay on the commencement stage.[121] In the summer of 1874, the LLS dedicated several meetings to the issue of whether it should support the Aeolioian Society in its quest to guarantee the right to public orations. According to the minutes on July 20, 1874, the LLS voted to publish the following message in the *College Review*: "The Ladies' Literary Society wish it to be understood that they are fully in favor of orations in all meetings of the Society both public and private and heartily approve of the request made by their Sister society that this privilege to be granted." As a result of their show of support, the two societies successfully petitioned the faculty to secure this right. At this time, they also formed the Union Society Association to better coordinate their joint activities.

In the 1880s, the two societies played an active role in connecting Oberlin's residents to broader public culture. They worked together to host public debates and bring the most renowned orators and musicians to campus.[122] One member, who was later renowned in her own right, gives us particular insight into the Aeolioian during this period. Mary Church Terrell was first a student in Oberlin's Preparatory Department and graduated from the college in 1884. She went on to be the first president of the National Association of Colored Women and a founding member of the National Association for the Advancement of Colored People. In her autobiography, *A Colored Woman in a White World*, Church Terrell states that "it would be difficult for a colored girl to go through a white school with fewer unpleasant experiences occasioned by race prejudice than I had."[123] She expanded her intellectual horizons in Oberlin because it provided a space in which to learn and grow. Her sense was that overt discrimination would have never been tolerated during her time there. One marker of her equality with her white counterparts was that she was twice selected to represent the Aeolioian in a public debate against the LLS, including in the showcase debate before commencement, a crowning achievement for women students in Oberlin's literary societies. She credits the Aeolioian with her knowledge of parliamentary procedure, which became very important in her leadership roles later in life. Moreover, the society gave her the "ability to speak effectively on [her] feet."[124] As formal prohibitions against women's rhetoric became a distant memory, generations of Oberlin students similarly carried their identities as debaters and club members with them into their future pursuits. During this time, graduated LLS members decided to activate an alumnae network dedicated to ensuring the sustainability of the argument culture they experienced at Oberlin.

Commemorating Oberlin's Debating Women

By 1936, one-third of all women graduates of Oberlin College had been members of the LLS or the Aeolioian.[125] Though their time together on campus was relatively short, the clubs fostered a sense of affiliation and connection to fellow members that extended far beyond Oberlin. The college's reputation as a pioneer in coeducation deepened a sense of coalition among its women graduates. Alumnae recognized the gravity of the club's early activities, and worked tirelessly to preserve memories of the past and to guarantee a future for the LLS. Emilie Royce Comings and Frances J. Hosford were leaders in collecting recollections from alumnae and narrativizing their history. The membership articulated a collective reverence for the debaters who had come before them, and alumnae could feel that they were part of something bigger than themselves. To be a "debating woman" at Oberlin, then, was both a description of participation in college activity and a lifelong social identity.

Securing and sustaining spaces for rhetorical activity was an ongoing issue, and alumnae were often at the center of fundraising efforts to ensure that women students would have a comfortable place to gather. The attic of Ladies' Hall remained the LLS meeting space for thirty years, though its spartan appearance was addressed over time. The unpainted floors were covered with a green and red flat weave carpet. The backless benches were replaced with cane-seated chairs. Meetings were no longer held by candlelight after the group purchased a kerosene lamp. They acquired a speaking platform for the room, as well as tables to distinguish the roles of president and secretary.[126] Yet room maintenance was a perennial functional and aesthetic concern for the students.[127] They made provisions for keeping the rooms tidy, and had to budget for kerosene to illuminate the space. The shared space became another point of collaboration between the societies. Aeolioian members requested that they be able to share the lamp that had been acquired by the LLS, as the two societies met in the same room on different days of the week.[128] In 1858, Aeolioian members debated "Resolved that the ladies' Literary Society should have a well finished, well furnished and cheerful, pleasant room for the weekly meetings."[129] When they moved to the second Ladies' Hall in 1865, the society room received a significant upgrade. It boasted an elegant Brussels weave carpet. As club member Emilie Royce Comings recalled: "we girls of the '70s used to follow with fluttering hearts its large diagonal green figures from the chairs at one end of the room to the platform at the other, where we met our fate. Some elegant high back walnut chairs were purchased for the president and the secretary, which added greatly to the adornment of the room."[130] That she was able to remember that level of detail about the room over thirty years later is indicative of the importance of the space in her understanding and experience of the argument culture it housed.

The room in the second Ladies' Hall was an ideal meeting space for a while, but shortcomings emerged over time. At an LLS meeting on June 24, 1874, for example, a committee was appointed to look into the room's ventilation to address a "disagreeable odor." The space was too cramped to accommodate the growing societies and had become dilapidated. In 1875, the LLS and Aeolioian mobilized to raise money to construct a building to accommodate society meetings. By 1881, they had raised $3,000 and convinced the college to match their funds. Alumna Susan Sturges donated $5,000 more, and thus Sturges Hall was built in 1884 with an assembly room on the first floor and two society rooms on the second.[131] This was fortunate for the society members, as the building they had been using burned to the ground in 1886. The Sturges Hall room was large, furnished with sturdy wooden chairs and tables, a large platform, and dramatic drapes covering large windows—quite a change from their earliest attic dwelling![132] While this attention to buildings and furnishings may seem superficial, we ought not forget that the physical space was important for the symbolic activity that would take place in the room. As Hosford argues, "it is significant that the girls of early Oberlin, amid the roughness of frontier life, made a home of their society quarters. It is even more significant that their successive improvements were remembered and passed into tradition, so that we know what they were."[33] Acquiring and decorating a room was not a frivolous pursuit for members and alumnae. Debating women at Oberlin had long moved on from the parlor debates of the secret society, yet still they desired a "home" for their activities. The preservation of the rhetorical space ensured a continuing presence for women's argumentation and debate. One ancillary effect of this preservation was the creation of a bridge between past, present, and future debating women.

A small group of LLS alumnae met for lunch in Brooklyn, New York, in 1903, and the plan to form a formal alumnae association was hatched. Throughout the early twentieth century, the new association made meticulous records of its members, did research into the history of the club, kept the alumnae up-to-date about present club activity, and established a scholarship for LLS members pursuing graduate education. Association correspondence emphasized that they were part of the oldest college women's club in the United States, and claimed 1835 as their founding date. The LLS alumnae association also planned a centennial celebration of the LLS on June 17, 1935. The program for the celebration included a business meeting, a "love feast," and speeches from living LLS graduates (the oldest in attendance was Emma Monroe Fitch, who graduated in 1869).[34]

The main event of the celebration, however, was a pageant performed by current LLS members. Each debater took on a "character"—a former member of the club—and performed a sketch dramatizing the founding and other key moments in the society's history. The origin story told in the pageant is of women debaters struggling to convince Marianne Parker Dascomb, the first Principal of the Female Department of the Oberlin Collegiate Institute, to let them organize in 1835. Their script supposes that founding members were actually attempting to meet in secret, but were found out by Dascomb, so they tried to cover by inviting her to be an honorary member. They actually wanted to put the word "debate" in their constitution, but were dissuaded by Dascomb:

BRANCH. Madame Chairman—July 21, 1835—We, the undersigned members of the Female Department of the Oberlin Collegiate Institute, associate ourselves to be called and known by the name of Young Ladies' Association of the Oberlin Collegiate Institute for the promotion of literature and *debate*.

MRS. DASCOMB. Well, really young ladies, do you consider debate quite genteel for our sex? And where was there any mention made of what should be your very first consideration?

CAPEN. (Sotto Voce) I knew it—Bible!

MOORE. (Hurriedly) Perhaps it would be more fitting to substitute *religion* for debate in Article I. I move it be adopted with that correction.[135]

This historical reconstruction obviously takes liberties, given the negligible evidence from 1835. That the LLS members of 1935 read a tradition of *debate* onto their predecessors that was in tension with Oberlin's dedication to religion is indicative of cultural changes then afoot.

After this initial scene, the pageant takes a strange turn, imagining that Adelia Field Johnston, Oberlin class of 1856 and the first woman faculty member and dean, has returned from the dead to forecast the future of the society for its original members. The Johnston character moves through the decades of the club, noting key members, while the LLS members of 1935 role-play their predecessors on the stage. Of the 1840s and 1850s, represented are

> *Antoinette Brown*, an ordained minister of the Congregational Church, until she herself was reformed from Orthodoxy to Unitarianism. *Lucy Stone*, foremost in the struggle for womens [sic] rights, so fearless that she could face a mob without a quickened heartbeat, so gentle that she could hush a crying child. Here is *Lucy Stanton*, the first colored woman to be admitted to a college club, or to receive a college diploma; and here is her friend and champion, *Sally Holley*, a northern woman of gentle birth and breeding, who will consecrate her life to the emancipation, and then to the education, of the colored race.[136]

Although it eclipses mention of the secret debating society, the pageant offers an alternative narrative by summoning the ghosts of Oberlin's

Figure 2. Alumnae at the LLS Centennial Jubilee, 1935. Photo courtesy of the Oberlin College Archives.

past debating women so that generations of women—young, aging, and dead—occupied the same space, at least momentarily. It cultivates a feminist heritage for current students and sustains the alumnae who assembled to celebrate the club. The specific details of their experiences may differ, yet there is something familiar about the tales of the historical women who have struggled to reach the podium that can serve as an inventional resource.[137] Generations of Oberlin alumnae cherished their membership and made a concerted effort to safeguard the memory and ensure the longevity of the hallowed club.

For a club to make it one hundred years is an impressive feat of longevity, especially because many intramural literary and debating clubs were transformed into intercollegiate debate teams during this period (Oberlin, too, fielded intercollegiate debate teams in the early twentieth century, even as the intramural societies were still active on campus). The Aeolioian and the LLS ultimately reunited in 1948 as a last-ditch effort to stay afloat as both societies faced dwindling membership. In 1952, they voted to disband for good. At a farewell tea, Ella Parmenter attempted to put this development into perspective, noting that Sturges Hall, once home to the LLS and the Aeolioian, would continue to house Oberlin's Department of Speech: "There, in the classrooms, women students gain many of the skills they used to gain in the literary societies. They have the added use of public address equipment and radio speaking to earlier skills. They learn and practice parliamentary procedure; they take part in panel discussions, they conduct forums, [and] participate in debate."[138] Parmenter's progress narrative is noteworthy, as it once again makes use of the idea of space to argue that the demise of the clubs was a sign of the transformation and expansion of opportunities for debating women in the twentieth century.

The Power of an Origin Story

Oberlin stands out as a leader in the history of coeducation and inter-racial education in the United States. Oberlin's women put pressure on the institution's ability to maintain gender-segregated spaces in the nineteenth century; they desired the same rhetorical education as men students, and this required securing and attending to physical spaces as part of the cultivation of their argument culture.

This discussion nuances our understanding of the first college women's debating society in the United States. Extant details of their efforts in both the secret society and the LLS lend considerable insight into the struggles women faced as they tried to access the benefits of a rhetorical education on a coeducational university campus. Ultimately, though, dating the original society back to the founding of the LLS in 1835 or the secret debating society in 1846 is not the main objective. As Lisa Tetrault reminds us in the context of another foundational feminist origin tale, "stories are made, not found."[139] Returning to such stories with an eye toward understanding how acts of remembering make events into myths need not discredit or render them false. Rather, it allows scholars to explore the power dynamics within the narratives, acknowledging that "an origins myth does not actually pinpoint a beginning so much as it acts as a filter that people use to impose a certain type of meaning onto a complex and contested landscape."[40] The Oberlin case underscores the rhetorical power afforded to one historical narrative on the basis that the debating society laid claim to the categories of "the first" and "women's."

Lucy Stone and Antoinette Brown Blackwell are the most well-known figures in this history, and the imprint of their time debating at Oberlin clearly made a difference in their lives as they pursued public careers that required oratorical excellence. The details of their secret debating society are murky—and that is precisely what makes the narrative inhabitable by generations of women debaters who came after them and by the scholars who study them. In taking both the secret debating society and the LLS into account, we have a much more expansive roster of debaters and a better sense of how an attic, a forest, a parlor, a classroom, and various campus buildings can serve as vital spaces for argument. This is a story characterized by exclusion and marginalization, but it is also much richer and more diverse than the origin story in popular circulation. It draws attention to the importance of a long-term cultivation strategy for argument cultures. That is, it required the deliberate and careful planning of debate alumnae to keep the momentum alive. As memories of previous generations of women debaters were passed down over this one hundred year period, the maintenance and improvement of their dwellings was a sign of their legitimacy within the institution. In doing so, LLS members charted new territory as they created and safeguarded a legacy for debating women at a coeducational institution of higher learning.

CHAPTER 2

"Women of Infinite Variety": The Ladies' Edinburgh Debating Society as an Intergenerational Argument Culture, 1865–1935

————·◆·————

From 1865 to 1935, predominantly middle- and upper-class white women of Edinburgh, Scotland, met monthly in the dining room of Sarah Elizabeth Siddons Mair's home to discuss and debate major political, social, literary, and aesthetic topics of the day. While Mair was the only member present for the society's entire seventy-year duration, other members often remained active for many years, revisiting previously debated topics and refining their arguments. The Ladies' Edinburgh Debating Society (LEDS) overlapped geographically and at times, concurrently, with better-known rhetorical theorists and practitioners. Prominent eighteenth-century Scots Hugh Blair, George Campbell, and Adam Smith lectured on belletristic rhetoric, which "sought to delineate and clarify aesthetic discursive qualities that affected listeners and readers."[1] Such teachings were popular in Scotland and widely influential in Europe and the United States.[2] Nineteenth-century theorists were less likely to publish their lectures than their eighteenth-century predecessors, yet student lecture notes provide contemporary scholars with a better sense of the rhetorical contributions of Scottish professors such as Alexander Bain and David Masson.[3]

Here is an opportunity to elucidate an understudied aspect of Scotland's history of rhetoric and education: women's participation in debate. At first glance, it is not difficult to understand why contemporary students of rhetoric might have studied Hugh Blair rather than Sarah Mair. As an educational campaigner and suffragist, Mair fought for women's right to gain access to courses where rhetorical theories were being taught as a part of formal university education. She did not formally lecture as a professor of Rhetoric or English Literature. Yet Mair and other members of the Ladies' Edinburgh Debating Society created an environment for rhetorical education and performance where argumentation was taught, presented, critiqued, and reflected upon. Participants tested ideas and considered their roles in Scottish society. As the result of ongoing deliberation, the group organically arrived at norms for sustainable argumentative engagement.

Rich archival materials attest to the group's activities as it transitioned from a literary society to a debating society. Early in the society's existence, the focus was divided between the publication of a literary journal for women and debates at the meetings. The journal, first known as *The Attempt* and later as the *Ladies' Edinburgh Literary Magazine*, provides insight into the argumentative activities of the LEDS because abstracts of the debates and future debate propositions were published for the benefit of the readership.[4] The unpublished minutes at this time were very sparse, recording only the propositions considered and debated, motions passed, and other organizational business. Later, as the person occupying the Secretary position changed, so too did the level of detail included in the minutes. In 1880, members voted to abandon work on the commercial enterprise of the journal in order to focus exclusively on their debates in society meetings. The final issue explains that the journal lacked the financial support and circulation it needed to thrive through subscriptions, yet the debates would "be carried on with unabated vigour, and, we hope, with still wider success."[5] Subsequent meeting minutes then began to include descriptions of arguments made in debates, rebuttals, critiques of the performances, and vote counts declaring a victor.[6] The decision to thoroughly record the content of arguments made in debates marks a momentous shift in the history of the society. Finally, an invaluable resource for rhetorical history lies in a commemorative volume published in 1936, one year after the LEDS voted to dissolve. Lettice Milne Rae's *Ladies in Debate: Being a History of the Ladies' Edinburgh Debating Society* includes reflections from different generations of LEDS members, a participant list, and a list of every proposition debated.[7]

Together, these resources span the years of the debating society's existence and serve to contextualize these Edinburgh women's rhetorical practices, including the evolution of arguments, ideas, and people, within a single organization across time. This chapter theorizes the Ladies' Edinburgh Debating Society as an "intergenerational argument culture." What rules or norms did the LEDS decide upon over the years to guarantee the sustainability of their argument culture? What is the value of intergenerational interaction in a debating society, and how does it relate to other cross-cutting, intersectional concerns? After placing the LEDS within the broader historical context of associational culture in the United Kingdom, moments where the society expressly hashed out a vision of its members' ideal argument culture are examined. Finally, I explore how the LEDS negotiated ideological and identity-based difference in its argument culture. In crafting its own argument culture, the LEDS demonstrates the potential and the problems with attempts to sustain debate across difference.

Associational Culture in the United Kingdom

The Ladies' Edinburgh Debating Society emerged out of an expansive social milieu of voluntary clubs and associations. Club culture in Scotland roughly maps onto Habermas's broad sketch of the political functions of the public sphere in Great Britain.[8] Philosophical, literary, and debating societies became mainstays of university and community life in Scotland's "Age of Improvement." Scots, and citizens of Edinburgh in particular, adapted to a number of changes in the eighteenth century that included the spread of capitalism and the loss of an Edinburgh-based governing body. The mushrooming of associational culture at the time can be traced to the ability of voluntary societies to create a space of experimentation and adaptation, a "means of asserting status for those outwith the established institutions and networks of state power."[9]

Associational culture often took the form of informal drinking, dining, or hobby clubs. Adult men of the middle classes dominated these activities, although social historian R. J. Morris maintains that "this adaptable and flexible form of social institution could never and was never limited to this group."[10] Community-based debating, which departed from the refined discussions of the salons, took place throughout the United Kingdom. In London, debating societies became more structured and thrived as a form of "rational entertainment" in the mid- to late eighteenth century. Public debates took place up to fourteen times a week, with some events drawing over one thousand audience members.[11] The shift from an "alehouse culture," full of beer, urination, yelling, fighting, and blasphemy, to more formal debates temporarily boded well for women wishing to watch the events.[12] Well-known clubs such as the Robin Hood Society first allowed women to attend the debates for free while men paid a fee. Soon thereafter, mixed-sex audiences were seen as an untapped economic opportunity.[13] Attempts to "feminize" an otherwise masculine and gritty debating activity were not met with much initial success, likely due to the high price tag of admission. Yet some Scottish groups, such as the Speculative Society of Dundee and the Pantheon Society, appear to have admitted women as audience members as early as the 1770s.[14] By 1780, women's participation in debate found new venues in four all-women London debating societies: La Belle Assemblée, the Female Parliament, the Female Congress, and the Carlisle House Debates for Women.[15]

One indication of the influence of debating societies is that they receive mention in eighteenth-century formal lectures and satirical performances. In his famous *Lectures on Rhetoric and Belles Lettres*, Scotland's preeminent rhetorical theorist, Hugh Blair, discusses the merits of debating organizations that allowed young men students to continue their studies by privately training for later public life. He claims that these societies aided better command of speaking, facility with expression, and a "copia verborum which could be acquired by no other means."[16] However, for Blair, the utility of debate only extends to elite, university-educated men. He shows little restraint in expressing his distaste for the more democratic organizations that functioned outside academia:

> As for those public and promiscuous societies, in which the multitudes are brought together, who are often of low stations and occupations, who are joined by no common bond of union, except a rage for public speaking, and have no object in view, but to make a show of their supposed talents, they are institutions of not merely a useless, but of a hurtful nature. They are in great hazard of proving seminaries of licentiousness, petulance, faction, and folly. They mislead those who, in their own callings, might be useful members of society, into phantastic plans of making a figure on subjects, which divert their attention from their proper business, and are widely remote from their sphere in life.[17]

Blair's use of the phrase "promiscuous societies" exhibits his classist assumptions about proper spheres of work, creating a clear division between those elite and educated men who could benefit from training in argumentation and the uneducated masses who were incapable of self-improvement and would only treat such associations as entertainment. Though commonly taken to refer to mixed-gender gatherings in the nineteenth century, the word "promiscuous" referred to a group "of mixed background, wealth, and education but had nothing to do with the presence—or absence—of women auditors" in Blair's time.[18] The idea that women would take part in debates was not a subject that needed to be explicitly discussed, given that he supported only those "academical associations" that would allow students to further explore university course material with the end goal of being "manly, correct, and persuasive."[19]

As debating societies gained prominence, so too did the humorists who sought to use them for a laugh. Stephen H. Browne argues that eighteenth-century satire was a "constitutive mode of cultural discourse" at the heart of classist and misogynist takes on the question of "who shall be eloquent?"[20] This point is exemplified in George Alexander Stevens's "Lecture on Heads," first presented in England in 1764. The satirical lecture became incredibly popular, and Stevens took it traveling in performances throughout England and Ireland, and in Boston and Philadelphia.[21] While many "heads" are lampooned in the lecture, his treatment of a woman moderator, or the President of a Ladies' Debating Society, is most intriguing:

> she would have physicians in petticoats, and lawyers with high heads, and French curls; then she would have *young* women of spirit to command our fleets and armies and *old* ones to govern the state:—she pathetically laments that women are considered as mere domestic animals, fit only for making pudding, pickling cucumbers, or registering cures for the measles and chincough. If this lady's wishes for reformation should ever be accomplished, we may expect to hear that an admiril is in histerics, that a general has miscarried, and that a prime minister was brought to bed the minute she opened the budget.[22]

Anxieties about women in power are expressed through purportedly funny gendered stereotypes—women are too feeble, too inclined toward domestic life, too prone to hysterics or other gendered ailments to pursue the avenues of power to which a debating society might lead them to believe they are entitled.[23] The idea that debating women of any class status would rank among the eloquent, academic, and influential was an uphill battle.

Nineteenth-century educational transformations slowly eroded this idea. While appeals for expanded educational opportunities date back much earlier, a campaign for women's higher education in the United Kingdom coalesced in the latter half of the nineteenth century. Girton College at Cambridge University was founded as the first residential, degree-granting women's college in 1869. In time, women's debating societies began to flourish in communities and at a number of elite universities, including the women's colleges at Oxford and Cambridge.[24] A caricature featured in an 1888 issue of *The Graphic*, a London-based illustrated weekly newspaper, demonstrates how mainstream women's debate had become.[25]

The image gently pokes fun at the number of different roles that can be inhabited at a debating society meeting at the same time that it provides a rare glimpse into the intellectual diversity present at such gatherings. At first glance, it seems that this image could be an example of an outsider looking in at debating women. However, upon closer inspection,

Figure 3. "Notes at a Ladies Debating Society," *The Graphic*, 1888. Photo used with permission of Look and Learn Ltd.

we see that the caricaturist represents herself: there she is, on the bottom right corner of the page, claiming the title of "the caricaturist, or the flippant debater" and working on her sketch of the Leader of the House. There are debaters who take their tasks very seriously, like the believer in facts and the debater preparing a crushing rejoinder. There are members who are silent, who listen more than they contribute, or who rely on other members to develop their opinions. Different gendered roles are represented: the masculine debater communicates her masculinity through stiff posture, a monocle, and a cane. Feminine debaters appear in frilly frocks and elaborate hats. Some are more concerned with their hourglass figures than with the facts of the debate, others are more concerned with waltzing than with the topic of the day. "The Neuter" appears as an elderly woman, seemingly much older than any other member of the society. Her label presumably refers to the common idea that women are gradually desexed and desexualized as they age. Yet her frustrated fist shaking may also indicate that her arguments have been neutered, that is, rendered ineffective, in the course of debate. As this cast of characters suggests, the study of nineteenth-century women's debating societies enables scholars to apprehend the kinds of argumentative encounters that might occur between a range of different personalities and backgrounds.

Outright resistance to the idea of debating women gradually wore away throughout the nineteenth century, but progress toward women's full participation in coeducational debating unions was "sporadic, halting and slow" well into the twentieth century.[26] For example, University College London was considered an early leader in university coeducation. The institution permitted women to attend lectures in the 1860s, and in 1878, voted to allow them to take degree examinations. Still, there was ambiguity on the subject of coeducational debating. In November 1878, the president of the Men's Debating Society at University College London wrote to the president of the university to inquire whether women could be admitted to the organization. The society's rules stipulated that members must be "current or former students." The matter in question was whether women fell under the university's definition of "students" (because they were not considered on equal terms with men until that year). Women students ultimately circumvented the issue by chartering their own society in December 1878.[27] Thus, as we consider debate during the late nineteenth and early twentieth centuries, it is important to note that the tendency toward gender-segregated, intramural societies was shaped both by larger ideologies and practical considerations as institutions grappled with the logistics of coeducation.

News of women's higher education in London, Oxford, and Cambridge traveled north, but Scottish coeducation had its own distinct trajectory. For one, Scotland had long prided itself on an educational system that was less elitist than England, often allowing working-class boys with intellectual promise a path into universities.[28] At the primary and secondary levels, mixed-gender schools were also more common in Scotland than they were in England. However, girls were excluded from the best schools.[29] As historian Jane McDermid explains, before Scotland's 1872 Education Act, the "combination of the democratic tradition in Scottish education and the Presbyterian patriarchy" meant these schools placed a primary focus on the boy students; girls were at a disadvantage in the system because they were less likely to be sent to schools in the first place, more likely to drop out, and had restricted options for classes.[30] The 1872 act made primary education mandatory, and the late nineteenth century was a time for some shifting views about secondary and higher education. Secondary schools began to include Latin and mathematics in addition to foreign languages, literature, classics, and subjects designed to enable a girl to run her own home as a married woman, such as cookery and sewing. Many girls enrolled in parish schools, which physically divided boys from girls through the use of separate entrances and playgrounds.[31] Yet full access to a university education was still a long time coming.

To compensate for these deficiencies, a multipronged campaign for women's education was launched in the 1860s. Largely due to the efforts of women who also held membership in the Ladies' Edinburgh Debating Society, university-level classes for women were established in 1867. By 1876, classes to prepare girls and women for examinations from the elementary to the university level began. Ten years after that, a teacher's training college, St. George's, was founded. Finally, St. George's High School opened its doors in 1888. In essence, these educational campaigners created their own system so that girls and women could receive a quality education through their life cycles.[32] This was necessary because it was not until 1892 that all institutions of higher education in Scotland were permitted to formally admit and grant degrees to women.[33]

Hence, when the Ladies' Edinburgh Debating Society was founded in 1865, the seeds of educational possibility were planted, but women could not formally partake in Scotland's universities. The society became an informal educational institution where women could gain knowledge through engagement with the topics of the day and train themselves in public speaking. Some LEDS members used skills learned in their meetings to other venues to agitate for change on a range of social issues, including coeducation and suffrage. For others, the fruits of an informal rhetorical education did not seem to extend far beyond the meeting space of their argument culture.

A Seat at the Table

The Ladies' Edinburgh Debating Society began as the Edinburgh Essay Society in 1865. Sarah Mair had recently completed her schooling, and sought to create a "small literary circle" with her former classmates, all eighteen- or nineteen-year-old Edinburgh women. On an afternoon stroll in Portobello, Mair told her father, Major Arthur Mair, of her plans to form the society.[34] While this plan might have been met with suspicion by other patriarchs of the time, Arthur Mair had a history of supporting women's access to wider forums for public speaking. One of Sarah Mair's earliest memories was of "seeing [her] father handing a lady on the platform to make a speech at a meeting," an anomaly at the time.[35] Denied the option of pursuing higher education in Scotland, a community-based debating society for women was born beyond the corridors of a university campus. There was no major quarrel, no scandal, and no secret escape plan needed for this group of debating women. In fact, the society's meetings were held with "cordial parental approval and encouragement" in the Mair family home.[36]

Sarah Mair came from a long lineage of people who challenged norms about the role of women in public life. She physically resembled her great-grandmother and namesake, Sarah Kemble Siddons, an illustrious stage actor of incomparable fame and talent in late-eighteenth-century

England. Siddons challenged gendered expectations in her powerful public theatre appearances (sometimes performed while she was visibly pregnant). She also appeared as a model in Gilbert Austin's *Chironomia* and Henry Siddons's *Practical Illustrations of Rhetorical Gesture and Action*, demonstrating the ideal form of bodily comportment and gesture promoted by the British elocutionary movement.[37] Sarah Mair's mother, Elizabeth Mair, was also theatrically gifted, though she was not in the habit of performing publicly until it became a necessity. When the family lost their fortune in railway shares, Elizabeth held dramatic Shakespearean readings in her drawing room to make extra money.[38] Sarah was the youngest of five children: she had three sisters, Frances, Harriot, and Elizabeth, and one brother, Colonel William Crosby Mair. Her sister-in-law was Mary Louise Wordsworth, granddaughter of William Wordsworth. Though her mother, sisters, and nieces sometimes participated in the LEDS, Mair was the respected founder, undisputed leader, and sole unwavering member.

Described as a place of "tradition and history" where life was "serenely disciplined and well-ordered," it is noteworthy that the Mair family home also housed the LEDS meetings.[39] Victorian homes were often physical manifestations of separate sphere ideology. As Vanessa D. Dickerson observes, "the house never had so powerfully, explicitly, and strictly defined society as it would in nineteenth-century Britain."[40] The layout of many middle-class homes included rooms meant to sequester, creating a domestic environment associated with privacy, interiority, and femininity.[41] Yet this domestic space was by no means inconsequential; what happened in the home was vital to the development of individual and national identities.[42] The Victorian home could be a place of expression and repression for women. The middle- and upper-class Edinburgh women who populated the LEDS were more likely to occupy their time with domestic leisure than with domestic labor. This is because many households in Victorian Scotland employed servants.[43] The Mair family was no exception. The labor of other women allowed the women of the house to trade cooking and cleaning for more pleasurable tasks such as reading, sewing, charitable organizing, and, indeed—debating.

The LEDS came together to transform yet another domestic space into a space for argument: the dining room. When the society was

founded, the family lived at 29 Abercromby Place, a grand Georgian terraced house in New Town, the center of the city.[44] Though the home had
a drawing room (where Elizabeth Mair held her readings), Sarah Mair and
her band of debaters chose to gather around a table in the dining room
for their meetings. In attempting to capture the spirit of the society, one
LEDS debater drew a contrast between the dining room and the drawing
room. In the former, "we were always allowed to express our views and
opinions, crude and imperfect as they might be, with a freedom that in a
drawing-room would have been considered presumptuous."[45] Amid rather
restrictive Victorian expectations about space and respectability—expectations defined by gender, class, and race—she found a unique freedom
to experiment with argument in the dining room.

A very reputable source describes the dining room as "finely propor-
tioned . . . with its mahogany furniture and air of solid Victorian comfort."[46]
The reputable source? *Ladies in Debate*, the club's commemorative volume,
includes an extended commentary from the perspective of the personi-
fied mahogany table! Though I leave it to others to sort out the meanings
of this commentary for object-oriented ontology, the Table's testimony is a
remarkable resource for understanding the materiality of this nineteenth
century domestic space. It provides details about the Mair home and
suggests how the furnishings and arrangement of the dining room may
have influenced the LEDS activities. For example, we learn that though
the home was not a prohibition house, that they enjoyed themselves with
drink but not so much that anyone drank themselves under the Table (no
one ever "found refuge beneath my kindly wings").[47] The Table's report
also provides insight into the physical configuration of LEDS meetings:
"at my head and at my foot are seated opposite each other the chosen
leaders, flanked by other duly elected officials and ordinary members."[48]
This formation delineated lines of stature by designating a place for those
in elected office, yet allowed all LEDS members to share in the power of
the space by gathering around the mahogany, claw-foot table. Mair always
occupied the head of the table because she perennially occupied one of
the President roles, but she invited her fellow members to have a seat at
the table—or, as we shall see, a space to stand at the table to deliver their
speeches during debates and discussion.

Despite the club's allegiance to change, the dining room, the table, and other material objects offered a real sense of stability to the debaters. Over its seventy-year history, the Mair family relocated only twice. They briefly moved to 25 Heriot Row before ultimately settling in a more modest (but still decidedly middle-class) abode in Edinburgh's quiet West End. Number 5 Chester Street is a stone-built terraced house, and the LEDS met in its dining room from November 1871 to November 1935. At Chester Street, the dining room had two large windows and a sizable fireplace. Red leather chairs and a sideboard were added to the collection of fine dining-room furniture.[49] Despite the change in location, the walls appeared just as they had been at Abercromby Place:

> [in] each successive dining-room hung the same fine proof engravings of the 'long-buried ancestors' on the maternal side of the family—the Kembles and Siddons. The great tragedienne herself [Sarah Siddons], as Queen Katherine in the Court scene, with stout Stephen Kemble as King Henry VIII., and John Kemble as Cromwell, adorned one wall, while the speaking countenance of Fanny Kemble, as well as the Tragic Muse, and the grave-featured John Kemble as Cato and as Hamlet, hung upon another. And over the mantelpiece, the military proclivities of the paternal side of the family was still represented by the historic print of the famous Wellington Banquet.[50]

The debater at the foot of the table faced the window; the head of the table faced the door. Debaters on one side of the table gazed upon a celebration of theatre; the other side gazed upon a celebration of war.[51] In many ways, this would have been an ideal backdrop for the debating society, which blends the performative and the competitive. Speakers could channel inspiration from the dramatic poses of Mair's thespian relatives into their rhetorical performances. A debater preparing a rebuttal could swell with national pride and gain competitive inspiration from the print celebrating military victory at the Battle of Waterloo.

In this room, LEDS members undertook a task that they were not, as least at the time the club was founded, allowed to do on a university campus. Here, they explored the limits of knowledge by claiming a right to speak and a stake in myriad topics. Although they certainly felt the gendered restrictions of the age, they transformed a domestic space into

Figure 4. The Ladies' Edinburgh Debating Society's meeting place from 1871 to 1935. Photo by Drummond Young, courtesy of Nigel Shepley.

a pedagogically oriented civic space—what they referred to as a "training school for women to fit them for public speaking of a high standard of excellence."[52] To do this in a home may have provided a sense of comfort, but it did not quell their lively and sometimes heated exchanges as they mulled over the rapidly changing cultural norms of their time.

An Omen of a Better Age

Edinburgh women's participation in arenas of public life were dramatically transformed between 1865 and 1935. When they began, reading in literature and arts was encouraged for middle- and upper-class women, but it was couched as a means of personal improvement rather than scholarly achievement.[53] University education was not an option; nor was voting. The society's motto, *auspicium melioris aevi*, or "an omen of a better age," nicely encapsulates how the aim of LEDS members was couched within hope for a broader women's rights movement as it flowered in the late nineteenth and early twentieth century.[54] In *Ladies in Debate*, Sarah Mair reflects on the scope of these changes:

> Starting in early Victorian days and travelling on into this Neo-Georgian age, I have watched and, to a small extent shared in, what may almost be called the Awakening of Woman. Not for a moment would I suggest that women of the eighteenth and nineteenth centuries were inferior intellectually to those of the present day. Indeed, the quiet sheltered homes of those earlier days produced many well-read women, whose minds were enriched by their love of literature and art. But their type was rather the exception than the rule, and the rank-and-file girl's life was apt to be somewhat pointless, even a 'blind alley.' But about the middle of last century, a spirit breathed on the quiet waters and roused certain women to realise that their brains were not given them merely to pilot them through a narrow round of more or less graceful trivialities.[55]

Mair's recollection charts the "Awakening of Woman" and eventual embrace of the "New Woman" at the end of the nineteenth century. During this period, Edinburgh women experienced relative freedom compared to their continental counterparts. They could walk around the city on their own without fear of harassment (except, perhaps, for the odd Scotsman who had had too many pints to drink).[56] Nearly every step in the transition to "New Woman"-hood—from the merits of women riding bicycles to smoking—was considered and debated by the LEDS. Certain members were known for bewailing the new attire and behaviors that came along with this shift in women's roles, while others firmly embraced the change. During a general discussion in 1899, for example, each LEDS member was asked to name her favorite heroine from history, romance, or real life. Mair declared the New Woman to be her favorite—"whose delightful combination of masculine sense, vigour, and public spirit . . . entitle her to that place."[57] By 1935, opinion had shifted so dramatically in favor of the "cigarette-smoking, bare-legged girl that tramps the Scottish country in shorts and sweater" that Mair suggested that members be allowed to smoke during debating society meetings.[58]

As a member from age nineteen to age eighty-nine, Mair's life was inextricably entwined with the LEDS. Yet it is necessary to stress that she is an important figure in Scottish women's history in her own right, active in many organizations that were outgrowths of LEDS debates and discussions. Her activism extended to a number of causes, including the Edinburgh Ladies' Educational Foundation, the St. George's School for Girls, the Hospital for Women and Children at Bruntsfield, and the Society for Equal Citizenship.[59] She was forever a champion of women's right to vote, right to education, and right to medical accreditation. For these combined efforts, and especially her work as an education campaigner, Mair was awarded an honorary Doctor of Laws (LL.D.) degree from the University of Edinburgh in 1920, and was named a Dame of the British Empire (D.B.E.) in 1931. Upon receiving the LL.D., Mair joked that though she had not earned the degree through the labors of formal scholarship, she had certainly "Lived Laborious Days" in the pursuit of women's rights.[60]

As a collective, the Ladies' Edinburgh Debating Society is also mentioned, but rarely explored, in historical studies of Scottish women's participation in movements for suffrage, education, and healthcare.[61] Many members of the LEDS created spin-off organizations dedicated to specific activist causes. For example, the Edinburgh Ladies' Educational Association developed out of Mary Crudelius's appeal for assistance at a LEDS meeting. This was the organization responsible for recruiting men professors, such as David Masson, a rhetoric professor at the University of Edinburgh, to deliver university-level lectures for women. Its members created women's courses at St. George's Hall, a training college for women teachers, and the St. George's High School for Girls.[62] While one very worthy approach would be to trace the movement of individual members in and beyond the group, this chapter is primarily concerned with the movement within the group—how the practice of intramural debate itself functioned as an organ of social change over its long and well-documented history. In order to better understand how the society created an argument culture where individuals and ideas could mature, the next section looks closely at the internal norms and practices of their meetings.

An Intergenerational Argument Culture

When the Society was founded in 1865, there were nineteen members. There was a constant influx of new members; on average, five to fifteen new members were added each year (which counterbalanced the loss of members to marriage, family life, relocation, or death). The membership roll for the LEDS comprised a number of distinguished women who went on to pursue a variety of positions in public life, including education campaigner Mary Crudelius; Charlotte Carmichael Stopes, Shakespearean scholar and mother to Marie Stopes, promoter of birth control in the United Kingdom; the poets Jeanie Miller Morison, Maria Bell, and Margaret Houldsworth; and Dame Louisa Lumsden, LL.D., headmistress, pioneer in the women's movement, and the first person to introduce lacrosse to Scotland. There were also members whose worldviews were inextricably connected to their family backgrounds. Flora Masson, for example, was the daughter of David Masson, an editor of his works, and an author in her own right. Grace Wood was the granddaughter of Thomas Chalmers, the preacher, mathematician, and Scottish Malthusian. At one LEDS discussion about favorite hobbies, Wood demonstrated that Malthusian ideas were alive and well when she "pleaded guilty to having a hobby for *Infanticide*, on the grounds that man was not a desirable product and that his existence on earth should, if possible, be put to an end!"[63]

While it certainly included people who would go on to be influential figures in women's rights, education, and literature, and members of prominent Edinburgh families, the society also hosted many members who were not renowned in public life. The member roll was filled with the names of women whose influence was focused on their immediate families and communities. These women may not have been well known during their lifetimes, and are largely forgotten in the vast history of Scottish associational culture. Membership in the LEDS was, in itself, a way to gain more widespread recognition and cultivate a network of homosocial bonding. The club's minutes noted when a member was sick or had a loss in the family. Many members remained active in debates until they died, and the club's minutes marked their passing. Typical of this kind of acknowledgment are these words about Adela Dundas, entered into the minutes on May 7, 1887: "Miss Dundas has been a member of the society for many years and one of its most efficient and interested supporters. Her charming papers were among the very best read at its debates, and her personal gentleness, courtesy and kindliness endeared her to all its members. Her memory will ever linger among us like the remembered sweetness of a woodland flower."[64] Even if their social interactions were limited in other spheres of activity, the debating society documented and valorized the contributions of its members.

The secret to the success and longevity of the LEDS was its ability to balance the needs and perspectives of "women of infinite variety."[65] As a community-based group, the LEDS avoided a problem identified in B. Evelyn Westbrook's study of the antebellum Clariosophic Society of South Carolina College: attitudinal and aspirational homogeneity. Since members of the Clariosophic Society were all "privileged white males who expected to become lawyers, ministers, or politicians," efforts toward "imagining and representing minority perspectives" fell short.[66] Westbrook concludes that the club was therefore limited in its ability to test members' ideas, challenge previously held beliefs, or engage in meaningful social critique. Long-time LEDS member Helen Neaves picks up on the value of heterogeneity in her comparison of college and community-based debating societies:

> I have had a slight experience of college debating societies, and without detracting from their merits and usefulness, I think the fact that the members live under the same roof and have the same ends in view, limits their sphere of action. In our Edinburgh Society the members represented widely different interests. We had among us women who had travelled far afield, women who had devoted themselves to education; others had taken up social work among the poor. There were also, amongst us, married women, the wives of professional men who could speak from experience on the upbringing of children; there was also a sprinkling of sports-loving young women who could put in a word for physical fitness.[67]

To Neaves, this mix of perspectives was unprecedented. Having members with a wide variety of experiences and perspectives better facilitated the ability to imagine and represent the multiple sides of a debate proposition.[68] There were members willing to defend both sides of questions about women's right to education, the franchise, role in parenting—even whether women should play field sports.[69]

To say that the LEDS was a bastion of diversity by contemporary standards is a rather precarious claim. By all accounts, members were well-connected white women of Edinburgh, and new members had to be sponsored and invited into the society. Yet because women were prevented from taking part in many forums for public speaking and debate, the LEDS monthly meetings brought together "a never-failing band of women—young, old, middle-aged, of many varied types and dispositions, of all shades of views (political, philosophical, social, theological)—of literary, scientific and artistic tastes, but all united by a love more or less developed of the True, the Good, the Beautiful."[70] This idea, that a culture could be created through argument despite differences in ideology, background, and identity, was a crucial one.

The LEDS was rooted in the idea of creating a community-based outlet for women's rhetorical performance. G. Thomas Goodnight suggests that when different generations unite in shared activity, there is a potential for "productive counterpoise" in which each generation "may inform the other, abstracting from history principles of prudent conduct even while adding to history the fresh vigor of optimism and progress."[71] "Generation" refers not only to difference in age but also to groups sharing temporal space with other groups. [72] In the next section, I show how the LEDS incubated intergenerational interaction on two levels.[73] First, there were different generations of debaters in the LEDS, based not on age, but on their past experiences with public speaking and debate. Through acts of deliberation and regulation, the society created an argument culture that catered to both experienced and novice debaters. Second, generational perspectives coalesced for LEDS members around life experiences, which affected their ability to draw on personal knowledge as evidence in debate. I chart how the debaters responded to topics about difference—age, gender, class, and race—by invoking their own experiences and group-based commitments.

Debates About Debate

The LEDS regularly engaged in "debates about debates," deliberating about the best conditions for creating and sustaining their argument culture. Most often these fell into the category of club business, when a member would propose a change in the society's operating procedure or comment on her vision of improving the quality of the debates and then propose a motion for consideration by other members. Occasionally, there were formal debates, where members actually defended sides of a proposition about the communicative norms of the very activity they were engaging in. Debates about debate, whether in the former or the latter form, took place regularly over the LEDS's seventy-year existence. Despite these ongoing changes, a deep sense of tradition and unwavering dedication to what they theorized as good deliberative practices were pervasive in the recollections of the members. They felt that the society was "the home of Tradition, for the rules laid down in the infancy of the Society were strictly adhered to through its prime and the 'rigour of the game' was never relaxed."[74] In other words, though there were motions to adjust debate practice as the society worked to accommodate a variety of different backgrounds, a basic dedication to excellence remained over the years.

As an intergenerational argument culture, the LEDS was animated by concerted efforts to provide all members with a site for rhetorical education and performance. These moments of reflection were aimed at creating an environment that balanced an ideal (traditionally masculine) vision of rational-critical debate where arguments could be tested with a supportive organizational *ethos* that mentored women with little past experience in debate. Accordingly, the best way to extend and develop the idea of an argument culture is to demonstrate how this argument culture adapted to the unique demands and constraints of bringing together women and debate in its time. Most important from this perspective is the way that the LEDS was fundamentally a cooperative enterprise.[75] How did the LEDS refine and adapt the rules and norms of debate in order to accommodate members with little debate experience? Are these moments of reflection examples of what we might term a cooperative argument culture?

The basic rules and procedures of the society remained relatively steady over the years. From its inception, the LEDS met in the Mair family dining room at eleven o'clock in the morning on the first Saturday of every month.[76] During each gathering, they discussed club business, chose a proposition to debate for the next meeting, listened to the debate of the day, and took a vote to chart which side of the proposition had garnered the most support. Each month, the society generated three possible propositions for each subsequent meeting, and decided on a suitable choice based on members' interest in the topics and ability to get members to agree to support either side of the question. The processes of choosing propositions and debaters "were as little to be missed as the debates themselves" because "views and preferences were frankly and controversially expressed."[77] The range of topics debated by the LEDS was vast. During any given year in the society's history, one might equally expect to hear a debate on a proposition like "should art represent only the beautiful?" or "should our government send out another Arctic expedition?"[78] The only propositions explicitly forbidden by the society were those of a religious nature or those dealing overtly with party politics. Even so, this regulation was adhered to only in the wording of the propositions. It would prove impossible to outlaw reference to religion or party politics during the course of the debates.

The society's name is a significant representation of its evolving self-image and focus. Mair reflected that the group's early name, the Edinburgh Essay Society, was a touch hubristic, suggesting "it was perhaps characteristic of this group of feminine literary aspirants to ignore the fact that men had already established literary societies in Edinburgh."[79] Despite Mair's opposition, the society voted to change the name to the Ladies' Edinburgh Essay Society in 1867.[80] These early names reveal the society's primary focus on writing for, editing, and publishing its journal, *The Attempt*. In 1872, the group's name changed to the Ladies' Edinburgh Literary Society, and in 1874, *The Attempt* became *The Ladies' Edinburgh Magazine* as it attempted to increase circulation under a new commercial publisher.[81] Debate was always a fixture of the group's meetings, and members had the opportunity to submit "really able thoughtful papers on the topics of debate" to be published in *The Ladies' Edinburgh Magazine*.[82] Yearly summaries of the topics debated were published in the magazine alongside reports of the major trends or policies regarding debate performance and etiquette. However, as time went on, the magazine's circulation continued to decline, so debating gradually became a more important focus of the society. During the final meeting of 1880, Mair proposed a motion that the society "devote its energies to the debates, and that efforts be made to enlarge the society—that several presidents be elected to manage the debates and that the rules regarding them be revised."[83] In 1881, the group changed its name to the Ladies' Edinburgh Debating Society and adopted a new set of rules.[84]

The rules adopted on February 5, 1881, laid out the expectations for club membership, participation, and leadership roles:

I. The Society shall be called 'The Ladies' Edinburgh Debating Society.'

II. The Society shall meet on the first Saturday of each month (August, September, and October excepted) at 11 o'clock am for the conduct of debates.

III. The members shall pay an annual subscription of half a crown.

IV. Nine members shall constitute a quorum.

V. Ladies wishing to be members of this Society shall be admitted on being proposed by one member and seconded by another, and on subscribing to the laws.

VI. Members, on withdrawal, shall send notice, in writing, to the Secretary.

VII. Three presidents, a secretary, and a treasurer shall be elected annually in December. Three only of these office bearers shall be elligible [*sic*] for immediate re-election.

VIII. The Presidents shall take it in turn to preside at the monthly debates of the society.

IX. The Secretary shall read the minutes of the Society, call the roll, send any necessary notices to the members, and take the vote on the debate.

X. The Treasurer shall receive the annual subscriptions of the Members, and read the accounts to the Society.

XI. The Presidents, with the help of the Secretary and Treasurer, shall submit, for the consideration of members, in January, a list of subjects proposed for debates during the ensuing year, which list shall be printed and circulated among the members.

XII. All debates shall be opened in the affirmative, and replied to in the negative, by two members previously appointed. Their speeches may be written or spoken; and each shall, when it is possible, be provided with a seconder.

XIII. After the debate has been opened by the proposers and seconders, all members shall be invited to take part in the discussion, at the close of which, the first speakers shall have the right of reply.

XIV. All members may vote who are present at the division. Should any member be obliged to withdraw before the division, she may leave her vote in writing with the Secretary, provided she has heard the entire opening speech or paper on each side.

XV. Members having undertaken to open a debate, and failed to do so, either in person, or by sending a written paper to the President, shall (unless they provide a substitute) be fined in a sum of five shillings.

XVI. Members shall be allowed to introduce lady visitors at the debates, but such visitors shall not be allowed to address the meeting or give a vote.[85]

These stipulations articulated the norms envisioned by the society as it shifted its focus from literary publishing and toward its own modifications of the rational-critical debate ideal. They do not clearly state whether the votes at the end of the debates were based upon the merits of the question (the voting member's beliefs) or the merits of the argument (the quality of debating performed). However, language in the minutes describing post-debate discussions ("Miss Neaves gave it as her opinion . . .") suggests that their votes reflected their beliefs or opinion shifts in light of the debate. These rules were taken quite seriously: the LEDS minutes document that it were unable to hold a debate in November 1889 because "a very distinguished and valued member having failed to prepare a paper on the subject of women's political associations paid the fine (five shillings)," according to the laws of the society. The secretary then added that it was an "incident on which comment is superfluous."[86] The distinguished member was the much-revered Sarah Mair, who, despite being the founder and president, paid the fine, emphasizing that no one was exempt from the regulations of the LEDS.

Over the years, various members sought to improve the quality of the debates by regulating particular logistical or stylistic preferences. One kind of proposed change sought to guide the rhetorical performance of the speakers: speaking times for speakers (twenty minutes for first speakers and ten minutes for second speakers), post-debate discussion, and the preferred style of delivery in debates.[87] During the April 1886 meeting, Mair proposed a measure that would require speakers to stand rather than sit during the post-debate discussions. Adela Dundas moved the motion, and then added an amendment that required debaters to speak rather than read their papers. The motion and amendment passed with eighteen votes of support and three votes against.[88] Although this was the first time that the society voted on whether members should read their speeches, it was not the first time that commentary about rhetorical genres and preferred delivery styles arose. In an 1878 edition of *The Ladies' Edinburgh Magazine*, the summary of debates for the year noted that while some members were skilled at speaking without notes, their experience had shown that writing out debate speeches in advance was still advised, at least for the first two speakers, because it allows "closer reasoning and more orderly information than even very good extemporaneous speaking, unless where it rises into oratory."[89] What precipitated the change in perspective about reading speeches almost ten years later? A likely explanation is that as the society placed a more exclusive focus on debate, members became more skilled at and interested in the premium that unscripted speeches placed on extemporaneous delivery tactics.

Two years after Adela Dundas's amendment to require speakers to speak rather than read their speeches, her sister Louisa clarified with another motion in which rebuttalists (known as "seconders") also must strive for extemporaneous delivery.[90] She argued that this approach would save time, because papers from second speakers were often redundant, repeating points made by the first speeches. If seconders were tasked with listening to the first speeches and then thinking on their feet to further the development of the debates, the overall quality of argumentation would improve. Although Louisa Dundas's motion was seconded, an amendment that augmented the motion so that seconders could still have the choice of whether to speak or read was ultimately adopted.[91] The issue seemed relatively settled until much later, when almost all of the previous members who had weighed in on the topic had cycled through the society. In 1934, one year before the LEDS dissolved, momentum for the debates was beginning to subside. Members requested to return to reading papers, but Mair once again affirmed the power of their collaboratively created regulations, expressing her opinion "that the Society should keep to its constitutions and continue to be a debating society."[92]

Another issue of interest for club deliberations was whether or not to keep the LEDS as a women-only group. The society never seriously considered the idea of welcoming men as permanent members, perhaps because the members had themselves been excluded from so many forums for public speaking. Instead, the controversy centered on whether the society should host promiscuous (mixed-sex) audiences—should men be allowed to come to the meetings as visitors or audience members observing the debates? In 1877, *The Ladies' Edinburgh Magazine* included a reference to a Ladies' Debating Club in London that admitted men as visitors who could participate in the debates once a year. Mair's comment on this practice was that it seemed "a rather daring act," but according to all accounts, "these mixed debates have been very successful."[93] Perhaps inspired by this, Louisa Dundas gave notice of her 1886 proposal "that the Society in future should not be limited to ladies."[94] Since the notice was given at the June meeting, the LEDS did not have a chance to discuss the issue until it reconvened in November. When the motion was debated, most members agreed that gentlemen could be considered as visitors but not as members of the society. However, they did not come to a resolution that satisfied a majority of the members, and because the attendance was low, further deliberation was stalled until the next meeting.[95] Dundas could not make the December meeting, and it seems that because she was not present to propose the motion again, the issue was dropped.

The topic was not reintroduced until six years later, when a persistent Louisa Dundas gave notice of a new motion to keep the LEDS in line with societal thinking: "that, the Edinburgh University having decided to admit women to its classes, the Ladies' Edinburgh Debating Society should reciprocate by admitting gentlemen, as visitors, to its debates."[96] When the LEDS addressed the issue in its November 1892 meeting, a lively discussion ensued. Members resolved to continue on as they had, without men visitors. According to the minutes, the main reason behind this decision was that men already had access to many societies, and that they should "be excluded from at least one paradise"![97]

Beyond these logistical qualms, LEDS debaters occasionally turned their attention to more substantive concerns about communicative norms. Some of these debates engaged in age-old debates about rhetoric and communication. An 1871 debate, for example, found that most members believed appeals to logic were superior to appeals to emotion.[98] The status of the art of conversation was the focus of a LEDS debate in 1903, in which four debaters drew from an assortment of examples to support the different sides of the question, "is the art of conversation dying out?" The first affirmative speaker, Miss Landale, argued that the art of the conversation was dying compared to historical accounts of French salons. In her estimation, conversational quality was suffering because although there was much study of recitation and speaking techniques made popular by the elocutionists, there was little emphasis placed on how to be a good listener. On the negative side, Mrs. Melville argued that these recollections of the good old days of quality conversation were subject to revisionist history. She suspected that such nostalgia was rooted in a taste for the manners of the past rather than a superior approach to communication, and predicted that in fifty years, others would look back on their own conversations as ideal. The seconder for the affirmative side bemoaned the specialization of conversation, where individuals felt that they could not speak on general topics but only on their particular hobbies and interests. The negative side's seconder gave a very short speech protesting Miss Landale's point about good listening habits, insisting that good listeners could ruin conversations with their "stony stares." At the end of the debate, observers of the debate were split on the status of the art of conversation. Twelve votes were cast in favor of the affirmative, thirteen were cast for the negative, and three members declined to vote.[99] The arguments made in these debates were not explicitly connected to debate practice within the society. However, members, even those who did not directly take part in the debates, were able to collaborate on a vision of ideal communication. Through argumentative encounter, they reflected on the best practices for their argument culture.

Yet the question that most directly bore on their debate practice was "does the habit of debate induce in the debater exaggerated and one-sided views?"[100] The LEDS cleverly decided that rather than hold a formal debate on the topic, it would allow each of the eighteen members attending the meeting to express her opinion on the subject. As if determined to perform the negative side of the question, the members expounded on a variety of different perspectives on the topic. Many members acknowledged the possibility that debate could lead to exaggerated or one-sided views, but thought that this likely occurred more among the young and in personal arguments rather than in formal debates. The "genial atmosphere of a debating society" guarded against this danger, because ritual argumentation and the friendship among the members promoted "tolerance and understanding of other people's views."[101] Some members thought that this broad-mindedness could be a liability because it made it difficult to form an opinion on a topic. Others thought that this could be a problem for audience members observing debates, but not for speakers. Sarah Mair argued that in having to prepare for a debate, debaters became aware of the arguments on both sides of the controversy, and were more likely at the end of the debate to have a fair reason for settling on an opinion. After each member said her piece, a vote was taken. Only two members voted affirmative, while the other sixteen felt confident that debate, on balance, did not lead to exaggerated or one-sided views.[102] One wonders what would have happened had the majority voted affirmative, since a cornerstone of the LEDS argument culture was a belief that testing ideas and justifying claims was a useful practice.

In addition to exhibiting self-reflexivity about their communicative norms, LEDS members were intentional in their efforts to encourage participation by their younger and less experienced colleagues. Even before the society made the formal move to focus exclusively on debate, members noted the need to recruit and support novice debaters. Adela Dundas's 1876 yearly summary in *The Ladies' Edinburgh Magazine* articulated the value of debate, stating that the society believed that "all persons [should be] required to think, to fix their minds upon any one topic, and to study it from all points of view . . . to be forced to put one's thoughts clearly before others and to state why one holds this rather than that opinion."[103] Adding that more participation by younger debaters would enhance these benefits for the whole society, Dundas urged her fellow members to think about how they might attain that goal. How does any argument culture socialize inexperienced participants into an activity that rewards competition and sharp wit? In their effort to answer this question, LEDS members coordinated concerted efforts to accommodate novice debaters in three areas: atmosphere, evidence, and topic and speaker selection.

While the LEDS cultivated an atmosphere of competition, its members were equally invested in developing an approachable atmosphere where mentoring could take place.[104] In this way, they demonstrated contemporary rhetorician David Zarefsky's point that though argument cultures may be combative, "argumentation is fundamentally a cooperative enterprise."[105] Sarah Mair set the tone for nurturing new generations of debaters. As Lettice Milne Rae recalls, their leader

> had infinite understanding and patience with those not thus endowed and could inspire confidence in the shyest and most awkward of what might be truly called 'maiden speakers.'. . . For not only did she exercise a supreme attraction for women of abler intellect and higher literary and intellectual attainments than her own, but she had the power, too, of drawing forth latent or unsuspected talent in what appeared on the surface very unpromising material.[106]

Mair created an atmosphere of supportive yet challenging debate education and performance. Especially early in the society's existence, this was quite a revolutionary innovation for young women. In contrast to dominant Victorian ideas about the necessary containment of women, the LEDS provided an open space to test ideas, however "crude and imperfect." Helen Neaves stresses that inexperienced debaters were simultaneously trusted with a forum for free-thinking but also had to consider that more experienced members would reign them in when necessary. Experienced generations of debaters within the LEDS "had it in their power to controvert [their] rash assertions, and it was undoubtedly one of the benefits conferred by the Debating Society that one had to prepare one's brief with care and circumspection if one wished to avoid a crushing defeat."[107] With the freedom to test ideas came the freedom to be tested by the superior acumen of a fellow LEDS member.

Another innovative way that the LEDS accommodated the different levels of experience present in the society was by valuing alternative forms of evidence. Members were valued for what they brought to the topics, whether it was knowledge learned in experience, books, or travel. Traditional debate evidence may include a quotation or a statistic from a scholarly book or journal, whereas LEDS debates were peppered with visual and hypothetical images, personal experiences, and illustrative talents. Propositions dealing with different geographical locations and cultures were made tangible through various members' travel tales. An 1871 debate on the superiority of German music over Italian music included vocal illustrations by both sides of the proposition.[108] When debaters felt intimidated by a philosophical topic like "is pain a necessity?" they could always fall back, as the speakers did in an 1889 debate, on poetry to help them to express their arguments.[109] By drawing on a range of skills and knowledge, and permitting alternative forms of evidence, the LEDS worked around certain barriers to debate participation, such as access to research materials and inadequate educational training.

Inevitably, though, there were moments in the society's history when inexperienced debaters were loath to volunteer for debates despite the resources that unique kinds of evidence afforded them. Mrs. Stitt describes her experience as an over-eager contributor at her first LEDS meeting:

> from a back seat my first question was lightheartedly asked and quite properly met with a kindly but firm suppression. The lesson was taken to heart, 'Do not say anything at all if you are not prepare to follow with an intelligent reason.' The hoped-for education had begun, and Ignorance hung its horrid head while the feeling of inferiority became almost worm-like.[110]

This anecdote demonstrates how the LEDS balanced two features of an argument culture identified by Zarefsky: cooperation and justification.[111] They encouraged participation by new members, such that Stitt felt comfortable enough to speak. Although Stitt felt embarrassed and inferior after her comment, it was not because other members had ridiculed her. Instead, Stitt's experience suggests that the society placed an emphasis on justifying one's claims. Her education in argumentation began that day, when fellow club members did not just allow her to get away with an inadequate contribution, but kindly held her responsible for reasoned interactions. They acculturated new members through careful mentoring balanced with a performance of their dedication to quality debate and discussion. Stitt, upon reflection, came to the same conclusion. Although the LEDS was intimidating and foreign to a newcomer,

> What might have seemed to me too lofty in thought and speech, was it not to help us become less selfish and more useful members of the community? There was no place in that room for flippancy or cheap wit. The debates, which even in my unregenerate days had been a pleasure and a delight, had they not always advocated noble and true causes? And in giving us many new lines of thought, had they not taught us that there are always two sides to a question? [112]

Stitt acknowledged that it was all done with the goal of making her a better debater, thinker, and member of the argument culture.

One obstacle that the LEDS encountered in convincing new generations of debaters to participate was the obscurity, abstraction, or specialization of certain debate propositions. To balance the needs of a debating society whose members saw themselves as "women of infinite variety," there was a perpetual pull between those debaters who saw the forum as a place to explore topics of global, theoretical, and philosophical importance, and those who felt only prepared to debate topics that bore directly on their lives in Edinburgh. How could inexperienced debaters be encouraged to participate in debates if the club decided to indulge the wishes of those who wanted the debates to cross intellectual frontiers?

A series of proposals and deliberations in 1870 demonstrate the contours of this matter. At several LEDS meetings in the previous year, debates had to be canceled because the LEDS had trouble getting members to represent each side of the proposition. In response, Miss Seton moved "that a law be passed which shall render compulsory the conducting of debates by all members of this society in turn" at the first meeting of the year in 1870. Not wanting to force people to debate against their better wishes, the society voted to support an amendment to instead create a list of volunteers who could debate on either side of a question when called upon.[113] The amendment represented the society's belief that no one ought to be forced to debate when she is unprepared in skill, background knowledge, or research and so temporarily solved a problem in speaker selection. However, it did not address the issue of how to craft a proposition that would encourage broader participation.

In June of the same year, the issue of topic selection came to a head. Although Dunlap's amendment succeeded in allowing the LEDS to schedule debate topics and debaters for the winter months, the group could not agree on a topic for the July debate. The three topics under consideration were "have we a sense of beauty independent of other sources of pleasurable sensation?," "is allegory an interesting and effectual mode of conveying secular instruction?," and "have we a natural consciousness of right and wrong?" Members objected to each of the subjects as being too abstract, and thus too difficult, to debate. After much deliberation, the society decided that it should instead hold a debate on a topic of current interest: "has the British government of India been beneficial to the natives of India?"[114] Despite its invocation of benevolent colonialism, LEDS members considered this topic debatable. Debaters for each side of the question lined up for the July debate. It also sent a message to members, who might have been intimidated by the more abstract debates proposed in June, that the society sought variety in topic selection. This same message was communicated seven years later in *The Ladies' Edinburgh Magazine*. In the summary of the year's debates, it was noted that although some members struggled with philosophical topics, the group decided that they had yielded some fascinating debates. As a consequence, the group decided to try to balance philosophical topics with practical topics because "variety is pleasing."[115] In 1880, Mair intervened in the normal topic selection process to better accommodate members who had not yet volunteered to debate. She claimed that they need not volunteer to speak on "deep philosophical subjects" and proposed her own list of simpler subjects to spark the interest of inexperienced debaters.[116]

Having only recently shifted to focus exclusively on debates, the society once again struggled with speaker selection for the debates in 1883. This time, the problem was more specific than the 1870 deliberations—they had plenty of members willing to be the second speakers, but had a shortage when it came to attracting volunteers to give the opening speeches in the debate. Louisa Dundas proposed a motion to form a committee that would, "in consulting upon measures, and framing rules . . . meet and obviate this difficulty." Dundas believed that "new members were scared by an imaginary idea that they *must* open the debates with long and elaborate papers—whereas the papers need not be long and would often be better if simplified." Here, she both diagnosed the problem and also set out a vision for better debates. Dundas cast the issue as a way of "equalizing" or sharing the workload as a courtesy to other members, so that the society would not turn into a forum where a small number of skilled performers debated each week and all others were perpetual audience members."[7]

The motion was passed at the April meeting, and a Committee on Rules for Debate was formed. Later that month, the committee called a special meeting where it generated the following new rules for consideration by the whole membership:

1) That there should be Honorary members, not more than 20 at a time, who on payment of a double subscription (5/) should be exempt from opening debates; these members were not to have the privilege of introducing visitors.

2) That the time for arranging the debate in the ordinary way shall henceforth not exceed ten minutes.

3) That in default of voluntary speakers, the President shall (after ten minutes have elapsed) call upon the ordinary members in turn to provide for the opening of a debate—by speaking or writing.

4) That any member so called upon must take the part assigned [or find a substitute] or pay a fine of 2/6?, 5/?[118]

5) That any member who has once been called upon from this manner should be exempted from speaking again for a year.

6) That no member shall be so called upon for three meetings after her entrance to the Society.

The Committee further recommended that the President shall keep the reserve list of subjects at hand on such occasions and that if any member compelled to take part in a debate should object to the subjects in the printed list, she may be allowed to choose from the reserved list or to suggest an entirely new subject, approved by the Society. The debaters being drawn by lot, the affirmative and negative sides to be left to themselves to decide.[119]

Although these proposed regulations could be faulted for giving members a way out of ever speaking in debates, the committee believed that doubling the fees would deter most from doing so. They more evenly distributed the debating load among ordinary members by exempting them for the rest of the year once they had been called upon. Rule 6, which allowed a period of acclimation to the norms of the society, ensured that new generations of debaters were prepared when they were called on to carry out a debate.

The full membership deliberated about these proposed rules in the May 1883 meeting. Mair explained the impetus behind each rule, suggesting that they grew out of various grievances the society had voiced in terms of finding suitable topics and speakers. Miss Oswald made a speech

> against the whole movement as a radical, not to say revolutionary one, that no amount of legislation would make good speakers out of those whom nature had not qualified to the task; and that if incompetent speakers were annoyed by being compelled to speak, the listeners would equally be forcibly [annoyed] having to listen to them.

Despite her impassioned speech, Oswald gained little support. Mair stressed that the measures did not disturb any of the existing laws adopted in 1880 and that debaters who wanted to volunteer were still given precedence. She reiterated Lumsden's point that the fate of the debate need not fully rely on the quality of opening speeches—a short or uninspired opening speech could still be enlightening through a "well-managed" post-debate discussion.[120] After hearing these points, the LEDS voted to adopt the new measures by a large majority. They succeeded in the goal of getting a wider variety of speakers to take on the opening speeches in debates for a while, with only a very few "honorary members" who never spoke on the society's roster.

Over time, however, the problem of finding speakers emerged again. In 1925, the topic was raised in regard to the numerous absences that members had accrued. Several motions to address the issue were brought up and defeated, including Miss Lee's motion that more speakers might be enticed to participate if they made the debates less "debate-like" by doing away with formal seconders.[121] In 1930, Alice Smith suggested that they change to a team debate format, with teams of four or six members on each side of the proposition. Other members were skeptical, but they agreed to try out a team debate for one debate.[122] The new format worked well on its trial run, and the team debate format was adopted for the majority of debates in the final five years of the society.

Despite these attempts to address the problem, it was ultimately the lack of volunteer speakers that led to the dissolution of the society in 1935. This examination of the LEDS rules, negotiations, and deliberative practices demonstrates the possibilities and the challenges that members faced as they carefully and deliberately attempted to balance the needs of its participants, old and new. Next, I explore how LEDS negotiated another delicate balance in its argument culture: ideological and identity-based difference.

Identity and Experience in Intergenerational Encounters

The Ladies' Edinburgh Debating Society hosted generations of people interested in argumentative encounter in the Mair family dining room. Generational thinking was particularly prominent when the society featured debates about age, class, race, and gender. To try to find out detailed information about each participant's identity-based affiliations and commitments would be a difficult and altogether different project. Moreover, given the archival materials available, to speculate on these differences would be a historically shaky endeavor. In this section, I ask, "is the age, gender, class, and race of the debater rhetorically significant?," much as Lorraine Code asks, "is the sex of the knower epistemologically significant?"[123] I resolve that the answer is yes, but not based on any essential quality emanating from these categories. Rather, debaters come to mobilize identity and experience-based knowledge as evidence to engage in debates about difference. An examination of how members chose to approach these sheds light on the way that the LEDS brought intergenerational perspectives into argumentative communion. In some instances, this yielded nuanced engagements with these issues that matured over time. However, especially in those debates pertaining to class and race, the members exhibited a remarkable shortsightedness and lack of reflexivity about their own privileged subjectivities.

The LEDS's debates about life changes—specifically, aging and marriage—are representative of generational argument. Goodnight suggests that generational argument is an act of translation requiring rhetorical invention:

> Because each generation passes through a different time, there persists in the public realm space for a plurality of informing sentiments, each capable of interrogation and generative of arguments that define the urgencies of the present and the relevant domain of future conduct. If such sentiments are not to collapse into blind rejection of the past or nostalgic longing for it, rhetorical invention is necessary to translate historical experience into a reasoned argument about the nature of present choice.[124]

In spaces specifically designated for ritual argument, such as debating societies, arguers can anticipate rebuttal and cross-examination and thus can generate argument strategies that draw from the past to guide present action. The society debated the question "do the years bring more than they take away?" twice, thirty years apart. The first debate was on April 6, 1889, when a young Miss Robertson argued for old age's "conversion of lessons from grievances into blessings," as a boon to individual, nation, and humankind. Maria Bell took the negative, drawing on "all poets and sages from Solomon downwards" who preferred the days of youth. At age thirty-seven, Bell conceded that old age was probably better than middle age, but maintained that childhood was much preferable to her current condition, that "burdened care-worn period of middle age." Though Bell had often written about old age, death, and the Christian afterlife in her poetry, she failed to convince the audience of LEDS members that youth was superior. [125] In the end, the affirmative won the debate by a margin of seven votes. [126]

When the society returned to the topic thirty years later, members only slightly changed the wording of the debate question to "do the years give more than they take away?" Isabella Landale supported the affirmative side, defending old age for its ability to make up for the arrogance of youth. Landale considered that the years may take away beauty, but then resolved that artists had captured the charm of old age. Besides that, "what young Adonis can compare with the old and dignified Sophocles?" She was steadfast in her belief that if a person maintained good hygiene, kept her mind sharp with mental gymnastics, and learned to read lips in preparation for hearing loss, old age was superior. Her opponent, Mrs. Wallace, maintained that youth brought hope and adaptability, whereas old age only brought a deteriorating body and a narrowing mind. She drew support from the seven stages of man in Shakespeare's *As You Like It*. By this time, there was more of an effort by the LEDS secretary to record the post-debate discussion by audience members. A dynamic discussion ensued, with members drawing from their personal experiences, ranging from work with children to their own feelings of dread as they aged and reactions to their friends passing on. Despite able arguments from the negative, in the end, the affirmative was once again victorious, this time by a margin of ten votes. [127]

LEDS members also brought their personal experiences to bear on the topic of marriage. When it formed as a group of young women in 1865, all members were unmarried. Over the years, however, members began to withdraw from the society in what Mair referred to as "losses by marriage." Mair, who never married, betrayed her feeling about this trend: "as was to be expected in a Society of maidens of eighteen and twenty years, especially when possessed not only of distinguished names, but of such charm in form, feature, and dress . . . wolves very soon began to attack the fold in the shape of husbands." [128] When the first of the members was married, they deliberated about whether the ranks of the society should be closed to married women. They ultimately resolved that matrimony should not disqualify members from participating in debating activities, and women "married and single, presently sat side by side around the Table with no apparent difference, mental or otherwise, to distinguish them." [129]

With the matter settled, the LEDS felt free to weigh in on debate topics related to the institution of marriage. The society returned to the subject because it was an enduring topic of interest for different generations of members, old and young, married and unmarried. The LEDS meeting minutes can be used to chart intergenerational approaches to argument about the topic as attitudes about marriage, romance, rules for courtship, and companionship gradually changed.[130] Four unmarried LEDS members compared competing visions of the proper role of marriage in 1881 with the question, "is the French *mariage de convenance* more conductive to the happiness of those concerned than the English system?"[131] Debaters on both sides of the proposition agreed that the question should be decided based on the well-being of the woman involved in the marriage. The affirmative side supported the French system based on the idea that women are better off with money and social position and that they needed some paternalistic guidance to guard against making foolish decisions. The negative team contested the culturally regressive idea that women were solely the property of their fathers. After the debate, "a great deal of interesting discussion followed in which all the married ladies present defended our practice and insisted that it was much better calculated as a measure of married happiness than any other."[132] The married members of LEDS must have been teeming with personal examples and anecdotes to defend the English system of matrimony that they had entered into. In the end, the affirmative side had only four supporters, and the negative carried the debate with thirteen votes. When the LEDS revisited the question in 1903, the society once again put the majority of its supporting votes behind marriage for love.[133]

Based on the propensity of LEDS members to reference personal experience, both the 1881 and the 1903 debate questions on marriage may have stacked the deck for the negative side. The married members had been united with their mates under the English system, and unmarried members presumably either had no interest in marriage in general, or, if they hoped to be married one day, would do so with some culturally derived sense of romance in mind. Both debate propositions focused the point of conflict on differing approaches to matching couples, rather than on a more radical probing of whether marriage was a desirable end goal. Not until 1914 did the society debate a proposition that questioned that assumption, asking, "are married persons generally more selfish than the unmarried?" The arguments made in this debate expose changing attitudes toward marriage at the time, including the idea that marriage may not be all that it is imagined to be for women.[134] The onset of World War I exacerbated fears about gender imbalances in the United Kingdom, and the large number of causalities during the war meant that many women who might have otherwise married remained single.[135]

The society returned to the topic of marriage in 1928. In this group-wide discussion, members once again engaged the question of the superiority of French versus English systems, as they had nearly fifty years earlier.[136] Predictably, the majority of members still argued in favor of the advantages of love-based coupling, but the range of perspectives on the purpose of marriage demonstrates the diversity of LEDS members. Issues of romantic love, procreation, and attitudes toward marriage in China and India were added to the mix. Importantly, the discussion gave voice to the idea that some could attain "complete freedom in marriage," while others might prefer to exercise the "freedom not to marry."[137] Although a presumed heterosexuality framed most of these discussions, the idea that one could have the "freedom not to marry" signaled how women were increasingly afforded agency in decision-making about their own lives.

Other questions about women's right to participate in public life were so frequently debated that it is beyond the scope of this chapter to detail each engagement. As Mair put it, "there was scarcely any advance made by women that did not find [ours] a friendly stage on which to air its ideas."[138] For example, an entire history of women's suffrage and access to education in Scotland could be told through the lens of LEDS debates. Scottish suffrage societies were active at the time, and activists gathered an estimated two million signatures on suffrage petitions between 1867 and 1876.[139] Some members of the LEDS were directly involved in the suffrage movement through organizations like the Edinburgh National Society for Suffrage (Mair became president of that organization in 1907).[140] However, the "infinite variety" in the LEDS included members who were against enfranchisement for women. As Mrs. Arnott put it, "opinion was naturally much divided . . . there was good deal of tension between different women's societies, and we remember gratefully what an asset to our Society was Miss S.E.S. Mair's wisdom, strength, and courage during those difficult years."[41]

The LEDS claims the distinction of being the first debating society in Scotland to debate the issue of suffrage in 1866. The group revisited the issue five more times before the right to vote was granted to women over thirty years of age in 1918.[42] There were spirited arguments on both sides of the suffrage question. The majority of the society voted against women's enfranchisement in 1866 and 1872. Subsequent debates held in 1883, 1891, 1905, and 1914 all resulted in majority votes for suffrage. There are many potential reasons for this gradual shift. Although the early 1880s were a relatively quiet period in Scottish suffrage activity, it gradually picked up steam. During this time, Scottish women gained the right to vote in municipal elections. In March 1884, Edinburgh was the site of the Scottish National Demonstration of Women, a mass gathering with suffrage meetings dispersed in homes and buildings throughout the city. Some LEDS members, including Sarah Mair and Charlotte Carmichael Stopes, spoke about suffrage at public meetings during this period.[43] The votes in the LEDS suffrage debates likely reflected both the quality of argumentation in each particular event and a genuine shift in public opinion about the issue in general. Another explanation is that LEDS membership grew significantly during this time, and a number of the new members were active campaigners for suffrage and women's education.

Recurring debates about women's education were not as focused as suffrage debates. The LEDS covered the value of home education versus school education for girls, whether classes should be coeducational, and whether women should be allowed to earn university degrees. Debates about education provided interesting moments of self-reflection for members, as the LEDS itself served as a form of self-education and there were quibbles over whether it was enough, or whether they should be fighting for access to universities. Just as with suffrage debates, education debates were complicated by the activist agendas of some members. Representative of this tension was a May 1886 debate on the question, "is it advisable that a training college for women intending to teach in secondary schools and private families be founded in Edinburgh?" In fact, a group of LEDS members were responsible for founding the St. George's Training School. Mair opened the debate by explaining the goal of a training college and

arguing for its value in Edinburgh. Miss Menzies "did not entirely disap-
prove of training colleges though she though them unnecessary and was
most sweeping in her condemnation of the St. George's Training College"
in particular. At the end of the debate, the society (perhaps convinced to
follow the lead of their president) voted affirmative by a margin of seventeen to one.[144] Taking that decisive win as a mandate, Mair proposed that
the LEDS donate twenty pounds of its surplus funds to the St. George's
Training School as a bursary. While there was some dissent by members
who thought that their funds should only be used to directly enhance
the debating society, Mair's proposal succeeded and the money was donated.[145] Members often expressed an interest in debating about higher
education and leveraged personal experience (usually regarding the next
generation of women—their daughters) about coeducation.

In addition to women's rights, the LEDS used its forum to debate
about gendered etiquette and the proper role of women.[146] Topics like "is
there a moral turpitude in dying the hair, and painting the complexion?"
were engaged with enthusiasm.[147] In 1924, members voted in support of
the idea that the modern girl had more charm than the Victorian maiden.[148]
Such debates often featured a reflection on women's roles of the past, and
where they thought they were going in the future. The LEDS discussion
about whether makeup was morally degrading, for example, was undertaken with a seriousness that might have accompanied a debate about
wartime provisions. As they took stock of their accomplishments (and
their ability to maintain charm despite new rights and responsibilities),
LEDS members reflected on their place in history, and were generally
satisfied with what they had achieved. Debate topics directly engaging
gendered identity were intermixed with other topics of literary, political,
social, and aesthetic importance. It is noteworthy, though, that they rarely
engaged in debates about men's roles or changing visions of masculinity.

One exception is a debate held on March 6, 1920. On this occasion,
the LEDS chose a topic that showcased how larger philosophical currents
intersected with gender in the lives of LEDS members: they debated on
the question "does Schopenhauer while decrying women unconsciously
do them honour?" The proposition refers to German philosopher Arthur
Schopenhauer's 1851 essay, "Of Women," in which he casts women as
mentally deficient, childish, vain, dependent, and utterly incapable of

mature reasoning and deliberation.'[149] The essay is peppered with misogyny, including Schopenhauer's claim that "you need only look at the way in which she is formed, to see that woman is not meant to undergo great labor, whether of the mind or body."'[150] That a group of women would even gather to debate this question puts pressure on Schopenhauer's characterization. However, the LEDS debaters did not craft the proposition to focus on whether Schopenhauer's claims were accurate or misguided. Instead, they challenged themselves to read against the grain, exploring how the essay could be potentially subversive.

Drawing on the work of British civil servant and sociologist Benjamin Kidd, Mair—the first affirmative speaker—attempted to invert Schopenhauer's argument that women's only value is to propagate the species. Kidd's theory of social evolution was an attempt to create a biological basis for societal progress.'[151] Mrs. Ivory, who suggested that Schopenhauer's essay was indicative of women's increasing influence, seconded Mair. She declared that he would not have dedicated the time to write about them if they did not occupy an important place in his thoughts. The negative team, composed of Miss (later Dame) Louisa Lumsden and Miss Frobel, declared that Schopenhauer's vitriolic rants left no room for creative interpretation. Responding directly to the affirmative side's argument about social evolution, Lumsden urged evaluating Schopenhauer's claims in light of his larger philosophy. Elsewhere, he discussed the "will to live" as a base human desire, and "this will is more or less strong in the masculine mind, but women have very little of it, and even their love for their offspring is merely instinctively evanescent [where] the father's love is at once more practical and more durable." In Schopenhauer's telling, women may propagate the species through reproduction, but they are not responsible for any social evolution as described by Kidd. Lumsden's seconder, Miss Frobel, argued that there was no way that "Of Women" could be interpreted as an honor. She lamented that Schopenhauer would position men and women in oppositional roles instead of speaking about their common humanity.

In the end, the audience members were not persuaded that "Of Women" could be more creatively interpreted as a compliment to women, and the vote resulted in a majority of five for the negative side with three members declining to vote.'[152] Prior knowledge of Schopenhauer's philosophical writings was a prerequisite for participation in this debate as a debater or as an audience member. If they had not heard of "Of Women" previously, the event created a reason for members to seek it out and read it. This episode illustrates how the Mair dining room was not just a gathering place to debate—it was also a space where Edinburgh women could incubate a more progressive gender ideology. They invented ways to critique sexist discourses, sharpening their critical skills and refuting the sexist discourses circulating in wider literary and public spheres.

True to the society's motto, many LEDS debates proved prescient in anticipating and arguing for social change for women. However, the society fell excruciatingly short when it came to seeing the intersections of multiple oppressions. For example, on a range of issues, from marriage to education, class played a prominent role, although the debaters did not always acknowledge it as such. Many LEDS members were involved in charitable work outside the club, yet it is clear that many of their activist efforts were oriented toward elevating women who shared their class status. One particularly heartbreaking illustration of this reality comes from Mary Walker's reflection on the efforts of some LEDS members to promote women's education at St. George's Training School. There, they caught Jane, the maid at the school, attempting to put her ear to the door of the lecture rooms. According to this account, had Jane "been born in a higher social stratum," she might very well have been sitting in the classroom instead of doing the housekeeping.[153] Rather than resisting this class-based exclusion by reaching out to Jane, the educational campaigners were content to leave it at that. Their efforts did not, at least at that time, extend to women of the working class. Another example of this class bias came in February 1878, when the LEDS debated whether the "servants of the present day [had] really deteriorated as a class from former times" (the majority voted for the affirmative).[154] When Ann Leask, the maid employed by the Mair family at 5 Chester Street, gave notice of her plan to retire, the LEDS voted unanimously to award her with five pounds and a leather purse for her many years of service. One of Leask's tasks in the home had been to prepare the dining room for the LEDS meetings.[155] Her labor supported and enabled the work on the debating society, but she was not invited to participate in its activities.

The class status of LEDS members manifested in the club's fee and fine structure, as well as in some of their discussions. One society discussion, held in 1901, also betrayed a particular class bias when it called for members to each contribute their "pet economy," or their favorite way to save money. While some members contributed tips about how to avoid wasting string or how to save on postage, Mair's suggestion was to travel first class in order to save money on luggage.[156] From the perspective of the poor and working classes of Edinburgh, this was not a very practical solution. Class privilege was not an issue that was acknowledged or directly engaged by the LEDS very often. For identity-based differences to be debatable in a forum like LEDS meetings, the topic needed to be articulated and there needed to be ample arguments on both sides of the debate question. Perhaps like the Clariosophic Society of South Carolina College, the LEDS's class-based homogeneity made representing a minority viewpoint on such issues difficult. Concern for the poor and working class was more likely to emerge in LEDS debates about charity work or deliberations about the best charitable organizations in Edinburgh should the society have any excess funds from member dues at the end of the year.

When it came to issues of race and ethnicity, the society similarly exhibited little critical awareness. There was no probing of the implications of members' own positionalities, no reflection on their assumptions about the entanglement of whiteness and Scottish or British identity. When race or ethnicity was specifically named in LEDS propositions, it was pursued at arm's length. Arguments centered on exotic Others and elided their own roles in perpetuating prejudice. Some members traveled to other countries through missionary and charity work.[157] However, LEDS members rarely referenced personal encounters with other races and ethnicities in the society's debates. The following examples, which include racist, anti-Semitic, colonialist, Orientalist, and victim-blaming justifications, offer a stark record of discriminatory arguments in circulation at the time; they also demonstrate the limitations and dangers of a racially and ethnically homogeneous group that perceived that it represented "women of infinite variety."

The first proposition that explicitly referenced race did not occur until 1915. Primarily preoccupied with World War I, other LEDS debates that year focused on issues like prohibition during wartime and women's work in munitions factories. In December, members turned their attention to the question, "can any race in the world be rightly considered as intrinsically subject?" The affirmative side, supported only by Helen Neaves (Mrs. Wallace had signed up to be the second affirmative speaker, but she was absent from meeting), built a case rooted in colonialist national policy. She suggested that the people of Egypt and India had proved to be intrinsically subject because they did not govern themselves. But the crux of the affirmative case was based on Neaves's interpretation of transatlantic conditions: she claimed that, despite emancipation and enfranchisement, African Americans had not gained true equality of citizenship in the United States. The negative team, Mrs. Inglis Clark and Sarah Mair, urged taking a longer view of racial hierarchy. Inglis Clark pointed to African Americans in higher education as evidence to negate Neaves's final argument. Mair argued that there was unity amongst all humans, and that "nature had imposed no barrier on the mingling of various races," though she acknowledged that there was social sanction against interracial marriage. The debate was a very close one, with five members voting affirmative, four voting negative, and three declining to vote.[158] Although it was not discussed in the debate, Scotland has a long and complex history with slavery. The number of slaves brought to Scotland was small compared to England, yet the growth of industries in Scotland's major cities was built upon the slave trade in the West Indies.[159] Later, many Scots, including some Edinburgh women, had a role in the transatlantic anti-slavery and abolition movements of the nineteenth century.[160]

It was not until fifteen years later that the LEDS took up another debate that was patently about race. This time, in February 1930, they focused on an issue that was only alluded to as a radical idea in 1915: "should social intercourse between white and coloured races be encouraged?" Both sides of the debate assumed that people of color were inferior. Arguments on the affirmative side were rooted in problematic arguments that may surprise the contemporary reader in their execution and scope. Miss Voge referenced anthropological studies of skull formation and shape now known to be the stuff of scientific racism and Miss Bury supported social intercourse between races as a way to expose inferior races to the civilizing behaviors of the dominant race. Though they supported interracial relationships, neither speaker uttered a word about the humanity or dignity of people of color.

On the negative side, Miss Greenlees led off the arguments against interracial social intercourse with a series of stereotypes. Her primary example was drawn from the United States, where she argued that African Americans remained intellectually and socially inferior despite emancipation from slavery. Greenlees's final argument was that white girls, especially in Scotland, tended to find something glamorous about black men, and that this often ended in tragedy. [161] Finally, Neaves seconded the negative side of the proposition.[162] Just as she had in the 1915 debate, she argued that the strength of the British Empire was based on the racial inferiority of Indians. At the end of the debate, the negative side garnered twenty-two votes, while the affirmative won only five, and three members did not vote.[163] Note that in this debate, neither the affirmative nor the negative side of the debate argued for the inherent value of all races. Both sides agreed that people of non-European descent were inferior and the disagreement in the debate revolved around the question of whether social intercourse could do anything to improve their status. Their arguments are steeped in vague and vicious generalizations. There was no acknowledgment of black communities in Britain, nor of the many prominent African American intellectuals who had traveled to the United Kingdom.[164] No mention was made of the number of African Americans pursuing higher education (many of whom were, in fact, also participating in intramural and intercollegiate debating) at that time.

The LEDS returned to a debate question about race and ethnicity four years later. Coincidentally, club business for the March 3, 1934, meeting included a discussion of a letter received from the Chinese Christian Association Debating Society in Singapore. The society expressed interest in the LEDS, and requested its assistance in developing their own debating group. The LEDS agreed to acknowledge the letter and write a letter back to the club expressing their mutual interest.[165] Other society business also took on a decidedly international turn; they decided that Lady Muir of Blair Drummond would give a talk at the next meeting about women in diplomatic posts. The debate of the day was on the question "has the influence of Jews in western civilisation been more beneficial than harmful?" The debate question must be historically situated, as it serves as a stark snapshot of the period, as Adolf Hitler had become Chancellor of Germany in 1933, and subsequently set into motion a series of efforts to restrict the rights and freedoms of Jewish people.

This debate was one of the LEDS's new "team debates" where each side included three speakers. Mrs. Burt began the debate by declaring that she had never personally known any Jews, but she had gone to school in Germany and learned much secondhand. She set out to research their positive influence on Western civilization, and had come with much to point to, especially in the areas of law, property, and family. Mrs. Arnott, the second affirmative speaker, suggested that conducting research on the debate topic had led her to better understand Jewish contributions in philosophy, music, art, medicine, journalism, and politics. For evidence of greatness, Arnott pointed to Albert Einstein and the actress Sarah Bernhardt. Her research had led her to believe that "we—the non-Jewish community—could not but love them." The third affirmative speaker, Miss Voge, reiterated the perspective that she had levied in the 1930 debate about interracial social intercourse. She argued that because "the Jew was not merely the equal to the Aryan but vastly his superior," intermarriage should be encouraged.[166] Each of the affirmative debaters argued on behalf of Jewish people, but from the perspective of outsiders looking in. We can surmise that no members of the Jewish community were members of the society based on the fact that the LEDS decided to debate this topic in the first place and that the debaters felt comfortable characterizing the audience as "we—the non-Jewish community." It is estimated that the total Jewish population in Edinburgh was 1,500 in 1914, and grew to only 2,000 by 1939 (compared to 15,000 in Glasgow by 1939).[167]

The negative team dealt in sweeping and pernicious anti-Semitic stereotypes. Miss Scott Moncrieff argued that Jews could not be considered civilized because they had always struggled to survive. Her seconder, Miss Fordyce Andrew, narrated Jewish history as a tale of nomadic people, arguing they were rightly regarded with suspicion. The third negative speaker, Miss Paterson, referenced her personal experience, which was limited to the poor and working-classes. The post-debate discussion entertained arguments on both sides of the debate. Most extreme was commentary from Lettice Milne Rae, who praised Jewish contributions to Western religion, philosophy, science, law, and public health in one breath but lobbied a post hoc fallacy in another: she argued that the discovery of tobacco by a Jewish person led to "excessive cigarette smoking among other wise innocent Christian women."[168] Akin to Greenlees's concern about black men in the 1930 debate, Rae's argument against an entire group of people was predicated on faulty reasoning based on harms to innocent white Christian women. In the end, however, the majority of the society found these arguments unpersuasive. The vote was overwhelmingly in favor of the positive contributions of Jewish people to Western civilization: nineteen votes for the affirmative, two for the negative, and three declining to vote.[169]

Although LEDS participants were not as infinitely diverse as they thought they were, they debated an array of topics, including many that summoned them to grapple with issues of age, gender, class, and race over time. This section lays bare how participation in the debating society may have succeeded in expanding their worldviews in some ways, yet limited it in others. It is a lesson in the possibilities and the painful pitfalls of ritual argument about issues of difference. Broaching a range of diverse topics is important, but it is not enough to ensure just representation and may, in fact, entrench bigotry when participants do not acknowledge the boundaries of their privileged positions.

Sustaining Practices

After seventy years of existence, the Ladies' Edinburgh Debating Society voted to dissolve in October 1935. Sounding a common theme, the members proposed a special meeting due to an ongoing problem with finding speakers for the debates. The debating society that had sustained itself through negotiations and innovations for so many years had finally reached a stopping point. The decision to dissolve was no doubt influenced by the advanced age of Sarah Mair, ever a dynamic presence in the society, who would go on to live only six more years.[170] In November, the society held its final meeting, and the idea for a publication detailing the LEDS history was proposed. The commemorative book was compiled by Lettice Milne Rae and published one year later. At Mair's request, proceeds from its publication were given to the Bruntsfield

Hospital for Women and Children. Eighteen members were not content
to stop debating, and a spin-off "daughter society" was planned. Funds
remaining in the LEDS bank account were split between a donation
for the daughter society, a gift for Isa Junes, the Mair family maid, and
publication of Milne Rae's book. Older members offered recollections
about the society, and Mair was thanked for all of her work over the
years before the final meeting concluded.[171] To the very end, she saw
the society as one that resisted inertia. In her contribution to the commemorative volume, she confessed

> Sometimes I dream that possibly some steadfast souls will develop and
> carry on our Society, handing it down to yet another generation busy
> with the problems of the twentieth century—perhaps even in 1965. If
> such there be, I would say to them, "Learn the lesson of progression
> truly, Do not call each glorious change decay." Growth—develop-
> ment—is the healthy condition of life: stagnation—obstinate resistance
> to change—is death.[172]

LEDS members were respectful of the older generations of debaters that
had come before them, mindful of their own legacy in Scottish history,
and concerned about the future generations of debaters to come. Though
one conclusion may be that the dissolution of the society suggests that
the LEDS never quite solved its internal tensions in balancing difference
and members' ideal vision of debate, their various efforts are instructive
as a model.

   In contrast to Tannen's sense of the static and monolithic argument
culture, the LEDS offers an example of an actual argument culture that
bore the imprint of different debaters, arguments, rhetorical styles, and
club deliberations over time. In other words, having debate at the center
of an organization does not guarantee the kind of ideal argument culture
that Zarefsky describes, but neither does it ensure the hostile terrain
that Tannen fears. Instead, a vibrant and sustainable argument culture
requires the ability to be self-reflexive and open to change, to redefine,
negotiate, and revisit the way that the group operates. The establishment
of basic rules and regulations, meta-moments of debate about debate,
constant efforts to accommodate different generations of arguers, and a

dedication to (if not a full realization of) perspectival diversity empowered members to have a stake in the argument culture they helped to create.

This chapter also points to the potential of studying historical argument cultures across time. By charting generations of arguers and ideas over the years, we can gain greater insight into the inner workings of such groups. The LEDS returned to various logistical issues regarding the debate process over the years. It also returned to various topic areas, with arguments and votes mirroring societal shifts. While work in feminist rhetorical history can (and should) focus on individual rhetors who go on to achieve public attention, we can also learn from the collective practices of those debaters who contributed to sustaining forums for discussion and debate, even those who will never be noted by name. For part of LEDS history, Sarah Mair and her fellow members did not have access to formal university lectures in rhetoric. Yet they created and documented their own rhetorical innovations, and ought to be taken seriously as powerful practitioners of nineteenth- and twentieth-century Scottish rhetoric. In studying the more mundane and quotidian decisions of groups like the LEDS, we may better appreciate rhetorical education and performance outside the rigid structures of top-down institutions. Moreover, we can see how this rhetorical education translated to civic participation in other arenas. The LEDS negotiated a cooperative argument structure rooted in tradition yet open to change as women's societal roles and deliberative goals changed.

In the physically stationary space of the Mair family dining room, there was movement—social movement—propelled by the force of argumentative encounter.[173] The debaters were travelers freed to move across spheres of knowledge, and, undoubtedly, the debates moved the needle toward social change for some on issues like suffrage and education. Yet as the previous section painfully demonstrates, the debates were not enough to confront the members' own ignorance and bigotry concerning class, race, and ethnicity. When LEDS members were denied proverbial seats at the tables of power—in universities, at polling places, in political organizations—they created their own space for argument by gathering around the table in the Mair family dining room. There is much to be celebrated in what they accomplished over the society's seventy years, but we must not lose sight of those who were denied a seat at that mahogany table as well.

CHAPTER 3

"Britain's Brainy Beauties": Intercultural Encounter on the 1928 British Women's Debate Tour of the United States

I

n 1928, three recent college graduates—Leonora Lockhart of Cambridge University's Girton College, Nancy Samuel of Oxford University's Somerville College, and Margery Sharp of the University of London's Bedford College—were selected to represent the United Kingdom in a debating tour of the United States. Transatlantic debate exchanges began in 1921 and grew in popularity throughout the 1920s, but never before had women held this honor.[1] An enthusiasm for international debating competitions combined with public curiosity about how these pioneering women would fare in their travels to ensure that the tour was destined to receive extensive media coverage in both countries. As tour participants, Lockhart, Samuel, and Sharp enjoyed a celebrity status that afforded them access to regional, national, and international platforms for public address and social commentary. As we endeavor to improve cross-cultural communication in an increasingly globalized world, this historical episode offers an opportunity to consider transnational advocacy as it was enabled by university-based argument cultures in the early twentieth century.[2]

The nineteenth and early twentieth centuries saw a variety of international alliances, including efforts to create an international suffrage movement, end slavery in the United States, and eradicate footbinding in China. These networks were sustained through international travel and correspondence.[3] Beyond concerted social justice campaigns, cosmopolitan sensibilities were cultivated in forums for rhetorical education and performance. Some U.S. Americans traveled abroad, but others experienced the world by learning about topics of global significance in local lyceums, public debates, and public lectures.[4] Though the debating societies discussed in previous chapters were grounded in specific geographical locations (the village of Oberlin; the city of Edinburgh), their debate topics were often global in scope and drawn from burgeoning transnational media cultures.[5] These historical debating societies simultaneously allowed for ritual argument *in situ* and for individual members taking their experiences to other sites.

The interwar period was a time of considerable expansion for U.S. intercollegiate debate programs, during which larger numbers of women joined and formed separate women's debating squads.[6] The locations for intercollegiate debate events were fairly predictable: debaters prepared and performed in educational spaces such as libraries, classrooms, lecture halls, and auditoriums. However, as travel became integral to the activity, argument cultures became progressively mobile. After months of preparation for their debates, the students wanted to take their show on the road—that is, they desired to embark on "debate trips" that would allow them to showcase their hard work and rhetorical skill at more than one site. In Egbert Ray Nichols's words, "an interstate and national outlook came to supplant the old satisfaction with provincial arrangements."[7] Debating, once an intramural activity rooted in local campuses and communities, became a vehicle for regional, interstate, and even transcontinental travel in the twentieth century.[8] International debate tours naturally followed as communication and transportation between countries became more viable, and as the need for a more global outlook became more acute. Discussion about debate topics and strategy spilled over to automobiles, train rides, and—in the case of international debate tours—ocean liners.

This chapter recovers the story of an international debate tour that has been largely forgotten. Though the participants went on to be standout figures in literature, linguistics, and politics, my aim is to detail how the 1928 British women's tour itself allowed the three debaters to go traveling in a series of events for campus and community audiences. It offers a fascinating case study in how Lockhart, Samuel, and Sharp were received and how they engaged with issues of difference as their status as British women debaters was highlighted in media accounts of the tour in college, local, and national newspapers. The chapter begins with a discussion of the importance of the international debate program in the 1920s before surveying newspaper coverage of the 1928 tour and its particular attention to gender, nationality, and argumentative style. I then examine how these dynamics were engaged as argumentative resources in a debate on coeducation with the Bates College debate team. Finally, I explore how the debaters transformed knowledge gained from the tour into cultural criticism in broader contexts.

The International Debate Program

An informal system of international debate exchanges can be traced back to 1921, when Bates College sent a delegation of three men students and a coach to debate at Oxford University in England.[9] U.S. debate coaches at individual colleges organized these exchanges through their personal contacts abroad. As interest in hosting international debates grew throughout the 1920s, responsibility for the coordination of the "international debate program" shifted to the Institute of International Education, an agency of the Carnegie Corporation.[10] The Institute of International Education was founded in 1919 on the premise that before the war, U.S. Americans had focused too narrowly on their own country, cultivating a "policy of comparative indifference to foreign affairs [that] was not conducive to the development of the 'international mind.'"[11] The war reoriented U.S. citizens to world affairs, and the institute sought to systematize what had earlier been ad hoc exchanges of students and professors between the United States and other nations.[12] Aided by the introduction of economical tourist class fares, approximately 250,000 U.S. Americans voyaged to Europe each year by the late 1920s.[13]

Initial debate tour visits to the United States involved teams composed exclusively of men students from Oxford or Cambridge. This began to change in the latter part of the decade. In 1928—the same year that Lockhart, Samuel, and Sharp traveled to the United States—men's debate teams from the University of Sydney, the University of the Philippines, and the United Kingdom also participated in U.S. tours. The year 1928 was also when the National Student Federation of the United States of America (NSFA), a student organization that developed out of the Intercollegiate World Court Congress, took over coordination of foreign debate exchanges.[14] The NSFA oversaw the logistics for the 1928 British women's debate tour, including the coordination of the schedule, finances, and travel details between stops. Institutions had to pay a $150 fee, guarantee lodging, and provide at least one night of hospitality in order to win a bid to host the debaters.[15] Another student organization, the National Union of Students, selected the debaters for the tour and handled logistics in the United Kingdom.

International debate tour events were renowned. Large audiences congregated to see the hometown team engage in an international competition. The international debate program was especially important to the cultivation of relations between the United States and the United Kingdom. The Anglo-American relationship was characterized by a friendly rivalry during the interwar years, as questions about economic and military power were being negotiated. Following Warren G. Harding's death, Calvin Coolidge assumed the U.S. presidency in August 1923. Coolidge inherited ongoing tensions in the transatlantic relationship regarding the repayment of war debts and the U.S. refusal to join the League of Nations, but sought to create alternative, less formal paths to international cooperation.[16] One such path was international debating. Shortly after Coolidge took office, Bates College President Clifton D. Gray wrote to inform him about an upcoming debate between men from Bates and Oxford. Coolidge's reply registered his support of the activity in no uncertain terms: "I think these international debating bouts, bringing together the representatives of both sides of the Atlantic, constitute one of the surest modes of promoting amity and true understanding between the English-speaking peoples."[17] "Silent Cal" was not so silent on the value of international debates![18]

Though the debaters were not formal political actors, there was an implicit recognition that these debates mattered in shaping public opinion and improving understanding across cultures. In 1928, Bates College men undertook a "world speaking tour" with stops in New Zealand, Australia, South Africa, and England. The debaters were regarded as silver-tongued ambassadors with the potential to resolve the world's differences through speech. A 1928 *Christian Science Monitor* article repeated Coolidge's sentiments, imagining the benefits of expanding international debating to other countries, stating, "in all of these countries, as in the United States and Great Britain, there are racial issues that press for solution. The relation between trade, tariff, and peace is a theme that is discussed with just as much vigor in the Orient as in the Occident. Any light thrown on these questions by the international debates under contemplation will be a clear gain for all peoples of the earth."[19] College students thus shouldered a heavy burden to facilitate intercultural argument and understanding on a global stage.

Debate exchange tours bring what Takuzo Konishi and I call "international argument cultures," or communities whose participants follow similar rules of argumentative engagement in diverse geographical contexts, into contact.[20] In addition to informal cultural exchange about food and customs, the tours allowed for a robust exchange of ideas about debate styles, formats, and arguments. The participants offered culturally specific perspectives on debate topics of common concern, rooting broad-based persuasive appeals in specific anecdotes from their experiences abroad. University debate methods had developed differently in the United States and the United Kingdom. British debating was modeled after the British Parliament, typically hosted informally within a local student union, and concluded with a vote from the audience. Intercollegiate competitions occurred infrequently, and the activity was almost always student-run. Like the range of questions featured in the Ladies' Edinburgh Debating Society's meetings, British university students tended to select topics based on social, cultural, and political values. Debates explored larger questions of what constituted the common good.

In the United States, intercollegiate debate tended to emphasize formal competition, teamwork, and the technical aspects of argumentation, including "the amount and significance of facts presented and their logical organization."[21] Members of university debating societies in the United States competed for spots on competitive debate squads through public tryouts, and also participated in off-campus debates for civic groups and high schools.[22] By the end of the 1920s, two popular formats were open forum debates with no decision at the end and expert decision debates, in which a panel of faculty members, administrators, or distinguished community members would render a decision.[23] Debate topics evolved toward issues of public policy, based in part in an American belief in the Constitution as the nexus of public argument.[24]

U.S. intercollegiate debate evolved to include debate coaches, usually faculty members with expertise in speech communication. International debate events were often the subject of critical attention from faculty scholars. The *Quarterly Journal of Speech* featured articles that used the tours as starting points for comparing American and British cultural and rhetorical differences, as manifested through their speaking styles. They also provided a catalyst for rethinking debate norms of the period.[25] Some academics believed that U.S. debate had developed superior methods and did not portray British debating in a very flattering light. For example, Egbert Ray Nichols argued that British debating of the 1920s and 1930s had more in common with U.S. lyceum and literary society debates of the 1880s and 1890s. In his assessment, it was a style that favored opinion over evidence, personality and humor over substance, and generally lacked the nuanced rebuttal skills that competitive intercollegiate debaters should learn.[26] However, it was also a style that tended to play better with public audiences. Though they had switched over to relying on expert judges in many domestic competitions, U.S. institutions followed the British tradition of audience voting at the end of international debate events.

Individual institutions in the United States had varied policies on the inclusion of women students, but their increased presence—at universities in general and on debate teams in particular—was undeniable. In one survey of Midwest colleges in 1927, nine out of ten reported having women students as participants in intercollegiate debates. The majority of the schools had separate men's and women's teams. Some debate coaches were enthusiastic about the growth of women's debate, while others said that it was a failed experiment at their institutions. Despite their growing numbers in the activity, attitudes toward women debaters were slow to change. One respondent to the survey maintained that this was simply because "women can't argue."[27]

In U.K. universities, men and women students participated in separate debating unions for much of the twentieth century. As Carol Dyhouse explains, at Britain's elite universities,

> misogyny was often fierce: in Oxford, where women had been admitted to degrees after the First World War, moves to control the number of women in the university were fueled by the argument that should Oxford become too 'feminized,' young men would opt for the more 'virile' environment of Cambridge (where women were not admitted to full membership until 1948).[28]

During this time, neither the Oxford Union nor the Cambridge Union Society allowed women as members, though they could sit in the balconies and speak on occasion. The march to coeducational debates was a long slog. In 1926, men in the Oxford Union enthusiastically voted for the affirmative on the motion that 'the Women's Colleges should be leveled to the ground' (and not, presumably, because they wanted the women to join them in the men's colleges).[29] Women students from Girton and Newnham Colleges at Cambridge lobbied for the right to join the Cambridge Union Society in May 1928, just months before the debate tour. A motion to allow their entrance into the union was debated for one hour and five minutes, but was defeated by an audience vote.[30] In July of the same year, the Representation of the People Act was expanded to allow women who were twenty-one or older to vote (women over thirty who met property-owning standards had been extended the right to vote in 1918). Given this dynamic, it was remarkable that three women, each in their early twenties, set off to represent not only the tradition of British debating, but the entire United Kingdom in October 1928.

English Girl Orators Here

The NSFA originally planned for the 1928 British women's tour to cover the Midwest and South, providing U.S. women's teams with the opportunity to participate in an international debate bout. However, in order to secure enough hosts over a seven-week period in November and December 1928, it was necessary to expand the tour to include hosts in New England and to permit debating with men's teams. The NSFA Vice President and Chair of International Debating, Martha H. Biehle, remarked that she was "very much disappointed to see how few women's colleges have debating teams," and found very few opportunities to schedule intercollegiate debates with women in New England.[31] The team ended up traveling as far west as Westminster College in Missouri, as far south as the University of North Carolina, and as far north as Bates College in Maine.[32]

The debaters selected for the tour had not traveled to the United States before, but each could be considered cosmopolitan for the period.[33] Lockhart and Samuel were called "daughters of British aristocracy" in U.S. newspapers.[34] Short biographies released to the press stressed their family connections, previous travels, and educational accolades. Leonora Lockhart was from a Scottish lowland family and had traveled to South Africa. It was often noted that she was a distant relation of Sir Walter Scott's biographer. As a senior at Girton College, Cambridge, Lockhart was active in political clubs and the debate society, receiving the prestigious Gardner Scholarship in History.

Nancy Samuel came from a well-known Jewish family in England. Her mother, Beatrice Franklin Samuel, was active in the Women's Liberal Federation. Press coverage of the tour never missed an opportunity to mention that Nancy was the daughter of Sir Herbert Samuel—member of parliament, member of the British cabinet, High Commissioner of Palestine, and later, liberal leader in the House of Lords.[35] As such, she had traveled extensively in Syria, Egypt, and what was then called Transjordania. Samuel earned her degree in philosophy, politics, and economics in 1928 from Somerville College, Oxford, where she was active in drama, debate, and local women's liberal clubs.[36] In addition to mentioning her famous father, news accounts mentioned her wit and good looks. For example, one article described her as "twenty-two years of age . . . an attractive girl with charming dark eyes" and an interest in politics.[37]

Margery Sharp was born in Wiltshire, England, but spent her childhood in Malta and traveling throughout Europe. She took time off from her education to be a secretary before she pursued her degree in French at the University of London's Bedford College.[38] She maintained an active interest in drama, journalism, literature, and poetry, and was a published author in *The Spectator* and *Punch*. As the least experienced of the three debaters on the tour, Sharp repeatedly told the press that she was selected to provide comic relief.[39] Since humor is one of the hallmarks of British debating, at least in the eyes of American audiences, this was no small role.

The debaters likely did not know each other before being selected for the tour. They were primarily linked by their overlapping affiliations—British, women, debaters—and were expected to represent each one of these groupings at public events. The British tour symbolized a national argument culture, in that they took the whole system of British debating traveling with them to international competitions. Yet the tour also sparked the creation of a new argument culture, one that Lockhart, Samuel, and Sharp created together through acts of collaborative, argumentative engagement. While the argument cultures created in Oberlin and Edinburgh were cultivated through decades of regular meetings, the international debate tour was a highly compressed schedule that focused on argument all day and every day.

Lockhart, Samuel, and Sharp wanted their tour topics to be similar to those debated by traveling men's teams on international tours. One sign that U.S. intercollegiate debate was still adapting to the increased presence of women is that, at least through 1928, there were separate national debate topics for men and women. In 1926, for example, men debated the McNary–Haugen Farm Relief Act, while women debated either trial by jury or the National Prohibition Act (the Volstead Act).[40] Before the tour began, the British trio offered their hosts the negative side of five possible debate propositions, which they deemed neither "threadbare" nor "frivolous":[41]

1. Resolved, that the popular reading of psychology is undermining morality.
2. Resolved, that democratic government appeals to prejudice rather than to reason.
3. Resolved, that the disadvantages of coeducation outweigh the advantages.

4. Resolved, that the centralization of government will destroy the political sense of the people.

5. Resolved, that it would be desirable to have an international language.

The first three options were the most popular on the tour, perhaps because they provided the most ground for the negative side.

Press outlets in the United States and United Kingdom took note of the tour's significance as the first of its kind to feature women debaters. What, reporters asked, would this tour mean for international and gendered power relations? Just days before their departure, the *Aberdeen Press & Journal* ran a story called "Women in Debate." In addition to commenting on the difficult job of being spokespeople for the entire United Kingdom, the anonymous author wondered aloud whether "academic emancipation thus side-by-side with men" in debate signaled a return to the *précieuses* of seventeenth century French salons or the intellectual bluestockings of eighteenth-century British society culture. They observed that women debaters were not ostentatious in speech, but were instead seen as "real" and "earnest," except for when the moment called for humor. One might think that this praise of women debaters would cast doubt on the idea that any particular gender has a natural inclination for debating ability. However, the article inverted the familiar argument that women are inherently inferior, instead arguing that debating is instinctual for women because "Eve debated the serpent and lost, but won when she turned her attention to Adam." It concluded with a message of support for Lockhart, Samuel, and Sharp, noting that their country will remain interested in their travels abroad, whether they meet women or men in competition.[42] Stateside newspapers ran a photo of the three smiling debaters as they boarded a train at Euston station in London with headlines announcing "English Girl Orators Here," and referring to them as "Britain's Brainy Beauties."[43]

The team departed for the United States aboard the White Star Line's RMS *Celtic* on October 20, 1928.[44] The ten-day journey originated in Liverpool, England, and ended in New York City in the United States. The ship's passenger list reveals that Lockhart, Samuel, and Sharp traveled alongside other residents of the United Kingdom. Their travel mates were men with a range of occupations, including a singer, an oil manufacturer, and an engineer. There were a number of other women on the ocean liner, too; most identified as housewives or listed no occupation.[45] Maritime historian Jo Stanley argues that the uptick in women travelers in the interwar period was the result of both supply and demand. Shipping companies needed new passengers once waves of wartime transport and migration subsided. Emboldened by their increased mobility during the war and their expanded citizenship rights, women sought new opportunities to travel abroad.[46] Ocean liners were a "place and space whose relations produced and reproduced social practices and discourses that affected how women passengers and crew could see themselves and their possibilities, within the wider space of the ocean and the world."[47] The transatlantic voyage was thus a liminal space for passengers to think beyond traditional boundaries of gender and nation. Though it requires a little creative license, we can imagine that the ten days aboard the ship was, for the debaters, a time to form their mobile argument culture. With only miles of blue waves in sight and the salty sea on their lips, Lockhart, Samuel, and Sharp were afforded time to get to know each other, time to share their anticipations about the tour ahead, and time to work together on the debate arguments they hoped would carry the day.

Upon their arrival in the United States, the team was quickly thrust into a travel schedule that included debates at twelve different universities. On each leg of the tour, Lockhart, Samuel, and Sharp received star treatment. For example, at one of the first stops at George Washington University in Washington, D.C., the debaters were "continuously entertained."[48] Dean of Women Anna Rose held a dinner in their honor at the American Association of University Women Clubhouse, and the Women's Advisory Council organized a tea for them. They debated the popular psychology motion in the university gymnasium. President Calvin Coolidge, British Ambassador Esme Howard, and other Washington elite were in attendance, and the British debaters reportedly won the audience's vote.[49] Itineraries on the tour regularly included visits to local women's clubs, meetings with important business and government representatives, and outings to experience the arts and culture that their host cities had to offer.

As the NSFA anticipated, the team primarily competed against women debaters at coeducational universities. However, in back-to-back stops at the University of North Carolina and the University of Kentucky, they debated men's teams. Due to the segregation of university debating societies in the United Kingdom, this may have been the first time that Lockhart, Samuel, and Sharp formally debated against men. The prospect of an international debate competition that pitted the United States against the United Kingdom and men against women made headlines. The mood was particularly electric as the hometown team prepared to debate on the topic of coeducation for a November 5th debate at the University of North Carolina (UNC). The student newspaper, the *Tar Heel*, teased its readership with small details about the debate throughout the fall to ensure a large crowd for the event. The debate team was quite popular at UNC in 1928, with over forty students aspiring to be on the team at the first meeting of the year. In preparation for the British event, they held practice debates on the coeducation question and had a faculty member lecture on the topic.[50]

The three debaters chosen to represent the university were J. C. Williams, E. H. Whitley, and Mayne Albright, all natives of North Carolina. Whitley and Albright were new to collegiate debate but had extensive high school debate experience, and Williams had represented UNC in previous debates against Alabama and Emory.[51] The *Tar Heel* ramped up publicity in the days before the event, billing the debate as a "clash" in which the "best of Carolina's debaters do battle for the honor of the university against a very select trio representing the pick of the women's colleges of the British Isles." It primed the audience by publishing an overview of the cultural differences between British and American approaches to debate. Here, the British style was described as more of a discussion than a debate, focused on general principles rather than specific details. The visitors would be "generally maturer than the American debaters and by the time they reach this country they have successfully defended their convictions dozens of times and consequently are able to play with their opponents, injecting considerable wit into the discussion at the expense of the other side."[52] When the team members arrived on campus, they were treated to a visit to the Playmakers Theatre and to tea with Lucetta Chase, wife of university president Harry Woodburn Chase.[53]

The debate was held on a Monday evening, and attracted a crowd of 900 students, faculty, and community members.[54] As predicted in the earlier *Tar Heel* article, Lockhart, Samuel, and Sharp were "witty," with a "dignified ease seldom possessed by American debaters."[55] They took the affirmative side of the motion, "Resolved, that the disadvantages of coeducation outweigh the advantages." Their case was that men and women had different educational needs on the basis of different interests and "masculine and feminine desires." The British debaters argued that women's colleges were best for balancing the intellectual and social lives of students. The UNC debaters maintained that coeducation was ideal for preparing students for the business world, as well as a "more intellectual and companionable social order." J. C. Williams, the second speaker for the negative side, was particularly dramatic in describing the stakes of the debate, arguing, "it is through the medium of universal education that the leaders of our nation hope to free the American people from the last clutching bonds of poverty."[56] Apparently, the audience agreed. Using the Oxford system of judging, the audience was asked to register their opinion about the topic before and after the debate. Before the debate, there was a slight preference for the affirmative side of the resolution. Ballots counted after the debate showed a shift to the negative side by a margin of thirty votes. The UNC team emerged victorious in front of their hometown crowd, but the British women were diplomatically reported to have possessed a "very adequate knowledge of the English language" and a "very well-defined knowledge of the scope of the problem."[57]

Not all observers of the debate, however, were so pleased with the performance of the UNC debaters. A column by student reporter Harry J. Galland suggested that the event was a harbinger of a shift in gender relations-as-usual. Written in a mocking style that simultaneously acknowledges and diminishes the rhetorical power of the women debaters, Galland chastised the UNC men for being "handicapped" by chivalry in their method of debate: the "girls . . . walk[ed] all over the poor boys with sarcasm and invective, while the gents continued to refer to the adversary as 'my fair opponent.'" Galland argued that the more assertive speech style on the part of the women debaters merited the men's abandonment of traditional gendered norms of politeness in the debate. Moreover, he feigned shock at the affirmative argument that women were better off without men in their colleges:

> This is a new construction of an idea with which all good Carolinians are carefully nurtured. We always thought we were conceding a place to the girls, and now the girls, or rather the debaters for them, turn around and say *they* are allowing us to stay, and are not particularly enthusiastic about it. Now we *are* mad. And all you gals can go buy your own chocolate shakes, and take your own notes on class. As for dates—well, that's a different matter.[58]

Galland's tongue-in-cheek ribbing demonstrates dominant assumptions and anxieties about gender and education at the time, especially when it comes to the mixing of intellectual and romantic worlds. Apparently, the very idea that Lockhart, Samuel, and Sharp would insist that coeducation should be seen from a woman-centered perspective was the stuff of giggles and snorts.

From Chapel Hill, the debaters traveled to Lexington, Kentucky, where they debated on the topic of governmental centralization in the Henry Clay High School auditorium. The University of Kentucky's team was composed of one first-year student, one sophomore, and one senior bound for law school.[59] Many will recognize the sophomore, Richard (Dick) Weaver, who would go on to become a well-known rhetorician and cultural critic. Clifford Amyx, Weaver's friend and teammate, attributes much of Weaver's rhetorical dexterity to the demands of their debate coach, William Sutherland: "he insisted we read Aristotle's *Logic* thoroughly, but then he sallied obliquely toward Bogoslavsky's 'functional logic'. . . . much of the incisive scorn in Weaver's *Ideas Have Consequences* derives from Sutherland's love of flaying contemporary fallacies."[60] The competition against Lockhart, Samuel, and Sharp is a highlight in stories about Weaver's time at the University of Kentucky. As the story goes, the Kentucky men were "crude as all get-out" when compared to the sophisticated visiting team. The British women's "debate style was all panache and grace and bitter irony and disrespect. They were commanding creatures, just overwhelming," as they argued that government centralization would destroy the political sense of the people, Amyx recalled.[61]

Weaver was Kentucky's only hope, and he fought to keep the team afloat with an approach described as "alert," "aggressive," and "somewhat strident." Sharp wooed the audience with her trademark humor, parodying Weaver's style. The British debaters ultimately won the audience vote, but the Kentucky debaters were made famous on their campus for having participated.[62]

The Bates Debate

Throughout November and early December, Lockhart, Samuel, and Sharp made stops in Virginia, Maryland, Pennsylvania, New Jersey, Missouri, Michigan, Indiana, and New York. Their final debate was in Lewiston, Maine, on December 13, 1928. Before and after the event, Lewiston newspapers published stories emphasizing gender and cultural differences between England and the United States.[63] Residents of the community were accustomed to attending and reading about debates in the local papers. As noted, Bates College was a leader in creating the international debate program and had enjoyed enormous competitive success in the 1920s under the direction of A. Craig Baird. The team included men of color, such as Benjamin Mays, who began debating in 1917 and later became President of Morehouse College and a mentor to Martin Luther King Jr.[64] In 1926, John P. Davis, an African American student, was elected as President of the Bates Debate Council. He protested the school's membership in Delta Sigma Rho, a national forensics honor society that required members to swear that they were "of good moral character" and "not a Negro." Bates maintained its chapter of Delta Sigma Rho, but put pressure on the organization to desegregate (a step that was not officially taken until 1935).[65]

Bates women debated in the coeducational Eurosophian and Polyhymnian literary and debating societies as early as the 1860s. By the turn of the century, the Bates College Debating Union had become coeducational, although women were never selected to participate in intercollegiate competitions. In the early twentieth century, following the creation of a very short-lived separate women's debating league, the faculty imposed new regulations that limited women's debating. The faculty demanded the end of coeducational literary society meetings, created separate divisions for the sophomore prize debates, and banned women from participating in intercollegiate debates. Bates women did not participate in their first intercollegiate debate against other women until 1924. One year later, they held their first mixed-gender intercollegiate debate. When Brooks Quimby took over as Director of Debating in 1927, he maintained the gender-segregated debate teams but allowed all debaters to work together under the auspices of the coeducational Debating Council.[66]

Quimby—who would later go on to write a Harvard master's thesis on international debate exchanges and serve on the national committee now known as the National Communication Association's Committee on International Discussion and Debate—collected and transcribed the speeches delivered in the December 13th debate with the British.[67] In this transcription, we have a rare and precious artifact of the time: a detailed record of six women's argumentation in an intercollegiate debating event. This transcript was published in *Intercollegiate Debates*, a yearbook of college debating featuring the best of the previous season's competition. As might be expected, the volume is full of the speeches of men debaters. The inclusion of the Bates debate was treated as evidence of a growing trend by editor Egbert Ray Nichols, who remarked, "it is fitting that a women's debate should appear occasionally in the pages of 'Intercollegiate Debates' . . . . in the forensic world they are doing all the things that men students do, and if interest keeps growing, will soon be doing these things quite as extensively as men."[68]

The British debaters defended the affirmative side of the coeducation resolution against three accomplished seniors from Bates: Miriam McMichael of Pittsfield, Maine, Yvonne Langlois of Philadelphia, Pennsylvania, and Eugenia Southard of Portland, Maine. Audience members paid fifty cents for admission to the debate at Bates Chapel. Each speaker had fifteen minutes for her main speeches, and both teams were permitted one six-minute rebuttal speech.[69]

Nancy Samuel opened the debate with pleasantries for her hosts at Bates, and some commentary on her impressions from the tour. She claimed that differences between the United States and England were exaggerated, using her stock phrase, "I am reminded of . . . ," as a way to introduce humorous anecdotes. Instead of discussing the substance of their cultural differences (which would soon be an important source of evidence during the debate), Samuel poked fun at the American use of the word "cream" to refer to many dairy products: "I am reminded of the story of the American who went to a hotel in England and he said, 'Here, waiter, bring me some coffee without any cream.' The waiter returned and said, 'I am sorry, sir, we haven't any cream. Will you have it without milk?'" This may seem a bit silly, but the anecdote accomplished the important rhetorical function of acknowledging and building a rapport with an international audience. Political philosopher Iris Marion Young notes that such acts of greeting, ritualized in Western political processes, can serve to "assert discursive equality and establish or re-establish the trust necessary for discussion to proceed in good faith."[70]

As Samuel moved into the crux of her speech, she admitted that her frame of reference for thinking about the topic had changed as a result of her experience on the tour (and perhaps she is alluding to the UNC debate here). Instead of suggesting that coeducation is intrinsically bad, the modified position stressed the advantages of gender-segregated education for everyone. Samuel proceeded to build the affirmative case with three main arguments:

1) *Sex differences in intellectual capacity.* Men excel in the sciences, and women excel in the humanities, so it does not make sense to teach them in the same way in higher education.

2) *Sex differences in competition/achievement.* Men and women shouldn't be treated the same in educational institutions because they are not being trained for the same world (men benefit from competition with each other as a source of "masculine preparation," whereas women's colleges allow women to prove their worth on their own merits).

3) *Coeducation turns education into a social club.* Citing evidence from their visits to Midwest colleges, where "dating carries as many hours as any other course," Samuel contended that is was a waste of time to date before mental maturity, and that the sex-segregated English system permitted time for the mind to "widen itself and improve itself to withstand 50 years of married life."[71]

After establishing these main arguments, the speech reached a crescendo when Samuel declared that coeducation was simply a symptom of American mass production. Perhaps their opponents could not see it because mass production was like a "fever . . . seeping over America," but Samuel claimed that her outsider status afforded her considerable perspective. While mass-produced goods like cars, soap, and clothes were admirable, "when individuals are put into the machine of standardization then their qualities are being wasted and pinched out of shape."[72] In a later assessment of the debate, Quimby contended that Samuel said more in a single speech than a whole team of Oxford men.[73]

Miriam McMichael took the podium as the first negative speaker for Bates. She utilized a straightforward, streamlined style typical of U.S. debate at the time to gradually build the argument that coeducation was the natural result of the more enlightened age in which they were living. After establishing the terms and scope of the debate topic, she reminded audiences that had the event taken place in 1828 instead of 1928, they would be discussing whether women should have access to higher education at all. The very presence of the traveling British women debaters was used as evidence and, indeed, an endorsement of women in higher education. World War I had transformed traditional assumptions about what women were capable of in the workforce, and women like Olympic swimmer Gertrud Ederle and aviator Amelia Earhart proved that "the old idea of woman as a mere will-o'-the-wisp or a clinging vine is decidedly passé."[74]

Upon taking the podium, Leonora Lockhart, second affirmative, pointed out that the odds were stacked against her team. She feared that she would "resemble the serpent" if she turned around and criticized the coeducational system at Bates after receiving such warm hospitality. Moreover, "for an English person to discuss coeducation before an American audience is rather like a South Sea-Islander attempting to instruct a Laplander on the construction of icebergs." However, she persevered, as she believed that in the case of iceberg construction and in coeducation, an outsider might be better positioned to see the topic impartially.[75] Lockhart introduced a new argument that took the debate in a decidedly different direction. She maintained that coeducation should be rejected for children as well as college students, referencing Freudian concerns about sexual consciousness. Educating girls and boys together risked that that they would be prematurely distracted by romantic attachments. She cited a recent headline about an American teenager who murdered his girlfriend as evidence that children were not emotionally equipped to deal with sexual thoughts.[76]

Lockhart also built upon Samuel's major arguments, contending that different intellectual predispositions called for more focused educational curricula because "we don't care to see a boy who does embroidery or a girl who plays football."[77] She argued that gender-segregated colleges were necessary in England because women were treated differently than men in public life. However, the argument that really seemed to get Lockhart's blood boiling was that coeducation turned colleges into social clubs, or "dating factories." Like Samuel, Lockhart extrapolated from her experience on the tour, citing as an example her interaction with one Midwestern student who claimed she had been on seventy-two dates in sixty days. A Dean of Women at one of their host institutions confided that many women students were only interested in one year of social activity before leaving college for matrimony. According to Lockhart, to have "more dates of this sort than dates of history"—to study college men instead of Graham Wallas's *Human Nature in Politics*—was a real shame.[78]

As the second negative speaker, Bates student Yvonne Langlois knew she could rely on the audience's predispositions in her speech. Imploring her audience to withhold judgment about the image of that "terrible creature, the 'co-ed'" created by the affirmative team, Langlois humorously pointed out that the President of Bates College, Clifton Gray, would likely never have married a co-ed if he knew how dangerous they were. She proceeded to provide a targeted, line-by-line refutation of the affirmative speeches, and even pointed out tensions between them: "Miss Samuel said women were superior intellectually, while Miss Lockhart said men were superior intellectually. We don't know which one to believe."[79]

Langlois's strategy was to stress that men and women benefited from each other's presence in classes and debates. Intermingling was necessary if they were going to be expected to live and work together in the future. Instead of just defending against the dating factories argument, she offered an argument to frame the social implications of coeducation:

Women learn not to blush and grow pale or vie with each other for his attentions when a man enters their company, while men are less inclined to be struck speechless or to want to show off in the presence of women; which reminds me of the terrible experience of poor Mr. Lennox-Boyd, one of the Oxford debaters who recently visited Bates. At a dance given in their honor at Vassar he was cut in on twenty-seven times. He described it as a horrible experience and thereby has taken an extreme aversion to women. We didn't notice any co-eds making wild dashes for him on the Bates campus.[80]

Langlois was able to draw on the recent visit of the Oxford men debaters, which many audience members would have fresh in their minds. Intended to amuse the audience, the image of a ravenous pack of romantically deprived Vassar students (stunted by a single-gender educational environment) worked well to counter the image of the "terrible creature, the co-ed" that Lockhart had offered. The women's college student, not the co-ed, was made frivolous and silly by the presence of men.[81]

Margery Sharp was accustomed to being the third affirmative speaker in tour debates. As she noted in her interviews with the press, Samuel and Lockhart had more experience and technical skill as debaters, but she was gifted with a humorous and self-deprecating style. In fact, her role in the debate was to defuse the momentum of the Bates team with a short, personal speech. She began by noting that she had been warned that American debaters began every speech with "Fellow citizens, I view you with alarm" and relied heavily on statistics. As she was neither a fellow citizen nor had any relevant statistics to offer, Sharp contended that she was at a distinct disadvantage, and would choose to focus on the part of the debate she knew about: McMichael's narrative of the progressive improvement of the status of women through the ages. The description of women's "undiluted misery" in the past was inaccurate, at least for white women of the upper classes, who managed to attain a high level of education, including knowledge of Latin and Greek. Sharp called upon the audience to remember figures like Louise Labbe and Lady Jane Grey. She argued that the Victorian woman was not "wholly the insipid creature depicted," blaming this inaccuracy on Charles Dickens and his inability to portray a "living woman" in his novels.[82]

In order to further diminish the caricatures created in the debate, Sharp offered personal evidence based on her own family history of working women. Her grandmother had worked alongside her grandfather in the ironworks business, and Sharp herself had worked as a stenographer in an office of ten to fifteen men before returning to the university. In both cases, they managed to get along perfectly fine. Taking offense at the idea that she might be lumped in with the overeager Vassar students, Sharp made her objection clear: "I am a product of a segregated college and I neither blush nor grow pale when a man enters my presence . . . at dances, I have often found time for conversation, as much as for the Charleston."[83] The purpose of coeducation could even be something else beyond heterosexual marriage. The specter of something else was not taken up later in the debate, but Sharp's decision to mention it in the space of the public debate event was significant. Though she was quick to minimize her contributions to the debate, a closer read reveals that Sharp deftly utilized personal experience and urged broader, more imaginative possibilities for women students. The Bates College student paper praised her as a skilled speaker who spoke "in a most disarming manner" and whose "cleverness of expression and ready wit kept the audience in a very receptive mood."[84]

Eugenia Southard's job, as the third Bates speaker, was to reinforce the strength of the negative team's arguments for any audience members who might have been taken with Sharp's bold style. She began by acknowledging that they had all enjoyed the previous speech, and then set about the task of swiftly refuting it with inside knowledge: "We heard that Miss Sharp was interviewed before she left England and she said that her purpose was to furnish humor. She has succeeded. She has not damaged coeducation hopelessly, however, as I am about to show you."[85] Southard continued on to demonstrate that she had done her research about the English system of higher education. She noted that when women were first admitted to Cambridge, a fainting room was established to accommodate their delicate natures. However, "since none collapsed[,] it was turned into a lecture room."[86] The fact that seven men (who were not the "effeminate type") and only two women had fainted when Bates College students had to get vaccinations was offered as further evidence that women had the fortitude to withstand the demands of coeducational life.[87]

Southard highlighted inconsistencies and discontinuities in the affirmative team's arguments, emphatically reminding the audience that Sharp did not extend or develop Lockhart's arguments about coeducation for children. To guard against the possibility that these arguments would resurface in the affirmative rejoinder, Southard again used her knowledge of the tour. Lockhart's Freudian reading of premature sex consciousness in schoolchildren was simply an example of the detrimental effects of the popular reading of psychology, a topic that the British debaters had recently engaged on the tour. She hoped to put the argument about intellectual differences to rest by citing the Binet–Simon Intelligence Tests, which found that intelligence was distributed equally between girls and boys.[88]

In response to the "dating factory" thread in the debate, she provided anecdotes from Smith College and Yale to prove that dating is a mainstay of higher education at both coeducational and gender-segregated institutions.[89] She admitted that women at coeducational institutions may be vice-presidents to the men presidents of student clubs, but suggested that such an arrangement was realistic training for gendered relations in the wider world. As vice-president of the Bates Debating Council (which was led by Walter O. Hodsdon), Southard again drew from her firsthand experience. To emphasize this point, she noted that the British women had debated almost exclusively at coeducational institutions in the United States because the women's colleges either did not have debate at all, or had it on a very limited scale.[90]

To close the debate, each team had the opportunity to offer six-minute rebuttals. In a final speech for the negative team, Miriam McMichael asked the audience to remember that the affirmative team was inconsistent and incoherent when they cast their ballots. They were indeed funny, but humor is no substitute for good argumentation. The negative team had offered a number of arguments in favor of coeducation, which all stemmed from the central idea that coeducation was preparation for real life. Samuel pointed out that the negative team members were so intent on refuting their arguments that they, too, had introduced contradictions. She boiled the affirmative case down to the idea that men and women will compete in the world, but that they could do so with different talents and different educational backgrounds. At the end of the debate, an audience vote was recorded. Audience members were instructed to vote on the basis of their individual convictions on the merits of the question, and the negative team from Bates was declared the victor.[91] The final vote tally was 296 in favor of coeducation, and 118 opposed.[92]

The transcript provides an extraordinary glimpse into the specific arguments made in a debate, even if we cannot fully relive the embodied performance of their speeches. Though all six of the debaters identified as women and students, they differed in their approaches to the subject based on their different national identities and argument cultures. True to competitive U.S. debate conventions, McMichael, Langlois, and Southard focused on defining terms, establishing agreed-upon facts, and citing statistics in order to argue for the advantages of coeducation. They approached the event as an international exchange of ideas, but one that was still fundamentally a contest. The Bates team bemoaned logical inconsistencies, contradictions, and discontinuities among the British team's speeches.

Lockhart, Samuel, and Sharp positioned themselves as sage outsiders. Their performance of white, upper class femininity was shaped by their experiences as British citizens who had experienced gender-segregated education firsthand and observed the effects of coeducation in their travels on the U.S. debate tour.[93] Inconsistencies between the affirmative speakers can be interpreted as representative of British debating style, and this is likely the case. Another complementary interpretation, however, is that their performance actively resisted agonistic forms of deliberation that ultra-competitive intercollegiate debating contests in the United States entailed. As Iris Marion Young argues, "restricting practices of democratic discussion to moves in a contest where some win and others lose privileges those who like contests and know the rules of the game. Speech that is assertive and confrontational is here more valued than speech that is tentative, exploratory, or conciliatory."[94] To be clear, Lockhart, Samuel, and Sharp knew the "rules of the game" of debate, and would certainly fall into the category of the educated elite who benefit from formalized norms of deliberation. They operated within a predetermined format, assertively articulated their arguments, and complied with the general expectations of public debate events. However, instead of creating a coherent, consistent affirmative case, they offered multiple arguments in multiple forms to prove coeducation's disadvantages. Their willingness to play with style—to add greetings, jokes, and narratives, and to see their performance less as a coordinated team battle and more as an intra- and inter-team exchange of ideas—certainly challenged the "norms of orderliness" of agonistic public forums.[95]

Beyond the intricacies of their arguments, both teams called upon the memory of past women and their educational struggles. As they moved between sometimes-conflicting arguments about women's roles in leadership, business, and home life, they demonstrated an awareness of their own roles within larger gendered and culturally inflected narratives. Both teams also relied on caricatures of the modern woman student, creating witty but biting portrayals that would surely have hit close to home as the debaters defended the merits of their own educational systems.

Debaters as Cultural Critics

So far, this chapter has focused on the practices of the 1928 British women debaters in and around their stops on the tour as they built their mobile argument culture. Indeed, one of the primary goals of this chapter is to take the rhetorical labor within such international public debates events seriously. However, debating was not the only occupation of the debaters on the tour. Outside of their debate appearances, they were consistently called upon to do comparative cultural analysis in press interviews. Lockhart, Samuel, and Sharp established *ethos* by virtue of their scholarly credentials, acumen honed in debates, and perspective as foreigners traveling the country. This knowledge transformed them from average young women into incisive cultural critics. The international debate exchange piqued the interest of U.S. audiences, eager to hear their comments on topics ranging from the amount of snow in British winters to highbrow culture.[96]

After the tour officially ended, the 1928 team remained in the spotlight. Margery Sharp is the member of the trio who achieved the most enduring fame for contemporary audiences. She traveled back to England and continued her career as a writer, regularly contributing to popular magazines and journals. Just two years after the tour, she published her first novel, *Rhododendron Pie*. Sharp went on to become an internationally revered author whose writing drew on the sharp wit she displayed as a debater. She penned a number of plays, short stories, and novels, but is best known for her children's book *The Rescuers* (later made into two animated Disney films, *The Rescuers* and *The Rescuers Down Under*). Perhaps unsurprisingly, Sharp's writings often featured women protagonists who bucked gender conventions (see, especially, Miss Bianca in *The Rescuers* and Sharp's *Martha* series).

Lockhart and Samuel stayed in the United States after the tour ended. Their commentary in interviews shortly thereafter focused primarily on observations about the quality of women students and the U.S. college experience overall. Carrying over some of their arguments from the debates, but emboldened now that their official tour duties were over, Lockhart and Samuel registered their frank assessment of American college life as "more social, more casual, less intellectual, and far less serious an undertaking than it is in England."[97] Moreover, although Samuel "declined to comment on her impression of American men," she offered her thoughts on American college women, taking particular aim at highly gendered co-ed activities like sororities and cheerleading. Consider this backhanded compliment: American "girls" were "extremely nice" and energetic, but lacked individuality. Sororities drained the college experience of the interesting tasks of finding oneself and finding one's own friends, and the cheerleaders she witnessed were rather lackluster, only swaying when they might have been turning cartwheels.[98] When *The Woman's Journal* featured an article on the dangers of coeducation in January 1929, Samuel provided testimony as a non-specialist source whose opinions supported the conclusions of expert researchers.[99]

Lockhart became a guest writer for a series of four articles that ran in the *New York Times* from 1929 to 1930. Although the debaters insisted that the differences between England and the United States were exaggerated when they were on the tour, each of Lockhart's articles, in title and content, foregrounded the ways in which the countries were dissimilar. The first two articles in the series ran in May 1929, expounding on the differences between the systems of higher education. The first, "Women's Colleges: A Striking Contrast," identifies class as a distinguishing cultural difference in women's education. Middle-class English students view their education as "an investment rather than a luxury," but members of the aristocracy "treat the women's colleges with a certain degree of condescension."[100] U.S. women are more likely to come to college from a range of class backgrounds, and to view the experience as preparation for all kinds of work, including domestic life. Lockhart views the development of women's education in the respective countries under consideration as reflective of broader cultural perspectives: namely, American universities focus on "good habits," while English universities focus on "the free development of personality." As Lockhart clarifies, American women participate in a system that is paternalistic down to the smallest policies, interpreting attendance requirements, quizzes, and faculty involvement in extracurricular clubs as further evidence of this brand of paternalism.[101]

A similar charge is levied in Lockhart's second article, "An English College Girl Studies Ours," where she regrets that U.S. students are handled with kid gloves and taken through various forms of first-year initiation in "an orgy of practical joking" that has no place in the English university.[102] Further, in a move that reads as rather Tocquevillian, Lockhart bewails the decline of interest in college organizations, which she attributes to a culture of individualism that resists the micromanaging of such groups. If U.S. women's debating societies are suffering, it is because they are "marred by over-rehearsal."[103] Finally, Lockhart noted that English college students have significant knowledge of public affairs, but do not participate in organized politics as American students do. She puzzles over the value and focus put into voting on U.S. campuses, which she sees as an intensified fervor that dies out between elections. Lockhart's discussion of student life moves from observations about debating to broader cultural diagnosis. She translated her translated her debate skills into incisive commentary of a civic and political nature.

In "The Professional Woman: A Contrast," Lockhart's third article in the series, she moved into a wider assessment of gender politics. In this article, the United States is declared the clear leader in smoothly paving married and unmarried women's paths into the workforce, an achievement that has coincided with a period of economic prosperity in the country. In retrospect, this appraisal is eerie, as it was rendered just months before stocks began falling in what would turn into the Great

Depression. Nonetheless, Lockhart firmly argues that economic enterprise supercharged progressive attitudes toward U.S. women, while English women were still forced to choose between domestic or professional life and faced much hostility if they chose the latter.[104] Beyond welcoming financial conditions, Lockhart makes a number of other observations about the success of U.S. women in the workplace. American attitudes about efficiency, she notes, spill over to gender relations in ways that ultimately benefit the married, working woman. In the name of efficiency, U.S. women have access to a number of appliances—from "the vacuum cleaner to the latest grapefruit corer"—that lessen their housework duties, freeing them up for leisure and work outside the home.[105] Pairing this with the rumor that American husbands were "an indulgent race of men," willing to share in household duties, Lockhart believed that women had a recipe for success.[106] Her thinking on gender relations had apparently evolved beyond the Bates coeducation debate. Freed from the requirements of the debate contest, and bolstered by months of observation of gender politics in the United States, the article is a shrewd piece of cultural criticism. Of course, the analysis assumes white, heterosexual, educated, middle- and upper-class people (she even comments on the "greater abundance and willingness of servants" in England), overlooking those who have never had a choice but to work.[107]

As for her own professional choices, Leonora Lockhart went on to pursue a successful career in linguistics. She worked at the London's Orthological Institute, a facility founded by linguist C. K. Ogden to promote Basic English, an international auxiliary language for second language learners.[108] Although she did not have much of an opportunity to debate the "international language" resolution on the 1928 tour, Lockhart dedicated her life to this pursuit. She has been called a "woman pioneer of Basic English," a scholar who played a crucial role in testing the language for its real world applications.[109] Lockhart authored and co-authored many books, including *Word Economy: A Study in Applied Linguistics* (1931), *The Basic Traveller: And Other Examples of Basic English* (1931), and *The Basic Teacher: A Course for European Students* (1950).

Lockhart produced her final article for the *New York Times* in May 1930, after she returned to London. It was from the perspective of the returned traveler that she was able to identify just how many attitudes and conventions had been absorbed by British culture, despite the long-held belief that "England is the cultural wet-nurse of America."[110] The article, entitled "American Ideas That Assail the Briton," maintained that such influence was significant, including the demise of the detached house and grand aristocratic family homes, distinctly American architecture, quick service food innovations like the waffle and the soda fountain, advertising, industrial psychology, a love of sports competition, jazz, Hollywood cinema, and standardized department stores.[111] This final development—that the character of British shops was transformed by influences such as Gordon Selfridge, the American-born businessperson who "like a prophet" dazzled Britons with "arresting window displays, his novelty lines, and his extraneous advertising activities"—should not be ignored.[112] Selfridge's vision of cosmopolitan entrepreneurship was ripe for anti-capitalist critique by British intellectuals such as G. K. Chesterton. Yet as British cultural studies scholar Mica Nava argues, department stores also provided "new social and work space for women."[113]

Nancy Samuel's experience after the debate tour ended is evidence of the kind of social and work space department stores provided. Samuel extended her stay by two months to "make a serious study of social, economic, and political problems" in the United States.[114] In order to do so, she applied to be a "shop girl" at Altman's department store in New York City. This decision came with the blessing of her high-profile political family in England, who "regard[ed] her insatiable craze for knowledge with admiration [and] some amusement."[115] With the curious eye of a social researcher, Samuel coordinated a grand experiment and went undercover as a shop assistant. England, "with its characteristic conservatism, progresses slowly in personnel work, so that comparatively few women have the opportunity of entering business from that angle," and Samuel's class background would have certainly kept her from such pursuits in her home country.[116] In New York, she wholeheartedly embraced the life of the workingwoman, living as her wages allowed by leasing a room in an apartment building that catered to single women.[117] Altman's placed her in the glass and china department, where she found her co-workers and the customers "good-tempered" with an "air of cheerfulness . . . which is a necessary part of prosperity."[118] After about five weeks of employment, her identity was discovered, and Samuel left her job in order to avoid the scores of reporters who had gotten wind of the story of an undercover British aristocrat conducting a sociological experiment.

Yet that was not the end of Samuel's study of U.S. labor. She instead answered an advertisement at a nearby factory, and was promptly hired as a "biscuit" packer.[119] The work was long and monotonous, but her co-workers, "unskilled workers" with "keen intelligence," kept things interesting. As Samuel recalled, "many had an intimate knowledge of two countries, for we were like a 'League of Nations' a little there. Some of the girls were Italian, some Scottish, some Irish, and many other nationalities were represented."[120] She reported getting along well with the factory workers, staying in the position for three and half weeks. A flurry of coverage commenced anew when the U.K. press found out that this "society girl" had lived as a "shop girl"—and biscuit packer.[121] Reporters consistently underlined Samuel's relationship to Sir Herbert Samuel. She maintained that she had engaged in the experiment in order to gain insight into social conditions.

Samuel viewed the debate tour and her time in the workforce as life experience that would allow her to better understand her fellow British citizens. When she returned to England, she became active in the Liberal party, and was a vital advocate in her father's quest for a return bid to the House of Commons in 1929.[122] In public speeches on the campaign trail and otherwise, Samuel told humorous anecdotes about her work in New York.[123] At one event, her shop experience was used against her. A heckler in the crowd interrupted Samuel's speech to accuse her of stealing a job from someone who needed it in the United States. As a special cable to the *New York Times* reported: "'I did no one of a job,' she retorted, 'there are many more positions in New York than there are people to fill them. I want to see the same here.'"[124] Years later, in an announcement of her engagement to Arthur Gabriel Salaman, Samuel's 1928 debate tour, stint in New York, activism in the Liberal Party, and assistance to her father's campaign were listed as her claims to fame.[125] Although she did not pursue national elected office, as was expected, Samuel remained a well-known and active participant in community political organizations for the rest of her life.

What, then, should we make of Lockhart's and Samuel's commentary? These developments provide crucial insight into the relationship between debate experience and activism in broader arenas of civic participation. Traditionally, mainstream debate is lauded for teaching skills that prepare participants for business, law, or politics. This exercise in tracing post-tour commentary lends historical grounding to Gordon R. Mitchell's notion of "argumentative agency," or "the capacity to contextualize and employ the skills and strategies of argumentative discourse in fields of social action, especially wider spheres of public deliberation."[126] Mitchell and Takeshi Suzuki identify six skills that can be translated between contemporary debating and public forums: panoramic argument vision, stasis distillation, on-point refutation, research, questioning, and topic selection.[127] The 1928 British women's tour demonstrates that beyond these skills, the activity also prepares its participants for cultural criticism, or the ability to understand, compare, and assess broader cultural currents. Through the travels and their adventures in argumentative engagement across the United States, Lockhart and Samuel gained knowledge that they were able to deploy as experts in their post-tour cultural criticism as they ruminated on a number of noteworthy themes. Some were a direct translation of arguments engaged in intercollegiate competition, and others demonstrated their range as public commentators. While on the tour, the British debaters mixed personal anecdotes with broader, more generalized arguments about their topics. They did not switch sides, as they were assigned the affirmative on each of their motions, but they likely did argue against their convictions, at least occasionally, for the purposes of debate. Once the tour ended, they seized multiple opportunities to develop, revise, and explore ideas encountered in their travels. They were able to acknowledge intercultural perspectives in their cultural criticism, distilling complex issues for a public readership. The process of international debate fed into future rhetorical engagements, connecting traditional argumentation skills to new spaces of public commentary.

Exchanging Arguments

This examination of the 1928 British women's tour is but one example to be explored in the vast history of intercultural debating, an activity that is worthy of continued attention in many global contexts.[128] Practical and intellectual considerations involving the cultural specificity of ideas and regionally inflected rhetorical norms continue as salient concerns for intercultural argumentation and public address. Lockhart, Samuel, and Sharp brought the British style of debating to public audiences, but national citizenship was but one affiliation among many. It was their status as white, class-privileged British women brought together for the purpose of debate that shaped their arguments and their later cultural criticism.

The story of the 1928 tour also has much to contribute to the history of debating women in the United States and the United Kingdom regarding space and mobility as opportunities for education and travel expanded for women. As they traveled on the RMS *Celtic* across the Atlantic, and in trains and automobiles through different states, Lockhart, Samuel, and Sharp honed their arguments with U.S. American audiences in mind. Their appearances on speaking platforms at various universities is an indication of the immense progress that women debaters had attained in accessing public spaces by the 1920s. Yet even as they moved into these new spaces and exercised their voices with greater legitimacy, they were treated as novelties. Press accounts marveled at their intellect and persuasive skill but could not help but mark their difference from the white, masculine, American norm in U.S. debate. Lockhart and Samuel's subsequent cultural criticism demonstrated that the rhetorical prowess of debating women was not limited to debate events. They were able to study another culture, offer commentary, and position themselves as experts in civic and political affairs.

The international debate program was unique in the 1920s in its ability to bring people together on the basis of debate. It coordinated and facilitated the movement of ideas, arguments, and people, enabling moments of intercultural encounter and public address. In this tour, debaters were able to experience other cultures through argument. They highlighted overlapping values in the quest for audience identification, and emphasized the aspects that made their cultural perspectives unique. This educational activity created a space for cosmopolitan alliances rooted in a shared appreciation for ritual argumentation and civic participation.

CHAPTER 4

"Your Gown Is Lovely, But . . .":
Negotiating Citizenship at Pennsylvania
State Colleges, 1928–1945

————— •◆• —————

I nstitutional tolerance of women's participation in intercollegiate and coeducational debate competitions vacillated throughout the late nineteenth and early twentieth centuries. However, intercollegiate debating underwent a "veritable explosion"[1] of popularity in the 1920s and 1930s, and by 1927, U.S. debating women had gained enough momentum for Mildred Freburg Berry to declare that "women have invaded the forensic field to stay."[2] That there were simply more women on college campuses across the United States at this time undoubtedly intensified this dynamic. Despite the Depression, the number of college women increased between 1930 and 1940 (from 10.5 to 12.2 percent of total student enrollment).[3] This cohort of women students also included representation from more diverse ethnic and religious backgrounds. "Equality with a difference" was the reigning mantra for women in higher education in the 1930s, signaling a demand for equal opportunities coupled with the belief that femininity set them apart.[4] Yet as economic worries ran high and budgets ran tight, arguments in support of university women's debating societies had to be carefully crafted.

The greater presence and legitimacy of women in academia gave rise to new considerations regarding their extracurricular activities. Between 1928 and 1945, debating women were offered unprecedented opportunities at universities, but their argument cultures were also subject to different kinds of institutional oversight. While intramural women's societies had allowed the members to generate their own topics for debate, participation in competitive intercollegiate debating meant that leagues or national forensics organizations like Pi Kappa Delta determined their debate topics. Moreover, the addition of faculty advisors to specifically oversee women's debating teams meant that they gained advocates with university administration, but had to give up control compared to student-run debating societies. Women's debating teams were, at times, in direct competition with their men counterparts for funding and access to campus resources.

In this chapter, I trace some of the tensions that arose when men's and women's debate teams shared academic spaces, locating strategies used to justify women's debate amid anxieties about the gendered politics of higher education between the Depression and World War II. How did debaters and their faculty advisors articulate reasons for sustaining women's teams during this critical period in U.S. history? Specifically, how did they construct a notion of the woman debater as citizen through particular articulations of gender, class, and race? The chapter begins by setting the scene to better understand some of the historical developments related to women, debate, and higher education during this period. I then analyze public arguments for ideological and material investment in women's debate at two coeducational Pennsylvania state institutions of higher learning: the University of Pittsburgh (Pitt) and the Pennsylvania State College (Penn State).[5] Under the purview of university administrations and the academic norms of the period, women students at Pitt and Penn State primarily debated in mainstream academic spaces, including classrooms, auditoriums, and lecture halls. However, as women constituted themselves as citizens through debate, the activity also took them traveling to contests at other schools, community organizations, and—in the case of Penn State—even to a nearby prison.

Educating the Woman Citizen

The 1930s were an uncertain time for college women.[6] While the New Deal propelled some women into positions of nationally prominent leadership, rising unemployment meant that professional opportunities were scant.[7] The economic concerns that dominated the historical landscape had many wondering whether higher education would simply prepare women to steal men's jobs. In part to alleviate strains on the labor market, Franklin D. Roosevelt's Federal Emergency Relief Administration began to provide to aid to students in 1934.[8] As many of the student debaters at Pitt and Penn State came from working-class backgrounds as the children of European immigrants, the decision to attend college was not one that was taken lightly.

On campus and in the community, women sought education about public speaking and argumentation as one way to gain steadier ground in shaky times. This demand yielded some interesting textual artifacts. Two public speaking textbooks published in the second half of the decade were specifically targeted at women, underlining the urgency in their need to acquire such skills. Eudora Ramsey Richardson's 1936 book, *The Woman Speaker*, sought to educate women's club members about public speaking basics. She argued that without rhetorical leadership, "women in our own country stand the chance of losing all that has been gained. Between 1920 and 1930 there was a distinct relaxing of our efforts, for it seemed that the woman movement had a sufficient start to be carried forward by its own momentum." The Depression required an awakening to the "realization that the ground that seemed solid was about to slip from under our feet."[9] In contrast, Jasper Vanderbilt Garland's 1938 textbook, *Public Speaking for Women*, took a decidedly less political approach in explaining the need for gender-specific instruction. As his preface asserts, women's desire to speak well is akin to their desire to dress beautifully: "their speeches, like their dress, must conform to accepted standards of manner and materials and yet bear the unmistakable flavor of individuality."[10] Though different in tone, both texts coupled exemplary speeches by women with specific, practical advice aimed at helping novice speakers organize their thoughts, overcome lack of confidence, and hone skills in verbal and nonverbal communication.[11]

A second textual juxtaposition contextualizes the dynamics of gender, debate, and the still relatively new discipline of speech communication during this period. The October 1937 issue of the *Quarterly Journal of Speech* provided back-to-back articles that excite the contemporary feminist rhetorical historian. The first is Doris G. Yoakam's article, "Pioneer Women Orators of America," which has been heralded as one of the earliest published works in the discipline to focus on women and women's issues.[12] In it, Yoakam analyzes nineteenth-century women speakers. After perusing that article, the *QJS* reader of 1937 would turn the page to find the final installment of Egbert Ray Nichols's three-part opus, "A Historical Sketch of Intercollegiate Debating." In it, he charts pivot points in the history of U.S. debating, including the international debate program, the rise of tournament debating, and changes in debate adjudication.[13] Women are mentioned, but only fleetingly. Thus, those of us concerned with women debaters within this history have these two ships, rubbing up against each other in the pages of the discipline's flagship journal, but ultimately passing in the night.

The economic precarity of the 1930s required the invention of strong rationales to support women's debating. Such rationales often developed the idea that debate helped extend citizenship practices to women. This is keeping with Margaret Nash and Lisa Romero's insight that expanded notions of citizenship undergirded prominent strategies to justify women's continued presence in the academy in the 1930s. As women were relatively new to the franchise, the jury, and other expanded rights, advocates argued that they needed higher education to learn about the responsibilities of citizenship. This angle seemed to fulfill a civic need without threatening scarce professional opportunities and "carried more weight in the face of the international rise of fascism."[14] Although the discursive frame of "racial uplift" was used when discussing women students of color, Nash and Romero find that most proponents of expanded opportunities for citizenship education had white, middle-class women in mind and "were framed within a discourse that preserved existing racial and gender boundaries."[15] Questions about women's intellectual capacities for higher education were largely settled, with advocates refocusing their efforts on how women could contribute to the common good by learning the broad and abstract norms of citizenship.[16] Many graduates of the 1930s went on to become wives and/or mothers, yet they also sought employment outside of the home or active involvement in voluntary associations. While educated women of the past had often felt pressure to choose between marriage and career, some in the interwar generation perceived the possibility (and the economic necessity) of a third choice that would allow both.[17] Thus, lessons learned in college were tentatively embraced for the potential to benefit both family and workforce.

The need for citizenship training took on a more focused, specific purpose in the 1940s. Large numbers of men and women students took military and civilian jobs to aid the war effort, at home and abroad.[18] Those students who remained on U.S. campuses found university life transformed by the arrival of active duty personnel in training, the enlistment of students and faculty members, and the need for wartime rationing. Women students at coeducational institutions outnumbered men, and they participated in a number of community volunteer efforts to support the war.

University debating was continually reframed in light of the historically specific demands of citizenship education in the 1930s and 1940s. Arguments for women's debate at Pitt and Penn State roughly map onto these evolving discourses of citizenship. I acknowledge that on its face, this is an unsurprising claim, as debate is often listed among the main expressions of citizenship in a democratic society. What is unique is that proponents of women debaters in the 1930s and 1940s were tasked with parting the waters during a time when the tides of gendered citizenship had not yet fully turned. Those seeking to limit women's participation in debate had a plethora of arguments to choose from, as enumerated in a 1945 article: "only a man has the stentorian voice to carry to remote recesses of an auditorium; woman's voice is squeaky, ineffective. Man's physique contributes to his persuasiveness; woman has to trade on her looks. Man's place is at the rostrum; women's is in the audience. And so on."[19] To be clear, this commentary showcased past attitudes toward women debaters in order to celebrate their successes, as women's squads experienced considerable growth.

How did these teams articulate their purpose and justify the ongoing inclusion of women debaters amid these historical developments? They framed debate as a cultural practice aimed at instilling citizenship through a distinctly feminine brand of conviction and poise. These were skills learned by individual debating women, but reconfigured as a way to contribute collectively to the community and the nation, especially during the war. As a strategy, it maintained the need for women's debate, but was sure not to rattle dominant gendered expectations too much. Debate was positioned as an activity that could help hone femininity, and femininity was positioned as an attribute that helped hone debating skill.

While elements of this strategy could likely be observed at many institutions across the United States during this period, Pitt and Penn State provide exemplary case studies. First, the universities were in close geographic proximity during a time of transition between public debate events featuring just two schools, triangular leagues, and the rise of tournament debating. Pittsburgh and State College, where Penn State is located, are approximately one hundred and fifty miles apart. As such, Pitt and Penn State debaters were regional competitors, reacting to similar evolutions in the activity and larger cultural trends. There were a number of debates between the two schools, such as a debate in 1928, in which Penn State's Helen S. Faust and Marie C. Snyder defended the proposition "that women's suffrage has been of practical benefit," against Pitt's Margaret Webb and Alice McAfee.[20]

Second, as relatively large, coeducational institutions, Pitt and Penn State are intriguing cases of coeducational argument cultures where women and men had distinct experiences with the debate activity.[21] On both campuses, gender-segregated teams were maintained with different competition schedules, yet at times, their faculty leadership, team identity, social activities, campus spaces, and funding overlapped. The teams were being constantly compared, creating an exigency for public discussion of gender dynamics in debate. Once access was secured, as shown in the ensuing analysis, the extent to which women debaters should be treated differently in the activity was a matter of dispute.

Finally, both universities have extensive, yet incomplete, archival materials about debate during this period.[22] The holdings do not include detailed minutes or transcripts that give a sense of what precisely happened within the debates of this period. However, programs and flyers for debate events, yearbooks, coverage in university and local publications, and personal correspondence are available. These documents are largely oriented toward presenting accounts of the Pitt and Penn State women's debating societies to broader public audiences such as the student body, administrators, and members of the community. As such, these materials detail goals, values, and strategies in advocacy for women's debate—discourses that both resist and map onto dominant gendered cultural currents.

Debating at the University of Pittsburgh

Debating at the University of Pittsburgh began with a men's literary society, when the institution was still known as the Western University of Pennsylvania. It was re-organized as a debating society in 1907, just one year before the institution was renamed.[23] Although they were never formally barred from the institution's charter, the first full-time women students were not admitted until 1895 and they did not enroll in large numbers until the School of Education was founded in 1910.[24] Faculty in public speaking, a division that separated from the English department in 1912, supervised the men's debating team.[25] Women students sporadically participated in debate in the early part of the twentieth century. Men and women appear together in the photograph of the debating team in the university's 1915 yearbook, for example, but there is no indication that they debated against each other, and the graduating women students list "girl's debating team" in their individual yearbook entries.[26] A separate Women's Debating Association (WDA) was officially formed at Pitt in 1921 "for the purpose of affording women students an opportunity to engage in debate and to enter into intelligent discussion of current problems."[27] The new organization was likely prompted by the hiring of Dean of Women Thyrsa Wealtheow Amos, a strong proponent of the leadership opportunities provided by women-only student organizations.[28]

Wayland Maxfield Parrish succeeded Frank Hardy Lane as Director of Debate in 1923. In the 1930s, Parrish oversaw all debate operations, while Richard Murphy and Theresa Kahn (later known as Theresa Murphy), both members of the public speaking staff, served as faculty advisors of the men's and women's societies.[29] Murphy and Kahn were former

Pitt debaters who hailed from western Pennsylvania. Murphy was raised in an Irish-German–Pennsylvania Dutch Methodist family, while Kahn grew up in a Pittsburgh Jewish family that had ties to the Guggenheims in New York.[30] According to their daughter, they attended Pitt because it was "the great working class University of the area and it provided an awful lot of opportunities, particularly in the Great Depression, after [their] families lost everything."[31] The men's and women's teams attended separate debate events, but coordinated for on-campus activities, including the end-of-the-year debate award banquets.

Parrish had strong opinions about how to organize debate activities, and he took measures to solidify the University of Pittsburgh's team identity at a time when many questions about best debate practices were in flux. He created a document called "The Pittsburgh Policy" to make the team's perspectives on intercollegiate debate clear to potential competitors at other universities. The Pittsburgh Policy is a list of aims, demands, and ethical expectations that the team wished to make public. It can also be read as a guiding document for the cultivation of conviction through debate—a policy that students would need to be aware of and consent to before representing the university.

The vision laid out in the Pittsburgh Policy was "to give students instruction and practice in Public Discussion," in contrast to making the activity "a major sport, a gladiatorial combat, or an advertising agency." Audience members for the events should not expect entertainment, but should be genuinely interested in the issues at hand, and see the forum as a space for "the molding of public opinion."[32] University of Pittsburgh-hosted events functioned as non-decision debates or used audience shift ballots in order to gauge how the audience was influenced by the debate. Audience members were asked to report their present opinion about the debate proposition before the debate by checking off yes, neutral, or no, and adding in any remarks they may have about the topic. After the debate, the audience members were asked to register their opinions by indicating whether their beliefs on the topic were affected by the arguments presented in the debate (as opposed to which team was better at debating). Rather than simply voting for the affirmative or negative team, the audience members were able to choose from a range of options. The audience shift ballots acknowledged that audience members had nuanced opinions and that there were shades of gray in their reactions to debate performance—it did not suppose that they would be able to make a definitive choice.[33]

The Pittsburgh Policy voiced the view that debate should be seen as an exercise in truth-seeking and judgment rather than winning: "each debater speaks on one side of a question only, and his choice of side is dictated by his own honest conviction after study of both sides. Whatever enthusiasm he feels is generated from the heat of conviction, not from a desire to win decisions."[34] This privileging of conviction over competitive success was a trademark feature of the University of Pittsburgh's debating societies at the time, instilling the idea that speech in public forums ought to reflect qualified opinions held by the speakers.

In her role as advisor to the women students, Theresa Kahn reinforced the message of the Pittsburgh Policy but was sure to underline that valuing conviction did not mean that debaters should be cloistered and rigid in their beliefs. Instead, debate was conceptualized as an exercise in critical thinking, cultivating belief, and making oneself open to potential criticisms. Kahn describes the process of analyzing a debate proposition from this perspective:

> We will think about the question, prepare a bibliography, read widely, and talk to people who know something about the resolution. We will probably read the same articles, because I must know your arguments if I am to answer them, and you must know mine. We will take notes, preferably on small cards, so that when we organize our material later on we can sift and arrange them with like points together.[35]

As debaters imagined their competition and anticipated arguments, they were able to refine and add nuance to their positions. As Richard Murphy noted, they often met their toughest critics in their own team members: "A debater on tour may feel tempted to stretch a point or two; but if he is debating against students in his own school, students who will take him to the library after the debate and point out any distortion, he will develop a respect for accuracy."[36] In other words, the critical spirit within the debating society, especially at a local level and against teammates, meant that debaters developed rigor in their intellectual pursuits.

Pitt debaters could not expect to rest on their laurels. In order to join the debating teams, students had to demonstrate that their skills met the tradition of excellence that was expected of the team. First-year students were welcome to try out, and even the veteran debaters had to prove that they hadn't become "dead timber" over the summer.[37] Rather than shielding them from criticism, Kahn's philosophy was to get as many students as possible interested so that the internal competition would be fierce. The tryout process for the women's debate team required students to prepare five-minute speeches on the debate propositions for the year.[38] Kahn selected up to fifteen students for the team. This approach allowed more students to have access to the benefits of debate education, and no one had the position of star varsity debater locked up at any given time. Moreover, Kahn contended that "discussions [were] more heated because more students take part, and competition is keen."[39] By creating opportunities for competition, and ensuring that no debater would take a position on the team for granted, the activity socialized students into a culture of criticism.

As her daughter later described, Kahn "believed that women should do what they wanted to do and that there was no reason why women couldn't do the same things that men do."[40] She navigated gendered restrictions of the period by suggesting that exposure to competition and criticism would help to develop feminine poise necessary for women citizens. Pittsburgh debaters had to steel themselves for criticism from multiple audiences. High schools, churches, and various branches of the League of Women Voters throughout western Pennsylvania hosted extension debates, which were the most frequent events on the WDA's schedule.[41] They also participated in a number of intercollegiate debate events throughout the Midwest and East against schools such as the University of Cincinnati, Cornell University, Oberlin College, and New York University.[42] In 1930, the final WDA event of the year was a radio debate about education, which aired on an evening broadcast of the local station, KDKA.[43]

Kahn believed that this mix of debate formats provided women college students with a prime opportunity:

> To stand before a critical audience and reason out a reply to a point that
> has been contested certainly develops poise. A debator [sic] learns to be

alert and accurate. To consider both sides of a question and weigh each thoroughly develops a keen reasoning ability.[44]

Debate allowed students to gain poise in front of an audience, to approach a speaking situation with grace and precision. Poise need not be learned in charm school, for debate provided a different kind of education—a way to attain balance and ease with one's public performance. Not only does the word *poise* have a quotidian sense that invokes the equilibrium of bodily comportment, but it also has etymological roots in the process of weighing ideas, and the quality of being heavy, significant, and important. Throughout the 1930s, this word was used to justify women's involvement in debate (and, it should be noted, was rarely used for men's debate). As late as 1937, the WDA described their group's general aim in the University of Pittsburgh yearbook as to "produce speakers of poise and ability."[45] This express goal provided symbolic heft to the activity, counterbalancing "the opinion of several million men that women merely gossip" and allowing WDA members to "prove that they have something to say and say it in an interesting as well as entertaining fashion."[46]

The coupling of poise and conviction through debate training created a class of women citizen-intellectuals, curious about the world and prepared to contribute to their communities. Pitt's women debaters met other women debaters who shared their common goals. As Kahn told the *Pitt Weekly*, debate stoked an "intellectual curiosity" in its participants that prepared women well for the workforce and daily conversation. Intercollegiate debates were particularly useful in creating a sense of community among women engaged in ritual argumentation:

> Here at Pitt, our policy of extension and collegiate debates offers the girl outside contacts with other girls whose interests are similar. Every girl who has debated with a team from another college has an experience worth remembering. If women are to take an active part in community life, then they should be able to talk intelligently on political and economic issues. Debating gives them this ability to think constructively.[47]

The activity provided an outlet or inquisitive women students of the thirties by providing an imperative to study current events, politics, and economics (rather than, say, an expectation that women's collegiate study would be limited to home economics). Curiosity was aroused in the topics selected for debate, and ideas were honed within the structure of debate competition, which provided students with opportunities for interaction with interlocutors who had similar intellectual interests. They were able to network and create connections through debate, an activity that prepared them for civic life. This was necessary, because in Kahn's view, the intellectual curiosity stimulated by debating was not meant to be limited to the activity; women would take their experience, training, and knowledge about current affairs, politics, and economics with them when they left college.

Student and faculty participants did not universally embrace the topics chosen for debate, but the topics are representative of Depression-era citizenship. There was an acute sense of the need to provide public debates that would serve the community in tough times. For example, the initial propositions for the 1930–1931 year were "Resolved, that the Eighteenth amendment should be repealed and the control of liquor traffic be placed in the hands of state legislatures" and "Resolved, that the emergence of married women into gainful occupations has been to the best interests of society."[48] However, these propositions were abandoned in favor of "Resolved, that the several states should enact legislation providing for compulsory unemployment insurance," because of its importance given the mass unemployment that plagued the nation.[49]

The issue of unemployment was never far from the minds of the debaters. As Pitt debater Helen Smith Schlenke remembered:

> During the depression years we had very little money. Most of the debaters were on scholarship—that's the only way they could attend school. And so we had to work very hard at our studies to remain in school. We saw a world, you must remember, that was pretty grim—full of joblessness, poverty. In the early '30s we went to college to get as much out of college as possible to start a career. Debate was an important part of our college education and student drive was in evidence among the debaters.[50]

The need to discuss the pressing issues of the time motivated students to research and hastened their wish to reach larger audiences. Noting that "the turnouts for home debates [had] been discouraging in the past," the debate team hoped "that since the question this year is of such current interest, there [would] be a greater response on the part of the students."[51] In keeping with national developments in the activity, Pitt's WDA made another change in 1930: it adopted the Oregon plan of debating. This style required three-person teams on both sides of the proposition. The first debater would present the constructive arguments of her team, the second debater would cross-examine her opponents, and the final team member would summarize their arguments.[52]

Marie Hochmuth (later known as Marie Hochmuth Nichols) joined the Women's Debating Association in 1928.[53] Contemporary rhetoricians know Marie Hochmuth Nichols as a prominent twentieth-century public address scholar and rhetorical critic, president of the Speech Association of America (now the National Communication Association), and the first woman editor of the *Quarterly Journal of Speech*. In the 1930s, Hochmuth was better known as a Pitt debater who went on to coach, first at Pitt, and then at the all-women's Mount Mercy College in Pittsburgh. She grew up in a large Catholic family in Dunbar, a small borough in Fayette County known as the "town of furnaces" for its contributions to the western Pennsylvania iron industry.[54] In high school, she was a member of the student newspaper staff and the debate team.[55] During her junior year, Hochmuth met Parrish when he served as a judge of a high school debate competition. Using a labor metaphor to describe her early relationship with Parrish, Hochmuth explained, "Professor Parrish had judged some high school debate colleagues of mine . . . and found their membership 'not in good standing.' It seemed to me at the time that qualifications for membership in his unions were pretty high. But in 1928 I applied, and I am still trying to qualify."[56]

Hochmuth was active on Pitt's intercollegiate women's debate team, graduating with bachelor of arts degrees in English and history in 1931. During her senior year, she was elected president of the WDA.[57] Hochmuth's experience and leadership position in the association meant that she often was a part of the three-person teams that represented the University of Pittsburgh during this time. She participated in five extension debates and traveled on both the "western trip" to Ohio Wesleyan University and Wittenberg College and the "eastern trip" to Cornell University,

Swarthmore College, New York University, Bucknell University, and Penn State. At Wittenberg, Hochmuth and her two teammates, Genevieve Blatt and Marjorie Hanson, debated against an all-men team for first time in the women's team's history.[58] Blatt, Hochmuth's frequent debate partner, eventually went on to a successful career in law and politics. She came to be known as the "First Lady of Pennsylvania Politics," was the first woman to hold statewide office in Pennsylvania, ran for the United States Senate, and as a Commonwealth judge presided over a landmark opinion that made it illegal for the state's high school sports teams to discriminate based on gender.[59]

Debate trips were incredibly exciting for western Pennsylvanians of the time.[60] As Jane Blankenship notes, "in addition to learning about argument, for many, particularly those who were daughters and sons of blue collar parents, debating allowed them to travel."[61] The WDA's intercollegiate debate trips clearly made an impact, even though they were not as extensive as the ones undertaken by the Men's Debating Association (MDA).[62] After the eastern trip, an article ran in the *Pitt Weekly* proclaiming:

> "Resolved, that we adopt a policy of more extensive debate trips in the future." These are the sentiments of the members of the women's debate team which has just returned from a long eastern trip, and it is a safe wager that it would not be easy to find an enthusiastic negative team to debate the question.[63]

Travel was a theme at the 1931 annual banquet, which was coordinated by the men's and women's associations. A flyer promoting the event spoofed a booking agency, "Debate Booking Bureau," and a travel agency, "Forensics Tours, Inc." For the Debate Booking Bureau, the flyer offered its unique services ("Our motto: two teams in twenty minutes! Have you tried our Oregon debates?"), promising entertaining debates on demand, and advertising the skills that debate experience offered ("Do you have the magnetic personality that insures success in every walk of life? Consult the Pitt Public Speaking staff to-day, Specialists in Debate").[64] The debaters were prepared to think on their feet, to debate any topic, in front of any audience at a moment's notice. Lampooning the more exaggerated claims of public speaking education, the debaters brought humor to their craft.

Wills, Kahn, Linn, Hochmuth, Blatt
Josselson, Hanson, Alter, Unkovich, Taimuty

Figure 5. University of Pittsburgh Women's Debating Association, 1931, *The Owl* yearbook. Photo used with permission of University Archives, University of Pittsburgh Library System.

The Forensics Tours Inc. offered "a peripatetic course, giving personally conducted instruction in the art of travel." Debate afforded students with opportunities to travel, but it also provided learning-in-motion, a chance to discuss rhetorical skills and topics of the day while en route to intercollegiate debate events. In addition to being able to "see the world from a Pullman," this parody claimed to teach recruits the tongue-in-cheek practical skills learned from debate travel, such as how to "meet college presidents," "pack evidence," and "keep fresh on 2 hours sleep."[65] The flyer, which was circulated to the banquet's attendees, showcases some of the skills claimed by debaters of the time. It also implies that debate was an activity that was enjoyable despite all the hard work it involved. By refiguring debaters as travelers, the document suggests that the students were provided with new experiences, and there was a social element of debate training that men and women debaters shared, even though the two groups did not travel together. The 1931 banquet marked the end of Hochmuth's career as a debater. She was awarded $15.00 as the top woman debater of the year, and was inducted into Delta Sigma

Rho, the national honorary forensics society, alongside two men debaters, Jess Spirer and Edward T. Crowder.[66]

In many ways, Hochmuth's experience as a debater, college student, and debate coach serves as a representative case for understanding tensions between traditional ideas about femininity and the popular image of debaters as smart, outspoken, and, indeed, masculine. Like many women students of the time, Hochmuth sought social work to aid the community during the tough Depression era years. After graduating from Pitt, she worked for the Allegheny County Emergency Relief Association as a field worker.[67] The association provided assistance to the unemployed sick and poor. They concentrated on creating short-term jobs of practical benefit to the community, such as training unemployed men to create home gardens.[68]

Later, Hochmuth returned to the University of Pittsburgh for a master's degree in speech. As she was finishing her degree program, she served as a faculty advisor for the WDA alongside her former coach, Kahn.[69] Parrish directed her master's thesis, "Richard Whately's *Elements of Rhetoric*, Part III, a Critical Edition."[70] This project was a continuation of Parrish's own study on Parts I and II, which, as Hochmuth recalls, was a tough act to follow: "I shan't go into all the details of his making me trace 132 allusions for an appendix, after I thought I had finished the greatest study on Whately—since his own, that is."[71] By the time she received her master's degree in 1936, she was well versed in Pitt's argument culture, as a debater and a debate coach. As a practitioner, she learned about the need for poise and conviction as she prepared for and took part in debates. As an instructor, she had to learn how to translate those elements into action for her students.

Hochmuth put her speech and debate skills to work when she taught courses and coached the debate team at Mount Mercy College (now Carlow University), an all-women's college in Pittsburgh, from 1935 to 1938. She taught a class on radio continuity and effectiveness, and was an active participant in groups such as the Pennsylvania Forensics Association, the Western Pennsylvania Speech Council, and the National Association of Teachers of Speech.[72] As a faculty debate coach, she was dedicated to challenging students and rewarding hard work, but she worried that the activity was not living up to its potential. She worked to reform debate in several areas, including the proposition subject areas, which she thought were "dull and adhere slavishly to newspaper headlines," and the announcement of the debate topic, which she believed should occur in the spring rather than the fall to allow students to work on debate throughout the summer.[73]

Employment at an all-women's college made Hochmuth even more attuned to gendered stereotypes in debate. In this role, she often played the provocateur, making statements to the *Pittsburgh Press* about the quality of college debating and suggesting, "women make more careful debaters than men. And, to give a woman poise, there is nothing better than a few trys [sic] at organized argument."[74] Hochmuth took advocacy for women debaters one step further, arguing for their superiority by virtue of their attention to detail. Note, too, that she also invokes poise as a benefit of debate for women. These statements were, predictably, rather incendiary for debaters in the region. Pitt's men debaters "rose in righteous indignation and demanded a showdown" almost one year to the day later after Hochmuth's claim. Their indignation must have been more "show" than "showdown," however, because when the teams ultimately met to debate whether the United States should cease using public funds for the purpose of stimulating business, it was decided that the teams should be split, with Mount Mercy's Veronica McGinley and Pitt's Saul Dizenfeld on the affirmative, and Mount Mercy's Anna Marie McConnell and Pitt's Abe Wolovitz on the negative.[75]

Using perspective gained as participant and coach, Hochmuth took the seeds of argument about citizenship through conviction and poise, and grew them into a critical assessment of women's debate in a time of transition. As the 1940s approached, she questioned how women were actually being treated in the activity, now that questions of access were largely settled. Central to Hochmuth's agenda of debate reform was her mission to redress the status of women debaters, who she feared were not taken seriously and did not take themselves seriously enough. In other words, she questioned the idea of "equality with a difference" if it meant that damaging stereotypes about femininity were keeping women debaters from gaining the full array of benefits offered to men in the activity. In 1939, she published "Your Gown is Lovely, but. . . ." in the *Bulletin of the Debating Association of Pennsylvania Colleges*.[76] Because she so rarely spoke about gender issues in academia or the ways that she navigated masculine institutions as a woman academic in her later career, "Your Gown is Lovely, but . . ." is an exceptional text. It identifies a problem in a speech activity and prescribes a solution for women debaters and their coaches. Moreover, it uses the lens of women's debate to test how far liberal feminism could go.

"Gentlemen, you may light your pipes and sit back smugly for the duration of this article, if you choose. Frankly, it is not intended for you." Marie Hochmuth's article begins with a jolt: debate coaches have put up with lackluster debaters for far too long, failing to provide intensive critique of their women students either because they do not consider them worthy of their time, or because they fear retribution. Whatever their reasons, Hochmuth asserts that the men debate coaches of Pennsylvania colleges share common feelings about having to judge mediocre women debaters: that "a strong man must have often felt like fleeing in desperation."[77]

Hochmuth is concerned with the gendering of citizenship education, which she fears had gone too far in the direction of catering to caricatures of femininity. She bemoans what she sees as harbingers of women's special treatment in debate, especially the selection of a Pi Kappa Delta debate topic for women and the publication of a public speaking textbook for women (the book in question is Jasper Vanderbilt Garland's *Public Speaking for Women*). The idea that women deserve special treatment, Hochmuth notes, is in sync with the view that women are inherently limited in what they can and cannot do (excepting, she says, "the very unusual women"). Not wanting to be seen as too radical, she acknowledges that women are essentially different from men, but questions how those differences manifest in rhetorical skill, insisting that "it remains to be proved that the best woman debater is not as good as the best man debater." Hochmuth suggests that Dorothy Thompson, *Time Magazine*'s most influential woman of the year after Eleanor Roosevelt in 1939, would never have been told that she could not debate. "I shall grant that Dorothy Thompson is an exception, and grant that there are far fewer excellent women debaters than there are excellent men debaters," she says, "but I insist that there are far fewer than there ought to be, or need to be."[78] Here, she is arguing against tokenism, wanting to expand the possibilities of excellence in debate to a wider circle of women beyond the chosen few who have somehow managed to rise to the top of an activity seemingly more hospitable to men debaters. She seeks to democratize debate, not by lowering standards of excellence to accommodate difference, but by suggesting a regimen that women debaters and their allies can pursue.

Hochmuth isolates five causes contributing to women's inferior debate performance. Echoing her dissatisfaction with a "women's debate question," the first cause is an unwillingness to study the tough subjects:

> Women, especially in the women's colleges, do not elect to study economics or political science, and only recently have they shown any interest in social studies. The announcement of a debate question involving a knowledge of economics or political science finds them wanting, and they throw up their hands in despair.[79]

For debate to provide proper citizenship training, students had to be willing to engage topics on equal footing. Moreover, students must learn about these topics in order to figure out their own convictions. She acknowledged that they may have weaknesses in their educational background because gender socialization tends to steer women away from such subjects, but she was also resolute in her conviction that time spent researching could make up for any weaknesses in prior exposure: "let her arm herself with a few good basic texts and make up for some of her weaknesses. The worst thing she can do, as far as her own morale is concerned, is put off coming to grips with difficult problems."[80] Consider this a point of personal philosophy that carries over to Hochmuth's later scholarship: she saw it as absolutely necessary for rhetorical critics to harbor an intellectual curiosity and do the heavy lifting to read about history, politics, and economics as part of their craft. Debate provided her with the ability to talk about these issues in a public forum in college, and she saw herself as rising to meet this challenge in all phases of her own life.

As the title "Your Gown is Lovely, but . . ." suggests, Hochmuth identifies the second cause for mediocre debating by acknowledging that some women debaters have imported (or been coached to import) charm school–style social graces into the activity rather than learning poise through exposure to argumentative criticism. She notes that some students have interpreted the function of the debating society as a social fraternity rather than an academic activity. For example, some women debaters expend extraordinary effort preparing the stage for a debate—more effort, she fears, than goes into the preparation of their arguments: "there are ferns and flowers; there is music which is a nuisance during intermission . . . ; and there are academic robes or formal gowns."[81] Hochmuth recognized the need for poise in debate, a lesson that Kahn had instilled in her as a debater. But poise represented a need for equilibrium in argumentation, not necessarily the selection of a formal gown. Debate should take precedence over adornment, and if one cannot balance the two, debate must be the thing that stays.

The third reason for mediocre debating also has to do with debate's potential to cultivate poise and self-confidence. She believes that there is a common and misguided sense that in order to be true women, they must be weak in their rhetorical performances. Hochmuth demonstrates her passion for debate and the airing of perspectives, stating, "no strong assertion of an honest opinion ever detracted from the dignity or charm of a woman, and to translate dignity into terms of a weak-kneed approach to debate work is to rob debate of the fire that really makes for good debating."[82] Hochmuth's alternative vision of what femininity can be offers debaters a way to transform any conflicted feelings they may have about being assertive speakers. Femininity is not incompatible with good argument. She does not, of course, give women debaters license to "rant and thunder on the debate platform," perhaps recalling Kahn's comparison of young debaters in rebuttal to Plato's comment about young philosophers: "like puppy dogs who delight to tear and pull at all who come near them."[83]

A fourth cause is that "women often appear to be just about ready to take a dose of some foul tasting medicine when they appear on the debate platform." Hochmuth believes that one cannot have perfection without passion; she considers "enthusiasm, or love for debate, to be of utmost importance to good debating."[84] She suspects that some women debaters may be in the activity for its prestige rather than for a genuine love of the activity.

Finally, Hochmuth shifts the blame for inferiority from the debaters to their faculty coaches. Debate educators are at fault for unsupportive practices, which fall into two categories: inadequate instruction and treating women debaters with kid gloves. Hochmuth is more sympathetic to those coaches who, because of their lack of knowledge about debate, or lack of time, are unable to help their debaters. She is much less tolerant of coaches who insist on "nursing" their women debaters through a variety of practices, including writing their speeches, and not permitting them to debate "non-cultural" topics: "women would probably be very comfortable if they were never called upon to do anything for themselves after they leave college . . . But this is not the case, and why colleges should continue to treat women as if they were living in the eighteenth century is a mystery."[85] Coaches should do what they can to foster an intellectual curiosity in their debaters, and this includes disavowing a double standard that prevents women from debating non-cultural topics.

Although she identified five obstacles to women debaters' attainment of excellence in debate, Hochmuth is hopeful that they will rise above mediocrity. Her ultimate recommendation for women debaters, especially those at women's colleges, is to recognize the value of public criticism. Similar to Hannah Arendt's later articulation of excellence as the result of public activities that require the presence of one's peers, Hochmuth's notion of excellence requires publicity, and intercollegiate debate provides a formal venue for structured criticism:

> women need audiences that will heckle instead of praise; they need to be taught to accept criticism without giving way to tears; they need to come in contact with really good debating more often they do . . . those who cannot bear the brunt should make way for those who can. Hard work is tiring; mental energy is painful; criticism is discouraging, but all of these things are essential to the woman debater who is to attain excellence.[86]

This little-known article should be viewed as an admonishment of women debaters who settle for anything less than excellence, but also as an attempt to pass on lessons on how to survive and excel in an activity dominated by men. Hochmuth's attitudes toward the activity, other women in debate, and the vision she developed for herself as a woman in academia are evident. Although she did not continue to coach debate teams in her later academic career, the elements of excellence that she expressed in "Your Gown is Lovely . . . but" would shape her approach to rhetorical criticism.[87] In her view of women's debate, Hochmuth extends some of the earlier themes about citizenship through instilling conviction and poise through criticism, but also questions whether discourses used to carve out a place for femininity in debate are giving students the short shrift. In doing so, her article provides a perspective that helps to round out this exploration of women debaters at the end of the interwar period.

Shortly after penning "Your Gown is Lovely, but . . . ," Marie Hochmuth left Pittsburgh to pursue a doctoral degree at the University of Wisconsin. She first met Henry Lee Ewbank, Director of Debate and her eventual dissertation advisor at Wisconsin, when she arranged for him to be a guest speaker at the Delta Sigma Rho Alumni dinner at the Pennsylvania Teacher's Association in 1938.[88] She recalled that she "was, at the time, dimly considering the alternatives of staying in my teaching position or striking out for work on a doctorate degree."[89] She elected to start graduate work at Wisconsin the next summer, and found in Ewbank an advocate and advisor for life.

In the time after Hochmuth's departure from Pittsburgh, the Pitt women's team underwent several transformations as the group's purpose evolved with the country's entrance into World War II. Wayland Parrish left the University of Pittsburgh for the University of Illinois in 1936. He had given his word about a contract for an instructor in the program at Pittsburgh, and when the university administration refused to renew it, he resigned.[90] Soon thereafter, Richard Murphy and Theresa Kahn departed for the University of Colorado. Charlotte McMurray took over as coach for the WDA in the 1938–1939 school year.[91] In 1940, the association changed its name to the Women's Speech Association (WSA) to better encompass its broader range of activities. That year, it took part in intercollegiate debates and fifty extension debates. It hosted ten tri-state colleges at a debating conference on the theme of "training the college girl for the world of tomorrow."[92] In Pitt's alumni magazine, Charles W. Lomas, the new Director of the Men's Debating Association, wrote that Pitt's debaters spoke in front of audiences totaling 20,000 people on topics ranging from "such intimate and personal problems as *Should Married Women Work?* to such highly technical questions as incorporation of labor unions and the desirability of the Anglo-American alliance."[93] During the

1941–1942 school year, Ruth R. Haun, an instructor of English and speech with a background in theatre, became the new faculty advisor for the WSA. That year, the members took part in the Intercollegiate Debate and Discussion Group at a symposium focused on the role of college students in the National Defense Program. They participated in intercollegiate debates with Penn State, Washington University, and Randolph Macon College. Their expanded range of activities included a poetry group that coordinated with a women's choral and modern dance organization.[94]

In the wake of the attack on Pearl Harbor in December 1941, the University of Pittsburgh quickly became involved in home-front war efforts. Many campus buildings were converted into spaces for cadet training. In 1942–1943, 11,961 cadets arrived on campus, sharing facilities with Pitt students: women, men who did not qualify for service, and recipients of draft deferments.[95] As historian Robert C. Alberts notes, Pitt's main academic building, the Cathedral of Learning, was "at the center of a large, important, and efficiently run military installation" by mid-1943.[96] The Key Center of War Information and Training was established on campus, as one of 140 units throughout the country designed "to serve as libraries of information and as clearinghouses for the development of morale building programs for schools, clubs, and community groups."[97]

Although their lives were undoubtedly transformed by war, those civilian students who remained on campus were encouraged to continue their studies and involvement in campus organizations as a way to perform the preservation of American life and the university ideal. As Helen Pool Rush, the newly appointed Dean of Women, explained in 1942, "being known and understood as an individual, . . . having a sense of belonging, of sharing in the planning the life of which the girl is a part in the University—all of these needs continue in wartimes because they are basic."[98] Her vision for women students included training in leadership, confidence, and social graces. University organizations provided women students with leadership opportunities that could easily adapt to wartime needs. In this context, the rhetorical talents of Pitt's debating teams merged with a specific wartime purpose. While previous years had described the benefits of the WDA/WSA in broad, abstract terms, they were transformed into caretakers of democracy and fervent advocates of free speech by 1943.

Lomas was put in charge of developing community leadership programs in civilian morale. He coordinated with Pitt's Department of Speech and university musical organizations, but the debating associations were at the center of these programs.[99] Coverage of the WSA and MDA in the 1943 edition of Pitt's yearbook showcases this new focus. A section heading titled "FREEDOM OF SPEECH" precedes pages on the speech and debating associations. The teams underlined the importance of reclaiming normalcy on campus as part of the war effort, declaring: "It is the little things, gossiping over a coke or cheering the team at a game, that constitute free speech. We must exercise this right to the best of our ability if we would preserve it."[100] Readers turn the page to witness a marked change in the WSA's self-presentation:

> Both in the Bill of Rights of the Constitution of the United States and President Roosevelt's statement of the Four Freedoms, the freedom of speech is specifically mentioned. It is to the preservation of the Freedom of Speech and to the development of intelligent discussion, both [of] which are basic in the fight for freedom, that the Women's Speech Association is dedicated.[101]

The yearbook pages thus presented freedom of speech as a concept that must be exercised in ways great and small. College speech and debate activities could not be written off as frivolous in wartime, for they were performances of free speech in a democratic society. As they went on to explain, WSA activities had been redirected to "develop within the University and community alert and progressive thinking" as part of the Key Center programming. WSA members continued their visits to local high schools, civic, and religious groups, where their former extension debates were exchanged for talks such as "What We are Fighting For," "Civil Liberties," "Elements of the Good Neighbor Policy," and "Problems of a Post-War World." The WSA specifically couched its efforts within a wider web of efforts by women's organizations on campus that aimed to "revaluate [sic] their aims in a nation at war."[102] The next page of the yearbook features the Men's Debating Association, under the direction of Lomas. This year, the text notes that "new significance" has been added to the MDA's activities, which coordinate with the Key Center: "speeches were planned, symposiums arranged, and debates prepared for the purpose of encouraging intelligent thought and discussion about our war effort and the post-war world."[103] The accompanying photo shows Lomas and thirteen men debaters, including three in military uniform.

In the following years until the end of the war, the aims and activities of the WSA and the MDA are largely consistent with those listed in the 1943 yearbook. By 1944, all men on the speech faculty had left the University of Pittsburgh for wartime duties. All speech and drama activities, including men's and women's debate, were taken over by Ruth Haun.[104] Tracing debate at Pitt from 1928 to 1945 reveals the transformation of gendered citizenship from the individual New Deal liberal citizen—rooted in a more abstract belief in poise and conviction—to a wartime citizen whose conviction centered on patriotism.[105] In State College, just northeast of Pittsburgh, similar themes were manifesting in a geographically proximate argument culture.

Debating at the Pennsylvania State College

Penn State (known then as the Farmer's High School) was founded in 1855 as an institution dedicated to agricultural science education. Due to financial hardship and declining enrollment numbers, it was also the first college in Pennsylvania to transition to coeducation.[106] The history of intercollegiate debate for Penn State men originated with a debate against Dickinson College in 1898.[107] As the story goes, this match was greeted with great enthusiasm by the student body and surrounding communities. A special train was chartered to bring more than 100 audience members to campus from the nearby borough of Bellefonte, and a local orchestra and mandolin club "furnished sweet interim music" for the event.[108] Pennsylvania governor Daniel H. Hastings was originally chosen to moderate, but the Spanish–American War prevented his attendance. Eighteen years later, Penn State women participated in their first intercollegiate debate against Swarthmore College on the topic of international treaties. Between 1916 and 1919, Penn State's women debaters participated in two more intercollegiate debates, both against Pitt women. In 1919, the women's team was "allowed to decline," until it was resurrected by John Henry Frizzell in 1926. Frizzell, who also served as College Chaplain and would later become the chair of the Speech Department, was a steadfast and enthusiastic champion of debate. As he told Penn State College President Ralph Dorn Hetzel, "when anything forward-looking and progressive in the field of speech is contemplated or accomplished, Penn State speech and debate men and women are more than generally found to be pushing it forward."[109] Penn State debate developed a team identity rooted in a "high level of gentlemanliness, courtesy, and fair play."[110] Frizzell was particularly proud of the team's reputation for honesty, hospitality, and innovation with new debate formats.[111]

Joseph O'Brien was hired to coach men's debate in 1928, and Clayton H. Schug was hired to coach women's debate in 1931. Frizzell continued to oversee the forensics program. Prior to his hire as debate coach and speech instructor at Penn State, Schug completed BA and MA degrees in speech at Ohio State University. He stayed at Penn State until his retirement at the rank of full professor in 1971, having coached a total of 1,072 women debaters over forty years.[112] Under Schug's direction, the women's squad grew substantially in size and scope, in line with a general surge of women student enrollment at the college throughout the 1930s.[113] Only five students came out for tryouts for the women's debate team in 1931. They ultimately recruited three more students from speech classes, for a total of eight students during the 1931–1932 season. That year, the team participated in eight intercollegiate debates and traveled an estimated eighteen hundred miles. Compare these statistics to the 1936–1937 year, when seventy-eight students tried out and forty-nine were chosen to participate in thirty-five debates (twenty-one were extension debates). That year, it was estimated that they traveled over four thousand miles.[114]

On May 5, 1932, the team participated in its first coeducational intercollegiate competition against Seth Low Junior College on the topic of capitalism versus socialism.[115] A bright orange flyer advertising the event, which was held in the Mineral Industries building on the Penn State campus, proclaimed: "He-She Debate TONIGHT." The team also started a program of well-attended extension debates, some of which were against men's teams. Even though the teams were gender segregated, Penn State debaters occasionally occupied the same stage at debate competitions. For example, in March 1933, the Penn State women's team debated the

Penn State men's team at Renovo High School on the national intercollegiate topic: Resolved, that the United States should cancel intergovernmental European war debts. Marie Mahoney and Sarah Ferree, on the affirmative side, won the judge's decision. The event also included performances by the high school orchestra and vocal solos by high school students during preparation time for the rebuttal speeches and during the time the judges took to deliberate.[116] Penn State debaters Helen Chamberlain and Myra Cohn competed against Pitt men in March 1935 on a resolution about the international shipment of arms and munitions. A panel of thirteen judges voted for Pitt on the affirmative, based on a shift-of-opinion ballot. A thousand people attended the event, which was held in nearby Altoona, Pennsylvania.[117] Gallitzen, a nearby coal-mining town, was a favorite community-based location for the debaters because locals would pack the auditorium and hang on every word when they debated labor topics. In such debates, "a lively open forum follow[ed] the debate proper, and autographs [were] demanded of the debaters by the younger set in the audience."[118]

Penn State debaters regularly participated in mixed-gender debates with other colleges. The Penn State men's team preferred to line up women's teams from other universities when they desired to deliberate on topics dealing with gender or social relationships. Pitt's Marguerite Swank partnered with Penn State's James W. Townsend to defend the affirmative side of the question, "should the male college graduate earning a minimum salary of $1,500 a year marry before he is twenty-five?" against Pitt's Marcella Leyton and Penn State's Roy J. Wilkinson. That debate, which was held in Penn State's Home Economics auditorium on February 28, 1935, asked audience members to record their personal opinion on the ballot before and after the debate. Shifts in opinion could be registered with a range of responses, including "more strongly in favor of the proposition," "in favor of the proposition," "undecided," "opposed," or "more strongly opposed to the proposition." Two hundred and thirty-four total ballots were collected after the debate, and the negative team won by a margin of twelve votes, with sixty-six audience members reporting that their opinions were unchanged.[119] As wider public discourses questioned whether college-educated women would forego their roles as wives and mothers, Pitt and Penn State debaters hashed out whether it was college educated *men* who were up to the task of fulfilling their family roles.[120]

In addition to their intercollegiate travels and community performances, another tradition unique to Penn State's women debate was inaugurated: Delta Alpha Delta (DAD). An honorary forensics society for women, the DAD chapter was founded in 1932 and remained active until 1972. Its membership was drawn from the top intercollegiate debaters on campus, who sought to "promote skill in public speaking and to develop a more general interest in these accomplishments among women students of the Pennsylvania State College."[121] In practice, this meant that DAD was responsible for providing hospitality to visiting women guests and organizing an intramural debate and discussion contest for sororities, dormitories, and other women's groups on campus.[122] In teaching their peers about the art of debate, DAD members took on an additional leadership role on campus. Intramural competitions focused on a range of subjects, from "frivolous" topics like "life: who gets more fun out of it—men or women?" to more serious topics like "can interfaith marriages succeed?"[123]

While the duties of DAD membership were mostly lighthearted, "the secret ritual of Delta Alpha Delta," an initiation ceremony for new members, was a rather serious affair. This was a private ritual, performed to create a sense of belonging within a small, cohesive group that sought to socialize members into a persuasive sensibility. Schug penned the script for a lively ceremony in which new inductees are referred to as "neophytes" and current members play the roles of Demegoria (representing public speech), Antilogios (representing debate), and Dikanikos (representing forensic speech). During the ceremony, the neophytes took an oath promising to improve their speaking skills, use their skills for good, and encourage speech and debate activities for Penn State women students. The seasoned members then presented a series of lessons that emphasized the importance of critical thinking, listening, and memory, while encouraging the inductees to be careful, be observant, and avoid jumping to conclusions. For example, a lesson on listening asks the neophytes to recite a line from the Bible, 1 Timothy 6:10. If the new students misquoted the line, stating "money is the root of all evil" instead of "*the love of* money is the root of all evil," they were scolded and reminded that one must not just listen, one must listen with accuracy.[124] On the whole, the ritual performed the belief that effective speech is all about power, but speech is powerless if it is not used correctly. The DAD ceremony stuck with the inductees. One debater related that the ceremony sprang to her mind whenever she heard anything about evil and money in the thirty years following her graduation from Penn State.[125] Through this ritual of rhetorical education, a distinct culture of debating was carved out specifically for women.

Men and women debaters shared in other gatherings on campus, and on the surface, relations between the gender-segregated teams were genial. Beginning in 1927, the women's team manager was allowed to attend meetings of the men-dominated Forensic Council, which determined travel schedules and coordinated other team logistics.[126] In 1936, the teams drew up a "Statement of Principles for the Coordination of Men's and Women's Debate at the Pennsylvania State College."[127] The document was a pragmatic agreement that divided up contacts with other university debate teams and community organizations among the two teams so that they would not run into scheduling problems or exhaust their audiences by double-booking events.

The two teams also held joint end-of-the-year celebrations, seemingly quite similar to Pitt's, where they celebrated the year's victories and performed humorous skits. The men debaters knew what happened on the women's trips, and vice versa. Because inside jokes abound, any attempt to understand the context or parse the good-natured razzing from the cruel-hearted bullying would be futile. However, a brief look at the "Forensic Follies"—the documents produced for the 1935 festivities—illuminates Penn State's argument culture, and its gendered dynamics. That year's celebration was done in a vaudeville theme, which included a "Hall of Fame" that awarded a "bouquet of flowers to Helen Chamberlain, Elsie Douthett, Myra Cohn, and Bunny Heagney for winning first place in debate at the Delta Sigma Rho tournament in Pittsburgh (we always thought our girls were the best)." Under a section titled "Worst (?) of the Year Pulled by Our Girls" are some groan-worthy puns—"Lehigh to a grasshopper" (presumably said in a debate against Lehigh University) and "we come from Punn State." The names of the debaters are then listed next to the names of famous actors, as if they were cast in one long melodrama over the debate season. Elsie Douthett would be played by

Mae West, Jean Kemp by Ruby Keeler, Bunny Heagney by the Bride of Frankenstein (men's team member Donald Frey was listed next to Frankenstein)—the list goes on.[128] The 1936 "Forensic Follies" included a program with two acts. The first was called "Skitsophrenia (concerning the split personalities of our debaters)," put on, it said, by the "Schug Stock Company." Act II was "resolved that the female of the species makes as good a debater as the male of the same."[129] The specifics of this debate are lost to history, but that they would choose this topic for entertainment at their yearly celebration indicates that gendered assumptions about argumentation were a common topic of discussion.

The "Forensic Follies" might be used as evidence of a lighthearted and porous relationship between the women's and men's teams, yet other documents indicate that the women's team struggled for meaningful recognition on campus. Marjorie Witsil Gemmill, who debated between 1935 and 1939, argued that representation in the Forensic Council did not translate to real decision-making power, stating, "how that Men's Team did try to walk all over us!"[130] There was little support for parity between the women's and men's team. Fluctuations in support for the women's team persisted throughout Schug's career, and the debaters remembered him as a "man who believed in equality for women when the idea was quite unpopular," one who "demonstrated with his lifework the belief that women were worth teaching."[131] Schug sought opportunities to speak publicly about the team's accomplishments, often reaching out to Penn State Dean of Women Charlotte E. Ray to note that "the constant struggle to gain and maintain for women's debate the place that one who is directly responsible for it feels that it should hold on our campus has been most discouraging at times."[132] Ray, who believed that debate was "one of the very important courses that our women students have," was a strong champion of the team within the institution.[133] Her vision, that all Penn State women would have an opportunity to learn public speaking and debate before they graduated, was one likely inspiration for Delta Alpha Delta. She often showed up to help adjudicate women's public speaking events on campus, and remained a steadfast supporter on campus until her retirement in 1946.

The tensions between the men's and women's teams that began to surface during the 1930s intensified during the war. In the early 1940s,

Penn State was subject to many of the same wartime pressures and transformations as Pitt. The student body mobilized quickly to fulfill various patriotic duties after the Pearl Harbor bombing, and college officials created a series of informal non-credit defense courses for undergraduates. Men and women undergraduates were encouraged to enroll, but the subjects of their course offerings differed. As a sort of proto-military training, men could learn about bomb control and marksmanship, while women "were offered instruction in community food canning, rehabilitation through crafts, the duties of table waitresses."[34] Yet this was not the only defense curriculum for women on campus at the time. Beginning in 1942, Penn State was one of eight locations chosen by Curtiss-Wright, a corporation that manufactures aircraft parts, to host an educational program to teach engineering to women. The "Curtiss-Wright Cadettes" were a group of students recruited to help meet the demand for skilled workers as many technicians were funneled into other war efforts.[35]

The composition of the campus community changed considerably as the cadettes and military personnel arrived and more students were drafted. Women were encouraged to take on campus leadership roles and move into academic fields previously dominated by men. By mid-1943, "women outnumbered men (1,764 to 1,150) for the first time in the College's History, with coeds even present in significant numbers in the engineering and agricultural curriculums."[36] This became an important issue for the debate teams, because their travel budgets were funded through a fee levied on the entire student body. This policy was started in 1922, when the women's debate team was defunct. When the women's team was re-instituted in 1926, it was decided that the budgets of each team would depend on the sex ratio of the student body. Before the war, the ratios strongly benefited the men's team, generating a budget large enough to send their top team to compete in Oxford, England. Travel for the women's team was concentrated in Pennsylvania, with notable excursions into other Mid-Atlantic states and Ohio.

As the number of men students on campus declined significantly during the war years, the gender politics of the period were brought into sharp focus. During this period, the men's debate team was approximately half of the size of the women's team, which averaged fifty to sixty members.[37] Class of 1945 debater Joan Huber recalls:

In the fall of 1944, the women's debate squad received more travel
money than the men's, owing to the fact that travel funds were distributed on the basis of enrollment by sex, and the women temporarily outnumbered the men. The men's coach was unhappy and called a meeting
to see if the women could be persuaded that men, in equity, should
have a larger share . . . the women had decided that, if men would give
us a fair share after the war, we would be delighted to share with them
currently. But no such agreement could be made. I still remember the
sense of shock that the men who wanted fair treatment in 1944 didn't
feel obliged to apply the same definition of fairness after the war.[138]

As this incident indicates, even though the war expanded opportunities
and increased leadership roles for women on campus, a sense of masculine entitlement persisted. Nevertheless, the women's team ultimately
voted to award the men's team with a larger budget than their portion
of the student fees warranted. Of course, budgets for both teams were
smaller than they had been pre-war, given the significantly smaller number of tuition-paying students on campus. Gas and tire rationing further
reduced the radius of permitted travel for debate competition to nearby
towns.

The idea that debating served a vital role in training women for citizenship was prevalent in the war years and beyond. Dean Ray envisioned
the war as a historical moment akin to the Civil War in widening the
horizons for women in industry and education if they would only take
advantage of the opportunity.[139] She was convinced of the connection between the activity, citizen education, and community betterment, arguing
that "every girl who has any experience in college debating is thereby better prepared to take her place as a leader in community and educational
affairs." It was particularly important—"with the new demands upon educated women"—that young women graduates of Penn State know how to
become leaders who could rise to the rhetorical demands of community
public speaking and know how to manage a meeting.[140]

The idea that debate provided citizen education through the cultivation of conviction and poise was further highlighted in the team's public
documents and media coverage. These documents dealt with the question of whether the assertive and direct speaking style demanded by

the activity would "detrac[t] from the dignity or charm of a woman," as Hochmuth says in "Your Gown is Lovely, but . . ."[41] At times, the argument for women's debate was couched in the idea that, in addition to developing traditional debate skills, the activity would allow participants to enhance their femininity or their preparedness for typical women's roles and occupations with additional conviction and poise. Other instantiations discursively positioned the students as having overcome the deficits of femininity (including but not limited to the lack of knowledge about current public and political topics, lack of bodily command, nerves, and vocal screeching).

An article in the April 1945 issue of *Penn State Alumni News* puts a spotlight on the supposed frictions between norms of traditional femininity and argumentation. The title of the article, "Varsity Debaters (Did They Ever Look Like This, Boys?)," paired with photos of debaters Rose Anne Wilson, Lois Fehr, Nancy Bartsch, Rosemary Halpin, and Jeanne Barinott, unambiguously registers the point that women—especially those whose gender expression is characterized by carefully curled hair, creamy white skin, and lipstick—are not what one would expect when picturing debaters. This presumed incongruity is both dispelled and maintained throughout the article, which sings the praises of the women debaters and their competitive successes while insisting on their unwavering feminine charm. Though their pictures frame the article, and the article is about their participation in the activity, the debaters were not interviewed. Instead, their competitive successes are narrated through an interview with Schug, who deploys the themes of conviction and poise to support his arguments for the value of women's debate.

Words like "sincerity," "belief," "fairness," and "honesty" and "earnestness" were peppered throughout the discussion of Schug's coaching philosophy. He claims that there is no single secret to coaching debaters, but stresses the position that they should not just argue for argument's sake. Debate is an activity that can help women locate and nurture their beliefs: "read, and study, and think about it until you know which side you sincerely believe in. Then you can do an earnest job."[42] Here, debate is less about freeing the expression of a pre-existing conviction. Liberal ideals are achieved not through switch-sides debate, but through the preparation that goes into a public debate performance.

Poise became a focus when Schug described the concrete skills and possible employment options available to women debaters. He maintains that "debating develops thinking on your feet, poise, personality, self-confidence, and underscores the importance of practice in almost any job or mode of life—gathering facts, organizing them effectively, and presenting them persuasively."[43] Ruth Zang Potts '38 echoed this emphasis in her assessment of the value of debate in a later letter to Schug: "I consider the self-confidence, self-command, and self-assurance gained through my debating experience to be the most important single contribution to my four years of college."[44] In terms of what this might mean for the students beyond their time at Penn State, Schug proposed that in addition to the need for a knowledge of public affairs in a legal or political career, poise under pressure would translate well to a career dominated by women: "Women debaters have done particularly well at practice teaching—a job that scares the daylights out of most students. School kids can put you on the spot if you're not used to talking to groups and meeting and answering questions and arguments."[45] Schug's comment underlines the argument that poise cannot be taught without practice in this passage; it is the result of being able to maintain one's cool time and time again in an activity that has exposure to public criticism and extemporaneous speech built into the format.

Yet even if they chose not to pursue careers outside of the home, Schug maintained that debate benefits women, making them "better and more enlightened citizens, and more interesting and intelligent companions and wives."[46] In isolation, it might seem bizarre—even insulting—that Schug would add "intelligent companions and wives" to the list of professions that debaters were prepared for. Yet this argument strategy is perfectly in line with women's education advocates of the 1930s, who took the fear that college-educated women would not marry and procreate, and turned it on its head. They argued that women of the era were more feminine than their predecessors. They would use what they learned in college to help them become better wives and mothers—thought to be an unproblematic social good on the whole, and good for the white middle class.[47] In 1945, this strategy made even more sense. As men and women deployed during the war began to return to the United States, marriage and birth rates surged.

Some, though certainly not all, college-educated women were encouraged to pursue domestic lives in the postwar employment landscape.[148] Such was the case of Joan Huber, the Penn State debater who related the funding dispute of 1944. Huber graduated in 1945, and was admitted to Radcliffe for graduate work in history, but did not attend due to a marriage proposal. As she put it, "we slipped into an easy domesticity after the war, using our intellects on the problems outlined in Spock and *Consumer Reports*. But all of us who were in debate are deeply in debt to Professor Schug because he believed that we had brains and could use them."[149] In this context, Schug's point about "interesting and intelligent companions and wives" resonated as a reason to continue to support women's debate.

In May 1945, the *Pittsburgh Press* ran an article entitled "They Have the Last Word," which reproduced similar themes and two of the photographs from the *Penn State Alumni Magazine*.[150] The article brings the accomplishments of the Penn State women's team to an even wider readership, making a concise argument about the extensive work that goes into preparation for debate, and underlining arguments about conviction and poise. *The Pittsburgh Press* does not include a comment on the translation of debate skills into domestic life, instead identifying the Penn State students as representative of women across the United States who were interested in increasing their involvement in political and community life as the war neared its end.

According to this representation, women debaters may appear traditionally feminine and delicate, but they can engage in the efforts necessary to overcome their deficiencies as thinkers and speakers. The photos in the spread depict the debaters preparing in four different contexts: researching in the library, practicing non-verbal communication, vocal training for radio debates, and speech transcription. In the article, Joan Huber and Ann Staltz are shown to challenge the idea that women do not possess developed convictions about public affairs by using their "time, brains, and perseverance" and posing with a book and a typewriter to depict the research process, as the caption proclaims "DEBATING IS HARD WORK." In the next photo, readers are reminded that a feminine preoccupation with appearance is actually a benefit in debate. Women like to primp in front of the mirror, which is also a great way to perfect body

They Have the Last Word

All over America, young women are showing an increasing interest in politics. The result is a revival of a venerable extra-curricular activity in high schools and colleges — debating. And the girls have found this practice of "having the last word" much to their liking and suited to the needs of those pointing for political or public careers.

At Pennsylvania State College this year, women debaters entered the Pittsburgh forum tournament, competed against men and came off with tie for first place. In a dozen years, the Penn State co-eds have engaged in 385 debates, have batted .746 in decision debates.

DEBATING IS HARD WORK as Joan Huber of State College and Ann Staltz of Pittsburgh know. Researching for facts and figures takes time, brains, perseverance. A good debate, they know, is made in the library, not on the platform.

APPEARANCE IS IMPORTANT and mirror practice helps. Nancy Bartch of Columbia, Pa., gets some help from Coach Clayton H. Schug—the girls call him Sugar. After the rudiments of gesturing and stance are mastered, girls learn how to speak with the whole body.

VOICE TRAINING is extensive at Penn State. Lois Feher of Sunbury, Pa., gets ready to record her voice while Roseanne Wilson of Pittsburgh does the monitoring. Microphone practice helps remove fear that seizes amateur speakers in radio debates.

HOW DOES IT SOUND is the question in the minds of Esther Pebley of Sharpsville, Pa., Ann Staltz and Roseanne Wilson as they listen to the playback of their voices. Defects not apparent to the speaker as she debates pop out at her in a cold transcription. Once, women debaters were taboo because they lacked force, were unimpressive, had squeaky voices. Proper training has overcome these obstacles.

Figure 6 (*opposite and above*). "They Have the Last Word," *Pittsburgh Press*, May 6, 1945. Photo courtesy of the *Pittsburgh Post Gazette*.

language for a debate. Nancy Bartsch appears next to a mirror alongside Schug, who provides guidance about proper gesture and stance.[51]

The remaining images suggest that women debaters can overcome their vocal deficiencies by practicing with technology. Lois Peher speaks into a microphone, while Roseanne Wilson monitors the voice recording in an effort to counteract that idea that women are too anxious be solid speakers in a radio debate. The image testifies to the idea that debaters could improve their poise, creating a steady and commanding voice, through practice. The final image shows Wilson, Stalz, and Esther Pebley playing and transcribing a voice recording in order to recognize "defects" that cannot be detected in a live oral performance. The caption claims, "Once, women debaters were taboo because they lacked force, were unimpressive, had squeaky voices. Proper training has overcome these obstacles." As such, the *Pittsburgh Press* coverage acknowledges the weaknesses that have been attributed to women speakers, but presents evidence that the current generation is willing to put in the hard work necessary to transcend feminine flaws of knowledge, bodily command, and voice. In doing so, the document offers a potent challenge to some stereotypes of the day. However, it is one that is rooted in refiguring rather than revaluing femininity, thus deploying some troubling stereotypes of its own.

Whether one believes that such publicity was ultimately helpful or harmful for the participants, it is difficult to deny that the link between citizenship and debate afforded opportunities for women debaters to challenge the boundaries of expected feminine behavior. In this way, training in conviction and poise worked subversively to justify exposing the debaters to some decidedly "unladylike" situations. Debate enabled women's presence in the community, on the public stage, on the microphone, and over the airwaves. It also meant that they got opportunities to debate in some other unexpected spaces.

Most unexpected for Penn State women was the State Correctional Institute at Rockview. The penitentiary was an active dairy farm that provided farm products to other prisons in the Pennsylvania state prison. It was also "wall-less" and averaged 12 escaped inmates per year in the 1930s.[152] Rockview is a mere six miles away from State College, in Bellefonte, Pennsylvania, making it an easy and affordable location to debate when travel opportunities were otherwise limited. According to Robert Branham, debate activities were often included in calls for prison reform in the 1920s and 1930s. Debate was a focus for prisoner education and rehabilitation at institutions like the Norfolk Prison Colony, where Malcolm X first learned to debate in the late 1940s.[153] Under the auspices of community participation and providing entertainment for the inmates at Rockview's medium-security facility, Penn State's Lois Notovitz and Sara Bailey debated the visiting Princeton University men's team on March 8, 1941, on the topic "Resolved, that the nations of the Western Hemisphere should form a permanent union." The four debaters were rather nervous before the debate. However, a letter written two days after the debate by Chaplain C. F. Lauer, Rockview's Director of Restoration indicates they did a good job of hiding their fear. Despite inhospitable weather, "close to seven hundred men listened with rapt attention for almost two hours."

The only problem with the smashing success of the event, according to Lauer, was that the inmates were so completely captivated: "how do you stop a debate? Our gang is hitting on all six. They are debating in groups of twos, sixes, and mobs. Coming from breakfast this morning, two of the birds wanted to settle this Western Hemisphere business with their fists."[54] The prisoners reportedly organized a follow-on forum to raise questions and share their knowledge on the topic. They insisted on more debates, causing Lauer to declare that "something has been started and it will take more than an empty promise to finish it."[55]

This was not a typical reaction. The prison had undertaken an experimental adult education program since 1935, and when outside lecturers were brought in, the prisoners were "much more critical than the average adult audience [and] prone to show their displeasure by walking out or making noises of disproval" if the speaker failed to adapt to the audience by talking above their heads, lacked pizazz, or failed to integrate some humor.[56] Given the positive reception of this debate, a yearly tradition of prison debates at Rockview began.

In the years that followed, Penn State women competed at Rockview against each other and against visiting men's teams from universities throughout the region. They were given the opportunity to move into a space that would be considered inappropriate for young college women were it not for their purpose as debaters performing an act that was framed as the epitome of citizenship. [57] They tested the limits of poise by presenting their arguments in front of a large and tough extension audience. As Lauer put it in a later letter, "any time you want to put your young folks to the fire test, send them on to us."[58] They cultivated conviction by debating in front of the convicted.

An Uneasy Integration

By 1927, "women had invaded the forensic field to stay."[59] By 1947, a national survey of over one hundred college and universities in the United States revealed "women students are in the minority in most forensic programs."[60] Emogene Emery corroborated these findings in 1952, perceiving a "marked post-war decline in women's debate activities" as programs redirected resources to men student veterans.[161] This chapter has focused on the period between these observations, a relative heyday for women debaters in terms of their sanctioned participation on university campuses.

This story of university debate illuminates some growing pains as coeducational institutions of higher learning welcomed larger numbers of women students into academic spaces. Women became increasingly present and integral to campus academics and activities, and universities had to rethink some policies while continuing to operate within social norms of the period. The Great Depression and World War II presented constraints on women's participation, but they also generated ingenuity in the name of expanded participation in an extracurricular activity closely tied to national identity and values. Women debaters and their advocates were able to use citizenship as a justification to support their wider scale participation in intercollegiate and community-based debates without too radically challenging expectations for gendered decorum.

We gain a better sense of the challenges of coeducational argument cultures in exploring the experiences of women debaters from 1928 to 1945. Previous chapters discussed women debaters within the rise of university coeducation in the nineteenth and twentieth centuries, though their argument cultures operated more or less on their own terms. Though certainly not free from institutional oversight, formal exclusions from particular educational venues meant that the Oberlin societies and Ladies' Edinburgh Debating Society held their intramural debates based on their own rules and on topics of their own choosing. While I do not wish to entirely romanticize those more enclaved interactions, there was a particular sense of freedom when women debated with and were judged by other women. The members of the 1928 British tour were tied to official organizations and U.S. university teams for tour logistics, but still largely shaped their own mobile argument culture.

As an extracurricular activity, debate allowed Pitt and Penn State women to take the stage at various campus and community events, occupying more prominent positions in more public spaces on a wider scale than ever before. They experienced the thrill of finding their voices through argument, of traveling to other campus and community spaces, and of representing their universities in a prestigious academic activity.

They gained confidence by exposing themselves to criticism, and they contributed to the war effort by using their rhetorical skills to perform and educate others about citizenship.

Examination of these gender-segregated societies at coeducational public institutions reveals how women's inclusion in the activity did not translate to equality or equity. It exposes how women debaters were held to different, and at times absurd, standards. As Marie Hochmuth's critique detailed, women debaters were expected to debate different topics and pursue those topics less rigorously than their men counterparts. They were expected to travel less and operate with less funding than the men's team. They were assumed to be in the activity for different reasons, with different career aspirations. Media outlets deployed a gendered frame that positioned the debaters as amusing anomalies. The fuller entry of women students into the academy in the twentieth century entailed new clashes over resources and rights to institutional space.

Faculty coaches and administrators—men and women—played pivotal roles in waging numerous public campaigns to maintain the continued presence of debating women on campus. They regularly advocated for parity and, in some cases, even argued for the superiority of women debaters. In addition to the traditional skill set of public speaking and argumentation, debate was justifiable because it offered women the ability to learn citizenship by cultivating conviction and poise. These arguments tended to be rooted in essentialist claims about feminine inclinations, but they also suggested that the real feminist move was in believing in the potential of debating women.

Conclusion

———•◆•———

Our journey through one hundred and ten years of women's debating history is coming to an end. Between 1835 and 1945, women mastered some skills that are considered traditional, ordered, and rational. They also experimented with argument norms such as style, evidence, format, and topic. A close examination of women's debating organizations over this period reveals understudied aspects of intramural and intercollegiate debating, including their role in establishing a legacy in educational institutions, facilitating intergenerational and intercultural encounter, and crafting a sense of gendered citizenship. Simply put, women were hardly "out of place" in intramural and intercollegiate debates. Even when they experienced formal exclusion from the activity, debating women made space for themselves.

By studying these argument cultures, *Debating Women* underlines the significance of debate in women's quest for higher education in the United States and United Kingdom. I have identified the germinal role that debate played in the lives of some famous figures who went on to make a name for themselves in social activism, politics, and education alongside hundreds of other debaters who might have otherwise been lost to history. The book acknowledges how debate participation brought women together to engage in rhetorical performances that supplemented, transcended, and in some cases substituted for university curricula. Their stories have much to convey about the power dynamics involved in debating, an activity at the heart of democratic societies. Their orientation to ritual argumentation meant that debating women engaged in a series of encounters with issues of gender, race, class, and nation over the years. At times, they were at the forefront of using argument to fashion progressive social change on these issues. At other times, they fell lamentably short. This final chapter revisits the themes of space and mobility featured in the book. Specifically, I contend that conceiving of argument as travel offers a promising alternative to the conflict-based metaphors that often structure discussions of public discourse. I conclude by discussing the implications of this history for ongoing efforts to diversify the study and practice of debate.

Argument as Travel

The integration of women students into nineteenth- and twentieth-century institutions of higher learning in the United States and the United Kingdom was by no means seamless. Gender-based spatial delineations cordoned off particular academic spaces, attempting to limit women's physical movement and access to forums for argumentation. Women were deemed "out of place" at the classroom podium (Oberlin), on the campus (LEDS), and in intercollegiate debate contests at various institutions (the 1928 British Tour; Pitt and Penn State). They responded by cultivating argument cultures in a forest, a parlor, a dining room, an ocean liner, a prison, and countless classrooms and auditoriums. They also took their arguments traveling with them on domestic and international debate trips and into other arenas that defined their lives and careers. The history of women's debate thus entails the claiming of space and the mobility of bodies, arguments, and ideas. *Debating Women* offers four case studies that showcase how varied women shaped and were shaped by debate. Each chapter reflects the specific historical period and cultural norms within which their argument cultures developed. Yet the case studies, together, offer powerful evidence of how women debaters were able to use the vehicle of debate to explore and engage the world around them.

Without question, space and mobility could be important themes in many studies of gender and education in the nineteenth and twentieth centuries. Often, one can understand layers of gendered history based on the architecture and layout of university campuses. Spatial demarcations reflect assumptions about who belongs in institutions of higher learning.[1] The study of debating adds a fascinating dimension to this history that shows how women struggled over the right to institutional and rhetorical space. Women had to argue to access and operate spaces for their debating organizations at the same level and with the same resources as their men counterparts. They also had to argue for rhetorical space: the right to be taken seriously and have their voices and arguments heard and thought worthy of development.[2] Despite various barriers, women were able to seize upon intramural and intercollegiate debate as a research-focused extracurricular activity that exists within and around educational institutions. Through debate, participants learned to engage in critique: sometimes that energy was funneled into reflexivity about topics; sometimes it manifested in debates about debate, or argumentation about ideal formats, rules, and behaviors; and sometimes it was aimed at challenging educational institutions themselves.

The desire to debate led some women to actually travel, violating gendered expectations about who should occupy spaces for argument. Yet even in physically fixed societies, debating women found ways to enlarge their worlds, interfacing with new topics, people, arguments, and ideas. This process comports with Hannah Arendt's evocative use of travel language in describing the social value of critical thinking:

> Critical thinking is possible only where the standpoints of all others are open to inspection. Hence, critical thinking, while still a solitary business, does not cut itself off from 'all others.' To be sure, it still goes on in isolation, but by the force of imagination it makes the others present and thus moves in a space that is potentially public, open to all sides;

in other words, it adopts the position of Kant's world citizen. To think
with an enlarged mentality means that one trains one's imagination to
go visiting.[3]

Historical debating societies and teams nicely illustrate Arendt's point
because in order to prepare well for a debate, one must anticipate competing perspectives. Preparation for a debate may have occasionally been
a solitary exercise for some debaters. More often than not, though, the
activity demanded collaborative co-presence: debaters tested their critical thinking with teammates, faculty advisors, and competitors.

The women-only intramural societies of Oberlin and Edinburgh
carved out spaces for debating women where they did not exist on university campuses. In both cases, women debaters focused on claiming
spaces for argument and then building legacies in those spaces. Oberlin
women attended classes but could not participate in classroom debates.
One version of the Oberlin women's debate origin story hinges on the
need to covertly travel to the woods behind the campus or to a parlor
in the village. The story of the LLS is told through various efforts to secure rooms and furnishings for their club. In making a "home" for their
rhetorical activities on campus between 1835 and 1935, Oberlin women
worked to ensure that future generations would have the legitimacy and
inspiration they needed to propel them forward. They did not have to
go far to get to their respective spaces for argument in Oberlin: ritual
argumentation "train[ed their] imaginations to go visiting" and prepared
them for civic life.[4]

Edinburgh women were not permitted to attend universities at the
time the Ladies' Edinburgh Debating Society was founded in 1865, so
they also made a "home" for themselves to debate—in a private home.
For seventy years, LEDS members gathered around a mahogany table in
the Mair family dining room. Of the four case studies, the debates of the
LEDS were the most geographically stationary. LEDS members are described as mobile and constantly moving through, cultivating knowledge
both inside and outside the society. As a community-based club that fash-
ioned itself as a training school, the LEDS only required travel within the
city of Edinburgh. However, as class-privileged women, many members
did have access to travel for leisure. Members had enough experience

with travel to be able to debate propositions such as "is a life of frequent travelling a better means of mental culture than a life spent at the house?"[5] Moreover, their varied debate topics prompted LEDS members to transport themselves to different perspectives and different geographical locations. This became a way to explore the world through research and argumentation. Although they considered themselves diverse and enlightened, viewpoints voiced in their debates concerning gender, race, and economic status demonstrate the limited scope of their travel across non-dominant social identities.

At the turn of the century and beyond, intercollegiate competitions and the rise of the "debate trip" allowed debaters to travel beyond their hometowns for the express purpose of argumentative engagement. The most potent example is the1928 British debate tour, when Lockhart, Samuel, and Sharp created a new, mobile argument culture out of a desire for interaction between two national argument cultures. They traveled across the Atlantic Ocean, across national borders, and between U.S. hosts, bringing their perspectives to bear in new spaces. Boats, trains, and automobiles moved their bodies. The trio's ideas and arguments also "moved," in that they were refined and revised in debates over the course of their time in the United States. The debate tour also enabled the movement of their arguments into other spheres and forums, from Lockhart's published cultural criticism to Samuel's participation in British politics.

The gender-segregated debate teams at the University of Pittsburgh and Penn State University illustrate the new opportunities and challenges for women university students and their increasing presence on the campuses between the Depression and World War II. There was fervor for intercollegiate debating competitions, especially those that involved travel throughout the United States. Women debaters at both institutions traveled to universities, high schools, and community civic spaces to engage in debate contests. Penn State women also performed in an unexpected space: a nearby penitentiary. Still, their treatment in the activity left much to be desired. As they worked to be taken seriously by men debaters, judges, faculty advisors, and university administrations, women debaters and their advocates identified poise and conviction as two unique benefits of participating in the activity for the woman citizen of the 1930s and 1940s. This strategy was their ticket to ride during tough economic times that severely limited travel.

Acknowledging the importance of space and mobility in this history implicates our cultural and theoretical understanding of the potential of argument and debate. As previously discussed, the most obvious symbolic resources to describe debating often rely on metaphors of verbal combat, violence, and war, which flow easily from the activity's competitive enterprise.[6] Feminist critics have demonstrated how the idea of argumentative combat is particularly constraining for women because the metaphor is "significantly compelled . . . by the persistent depiction of the 'man of reason' as consistently battling aspects of unreason regularly constructed as womanly or 'feminine.'"[7] Some debaters embrace the frame in the spirit of friendly competition, but the antagonistic excesses of this view can impoverish civic discourse. When public issues are framed in terms as winners and losers of a verbal battle, everybody loses, because victory and domination become debate's sole purpose. We are no longer focused on the potential of debate to transform knowledge and people.

Historically, contesting the argument as war trope has been central to the task of using speech and debate education in the service of the broader civic good. Richard Murphy, the faculty advisor to the men's team in Pittsburgh and later, Hochmuth's colleague at the University of Illinois, noted the need to transform militaristic metaphors in his 1929 radio talk on the rules and ethics of debating. Here, Murphy acknowledges the damaging effects of conceiving of argument as war, and charts his own vision for changing it:

> In considering the etiquette of debating let us remember that debate is not verbal combat in which clever young men and women try to evade issues or trap their opponents. I think debating suffers from analogies of war that occur in our textbooks. Phrases like these mislead the debater: "when to use light cavalry"; "when to use artillery"; "how to plan an ambuscade, and how to retreat." Others are: "bottling up the enemy"; "drawing the enemy's fire"; "planting mines." The result is that the young debater sees debate as a verbal combat, a war of nouns and verbs. He draws the corollary that all is fair. He sees debate as a war with rhetorical bombs bursting in the air. He directs his efforts not toward

the arrival at issues, but toward confusing or wounding the "enemy." He concentrates on hurling polysyllabic projectiles, and in floating rhetorical smoke screens. It is time for some disarmament in debating.[8]

That a faculty advisor in the 1920s agrees with some of the points made by contemporary feminist critics in calling for debating disarmament is significant. Change may be slow within any particular argument culture, but Murphy's call serves as evidence that there are always people working towards it. When we move away from argument as war as an exclusive frame, we can actualize the potential of this rhetorical activity.

This study of debating women offers an alternative frame—argument as travel—which is suggestive of the range of perspectives and skills afforded by the activity, and made clear by this exploration of historical women's debating organizations. To be sure, debating women engaged in verbal battle; many found the thrill of competitive success exhilarating and were quite content to exhibit adversarial styles. Yet by choice or by necessity, they also explored other purposes for debate. For example, when members of the Ladies' Edinburgh Debating Society described their argument culture, they did not reject the idea of debate as a combat. However, they did use the ethic behind argument as travel to ensure that they did not foster a hostile argument culture. Writing from the perspective of the mahogany table, Sarah Mair explains:

> And never as I 'summon to the sessions of sweet silent thought' the long array of debaters who have drawn swords as it were across my board, never does one painful clash, one unworthy thrust, one hit below the belt, present itself to my remembrance. Keenness and wide divergence of opinion, but never anything mean has marred the healthful combat of words. Pleasant raillery sometimes, but never bitter sarcasm; a skillful thrust, but never a mean advantage; a happy laugh, perhaps, when one side recognizes a specially good retort, but never a note of scorn or unkindness.[9]

Perhaps inspired by the military artifacts that adorned the Mair family dining room, this reflection reveals that the debaters were very specific about how they conceived of the activity and careful about how they conducted themselves. In addition to using the language of combat to describe their activities, Mair also used the language of travel. The dining room that hosted the LEDS debates was referred to as a "roadside inn where weary travellers could stop and rest a while."[10] That the same physical space could host verbal combat and offer respite to debaters suggests that LEDS members enjoyed a range of benefits from the activity. They engaged in competition, but they were also dedicated to cultivating and sustaining relationships. In order to do both, they had to be open to movement and change, such as the way that a really good argument from an opponent might transform their thinking on a topic.

Expanding argument's symbolic resources helps us to understand that interlocutors ought not be seen as foes to dominate and destroy. In the 1970s, argumentation scholar Wayne Brockriede engaged in a similar thought experiment in which he suggested that we conceive of arguers as lovers.[11] Based on a woman-centered history of debate, I propose a schema in which debaters are co-travelers using argument as a method of intellectual inquiry. This approach acknowledges that ritual argumentation is about the desire to journey to new knowledge and perspectives. It entails self-risk, but ideally, the traveler will embark on a voyage with a spirit of adventure, trying new things, and exhibiting a genuine concern for engagement with new places and peoples. However, the travel metaphor also sensitizes us to some less desirable attitudes toward argumentation. For example, a debater might act as a careless tourist, content to see the sights and buy some souvenirs, but remaining largely indifferent to the people and places visited. This kind of shallow argumentation is on display when debaters fail to adequately do their research or fail to take arguments in a debate on their merits, trading soundbite barbs instead of sincere engagement. Worse yet, debaters can adopt the orientation of a traveler as conqueror, exploiting new terrain and viewing people living there in purely instrumental terms while propagating racist, sexist, classist, and nativist perspectives and failing to take their own subject positions into account. In other words, conceiving of argument as travel does not solve all of the problems of the argument culture. Instead, the travel metaphor orients us to the possibilities of argument cultures that allow participants to generate meaning with a spirit of curiosity and collaboration. My suggestion for an alternative constellation of metaphors grounded in travel participates in the history, some of which I have documented here, of recognizing the value of argumentation and debate while attempting to revise its norms to be more inclusive.

Space for Improvement

Debating Women makes space for women in prevailing accounts of intramural and intercollegiate debate, augmenting histories of rhetoric and education. Still, there is much more work to do in understanding the full range of diverse participants, styles, topics, and formats. My hope is that this project opens up space for future studies about debate and historically marginalized groups. Due to an unfortunate and increasingly divergent path between competitive debate teams and academic research departments, intramural and intercollegiate debating organizations have not received the scholarly attention they are due.[12] Opportunities abound to explore debating societies in spaces such as women's colleges, historically black colleges and universities, and educational institutions beyond the United States and the United Kingdom.[13] Likewise, this project only scratches the surface in studying the cosmopolitan alliances forged between a number of different countries through the international debate exchanges. In traveling into these new research spaces, future projects could shape our historical knowledge of education, argumentation, and public address in ways that substantially revise dominant narratives about civic participation.

During the historical period covered in this book, debating organizations held a coveted role as a premier extracurricular activity on many university campuses. I encourage other researchers to delve into the history of debate at their own universities in order to better understand and articulate its legacy in institutional histories. Debate practitioners may find in historical research the ability to create intergenerational dialogue among alumni. For example, while conducting archival research at Penn State, I had the good fortune to meet Mimi Barash Coppersmith, a successful businessperson and a Penn State alumna who debated in the early 1950s. Coppersmith articulated her experience as crucial to her own intellectual and civic development: "Debate was great for women, most of whom are very real feminists today. They didn't have to learn how to be feminists, they already were. They had minds. They were willing to share their thoughts. They were willing to be criticized, helped, and brought along."[14] Her candid assessment of the value of her education through debate helped me to better understand the argument culture of women's debate on the campus under the direction of Clayton Schug. Oral history and ethnographic interviews offer a particularly enticing methods for understanding the experiences of diverse debate participants in the latter half of the twentieth century.

As debating women entered into new academic spaces in the nineteenth and twentieth centuries, they found in debate organizations opportunities to converse, reflect upon, and revise settled norms. There is value in knowing and understanding this history as we strive to do better in our time. Of course, the landscape of higher education is very different in the twenty-first century. Women students now outnumber men on college campuses in the United States and the United Kingdom. Educational trends change over time, but the ability to think critically, communicate and defend one's position, and speak eloquently is of enduring importance.[15] Likewise, by many measures, participation in contemporary intercollegiate debate is more diverse and inclusive than it has ever been. Debaters across the world are changing what debate is and can be. There are active and ongoing discussions in competitive debating communities about how to make the activity more accessible and meaningful for people of all genders, sexualities, races, classes, and physical abilities. Diverse debaters participate and achieve remarkable success in the highest echelons of competition.[16] In the twenty-first century, these educational spaces are, hypothetically, open to all.

In practice, we know this is still not true. Despite these and countless other successes, this is not a simple progress narrative. Universities struggle with meaningful diversity and inclusion programs to support students once they enter these academic spaces. Over the past thirty years, numerous scholars have identified how debate competitions continue to be spaces dominated by privileged white men and have consistently if sometimes unintentionally devalued the contributions of women, people of color, and other marginalized groups.[17] For example, Emma Pierson's statistical analysis of over 35,000 speeches by over 2,000 debate teams at the European University Debate Championship and the World University Debate Championship between 2001 and 2013 exposed a "simple and incontrovertible" result: "across all tournaments, male speaker scores are higher than female speaker scores by an average of 1.2 points per round, a highly statistically significant discrepancy." Moreover, the study found that being part of a mixed-gender team helped women debaters, while it hurt men debaters.[18]

Debating Women offers historical evidence of the exclusions and inequities that still haunt the activity, but I hope that contemporary debaters will also find an alternative account of debate that is full of hope and inspiration. In the stories of historical debating women, we have a way to "complicat[e] our understanding of current practice through a disruption of familiar genealogies."[19] These narratives lay to rest the idea that white men were the only agents in this history. Debating women were present and persistent in their pursuit of argument in spaces that worked for them. Knowing this history is especially important in a moment in which spaces purposefully designated for women and gender minorities are re-emerging in the form of the Women's Debate Institute, the North American Women's Debating Championships, the Celebration of Women in Debate Tournament, and the Oxford Women's Open.[20]

In a world in which hostility, bullying, and partisanship seem to reign supreme, it can be easy to diminish the value of debate and decry the state of civic discourse. Yet the answer is not to shy away from argumentative engagement in polarized times. Colleges and universities have the opportunity to invest in debate, an activity that can support educational goals, encourage critical thinking, and activate new arenas of knowledge. Scholars of rhetoric and communication have an important role to play in researching and teaching about quality argumentation. I join my colleagues in the call for a "renaissance in speech and debate education."[21] Yet this study also highlights the necessity to craft argument cultures that are inclusive, sustainable, and open to change. We should not reject debate for its sometimes marginalizing and exclusionary practices, and we must actively work to address them as we seek to improve civic participation on a broader scale. Who is told that they are "out of place" in debate today? How can we share in the affordances of institutional and rhetorical space? How can we ensure that an education in speech and debate in the twenty-first century moves students to where they need to be? The history of women's debate demonstrates that one size does not fit all when it comes to the value, format, style, and purpose of rhetorical education.

Finally, the insights of *Debating Women* may be scaled up to consider ongoing issues of gender, communication, and space whenever debating women are told they are "out of place." Here too, the progress narrative is complicated. In theory, there is no public role, no powerful position, no political office that is off limits. Yet when women across the globe enter political debates, the story is depressingly familiar:

- British Prime Minister David Cameron told shadow treasury minister Andrea Eagle to "calm down, dear" during a House of Commons debate, while other women members of Parliament reported being mocked for their high-pitched voices in 2013.[22]
- Spanish Popular Party candidate Miguel Arias Cañete blamed gender for his poor performance in a 2014 debate against Socialist candidate Elena Valenciano, explaining, "a debate between a man and a woman is very complicated, because if you abuse your intellectual superiority, or whatever, you come across as a male chauvinist who is cornering a defenceless woman."[23]
- The 2016 U.S. presidential debates between Hillary Clinton and Donald Trump were consistently framed as a "battle of the sexes." Media coverage of the first debate, for example, noted that it was "not as bloody as some expected" but that Trump's "gloves might come off in a future debate."[24]

Debating Women provides a historical perspective on this troubling sample of gender politics in contemporary public discourse. Its lessons should prompt us to ponder how these exchanges could be different.[25] How can we maintain the benefits of this age-old civic activity while ensuring that it is genuinely hospitable to all? What would these events look and sound like if the debates were framed through the language of travel (about exposure to new ideas and perspectives) instead of the language of war (cut-throat competition)? How might changes to the topics, formats, and style of the debates contribute to a more equitable and productive rhetorical exchange?

In the end, there is no easy remedy for overcoming pervasive stereotypes about gender and debate—issues that have long plagued women who seek to gain knowledge and power.[26] There is nothing original about telling women they are too shrill and emotional, that they can't or shouldn't argue, that they are intruding on a masculine domain, and that they cannot hold their own in verbal combat. Yet when women insist on taking the stage despite these rebukes, when they refuse to hear that they do not belong, when they demand to share in the benefits of this civic activity, they are continuing the work of a long and storied tradition of debating women.

Notes

—·◆·—

PREFACE

1. *Prospectus of the Vassar Female College, Poughkeepsie, N.Y.* (New York: C.A. Alvord, 1865), 3.

2. *Prospectus of the Vassar*, 18.

3. *Prospectus of the Vassar*, 18. Spelling in the original. In practice, this belief was untenable for long. In 1867, the school's ailing founder, Matthew Vassar, wrote to his doctor declaring that he would set aside money in his will for what he called the "Vassar College Offhand Speaking Society," which would host extemporaneous debates four times a year. Matthew Vassar to John H. Raymond, 5 February 1867, Matthew Vassar Papers, MVP 6.157 001–002, Vassar College Digital Library, http://digitallibrary.vassar.edu/islandora/object/vassar:48564/pages. I first learned of the reference to debating in the Vassar prospectus in Frances Juliette Hosford's *Father Shipherd's Magna Charta: A Century of Coeducation in Oberlin College* (Boston: Marshall Jones Company, 1937). For a discussion of

subsequent rhetorical education at Vassar and the Seven Sisters Colleges, see Kathryn M. Conway, "Woman Suffrage and the History of Rhetoric at the Seven Sisters Colleges, 1865–1919," in *Reclaiming Rhetorica: Women in the Rhetorical Tradition*, ed. Andrea A. Lunsford (Pittsburgh: University of Pittsburgh Press, 1995), 208. A review of debating in later years at Vassar is available in Helen C. West, "The History of Debating," *The Vassar Miscellany: Fiftieth Anniversary Number* (October 1915): 144–61.

4. *Prospectus of the Vassar*, 20.

5. *Oxford English Dictionary Online*, s.v. "incongruous."

6. Tim Cresswell observes that "place" is sometimes a referent for a physical location, yet common phrases like "know your place" reveal that the word also can also be used to imply a strong sense of propriety. In these cases, *"expectations* about behavior . . . relate a position in a social structure to actions in space." Tim Cresswell, *In Place/Out of Place: Geography, Ideology and Transgression* (Minneapolis: University of Minnesota Press, 1996), 3. The idea that there is a "culturally awkward relationship between the voice of women and the public sphere of speech-making, debating and comment" and that efforts are often made "not only to exclude, but to parade that exclusion" is a phenomenon that classicist Mary Beard traces back to Greek and Roman antiquity in "The Public Voice of Women," *Women's History Review* 24, no. 5 (2015): 810. This is a claim that has been substantiated by feminist historians and rhetoricians studying a vast array of historical periods.

7. It is debate as part of a democratic ideal that I want to stress here as a backdrop for understanding gendered exclusions. As Robert Branham argues, democracies may spotlight the importance of public debate in governance and policy, but the practice of debate takes place in all societies—"even the most feudal, doctrinaire, and totalitarian." See *Debate and Critical Analysis: A Harmony of Conflict* (Hillsdale, NJ: Lawrence Erlbaum Associates, 1991), 4–5.

8. Branham, *Debate and Critical Analysis*, 15–16.

9. Deborah Tannen, *The Argument Culture: Moving from Debate to Dialogue* (New York: Random House, 1998), 25. A number of scholars complicate this diagnosis by demonstrating alternative possibilities within a culture that continues to use argument as an important means for fleshing out public issues. For example, Gordon R. Mitchell takes Tannen's critique as a starting point to explore role-play simulation as an alternative approach to modeling public argument in the classroom in his "Simulated Public Argument as Pedagogical Play on Worlds,"

Argumentation and Advocacy 36, no. 3 (2000): 134–51. Gerald Graff takes exception to Tannen's sense of academia as ritualized combat in "Two Cheers for the Argument Culture," in *Clueless in Academe: How Schooling Obscures the Life of the Mind* (New Haven: Yale University Press, 2003), 83–95.

10. Jürgen Habermas, *The Structural Transformation of the Public Sphere: An Inquiry into a Category of Bourgeois Society*, translated by Thomas Burger (Cambridge: MIT Press, 1991), 36.

11. Jessica Enoch, *Refiguring Rhetorical Education: Women Teaching African American, Native American, and Chicano/a Students, 1865–1911* (Carbondale: Southern Illinois University Press, 2008), 7–8.

12. See J. Michael Hogan, "Public Address and the Revival of American Civic Culture," in *The Handbook of Rhetoric and Public Address*, ed. Shawn J. Parry-Giles and J. Michael Hogan (Oxford: Wiley-Blackwell, 2010), 431–36; J. Michael Hogan et al., "Speech and Debate as Civic Education," *Communication Education* 65, no. 4 (2016): 377–81; G. Thomas Goodnight and Gordon R. Mitchell, "Forensics as Scholarship: Testing Zarefsky's Bold Hypothesis in a Digital Age," *Argumentation and Advocacy* 45, no. 2 (2008): 81; Richard Graff and Michael Leff, "Revisionist Historiography and Rhetorical Tradition(s)," in *The Viability of the Rhetorical Tradition*, ed. Richard Graff, Arthur E. Walzer, and Janet M. Atwill (Albany: State University of New York Press, 2005), 24–27.

13. Histories of debate that emphasize the lack or small number of women participants include L. Leroy Cowperthwaite and A. Craig Baird, "Intercollegiate Debating," in *History of Speech Education in America*, ed. Karl R. Wallace (New York: Appleton-Century-Crofts, 1954), 259–76; William M. Keith, *Democracy as Discussion: Civic Education and the American Forum Movement* (Lanham, MD: Lexington Books, 2007); Jarrod Atchison and Edward Panetta, "Intercollegiate Debate and Speech Communication: Historical Developments and Issues for the Future," in *The Sage Handbook of Rhetorical Studies*, ed. Andrea A. Lunsford, Kirt H. Wilson, and Rosa A. Eberly (Thousand Oaks, CA: Sage Publications, 2009), 317–33; Michael D. Bartanen and Robert Littlefield, *Forensics in America: A History* (Lanham, MD: Rowman and Littlefield, 2014). There are some exceptions that view women's debate as central, such as Lisa Mastrangelo, "'They Argued in White Shirtwaists and Black Skirts': Women's Participation in Debate Competitions," in *Contest(ed) Writing: Reconceptualizing Literacy Competitions*, ed. Mary Lamb (Newcastle: Cambridge Scholars Publishing, 2013), 115–38; and Sarah Wiggins, "Gendered Spaces and Political Identity: Debating Societies in

English Women's Colleges, 1890–1914," *Women's History Review* 18, no. 5 (2009): 737–52. Other examples of scholarship focused on women's debating in single institutions or regions are discussed in the next chapter.

14. Atchison and Panetta, "Intercollegiate Debate," 324.

15. Bartanen and Littlefield, *Forensics in America*, 271. Bartanen and Littlefield problematize this paradigm and devote chapters to African American and women forensics participants in the last section of their book, entitled "The Sociocultural Dimensions Contributing to the Evolution of Forensics."

16. See Bartanen and Littlefield, "Organizational Structures and Their Influence on Forensics Practice," in *Forensics in America*, 79–118.

17. Throughout the book, I endeavor to be as precise as possible in my use of language and pronouns while also using terminology that will be recognizable to readers. For example, I use the term "women" in the title to denote a cultural rather than a biological category; "men" and "women" were labels used to distinguish between debating organizations and structured campus and community spaces. The marking of terms with "women" or "men" is deliberate to reflect formal and informal policies in campus organizations or debate competitions. This is also done to denaturalize the idea of the unmarked debater or student as man. I do use the term "female" when it refers to a named organization, like the Female Department at the Oberlin Collegiate Institute.

18. Scholars from English, history, communication, and gender studies have shaped this burgeoning area of research. Attempts to include women in the history of rhetoric can be traced back to early works such as Doris G. Yoakam's "Pioneer Women Orators of America," *Quarterly Journal of Speech* 23, no. 2 (1937): 251–59; and Lillian O'Connor's *Pioneer Women Orators: Rhetoric in the Ante-bellum Reform Movement* (New York: Columbia University Press, 1954). Calls for additional efforts to recover women's voices in this history followed in Karlyn Kohrs Campbell's *Man Cannot Speak for Her: A Critical Study of Early Feminist Rhetoric*, vol. 1 (New York: Praeger, 1989); Andrea A. Lunsford, ed., *Reclaiming Rhetorica: Women in the Rhetorical Tradition* (Pittsburgh: University of Pittsburgh Press, 1995); and Cheryl Glenn, ed., *Rhetoric Retold: Regendering the Tradition from Antiquity through the Renaissance* (Carbondale: Southern Illinois University Press, 1997). Lindal Buchanan and Kathleen J. Ryan's edited volume, *Walking and Talking Feminist Rhetorics: Landmark Essays and Controversies* (West Lafayette, IN: Parlor Press, 2010), frames and compiles the major contributions to this flourishing subfield. While it is not possible to note all of the work in this

area, other book-length scholarship that most strongly influenced my thinking on the subject includes Mary P. Ryan, *Women in Public: Between Banners and Ballots, 1825–1800* (Baltimore: Johns Hopkins University Press, 1990); Susan Zaeske, *Signatures of Citizenship: Petitioning, Antislavery, and Women's Political Identity* (Chapel Hill: University of North Carolina Press, 2003); Angela G. Ray, *The Lyceum and Public Culture in the Nineteenth-Century United States* (East Lansing: Michigan State University Press, 2005); Ronald J. Zboray and Mary Saracino Zboray, *Everyday Ideas: Socioliterary Experience among Antebellum New Englanders* (Knoxville: University of Tennessee Press, 2006); Jacqueline Jones Royster, *Traces of a Stream: Literacy and Social Change among African American Women* (Pittsburgh: University of Pittsburgh Press, 2000); Enoch, *Refiguring Rhetorical Education*; and Lindal Buchanan, *Regendering Delivery: The Fifth Canon and Antebellum Women Rhetors* (Carbondale: Southern Illinois University Press, 2005).

19. I resist labeling their communicative style as "masculine" or "feminine" in favor of a more fluid understanding of how a range of styles can be deployed in the course of argumentative performance. See Catherine Helen Palczewski, "Argumentation and Feminisms," *Argumentation and Advocacy* 32, no. 4 (1996): 161–69; M. Lane Bruner, "Producing Identities: Gender Problematization and Feminist Argumentation," *Argumentation and Advocacy* 32, no. 4 (1996): 185–98.

20. The public address tradition of rhetorical studies might take a speech text as an expression of the convictions of the speaker, whereas debaters may argue against their convictions in the spirit of investigating both sides of an argument. In other words, historical records might reveal that a debater defended the affirmative or negative side of a resolution, but it is not always clear whether this reflected their personal opinions or whether they were testing ideas for the purposes of having representation on both sides. Speeches given within the semi-public spaces of debating society meetings, or in intercollegiate competitions, can be indicative of wider cultural values and of the arguments in circulation at the time, but are of limited value in identifying an individual rhetor's perspective unless they are repurposed in other forums of public argument because of the possibility that they represented that side of the proposition out of logistical necessity. The cultural criticism of members of the 1929 British women's debate tour, explored later in this volume, is an example of this repurposing. The Pittsburgh Policy, also discussed later, represents one university's view on the ethics of "switch sides" debate.

21. The study of public address, once dominated by studies of people in positions of power on the public stage, has turned its attention to the operations of power and persuasion in public culture through a wider range of artifacts and texts. See Kathleen J. Turner, ed., *Doing Rhetorical History: Concepts and Cases* (Tuscaloosa: University of Alabama Press, 1998), 2; Shawn J. Parry-Giles and J. Michael Hogan, "The Study of Rhetoric and Public Address," in *The Handbook of Rhetoric and Public Address*, ed. Shawn J. Parry-Giles and J. Michael Hogan (Oxford: Wiley-Blackwell, 2010), 3. David Zarefsky's catalogue of the major developments in rhetoric and public address since the 1960s includes the study of social movements, marginalized figures, "texts" and artifacts beyond formal speeches, broader cultural practices, reconsideration of traditional or canonical texts, institutions and other organized bodies, and heightened attention to identity in "Public Address Scholarship in the New Century: Achievements and Challenges," in Parry-Giles and Hogan, *The Handbook of Rhetoric and Public Address*, 69–70. See also Lester C. Olson, "Rhetorical Criticism and Theory: Rhetorical Questions, Theoretical Fundamentalism, and the Dissolution of Judgment," in *A Century of Transformation: Studies in Honor of the 100th Anniversary of the Eastern Communication Association*, ed. James W. Chesebro (New York: Oxford University Press, 2010), 37–71.

22. I consulted archival materials housed at Oberlin College, the National Library of Scotland, University College London, Bates College, University of Illinois Urbana–Champaign, University of Pittsburgh, and Pennsylvania State University, as well as numerous digital collections. My approach to evaluating and interpreting these materials generally follows the guidelines of archival research in rhetoric laid out by Lynée Lewis Gaillet. This process includes developing highly revisable research questions, recording and categorizing artifacts by genre, consulting related primary and secondary sources in order to contextualize materials, determining the contemporary and historical rhetorical significance of the materials (including the original audience, reception, and subsequent impact of the artifact), and crafting a narrative strategy that reflects the available evidence. See Lynée Lewis Gaillet, "Archival Survival: Navigating Historical Research," in *Working in the Archives: Practical Research Methods for Rhetoric and Composition*, ed. Alexis E. Ramsey, Wendy B. Sharer, and Barbara L'Eplattenier (Carbondale: Southern Illinois University Press, 2009), 34–36. While there are many useful theoretical engagements with archival research, Gaillet's chapter provides a detailed and practical guide to the archives for rhetorical scholars.

Where possible, my methods also include personal correspondence and oral history interviews. For more on the benefits of archival research in the history of speech communication and forensics, see William M. Keith, "Crafting a Usable History," *Quarterly Journal of Speech* 93, no. 3 (2007): 345; Robert S. Littlefield, "Gaining a Broader Focus: The Benefits of Archival Research Exploring Forensic Education and Activity in the 20th Century" (paper presented at the National Communication Association convention, Chicago, IL, November 16, 2007).

23. This approach roughly maps onto Burton's material method of "rhetorical accretion," or "the process of layering additional texts over and around the original text," in Vickie Tolar Collins, "The Speaker Respoken: Material Rhetoric as Feminist Methodology," *College English* 61, no. 5 (1999): 547. Jennifer Clary-Lemon makes the case for extending rhetorical accretion to include an examination of "location, relationships, positionalities, images, and contexts" in "Archival Research Processes: The Case for Material Methods," *Rhetoric Review* 33, no. 4 (2014): 387.

INTRODUCTION

1. Though it is often traced back to the legal and political argument of ancient Greece and Rome beginning around the 5th century B.C., scholars have unearthed debate's importance as a method of educational and religious inquiry in other locales, such as China, Japan, and India. See Kenneth T. Broda-Bahm, Daniela Kempf, and William J. Driscoll, *Argument and Audience: Presenting Public Debates in Public Settings* (New York: International Debate Education Association, 2004), 29–34; Robert James Branham, *Debate and Critical Analysis: A Harmony of Conflict* (Hillsdale, NJ: Lawrence Erlbaum Associates, 1991), chapter 1.

2. *Oxford English Dictionary Online*, s.v. "debate, v.1"; *Oxford English Dictionary Online*, s.v. "debate, n.1."

3. The slipperiness in these terms is also reflected in argumentation scholarship. Daniel J. O'Keefe argues that it is crucial to distinguish between two senses of argument—it can be something that one creates ("I made an argument about charter schools") or an exchange that one has ("they had an argument about public education"). See Daniel J. O'Keefe. "Two Conceptions of Argument," in *Readings in Argumentation*, ed. William L. Benoit, Dale Hample, and Pamela J. Benoit (Berlin: Foris Publications, 1992), 79–90. In the same volume, Dale

Hample argues for a third sense—argument-as-cognition, or "the mental processes by which arguments occur within people" in his "A Third Perspective on Argument," 92.

4. Branham, *Debate and Critical Analysis*, 1.

5. Diverse approaches to the academic study of argumentation have emerged across the globe, yet there is also general consensus that the term "arguing" signals the "offering or exchange of reasons," as described by Robert C. Pinto, "Argumentation and the Force of Reasons," *Informal Logic* 29, no. 3 (2009): 268, DOI: 10.22329/il.v29i3.2844.

6. G. Thomas Goodnight, "The Re-Union of Argumentation and Debate Theory," in *Dimensions of Argument: Proceedings of the National Communication Association/American Forensics Association Alta Conference on Argumentation*, ed. George Ziegelmueller and Jack Rhodes (Annandale, VA: Speech Communication Association, 1981), 416.

7. Lisa Mastrangelo also comments on this conundrum in "'They Argued in White Shirtwaists and Black Skirts': Women's Participation in Debate Competitions,'" in *Contest(ed) Writing: Reconceptualizing Literacy Competitions*, ed. by Mary Lamb (Newcastle: Cambridge Scholars Publishing, 2013), 116–17.

8. James Jasinski, *Sourcebook on Rhetoric: Key Concepts in Contemporary Rhetorical Studies* (Thousand Oaks, CA: Sage Publications, 2001), 146.

9. For more on the Beecher–Grimké exchange, see Alisse Portnoy, *Their Right to Speak: Women's Activism in the Indian and Slave Debates* (Cambridge, MA: Harvard University Press, 2005), 160–202; Stephen Howard Browne, *Angelina Grimké: Rhetoric, Identity, and the Radical Imagination* (East Lansing: Michigan State University Press, 1999), 83–110. At this time, Grimké was regularly engaged in public speaking, but her debates with both Beecher and Theodore Weld unfolded through correspondence in 1837. For a thorough discussion of the exchange with Weld, see Browne, *Angelina Grimké*, 111–38.

10. G. Thomas Goodnight, Zoltan P. Majdik, and John M. Kephart III, "Presidential Debates as Public Argument," in *Concerning Argument: Proceedings of the 2007 National Communication Association/American Forensics Association Alta Conference on Argumentation*, ed. Scott Jacobs (Washington, DC: National Communication Association, 2009), 267. The authors note that many scholars treat presidential debates as "pseudo-argumentation" when they ought to treat them as public argument. This trend is based on a definition of "real debate" provided by Jeffrey Auer in 1962 (one that seems better suited for contest

debating than public debating). Though Auer sources his definition to a tradition of American public debate detailed by nineteenth-century author Reuben Davis, Goodnight, Majdik, and Kephart's re-reading argues that Auer was reliant on a false nostalgia: "in the United States, our national debates have been as much open, social, self-forming, entertaining exchanges as they have resembled the senatorial confrontations of Webster and Hayne or the mythologized Lincoln–Douglas exchange" (269). The latter two categories of debate treated here, intramural and intercollegiate debate, have received less scholarly attention but are important developments in the history of rhetoric, education, and public address.

11. David Zarefsky, *Lincoln, Douglas, and Slavery: In the Crucible of Public Debate* (Chicago: University of Chicago Press, 1990), especially chapter 8.

12. However, members of debating societies and teams do sometimes participate in public debate events, especially in front of community civic organizations.

13. David Potter, "The Literary Society," in *History of Speech Education in America: Background Studies* (New York: Appleton-Century-Crofts, 1954), 242–43. The deliberate decision to shift from a literary to a debating focus is reflected in the minute books and names of some societies—including one studied in this book, the Ladies' Edinburgh Debating Society.

14. James Gordon Emerson, "The Old Debating Society," *Quarterly Journal of Speech* 17, no. 3 (1931): 364. Martin J. Medhurst notes that formal rhetorical instruction in U.S. colleges and universities during the nineteenth century was parceled into distinct areas of study such as literature, drama, grammar, or composition. Oral rhetoric was practiced primarily in schools of elocution, literary societies, and debate clubs. He credits the 1895 publication of George Pierce Baker's *The Principles of Argumentation* with providing debate clubs the theoretical justification needed for more formal integration in to the university curriculum. See Martin J. Medhurst, "The History of Public Address as an Academic Study," in *The Handbook of Rhetoric and Public Address*, ed. Shawn J. Parry-Giles and J. Michael Hogan (Oxford: Wiley-Blackwell, 2010), 21–22.

15. As recalled by one of its members, Robert Waters, a Scottish-born American educator. See Robert Waters, *Intellectual Pursuits, or, Culture by Self-Help* (New York: Worthington Company, 1892), 120.

16. This point has also been observed of debating societies in earlier periods. As historian Carolyn Eastman writes in her study of young men's debating societies in the early American republic: "belonging to a debating society announced one's

lack of position more than the reverse, since these groups promised to further a young man's entry into public life by cultivating his speech, conduct, and relationships." Carolyn Eastman, *A Nation of Speechifiers: Making an American Public After the Revolution* (Chicago: University of Chicago Press, 2009), 115.

17. Angela G. Ray, "The Permeable Public: Rituals of Citizenship in Men's Antebellum Debating Clubs," *Argumentation and Advocacy* 41, no. 1 (2004): 1.

18. Ray argues that though these debates often served to re-entrench dominant opinions of the Other, the recurrence of these issues as legitimate topics for debate exposed the influence of counterpublic agitation on rational-critical debate and at least suggested that there was ground for a two-sided argument ("Permeable Public," 14).

19. There have been many calls to action in this regard, but see especially Andrea A. Lunsford, ed., *Reclaiming Rhetorica: Women in the Rhetorical Tradition* (Pittsburgh: University of Pittsburgh Press, 1995); Cheryl Glenn, ed., *Rhetoric Retold: Regendering the Tradition from Antiquity through the Renaissance* (Carbondale: Southern Illinois University Press, 1997); Jacqueline Jones Royster, Gesa E. Kirsch, and Patricia Bizzell, "Documenting a Need for Change in Rhetorical Studies," in *Feminist Rhetorical Practices: New Horizons for Rhetoric, Composition, and Literacy Studies* (Carbondale: Southern Illinois University Press, 2012), 13–25.

20. Mary Thale, "Women in London Debating Societies in 1780," *Gender & History* 7, no. 1 (1995): 5–24; Donna T. Andrew, "'The Passion for Public Speaking': Women's Debating Societies," in *Women & History: Voices of Early Modern England*, ed. Valerie Frith (Toronto: Coach House Press, 1995), 165–88.

21. See Eastman, *Nation of Speechifiers*, chapter 2; Mary Kelley, *Learning to Stand and Speak: Women, Education, and Public Life in America's Republic* (Chapel Hill: University of North Carolina Press, 2006), chapter 4.

22. See Elizabeth McHenry, *Forgotten Readers: Recovering the Lost History of African American Literary Societies* (Durham, NC: Duke University Press, 2002); Shirley Wilson Logan, *Liberating Language: Sites of Rhetorical Education in Nineteenth-Century Black America* (Carbondale: Southern Illinois University Press, 2008); Phyllis M. Belt-Beyan, *The Emergence of African American Literacy Traditions: Family and Community Efforts in the Nineteenth Century* (Westport, CT: Praeger, 2004); Jacqueline Bacon and Glen McClish, "Reinventing the Master's Tools: Nineteenth Century African-American Literary Societies of Philadelphia and Rhetorical Education," *Rhetoric Society Quarterly* 30, no. 4 (2000): 19–47; Angela

G. Ray, "'A Green Oasis in the History of My Life': Race and the Culture of Debating in Antebellum Charleston, South Carolina" (lecture given at the twenty-eighth Annual B. Aubrey Fisher Memorial Lecture, University of Utah, Salt Lake City, 2014); Angela G. Ray, "Warriors and Statesmen: Debate Education among Free African American Men in Antebellum Charleston," in *Speech and Debate as Civic Education*, ed. J. Michael Hogan et al. (University Park: Pennsylvania State University Press, 2017); Brittany Cooper, "Take No Prisoners: The Role of Debate in a Liberatory Education," in *Using Debate in the Classroom: Encouraging Critical Thinking, Communication, and Collaboration*, ed. Karyl A. Davis et al. (New York: Routledge, 2017), 12–13.

23. A. O. Bowden claims that women's clubs focusing on the "philanthropic and literary" date back to the 1730s in the United States, though the "real" women's club movement, which focused on "self-development and growth," took shape in the nineteenth century. See A. O. Bowden, "The Woman's Club Movement: Appraisal and Prophecy," *Journal of Education* 111, no. 9 (1930): 258. Focused as they are in serving particular communities, these societies can be seen as part of a larger education movement in the nineteenth century, which took the form of lyceums, Chautauqua, and later, the discussion movement in the United States (William Keith, *Democracy as Discussion: Civic Education and the American Forum Movement* [Lanham, MD: Lexington Books, 2007]). In the United Kingdom, this movement manifested in Mechanics' Institutes, the People's College, and university extension programs. See Robert Axford, "The Background of the Adult Education Movement," in *Transactions of the Wisconsin Academy of Sciences, Arts, and Letters*, vol. 1, ed. Stanley D. Beck (Madison: Wisconsin Academy of Sciences, Arts, and Letters, 1961), 345–51, http://digital.library.wisc.edu/1711.dl/WI.WT1961.

24. Anne Ruggles Gere, *Intimate Practices: Literacy and Cultural Work in U.S. Women's Clubs, 1880–1920* (Urbana: University of Illinois Press, 1997), 3. As she explains, "women's clubs were part of public life, but as intermediate institutions located between the family and the state, they also fostered intimacy among members" (Gere, *Intimate Practices*, 13). See also Wendy B. Sharer's *Vote and Voice: Women's Organizations and Political Literacy, 1915–1930* (Carbondale: Southern Illinois University Press, 2004). For a rhetorical analysis of black women intellectuals and their roles in nineteenth-century churches and clubs, see Shirley Wilson Logan, *We Are Coming: The Persuasive Discourse of Nineteenth Century Black Women* (Carbondale: Southern Illinois University Press, 1999).

25. Gere, *Intimate Practices*, 2.

26. Peter Gordon and David Doughan, *Dictionary of British Women's Organizations, 1825–1960*, 2nd ed. (Oxford: Routledge, 2013), 1–10.

27. See Christine D. Meyers, *University Coeducation in the Victorian Era: Inclusion in the United States and the United Kingdom* (New York: Palgrave Macmillan, 2010).

28. See Carol Dyhouse, *No Distinction of Sex? Women in British Universities, 1870–1939* (London: University College London Press, 1995); Wiggins, "Gendered Spaces"; L. Jill Lamberton, "Claiming an Education: The Transatlantic Performance and Circulation of Individual Identities in College Women's Writing" (PhD diss., University of Michigan, 2007), chapters 3 and 4.

29. Fawcett's speech was significant because it illustrated that women could stand and speak on the debating hall floor, rather than sitting as audience members in the balcony as they had previously. See Elizabeth Crawford, *The Women's Suffrage Movement in Britain and Ireland: A Regional Survey* (New York: Routledge, 2006), 100; Oxford Union Society, *Proceedings of the Oxford Union Society, Michaelmas Term, 1904, to Easter Term, 1905* (Oxford: Geo. Bryan and Co., 1905), 12.

30. Eugene Chenoweth and Uvieja Good, "The Rise of Women and the Fall of Tradition in Union Debating at Oxford and Cambridge," *Speaker & Gavel* 9, no. 2 (1972): 31–32.

31. There was a failed attempt to unite into a coeducational union due to a decline in membership in the interwar years. See University of Edinburgh, "Edinburgh University Union," Our History, http://ourhistory.is.ed.ac.uk/index.php/Edinburgh_University_Union.

32. Barbara Miller Solomon, *In the Company of Educated Women: A History of Women and Higher Education in America* (New Haven: Yale University Press, 1985), 44, table 1.

33. Marie Hochmuth and Richard Murphy, "Rhetorical and Elocutionary Training in Nineteenth-Century Colleges," in Wallace, *History of Speech Education in America*, 153.

34. Emerson, "The Old Debating Society," 363.

35. As Lisa Mastrangelo states, "our own historical sense is at odds with a story that places women in public forums of argumentation during a period that we normally associate with their silence" ("'They Argued in White Shirtwaists,'" 118). See 121–25 of the same chapter for Mastrangelo's extensive research into debates that broke the trend during this period; Helen C. West, "The History of Debating," *The Vassar Miscellany: Fiftieth Anniversary Number* [October 1915]:

144–61; Kathryn M. Conway, "Woman Suffrage and the History of Rhetoric at the Seven Sisters Colleges, 1865–1919," in Lunsford, *Reclaiming Rhetorica*, 215–16; Robert J. Branham, *Stanton's Elm: An Illustrated History of Debating at Bates College* (Lewiston, ME: Bates College, 1996), 22–23; Otto F. Bauer, "A Century of Debating at Northwestern University: 1855–1955" (master's thesis, Northwestern University, 1955); Meyers, *University Coeducation*, 125–26. Thanks to Angela G. Ray for bringing the Bauer thesis to my attention.

36. Potter, "The Literary Society," 241.

37. Andrea G. Radke-Moss, *Bright Epoch: Women and Coeducation in the American West* (Lincoln: University of Nebraska Press, 2008), 91–101. For a discussion of debating at normal schools, see Suzanne Bordelon, "'Resolved That the Mind of Woman Is Not Inferior to That of Man': Women's Oratorical Preparation in California State Normal School Coeducation Literary Societies in the Late Nineteenth Century," *Advances in the History of Rhetoric* 15 (2012): 159–84, DOI: 10.1080/15362426.2012.697679; Beth Ann Rothermel, "A Sphere of Nobel Action: Gender, Rhetoric, and Influence at a Nineteenth-Century Massachusetts State Normal School," *Rhetoric Society Quarterly* 33, no. 1 (2003): 35–64.

38. Radke-Moss, *Bright Epoch*, 93.

39. Radke-Moss, *Bright Epoch*, 93–94. For example, the University of Nebraska's Palladian Society held a debate in 1872 in which Miss J. C. Kelley debated alongside four men about whether the liquor trade should be abolished. The same society re-organized into separate debating clubs for men and women in the early 1880s (Radke-Moss, *Bright Epoch*, 93–94, 96). Donald Olson reports that the University of Nebraska chancellor's daughter was the first secretary of the Palladian. According to his findings, although the early society was coeducational, women did not play an active role at the beginning. See Donald Orrin Olson, "Debating at the University of Nebraska" (Master's thesis, University of Wisconsin, 1947), 3. A similar story of coeducational societies turned gender-segregated comes from Iowa Agricultural College (now Iowa State University) during the same period. There were four active literary societies on campus: three were coeducational and one was for men only. The Crescent Literary Society required its members to do three-minute impromptu responses to subjects of the day. Men's responses came in the form of oratory, while women wrote essays and gave recitations. Carrie Clinton Lane reportedly broke convention by delivering her response as an oration. This breaking of norms caused such a stir on campus that she formed a separate debating club "where the girls could debate among themselves awhile,

until they had the courage to venture combat with the men" (see Elizabeth Storm, "Mrs. Catt Delivers Oration at Ames," *Des Moines Register*, June 17, 1921). Lane, better known by her later name—Carrie Chapman Catt—graduated in 1880 and went on to be a renowned activist in the suffrage and peace movements.

Thank you to Becky S. Jordan and Tanya Zanish-Belcher at the Iowa State University Special Collections for pointing me to this article and providing useful background information on Carrie Chapman Catt.

40. Robert J. Connors, *Composition-Rhetoric: Backgrounds, Theory and Pedagogy* (Pittsburgh: University of Pittsburgh Press, 1997), 44.

41. Connors, *Composition-Rhetoric*, 50.

42. For an overview of this scholarly exchange, see Buchanan, *Regendering Delivery*, 42–44. See also Roxanne Mountford, "The Feminization of Rhetoric?" *JAC* 19, no. 3 (1999): 485–92; Conway, "Woman Suffrage," 203–26; Lisa Mastrangelo, "Learning from the Past: Rhetoric, Composition, and Debate at Mount Holyoke College," *Rhetoric Review* 18, no. 1 (1999): 46–64; Lisa Reid Ricker, "'Ars Stripped of Practice': Robert J. Connors and the Demise of Agonistic Rhetoric," *Rhetoric Review* 23, no. 3 (2004): 235–52; Susanne Bordelon, "Contradicting and Complicating Feminization of Rhetoric Narratives: Mary Yost and Argument from a Sociological Perspective," *Rhetoric Society Quarterly* 35, no. 3 (2005): 101–24; Mastrangelo, "'They Argued in White Shirtwaists,'" 117–18. Connors did temper his claims in response to these critiques. Radke-Moss's discussion of University of Nebraska literary societies in the nineteenth century points to evidence of men actively encouraging women's debate participation in *Bright Epoch*, 95.

43. Keith, *Democracy as Discussion*, 59. A connection between intramural societies and the intercollegiate debating competitions of the late nineteenth and twentieth centuries seems all but taken for granted by communication scholars. For example, James Gordon Emerson suggests that literary societies gave way or transformed into other activities due to broadened opportunities for entertainment in other aspects of U.S. culture, the rise of specific courses dedicated to public speaking, and the creation of intercollegiate debate squads (in "Old Debating Society," 367–68). Yet Connors reads a decline in women's debate participation at the turn of the century as support for broader claims about the decline of "oral agonistic rhetoric." He even goes so far as to suggest that intercollegiate debating after 1880 is best seen as a "forced blossom of agonism made to grow artificially in a place where it no longer took natural root" (*Composition-Rhetoric*, 59). He acknowledges that debate never completely faded

away from U.S. colleges, but writes intercollegiate debate off as dominated by men until the 1930s. This, I think, unfairly ignores the participation of women in literary and debating societies during this time. This book offers evidence to the contrary. Given the mutual interest in the topic, additional research and conversation between rhetorical scholars in composition and speech communication on this topic would be beneficial.

44. Egbert Ray Nichols's trio of *Quarterly Journal of Speech* articles, published in 1936 and 1937, categorizes the history of U.S. intercollegiate debating into three phases. The debates of 1893–1902 laid the foundations, usually based upon yearly debate contests between rival universities; 1903–1913 saw the sophistication of league debating and the rise of debate organizations and honor societies. With a notable slowdown during World War I, the final phase, 1913–1923, was characterized by an expansion in the number of universities participating in the activity, the number of debates held per year, and the number of women participants. Although imperfect in capturing the details of each participating university in the United States, Nichols's timeline provides a useful starting point that we may tweak and revise as additional research emerges. See Egbert Ray Nichols, "A Historical Sketch of Intercollegiate Debating: I," *Quarterly Journal of Speech* 22, no. 2 (1936): 213–20; Egbert Ray Nichols, "A Historical Sketch of Intercollegiate Debating: II," *Quarterly Journal of Speech* 22, no. 4 (1936): 591–603; Egbert Ray Nichols, "A Historical Sketch of Intercollegiate Debating: III," *Quarterly Journal of Speech* 23, no. 2 (1937): 259–78. This system of contest debating represents a distinct difference in the debating cultures of the United Kingdom and the United States, which would not meet until the international debate competitions of the 1920s.

45. L. Leroy Cowperthwaite and A. Craig Baird, "Intercollegiate Debating," in Wallace, *History of Speech Education in America*, 260.

46. Cowperthwaite and Baird cite Ralph Curtis Ringwalt's claim that the first intercollegiate debate was between Harvard and Yale in 1892; Otto F. Bauer claims that intercollegiate debating between Northwestern University and University of Chicago literary societies occurred earlier in "The Harvard–Yale Myth," *The AFA Register* 11 (Winter 1963): 20. More recently, Jamie McKown traces the development of intercollegiate debates by drawing on recently digitized newspapers of the period. He has found evidence of a number of debates dating back to the 1880s, including Rutgers–New York University and Emory–Mercer–University of Georgia. See his "Renewing a 'Very Old Means of Education': Civic

Engagement and the Birth of Intercollegiate Debate in the United States," in Hogan et al., *Speech and Debate as Civic Education for Citizenship*.

47. For an overview of this change, and the relative deficiencies of intramural literary and debating societies, see Jarrod Atchison and Edward Panetta, "Intercollegiate Debate and Speech Communication: Historical Developments and Issues for the Future," in *The Sage Handbook of Rhetorical Studies*, ed. Andrea A. Lunsford, Kirt H. Wilson, and Rosa A. Eberly (Thousand Oaks, CA: Sage Publications, 2009), 319–20.

48. Nichols, "A Historical Sketch of Intercollegiate Debating: I," 219.

49. Cowperthwaite and Baird, "Intercollegiate Debating, 263. The need to frame debate as both an intellectual and a competitive endeavor has long plagued the activity. In her examination of intercollegiate debate at Emory University, New York University, and the University of Chicago from 1900 to 1930, Claudia J. Keenan finds the comparison of intercollegiate debate with sports superficial because debate research was intense, challenging, and difficult for lay audiences to understand. See Claudia J. Keenan, "Intercollegiate Debate: Reflecting American Culture, 1900–1930," *Argumentation and Advocacy* 46, no. 2 (2009): 80. Indeed, this problem with translating insular debate practices and vocabulary and the problem of financial concerns are two issues precipitating the rise of the tournament system of debating in the 1920s, where many schools would come together at a host campus. The relative accuracy of the "sportification" of intercollegiate debate must have varied by college campus. My research at the University of Pittsburgh suggests that debaters in the early to mid-twentieth century were treated with great respect, on par with the collegiate sports heroes of the day. There were also concerted steps taken to balance the specialization of intercollegiate debate with efforts to engage in public outreach through extension debating (and later, at Pittsburgh, a community-oriented radio and television series). As a researcher keenly interested in the metaphors that surround argumentation, I try to avoid the sports metaphors that describe contemporary debate. Needless to say, in this historical context, connections between debate and athletics were exclusionary to women because intercollegiate athletics often did not include women—the claim that debate functioned as an "intellectual sport" surely wasn't making an analogy to the women's volleyball team. However, the comparison is useful in thinking about the way that early intercollegiate debate practitioners saw themselves as representatives of the school.

50. Nichols, "A Historical Sketch of Intercollegiate Debating: II," 591.

51. Cowperthwaite and Baird, "Intercollegiate Debating," 265. Obviously, debate "questions" were phrased as questions, whereas propositions or resolutions were phrased as sentences that could be affirmed or negated.

52. See, for example, Richard Murphy, "The Ethics of Debating Both Sides," *Speech Teacher* 6, no. 1 (1957): 1–9; Keith, *Democracy as Discussion*, 68–83; Ronald Walter Greene and Darrin Hicks, "Lost Convictions: Debating Both Sides and the Ethical Fashioning of Liberal Citizens," *Cultural Studies* 19, no. 1 (2005): 100–126; Eric English et al., "Debate as a Weapon of Mass Destruction," *Communication and Critical/Cultural Studies* 4, no. 2 (2007): 221–25; and Darrin Hicks and Ronald Walter Greene, "Managed Convictions: Debate and the Limits of Electoral Politics," *Quarterly Journal of Speech* 101, no. 1 (2015): 99–102, DOI:10.1080/0 0335630.2015.994903. Hicks and Greene provide a history of this concern in three episodes in intercollegiate debating: in the 1910s and 1920s, in the 1950s and 1960s, and twenty-first century controversies over the politics of debate performance.

53. Keith identifies these issues as central controversies over debate in *Democracy as Discussion*, 67–83. See also Michael D. Bartanen and Robert Littlefield, "Tensions that Shaped the Evolution of Forensics," in *Forensics in America: A History* (Lanham, MD: Rowman and Littlefield, 2014), 119–41.

54. See Herman Cohen, *The History of Speech Communication: The Emergence of a Discipline, 1915–1945* (Washington, DC: Speech Communication Association, 1994), 29–30; Pat J. Gehrke and William M. Keith, eds., *A Century of Communication Studies: The Unfinished Conversation* (New York: Routledge, 2015); Pat J. Gehrke, *The Ethics and Politics of Speech* (Carbondale: Southern Illinois University Press, 2009).

55. Cowperthwaite and Baird, "Intercollegiate Debating," 266.

56. Nichols, "A Historical Sketch of Intercollegiate Debating: I," 219.

57. See Frank Hardy Lane, "Faculty Help in Intercollegiate Contests," *Quarterly Journal of Public Speaking* 1, no. 1 (1915): 9–16; William Hawley Davis, "Is Debating Primarily a Game?" *Quarterly Journal of Public Speaking* 2, no. 2 (1916): 171–79; J. M. O'Neill, "Game or Counterfeit Presentment," *Quarterly Journal of Public Speaking* 2, no. 2 (1916): 193–97; Keith, *Debate as Discussion*, 68–82.

58. Cowperthwaite and Baird, "Intercollegiate Debating," 274.

59. Cowperthwaite and Baird, "Intercollegiate Debating," 274. Debaters and faculty advisors dealt with the question of whether debates should be decided by an audience (who may be swayed by their opinions on the proposition rather than

which team did the better debating) by creating innovations such as the "non-decision" debate and the "shift-of-opinion" ballot, which asked audience members to register their feelings about a topic before and after the debate. Cowperthwaite and Baird, "Intercollegiate Debating," 272–73. The focus on audiences was renewed when universities across the country were exposed to Oxford-style debating during international debating tours that date back to the 1920s, which is discussed later in further detail. The British debaters focused on audience persuasion rather than debate as an intellectual sport. See A. Craig Baird, "Shall American Universities Adopt the British System of Debating?" *Quarterly Journal of Speech Education* 9, no. 3 (1923): 215–22.

60. Gordon R. Mitchell explores this question in the context of contemporary academic policy debate in "Pedagogical Possibilities for Argumentative Agency in Academic Debate," *Argumentation and Advocacy* 35, no. 2 (1998): 41–60.

61. Cowperthwaite and Baird, "Intercollegiate Debating," 269. This consensus about women's participation in intercollegiate debating is cited by Keith, *Democracy as Discussion*, 62–63, and Atchison and Panetta, "Intercollegiate Debate and Speech Communication," 324.

62. Anonymous, "Co-Eds," *The Owl* (Pittsburgh, University of Pittsburgh, 1914), 427, http://digital.library.pitt.edu/d/documentingpitt/yearbooks.html.

63. The joke was published under the headline "Too Much for the Club" in the *New York Times*, November 23, 1904. I also found evidence that the joke circulated, appearing in the *Washington Star* and in the Wellington, New Zealand-based *Evening Post* with a series of jokes under the headline "Where Ignorance—," July 29, 1922. A similar scene is described in Hildegard Gordon Brown's *Conclusions of an Everyday Woman*, which pokes fun at community debating societies composed of women who primarily stay at home. In Brown's humorous story, a ladies' debating society attempts to debate the merits of Milton's *Areopagitica* compared to his *Apologia*. The story is a comedy of errors that plays on the idea that women debaters are unprepared as both speakers and thinkers to engage serious literary topics. Mrs. Adair, who is hosting the meeting, is utterly confused about debating society business. A large portion of the society, including the primary debaters, presumably scared off by the topic, fail to show up to the meeting, claiming various ailments. After bumbling through the minutes, disregarding time limits, and confusion over the order of the debate, it becomes painfully clear that few in the club have actually read the literary works in question, and no one can pronounce *Areopagitica*. At the end of the debate, after Mrs. Adair has played the

roles of chairwoman, president, opposer, seconder, debater, and minutes writer, her aunt asks her how much she actually knows about the topic. Adair responds that she knows nothing. The message of the tale is clear: women's debating societies are pale imitations of the rational-critical ideal. See *Conclusions of an Everyday Woman* (London: John Lane, The Bodley Head, 1908), 85–94.

64. Waters, *Intellectual Pursuits*, 111–12. The "yellow peril" referred to the fear of the expansion of Asian countries, and a growing unease with the presence of Chinese and Japanese immigrants in western countries. Historians believe that the racist image of a "yellow peril" originated in European newspapers. Roger Daniels describes how fear of the yellow peril came to the United States in the late nineteenth century as "the bogus specter of the invasion of the continental United States by an Asian army," and discusses its use as a foundational part of anti-Asian propaganda. See his *Asian America: Chinese and Japanese in the United States Since 1850* (Seattle: University of Washington Press, 1988), 39.

65. Some exceptions can be found at individual institutions. For example, Lisa Mastrangelo cites a 1897 intercollegiate debate between Boston University and Harvard/Radcliffe that included Maud Wood Park in "'They Argued in White Shirtwaists,'" 122. When Ohio Wesleyan University held tryouts for the 1898–1899 advanced debate squad, twenty-six students vied for a spot. Two women, Miss Winterbottom and Miss Mary Beal, were selected for that year's five-person squad. Beal competed alongside two male teammates in a debate contest against Oberlin in 1899, the third intercollegiate debate in the Ohio Wesleyan's history. See William Roy Diem and Rollin Clarence Hunter, *The Story of Speech at Ohio Wesleyan* (Columbus, OH: F.J. Heer Printing Company, 1964), 119. However, the attempted inclusion of women debaters was controversial in other cases. For example, in 1908, Cornell University senior Elizabeth Ellsworth Cook was selected for a triangular league contest with Columbia University and the University of Pennsylvania. Columbia's men debaters objected, arguing that Cook's presence would influence the judges: "they would admire her nerve, and it wouldn't matter what she said. We wouldn't dare to attempt to answer her argument without apologizing first." See "Object to Woman Debater," *Cornell Alumni News*, January 29, 1908, eCommons.cornell.edu. Though Cook was ultimately allowed to participate, she was an exceptional case (coverage of the event also marveled that one of the Columbia debaters was Chinese). An account of the Cornell–Columbia matchup in the *Cornell Alumni News* noted "the presence of a woman on one team and of a Chinaman [*sic*] on the other

. . . Miss Cook was the first speaker for Cornell and it was her task to outline the question and the position of the affirmative. She acquitted herself well. Her arguments were forceful and her manner was pleasing. Mr. Koo was perhaps the least self-conscious speaker of the evening, and his rebuttal speech was incisive and pithy. The judges deliberated fifteen minutes before their decision [in favor of the negative team from Columbia] was announced." See "Cornell Loses in Debate," *Cornell Alumni News*, March 4, 1908, eCommons.cornell.edu. Cook would have her revenge one month later, when she beat out five male competitors for Cornell's Woodford Prize in Oratory competition (*Cornell University Woodford Prize in Oratory*, April 25, 1908, program, Miller NAWSA Scrapbooks, 1897–1911, Scrapbook 6, page 62, Library of Congress).

66. Cowperthwaite and Baird, "Intercollegiate Debating," 269; Nichols, "A Historical Sketch of Intercollegiate Debating: III," 259. Cowperthwaite and Baird have a slightly different interpretation than Nichols of women's debating during the First World War. The former contend that women did not appear on intercollegiate platforms in "appreciable numbers" until after the war, while the latter credits women for sustaining interest in the activity during the war. Nichols's attention to intramural debating likely accounts for this distinction.

67. Cowperthwaite and Baird, "Intercollegiate Debating," 270.

68. See Carly S. Woods, "Taking Women Seriously: Debaters, Faculty Allies, and the Feminist Work of Debating in the 1930s and 1940s," in Hogan et al., *Speech and Debate as Civic Education*, 53–63.

69. For a cohesive overview of feminist critiques of the public/private distinction, see Seyla Benhabib's "Models of Public Space: Hannah Arendt, the Liberal Tradition, and Jürgen Habermas," in *Feminism, the Public and the Private*, ed. Joan B. Landes (Oxford: Oxford University Press, 1998), 85–92. In a desire to open up a space for diverse paths to civic participation, many have reoriented around the idea of "nonliberal, nonbourgeois, competing public spheres." Nancy Fraser, "Rethinking the Public Sphere: A Contribution to the Critique of Actually Existing Democracy," in *Habermas and the Public Sphere*, ed. Craig J. Calhoun (Cambridge: MIT Press, 1992), 115. For examples of these alternate paths to public participation for women in the nineteenth century U.S. and British contexts, see Mary P. Ryan, "Gender and Public Access: Women's Politics in Nineteenth-Century America," in Landes, *Feminism*, 197; Leonore Davidoff, "Regarding Some 'Old Husbands' Tales': Public and Private in Feminist History," in Landes, *Feminism*, 164–94.

70. Thomas B. Farrell argues that rhetoric is the "primary practical instrumentality for generating and sustaining the critical publicity which keeps the promise of the public sphere alive" in his *Norms of Rhetorical Culture* (New Haven: Yale University Press, 1995), 199. For a sense of the vast contributions of rhetorical scholarship to public sphere studies, see, among others, Farrell, *Norms of Rhetorical Culture*, especially chapter 5; Robert Asen and Daniel C. Brouwer, eds., *Counterpublics and the State* (Albany: State University of New York Press, 2001); G. Thomas Goodnight and David B. Hingstman, "Studies in the Public Sphere," *Quarterly Journal of Speech* 83, no. 3 (1997): 351–99; Gerard A. Hauser, *Vernacular Voices: The Rhetoric of Publics and Public Spheres* (Columbia: University of South Carolina Press, 1999). "Actually existing" comes from the subtitle of Fraser's critique of Habermas—"Rethinking the Public Sphere: A Contribution to the Critique of Actually Existing Democracy."

71. G. Thomas Goodnight, "The Personal, Technical, and Public Spheres: A Note on 21st Century Critical Communication Inquiry," *Argumentation and Advocacy* 48, no. 4 (2012): 261. In the 2012 article, Goodnight comments reflects on his original article, "The Personal, Technical, and Public Spheres of Argument: A Speculative Inquiry into the Act of Public Deliberation," *Journal of the American Forensic Association* 18 (1982): 214–27.

72. Goodnight, "The Personal, Technical, and Public Spheres: A Note," 260.

73. In what she terms a "revisionist historiography of the public sphere," Fraser notes that many marginalized groups have created "subaltern counterpublics" aimed at creating oppositional discourses that expressed the needs of their group ("Rethinking the Public Sphere," 123). In the intervening years, there has been a great deal of conceptual innovation that aimed to better represent the complex ways that subordinate social groups come together as publics. See especially Margaret Zulick and E. Anne Laffoon, "Enclaved Publics as Inventional Resources: An Essay on Generative Rhetoric," in *Argument in Controversy: Proceedings of the Seventh SCA/AFA Conference on Argumentation*, ed. Donn W. Parson (Annandale, VA: Speech Communication Association, 1991), 249–55; Catherine R. Squires, "Rethinking the Black Public Sphere: An Alternative Vocabulary for Multiple Public Spheres," *Communication Theory* 12, no. 3 (2002): 446–68.

74. For example, Rita Felski focuses on the "diverse forms of recent artistic and cultural activity by women" such as literature and art in order to understand how feminist ideology emerged to challenge oppression in her *Beyond Feminist Aesthetics: Feminist Literature and Social Change* (Cambridge, MA: Harvard

University Press, 1989), 164. She conceives of a feminist public sphere as one that is at once oppositional and outwardly directed. It is oppositional insofar as the experience of subordination motivates its development, yet outwardly directed as it aims to circulate arguments throughout broader culture (Felski, *Beyond Feminist Aesthetics*, 167). There are also several book-length studies that explore women's involvement as writers and readers of treatises on dialogue and conduct books as modes of participation. See Lawrence E. Klein, "Gender, Conversation and the Public Sphere in Early Eighteenth-Century England," in *Textuality and Sexuality: Reading Theories and Practices*, ed. Judith Sill and Michael Worton (Manchester: Manchester University Press, 1993), 100–115; Jane Donawerth, "Conduct Book Rhetoric: Constructing a Theory of Feminine Discourse," in *Conversational Rhetoric: The Rise and Fall of a Women's Tradition, 1600–1900* (Carbondale: Southern Illinois University Press, 2012), 41–72; Ingrid H. Tague, *Women of Quality: Accepting and Contesting Ideals of Femininity in England, 1690–1760* (Suffolk: Boydell Press, 2002). For a sense of the range of scholarship on contemporary cases of counterpublicity, see Asen and Brouwer, *Counterpublics and the State*; Daniel C. Brouwer and Robert Asen, eds., *Public Modalities* (Tuscaloosa: University of Alabama Press, 2010).

75. Angela G. Ray's work on rhetorical rituals is immensely helpful in thinking about the relationship between embodied rhetorical practices and greater civic conversations. She sees men's debating clubs as engaging in "rituals of citizenship" in "Permeable Public," and coins "rhetorical ritual" to emphasize the public orientation and persuasive function of performances evident in Reconstruction-era women's voting in her "The Rhetorical Ritual of Citizenship: Women's Voting as Public Performance, 1868–1875," *Quarterly Journal of Speech* 93, no. 1 (2007): 3. Here Ray notes that rituals "may or may not be addressed to observers susceptible to influence," a point that is also true of some of the women's debating societies featured in this book ("Rhetorical Ritual," 3).

76. Wayne Brockriede, "Where Is Argument?" in *Readings in Argumentation*, ed. William L. Benoit, Dale Hample, and Pamela J. Benoit (Berlin: Foris Publications, 1992), 73. As Manfred Kraus explains, since Stephen Toulmin's articulation of the field-dependency of arguments, and Chaïm Perelman and Lucie Olbrechts-Tyteca's attention to audiences, argument scholars such as G. Thomas Goodnight and Raymie McKerrow have developed related theories of fields, spheres, and communities. See Manfred Kraus, "Cognitive Communities and Argument Communities," in *Argumentation: Cognition and Community;*

Proceedings of the 9th International Conference of the Ontario Society for the Study of Argumentation, ed. F. Zenker (Windsor, ON: University of Windsor, 2011), 1–11, http://scholar.uwindsor.ca/ossaarchive/OSSA9/papersandcommentaries/23.

77. David Zarefsky, "What Does an Argument Culture Look Like?," *Informal Logic* 29, no. 3 (2009): 296–308. Zarefsky is responding to Deborah Tannen, as referenced in the preface. His detailed orientation to argument is most suitable to describe debating societies as argument cultures, though we may also find considerable insight from Farrell, who defined a rhetorical culture as "an institutional formation in which motives of competing parties are intelligible, audiences available, expressions reciprocal, norms translatable, and silences noticeable" (*Norms of Rhetorical Culture*, 1). The norms of a rhetorical culture are likewise changed through debate. See Farrell, *Norms of Rhetorical Culture*, 12–13.

78. Zarefsky, "What Does an Argument Culture Look Like?," 298–303. He stresses that these features are meant to be descriptive rather than prescriptive or necessary conditions, leaving it to other scholars to identify moments where actual argument cultures coalesce. Zarefsky also offers five productive tensions among these features of an argument culture: contingency–commitment, partisanship–restraint, conviction–sensitivity to an audience, reasonableness–subjectivity, and decision–nonclosure.

79. Zarefsky, "What Does an Argument Culture Look Like?," 297.

80. Susan Zaeske and Sara Jedd emphasize the need to "shift the focus from women as subject of research to gender as a category of analysis" that examines power relationships in rhetorical performances across the gender spectrum (Susan Zaeske and Sarah Jedd, "From Recovering Women's Words to Documenting Gender Constructs: Archival Research in the Twenty-First Century," in Parry-Giles and Hogan, *The Handbook of Rhetoric and Public Address*, 195). I agree with this assessment, but also note that because debating activities were gender-segregated in communities and on college campuses I study, the historical records tend to be as well. Thus, while I draw on the historical category of "woman" as an organizing term throughout the historical periods covered in the book, I am acutely aware that it is gender ideology that manifests in the materials. A feminist rhetorical lens allows me not simply to view women as marginalized, feminine "others," but to examine debating as one historically specific practice through which "cultural descriptions of gender are produced and circulated"; see Nancy Fraser, *Fortunes of Feminism: From State-Managed Capitalism to Neoliberal Crisis* (London: Verso Books, 2013), 140. I explore "debating women" as an idea, a

construction, and a social identity, while questioning whether a narrow view of debate as a competitive verbal battle serves anyone well.

81. David Zarefsky, "Four Senses of Rhetorical History," in *Doing Rhetorical History: Concepts and Cases*, ed. Kathleen J. Turner (Tuscaloosa: University of Alabama Press, 1998), 29. Zarefsky's discussion of the four senses of rhetorical history is an essential heuristic for thinking through those "distinctions that do matter" in the way rhetoricians have approached history. As he notes, "these distinctions are useful not for boundary drawing but for understanding the richness of our field" and tend to "cross-fertilize" (26). My approach to studying the history of debating societies most closely fits within the sense of historical studies of rhetorical practice but one that is self-consciously consumed with the history of rhetoric, of the "development, from classical times to the present, of principles of effective discourse" (26). My approach is also informed by readings in the rhetoric of history and, with a little tweaking, could easily be considered under the banner of "rhetorical studies of historical events."

82. Raymond Williams, *Keywords: A Vocabulary of Culture and Society*, 2nd ed. (New York: Oxford University Press, 1985), 87–88.

83. Daphne Spain, *Gendered Spaces* (Chapel Hill: University of North Carolina Press, 1992), 143.

84. Many theorists have argued for more precision in the use of "space" versus "place," as the two terms are often conflated. In this book, I am interested in both the places—the geographical or built environments—and the spaces—the more abstract movement and comingling of bodies, ideas, and arguments—created and inhabited by women debaters. A sense of decorum relies heavily on the idea of "place"—some belong, and others do not. As Michel de Certeau explains in *The Practice of Everyday Life*, vol. 1, "the law of the 'proper' rules in the place: the elements taken into consideration are *beside* one another, each situated in its own 'proper' and distinct location, a location it defines. A place is thus an instantaneous configuration of positions. It implies an indication of stability" (Berkeley: University of California Press, 1984), 117. Space, in contrast, implies not stability or propriety, but is instead "composed of intersections of mobile elements . . . actuated by the ensemble of movements deployed within it . . . the effect produced by the operations that orient it, situate it, temporalize it, and make it function in a polyvalent unity of conflictual programs or contractual proximities" (*Practice of Everyday Life*, 117). Space, then, is place as it has been constituted and shaped by practices—Certeau provides the example that streets

are created by urban planners (place) but are spatialized by the active movements of people moving through the city (*Practice of Everyday Life*, 117). *Debating Women* is primarily concerned with how the practice of debating transforms classrooms, auditoriums, parlors, dining rooms, forests, and prisons into "spaces of argument." Therefore, like many of the feminist theorists I draw from in my analysis, I prefer the term "space" but also will use "place" when appropriate. I agree with Doreen Massey's assessment that "particular ways of thinking about space and place are tied up with, both directly and indirectly, particular social constructions of gender relations." See her *Space, Place, and Gender* (Minneapolis: University of Minnesota Press, 2004), 2.

85. See, for example, David N. Livingstone, "The Spaces of Knowledge: Contributions toward a Historical Geography of Science," *Environment and Planning D: Society and Space* 13, no. 1 (1995): 5–34.

86. Francesca Bordogna's working definition of "geography of knowledge" is "the entire arrangement of the disciplines, and the configuration of their conceptual and methodological relationships as well as the 'social' relationships among practitioners of different disciplines," in *William James at the Boundaries: Philosophy, Science, and the Geography of Knowledge* (Chicago: University of Chicago Press, 2008), 26–27. Paul Stob further develops this line of inquiry by analyzing James's intellectual discourses in his late-nineteenth-century book reviews and public lectures. See Paul Stob, *William James and the Art of Popular Statement* (East Lansing: Michigan State University Press, 2013), 39–72.

87. Gillian Rose, *Feminism and Geography: The Limits of Geographical Knowledge* (Minneapolis: University of Minnesota Press, 1993), 4.

88. Linda McDowell includes a helpful diagram that charts these supposed associations, "masculine: public, outside, work, work, production, independence, power" in contrast with "feminine: private, inside, home, leisure/pleasure, consumption, dependence, lack of power," in her book, *Gender, Identity, and Place: Understanding Feminist Geographies* (Minneapolis: University of Minnesota Press, 1999), 2.

89. It is the job of critical feminist work to point out where these assumptions have been naturalized, and where they might be denaturalized. See McDowell, *Gender, Identity, and Place*, 12.

90. Lorraine Code, *Rhetorical Spaces: Essays on Gendered Locations* (New York: Routledge, 1995), x.

91. See especially Katherine McKittrick and Clyde Woods, eds., *Black Geographies*

and the Politics of Place (Cambridge, MA: South End Press, 2007); Katherine McKittrick, *Demonic Grounds: Black Women and the Cartographies of Struggle* (Minneapolis: University of Minnesota Press, 2006); Lisa A. Flores, "Creating Discursive Space Through a Rhetoric of Difference: Chicana Feminists Craft a Homeland," *Quarterly Journal of Speech* 82, no. 2 (1996): 142–56.

92. Roxanne Mountford, *The Gendered Pulpit: Preaching in American Protestant Spaces* (Carbondale: Southern Illinois University Press, 2003), 17.

93. See, for example, Jessica Enoch, "A Woman's Place Is in the School: Rhetorics of Gendered Space in Nineteenth-Century America," *College English* 70, no. 3 (2008): 275–95; McHenry, *Forgotten Readers*, 10; Mountford, *The Gendered Pulpit*, especially chapter 1.

94. Cheryl Glenn, "Remapping Rhetorical Territory," *Rhetoric Review* 13 (1995): 287–303. For a more thorough elaboration of this argument, see Carly S. Woods, "(Im) Mobile Metaphors: Toward an Intersectional Rhetorical History," in *Standing in the Intersection: Feminist Voices, Feminist Practices in Communication Studies*, ed. Karma Chávez and Cindy Griffin (Albany: State University of New York Press, 2012), 78–96. My thinking about the relationships between the politics of location versus relation in rhetorical history is shaped by Aimee Marie Carillo Rowe's "Be Longing: Toward a Feminist Politics of Relation," *NWSA Journal* 17, no. 2 (2005): 15–46. Moreover, feminist geographer Doreen Massey's work also advocates thinking in terms of relationality. Her conceptualization of space is one that "stresses the construction of specificity through interrelations rather than through the imposition of boundaries and the counterpoint of one *against* the other . . . the argument is that the need for the security of boundaries, the requirement for such a defensive counterpositional definition of identity, is culturally masculine," in *Space, Place, and Gender*, 7.

95. This view is informed by scholarship in mobility studies, especially Tim Cresswell's *On the Move: Mobility in the Modern Western World* (New York: Routledge, 2006). There has been a pronounced turn in rhetorical studies toward critical rhetorics of space, place, mobility, and regionalism. See especially Alessandra Beasley Von Burg, "Mobility: The New Blue," *Quarterly Journal of Speech* 100, no. 2 (2014): 241–57; Jenny Rice, "From Architechtonic to Tectonics: Introducing Regional Rhetorics," *Rhetoric Society Quarterly* 42, no. 3 (2012): 201–13; Joshua P. Ewalt, "Rhetorical Constellations: On the Materiality and Mobility of Arrangement and Invention" (PhD diss., University of Nebraska–Lincoln, 2015); Carly S. Woods, Joshua P. Ewalt, and Sara J. Baker,

"A Matter of Regionalism: Remembering Brandon Teena and Willa Cather at the Nebraska History Museum," *Quarterly Journal of Speech* 99, no. 3 (2013): 341–63; Joan Faber McAlister, "Ten Propositions for Communication Scholars Studying Space and Place," *Women's Studies in Communication* 39, no. 2 (2016): 113–21; Woods, "(Im)Mobile Metaphors"; Alyssa A. Samek, "Mobility, Citizenship, and 'American Women on the Move' in the 1977 International Women's Year Torch Relay," *Quarterly Journal of Speech* 103, no. 3 (2017): 207–29, DOI: 10.1080/00335630.2017.1321134. Some public sphere scholarship likewise focuses on the movement of publics and how they oscillate between enclaved configurations and more traditionally public discursive arenas. See Daniel C. Brouwer, "ACT-ing UP in Congressional Hearings," in Asen and Brouwer, *Counterpublics and the State*, 87–110.

96. See Tannen, *The Argument Culture*, 4.

97. See Catherine H. Palczewski, "Argumentation and Feminism," *Argumentation and Advocacy* 32, no. 4 (1996): 164.

98. Goodnight, "The Personal, Technical, and Public Spheres: A Note," 260.

99. Woods, "(Im)Mobile Metaphors," 79–80.

100. Massey, *Space, Place, and Gender*, 11.

101. Mindful of ongoing debates about whether we ought to focus on the great, well-known orators or the quotidian practices of everyday people, I selected cases that would constitute a middle ground between these two poles, focusing on the little-known debating experiences of some well-known figures, as well as the significant debating experiences of some little-known figures. Barbara Biesecker and Karlyn Kohrs Campbell's exchange in *Philosophy & Rhetoric* about the value of studying the individual speaking subject as opposed to collective rhetorical practices remains a significant methodological rift in feminist rhetorical history. See Barbara Biesecker, "Coming to Terms with Attempts to Write Women into the History of Rhetoric," *Philosophy & Rhetoric* 25, no. 2 (1992): 140–61; Karlyn Kohrs Campbell, "Biesecker Cannot Speak for Her Either," *Philosophy & Rhetoric* 26, no. 3 (1993): 153–59; Barbara Biesecker, "Negotiating with Our Tradition: Reflecting Again (without Apologies) on the Feminization of Rhetoric," *Philosophy & Rhetoric* 26, no. 3 (1993): 236–41. Kate Ronald identifies the exchange as one of two major methodological issues in the development of feminist rhetorics in "Feminist Approaches to the History of Rhetoric," in Lunsford, Wilson, and Eberly, *Sage Handbook of Rhetorical Studies*, 139–52, while Lindal Buchanan and Kathleen J. Ryan feature Biesecker's original article and Campbell's reply as a

landmark controversy in their volume, *Walking and Talking Feminist Rhetorics: Landmark Essays and Controversies* (West Lafayette, IN: Parlor Press, 2010).

CHAPTER 1. "THE FIRST GIRLS' DEBATING CLUB": CREATING A LEGACY AT OBERLIN COLLEGE, 1835–1935

1. Robert Samuel Fletcher, *A History of Oberlin College: From Its Foundation through the Civil War*, vol. 2 (Oberlin: Oberlin College, 1943), 523.

2. Alice S. Rossi, ed., *The Feminist Papers: From Adams to de Beauvoir* (Lebanon, NH: Northeastern University Press, 1973), 341.

3. Karlyn Kohrs Campbell, *Women Public Speakers in the United States, 1800–1925: A Bio-Critical Sourcebook* (Westport, CT: Greenwood Publishing Group, 1993), 64; Beth Waggenspack, "Women Emerge as Speakers: Nineteenth-Century Transformations of Women's Role in Public Arenas," in *The Rhetoric of Western Thought*, ed. James L. Golden, Goodwin F. Berquist, William E. Coleman, and J. Michael Sproule (Dubuque, IA: Kendall-Hunt Publishing Company, 2004), 219; Bernard K. Duffy and Halford Ryan Ross, *American Orators before 1900: Critical Studies and Sources* (Westport, CT: Greenwood Press, 1987), 358.

4. Robert J. Connors, *Composition-Rhetoric: Backgrounds, Theory and Pedagogy* (Pittsburgh: University of Pittsburgh Press, 1997), 55. Michael D. Bartanen and Robert Littlefield's *Forensics in America: A History* (Lanham, MD: Rowman and Littlefield, 2014) credits the Oberlin Collegiate Institute as the home of the first college women's literary society, but states that it was formed in 1839 (277).

5. Lindal Buchanan, *Regendering Delivery: The Fifth Canon and Antebellum Women Rhetors* (Carbondale: Southern Illinois University Press, 2005), 56–67; Kathryn M. Conway, "Woman Suffrage and the History of Rhetoric at the Seven Sisters Colleges, 1865–1919," in *Reclaiming Rhetorica: Women in the Rhetorical Tradition*, ed. Andrea A. Lunsford (Pittsburgh: University of Pittsburgh Press, 1995), 206. Mastrangelo follows Conway's chronology in stating that "women had been engaging in debate with each other at Oberlin since 1846, when Antoinette Blackwell and Lucy Stone had created a secret debating society that later became the Young Ladies Literary Society" in "'They Argued in White Shirtwaists and Black Skirts': Women's Participation in Debate Competitions," in *Contest(ed) Writing: Reconceptualizing Literacy Competitions*, ed. Mary Lamb (Newcastle: Cambridge Scholars Publishing, 2013), 129.

6. Andrea Moore Kerr, *Lucy Stone: Speaking Out for Equality* (New Brunswick,

NJ: Rutgers University Press, 1995), 37; Elizabeth Cazden, *Antoinette Brown Blackwell: A Biography* (Old Westbury, NY: The Feminist Press, 1983).

7. Naomi Wolf, *Fire with Fire: The New Female Power and How to Use It* (New York: Vintage, 1994), 171.

8. Laurel Collins, *The Firebrand* (New York: Kensington Publication Corp., 1997), 379.

9. As Daniel Morgan Rohrer points out, the LLS was "distinctly the first 'non-male' organization in America's colleges," but similar societies for women emerged at other colleges during this period, including the Clever Girls Society of Albion College (1844) and the Ladies' Literary Union of Hillsdale College (1857), among others. See Rohrer's "Young Ladies Literary Society of Oberlin College, 1835–1860" (master's thesis, University of Wisconsin, 1969), 14–15.

10. Anne Ruggles Gere notes a general preference for the term "women" over "ladies" in her study of U.S. women's clubs, 1880–1920, and suggests that this change may have signaled a desire to shed the upper-class label of "lady" or an alignment with the feminist ideal of new womanhood. See Anne Ruggles Gere, *Intimate Practices: Literacy and Cultural Work in U.S. Women's Clubs, 1880–1920* (Urbana: University of Illinois Press, 1997), 7.

11. Later, LLS members came to appreciate the club's earlier name as part of their inheritance in a pioneering women's club: "like the willow-pattern china, it was not quite the thing for daily use, but is carefully preserved on the top shelf." "History and List of Members of the L.L.S. Society of Oberlin College (founded in 1835) and of the L.L.S. Alumnae Association," 13–14, pamphlet, RG 19/3/4, Ladies' Literary Society, Subgroup 1, Series 5. Historical File 1850–1950, Folder: Constitutions, Bylaws, History, 1874–1840, Oberlin College Archives. See also Frances Juliette Hosford, *Father Shipherd's Magna Charta: A Century of Coeducation in Oberlin College* (Boston: Marshall Jones Company, 1937), 54. For ease of understanding, I refer to the group as the LLS throughout this chapter.

12. Rachel F. Seidman, "The Ladies' Literary Society: Oberlin's Early Feminists," *Oberlin Alumni Magazine* 83, no. 4 (1987): 14.

13. For the purposes of consistency across the chapters in this book, I will refer to the debaters by the names they went by at the time of their participation in their debating organizations, even though many later changed their names after marriage. Therefore, I will refer to Antoinette Brown, even though she is better known in her later life as Antoinette Brown Blackwell. Bibliographic entries are listed as they appeared in their publications.

14. Alice Stone Blackwell, *Lucy Stone: Pioneer of Women's Rights* (Charlottesville:

University Press of Virginia, 1930), 1.

15. Seidman, "The Ladies' Literary Society," 14. The date that the society's name change became official is another point of discrepancy—some sources say 1850, while others say 1846 and 1840.

16. Again, this is difficult to delineate because debating was a principal activity in most nineteenth-century literary societies. Robert J. Connors points to Oberlin and the LLS as evidence for broad claims about the trajectory of nineteenth-century rhetorical education. While he mentions the secret society in his account, it is not clear how it functions for his argument. This is yet another reason why the various versions of the origin story are worthy of further investigation. Even though we don't know all of the details of what happened in the secret society, we do know that Stone and Brown were trying to do something different there than they did as LLS members—and that the difference in aim was oriented around the desire to effectively participate in public, persuasive speech. While my review of the extant materials does not fully settle the question of whether LLS members participated in agonistic/oral or irenic/written argumentation, the overlapping aims, practices, and members in the two societies strongly indicate that women students actively created spaces for debate during this period (and thus I side with those who have questioned the feminization of rhetoric claim).

17. I see this move as in line with what Jessica Enoch calls the "rhetorical act of remembering women," in her "Releasing Hold: Feminist Historiography without the Tradition," in *Theorizing Histories of Rhetoric*, ed. Michelle Ballif (Carbondale: Southern Illinois University Press, 2013), 58–73. While this chapter is also concerned with recovering historical materials involving women rhetors, the celebration and commemoration of the origin story by LLS members in the late nineteenth and early twentieth centuries and by contemporary scholars is an important component of the argument of this chapter.

18. Antoinette Brown Blackwell and Sarah (Mrs. Claude U.) Gilson, "Antoinette Brown Blackwell: The First Woman Minister," MS, 1909, Blackwell Family Papers, A-77, Folder 4, Sequence 47–48, Schlesinger Library, Radcliffe Institute, Harvard University, Cambridge, MA, http://pds.lib.harvard.edu/pds/view/46848362.

19. Fletcher, *A History of Oberlin College*, vol. 2, 509.

20. See Fletcher, *A History of Oberlin College*, vol. 2, 507–522, for a discussion of Oberlin's early admission process. Silas R. Badeau to R. E. Gillett, February 6, 1837, quoted in Fletcher, *A History of Oberlin College*, vol. 2, 515.

21. Roland M. Baumann, *Constructing Black Education at Oberlin College: A Documentary History* (Athens: Ohio University Press, 2010), 15. The reference to "colonists" in this quote refers to the founding of Oberlin as a colony in 1833.

22. Baumann, *Constructing Black Education at Oberlin College*, 24–25.

23. According to Oberlin College's minority student records, James Bradley was the first man of color admitted, in 1835, and Sarah J. Watson Barnett was the first woman of color admitted, in 1842. However, Lucy Stanton (discussed later) was the first woman of color to graduate from the Literary Course in 1850. Oberlin College Archives, "Catalogue and Record of Colored Students," RG 5/4/3, Minority Student Records, 1835–1862, Oberlin College Archives.

24. For example, in 1853, a white slave-owner from Tennessee wrote to request admission for a fourteen-year-old black girl. He intended to free her from slavery, but wanted her to attend Oberlin because he believed she would not be "fit for freedom without some education." H. E. Ring to J. M. Fitch, 1853, quoted in Fletcher, *A History of Oberlin College*, vol. 2, 517.

25. The best records available estimate that the number of black students enrolled at Oberlin College between 1835 and 1865 was two to five percent of the total student body, according to Ellen N. Lawson and Marlene Merrill, "The Antebellum 'Talented Thousandth': Black College Students at Oberlin before the Civil War," *Journal of Negro Education* 52, no. 2 (1983): 143, DOI: 10.2307/2295031.

26. Shipherd quoted in Hosford, *Father Shipherd's*, 5. For more on Oberlin's coeducational practices, see Carol Lasser, ed., *Educating Men and Women Together: Coeducation in a Changing World* (Urbana: University of Illinois Press, 1987).

27. Lori D. Ginzberg, "The 'Joint Education of the Sexes': Oberlin's Original Vision," in Lasser, *Educating Men and Women Together*, 69. This observation is representative of larger views on women's education at the time. That is, some people believed women were intellectually inferior, but even among those who believed that women could compete academically with men, there was not necessarily an accompanying belief that gender roles or expectations would change. As Margaret A. Nash writes, "for the most part, a belief in women's capacity for high intellectual attainment did not go hand in hand with a belief in full gender equality." See Margaret A. Nash, *Women's Education in the United States, 1780–1840* (New York: Palgrave MacMillan, 2005), 1.

28. Robert Samuel Fletcher, *A History of Oberlin College: From Its Foundation through the Civil War*, vol. 1 (Oberlin: Oberlin College, 1943), 291.

29. Fletcher, *A History of Oberlin College*, vol. 2, 512.

30. Cazden, *Antoinette Brown Blackwell*, 25.

31. Hosford, *Father Shipherd's*, 40–41.

32. Karlyn Kohrs Campbell, ed., *Man Cannot Speak for Her: A Critical Study of Early Feminist Rhetoric*, vol. 1 (New York: Praeger, 1989), 9.

33. See, for example, Carolyn Eastman, *A Nation of Speechifiers: Making an American Public After the Revolution* (Chicago: University of Chicago Press, 2009), especially chapter 2; Mary Kelley, *Learning to Stand and Speak: Women, Education, and Public Life in America's Republic* (Chapel Hill: University of North Carolina Press, 2006), chapter 4; Lindal Buchanan, *Regendering Delivery: The Fifth Canon and Antebellum Women Rhetors* (Carbondale: Southern Illinois University Press, 2005). As Buchanan puts it, "late eighteenth and early nineteenth century schoolgirls actually learned about delivery in reading classes and textbooks, which introduced them to basic principles of elocution as well as models of civic discourse" (*Regendering Delivery*, 11). See Angela G. Ray, "Rhetoric and Feminism in the Nineteenth-Century United States," in *The Oxford Handbook of Rhetorical Studies*, ed. Michael J. MacDonald (Oxford: Oxford University Press, 2017), DOI: 10.1093/oxfordhb/9780199731596.013.046.

34. Barbara Welter, "The Cult of True Womanhood: 1820–1860," *American Quarterly* 18, no. 2 (1966): 151–74. As Susan Zaeske argues, in order to substantiate their desire to address promiscuous (mixed sex) audiences, women orators in the 1830s employed rhetorics of female morality and benevolence that reinforced narrow views of femininity. She contends that emphasis hindered women's more overt political activism in the 1840s in "The 'Promiscuous Audience' Controversy and the Emergence of the Early Women's Rights Movement," *Quarterly Journal of Speech* 81, no. 2 (1995): 191–207.

35. Hosford, *Father Shipherd's*, 81.

36. Hosford, *Father Shipherd's*, 50.

37. Sarah C. Little, "Oberlin and the Education of Women," in *The Oberlin Jubilee, 1833–1883*, ed. W. G. Ballantine (Oberlin, OH: E.J. Goodrich, 1883), 151.

38. Lucy Stone, "Oberlin and Woman," in Ballantine, *The Oberlin Jubilee*, 316–17.

39. Emilie Royce Comings published this list of probable members of the original group: Emily Ingraham Briston, Mary Williams Mabbs, Sarah Capan Putnam, Elizabeth Leonard Morgan, Mary Thompson Keep, Mary Rudd Allen, Betsy Branch Hudson, Mary Adams Conklin, Frances Cochran Steele, Catherine Moore Barrows, and honorary member Marianne Parker Dascomb. Comings

also suggests that this meeting took place in Slab Hall (known more formally as Cincinnati Hall). See "The Pioneer Woman's Club," *Club Notes for Women* 8, no. III (1907): 83. Hosford explains that the lower hall of the seminary could refer to several places on campus at the time, and provides the best evidence that it was likely Oberlin Hall in her *Father Shipherd's*, 45–46.

40. Interest in the men's lyceum was reinvigorated in the 1840s.

41. Hosford, *Father Shipherd's*, 47.

42. Hosford amusingly calls this "a clumsy peace offering if intended to appease righteous wrath" in *Father Shipherd's*, 47; Comings, "Pioneer Woman's Club," 84.

43. Comings, "Pioneer Woman's Club," 84.

44. Mary Ann Adams et al. to John Keep, July 10, 1839, quoted in Fletcher, *A History of Oberlin College*, vol. 2, 761–62. As Roland Baumann explains, trustees John Keep and William Dawes were able to raise £6,000 in financial support for Oberlin from philanthropists in England and Scotland in 1839–1840. See his *Constructing Black Education*, 36.

45. *Oberlin Evangelist*, September 1, 1858, 141.

46. Hosford, *Father Shipherd's*, 26–27.

47. Minutes of the Young Ladies' Association of Oberlin College Institute, 1846–1850, June 16 and June 23, 1847, RG 19/3/4, Series 1, Box 1, Oberlin College Archives. Hereafter cited as Minutes of the LLS.

48. Minutes of the LLS. "Ladies' Literary Society" was used in the late 1840s, but was not officially instituted in the minutes of the organization until 1850.

49. Though membership was restricted to "young ladies," the society was in regular conversation with men's groups and even occasionally attended public meetings at their invitation. For example, in 1846, the Young Men's Lyceum extended an invitation to attend its public meeting in the chapel. The LLS deliberated and voted to accept the invitation. Minutes of the LLS, May 6, 1846.

50. Minutes of the LLS, June 27, 1846.

51. Minutes of the LLS, February 26, 1847.

52. Minutes of the LLS, June 2, 1847.

53. Emilie Royce Comings and Frances J. Hosford, "The Pioneer Women of Oberlin College," *Oberlin Alumni Magazine*, March 1927, 11. RG 19/3/4/, Folder: LLS Const., Bylaws, Box 1, Oberlin College Archives.

54. "History and List of Members," 15.

55. Recall that Vassar also appears to have dwelled on this hair-splitting distinction between written or sedate oral communication on one hand and oral

argumentation and debate on the other.

56. Hosford, *Father Shipherd's*, 94.

57. Blackwell, *Lucy Stone*, 49. See pages 42–61 for a thorough account of Stone's time at Oberlin.

58. Cazden estimates that more than ten percent of the residents of Oberlin were black or multiracial when Brown arrived in Oberlin in 1846 (*Antoinette Brown Blackwell*, 23). Ellen NicKenzie Lawson notes that the number rose to twenty percent in 1860. See her "Observations on an Antebellum Interracial Utopia," *Oberlin College Observer*, March 4, 1982, 4. RG 30/157, Ellen Lawson-Marlene Merrill Papers, Folder: Town of Oberlin, Box 3, Oberlin College Archives.

59. J. Brent Morris, *Oberlin, Hotbed of Abolitionism: College, Community, and the Fight for Freedom and Equality in Antebellum America* (Chapel Hill: University of North Carolina Press, 2014), 2.

60. Blackwell, *Lucy Stone*, 51.

61. Morris, *Oberlin*, 85.

62. Carol Lasser and Marlene Deahl Merrill, *Friends and Sisters: Letters Between Lucy Stone and Antoinette Brown Blackwell, 1846–93* (Urbana: University of Illinois Press, 1987), 9.

63. Cazden, *Antoinette Brown Blackwell*, 25.

64. Lucy Stone married Henry Blackwell (Samuel's brother) in 1855, but famously chose not to change her last name upon marriage. Even today, a "Lucy Stoner" refers to a woman who keeps her surname. It is therefore a slightly amusing but cruel joke of history that I came across a folder with newspaper clippings about Stone labeled "Mrs. Henry Blackwell" in the Oberlin College Archives. Antoinette Brown became known as Antoinette Brown Blackwell when she married Samuel Blackwell in 1856.

65. Antoinette Brown Blackwell remembers the debating society forming in secret during her first year at Oberlin, though she does not specify when during the year it happened. The chronology is particularly difficult to piece together, as she actually reports her entry into Oberlin as 1845 in some places and 1846 in others. See Antoinette Brown Blackwell, "Reminiscences of Early Oberlin," February 1918, Blackwell Family Papers, 1784–1944, 1832–1939, Folder 1, Schlesinger Library. Sequence 25 and 30 demonstrate the discrepancies in reported entry dates; I believe the correct time for Brown's arrival is winter/spring 1846. Some sources claim that the secret debating society was founded in May 1846. This is entirely possible; however, this claim appears to be based primarily on seeing the

LLS and the secret society as the same group, because the extant minutes of the LLS also begin in May 1846. For example, Cazden's biography *Antoinette Brown Blackwell* describes the LLS as a secret society that met in the woods beginning in May 1846 (28–29) and says that the Thome rhetoric class incident (described later) occurred the following fall. My hypothesis is that the secret debate society was founded in late 1846 or early 1847, after the September 1846 visit of Abby Kelley Foster and Stephen Foster. This event underlined the need for Stone to gain practical public speaking experience as her post-graduation goal of being a lecturer crystallized.

66. Stone and Brown experienced literary society activities in other locales, so they had some basis of comparison with the LLS. Stone was enrolled in the Wilbraham Academy in Massachusetts for a short time before she came to Oberlin. On June 18, 1840, she wrote from Wilbraham to her brother, referencing a literary society there: "it was decided in our Literary Society the other day that ladies ought to mingle in politics, go to Congress, etc., etc. What do you think of that?" (quoted in Blackwell, *Lucy Stone*, 40). In the winter of 1847, Brown taught at the Rochester Academy in Rochester, Michigan. During that time, she wrote to Stone to tell about her experience with a literary society there. She reports:

> We have a good constitution & the order of exersises thus far have been the following Two composition, three declamation, two other composition, a discussion contents of the budget box . . . There are *some* young ladies here of superior talent—*all take a deep* interest in the exercises & I must say I have never before improved so rapidly in my life in the use of the tongue. How I wish we had such a society at Oberlin such exercises & such fearlessness & eagerness in the path of improvement. (Brown to Stone, quoted in Lasser and Merrill, *Friends and Sisters*, 20)

Lasser and Merrill surmise that this experience may have inspired the creation of the secret debating society at Oberlin, though others believe the secret society began in 1846, as I have already detailed. Lisa M. Gring-Pemble explores this version of chronology in footnote 10 of her "Writing Themselves into Consciousness: Creating a Rhetorical Bridge between Public and Private Spheres," *Quarterly Journal of Speech* 84, no. 1 (1998): 41–61. The last sentence of the letter certainly seems to support Lasser and Merrill's interpretation if we view it in terms of a comparison of the Rochester society to the LLS, where

Brown was highlighting what a literary society *could* be. However, if we consider that Brown and Stone treated the secret society and the LLS as separate groups, I do not think that this letter bears definitively on the origin date of the secret society. Brown's "Reminiscences of Early Oberlin" (sequence 25) indicates that the secret society was founded during her first year at Oberlin (1846), and though her writing style does not allow for a clear chronology of events, she does write about the teaching position in Rochester after discussing the debating society in the woods and the incident in Thome's classroom.

67. Lillian O'Connor did some remarkable archival sleuthing to uncover this insight—she went back in the charging records of the library and matched the book number to Stone's account. According to O'Connor, Stone checked out the Blair book for two weeks and paid a fine upon its return. *Pioneer Women Orators: Rhetoric in the Ante-bellum Reform Movement* (New York: Columbia University Press, 1954), 69.

68. Sally G. McMillen, *Lucy Stone: An Unapologetic Life* (Oxford: Oxford University Press, 2015), 61. A transcript of Stone's speech is available in the Robert S. Fletcher Papers, RG 30/24, Oberlin College Archives. Stone was called before the Ladies' Board and questioned about the speech the next day (Blackwell, *Lucy Stone*, 63). That Stone's speech would have been delivered in front of a "mixed audience" in terms of both race and sex is the subject of a fictionalized exchange between Stone, Brown, and Ladies' Board director Mrs. Mahan in Maud Wood Park's *Lucy Stone: A Chronicle Play* (Boston: Walter H. Baker Company, 1938), 39.

69. For a fuller account of the Foster lectures in Oberlin, see Ron Gorman, "William Lloyd Garrison and Frederick Douglass Debate in Oberlin," *Oberlin Heritage Center* (blog), June 19, 2013, http://www.oberlinheritagecenter.org/blog/tag/abby-kelley-foster.

70. Blackwell, *Lucy Stone*, 60–61. This quote, and several quotes throughout this book, use outdated terms to refer to people of color. I reproduce the terms as they appeared in the original texts for the sake of historical accuracy, but want to make clear that I do not endorse this terminology.

71. Jens Brockmeier, *Beyond the Archive: Memory, Narrative, and the Autobiographical Process* (Oxford: Oxford University Press, 2015), 14.

72. Here, we describe the translation of memory to history, as described by Pierre Nora in "Between Memory and History: Les Lieux de Mémoire," *Representations* 26 (1989): 7–24. As Nora writes, "Memory, insofar as it is affective and magical, only accommodates the facts that suit it; it nourishes recollections that might be

out of focus or telescopic, global or detached, particular or symbolic—responsive to each avenue of conveyance or phenomenal screen, to every censorship or projection. History, because it is an intellectual and secular production, calls for analysis and criticism" (8–9).

73. Stone and Brown graduated in 1847, though Brown studied at Oberlin's theological seminary until 1850. She was permitted to sit in on the classes, but was not awarded a degree because of her sex. Oberlin later awarded Brown an honorary Master of Arts degree (1878) and an honorary Doctor of Divinity (1908). The General Federation of Women's Clubs met at Chicago's Palmer House, May 11–13, 1892 (Lasser and Merrill, *Friends and Sisters*, 262).

74. Brown Blackwell to Stone, April 20, 1892, quoted in Lasser and Merrill, *Friends and Sisters*, 260–61.

75. Brown Blackwell to Stone, April 20, 1892, quoted in Lasser and Merrill, *Friends and Sisters*, 261.

76. Stone to Brown Blackwell, May 5, 1892, quoted in Lasser and Merrill, *Friends and Sisters*, 263. Historian Mary Kelley derived the title of her book from this exchange—*Learning to Stand and Speak: Women, Education, and Public Life in America's Republic*. Like Brown, Lettice Smith (Holmes) stayed on to study theology at Oberlin after graduating.

77. Lasser and Merrill believe that this reference is to John Mercer Langston, but that it "appears to be in error, however, since Langston's father, a white planter, died when the child was quite young, and while Langston attended Oberlin, he was under the care of a guardian" (*Friends and Sisters*, 263). Langston's parents were Captain Ralph Quarles, a Virginia plantation owner, and Lucy Jane Langston, a woman of Native American and African descent, who was enslaved by Quarles until 1806. Both parents died when John Mercer Langston was a small child. See William F. Cheek and Aimee Lee Cheek, *John Mercer Langston and the Fight for Black Freedom, 1829–1865* (Urbana: University of Illinois Press, 1989), 13–19.

78. I have not been able to locate a script for Brown's speech, but Alice Stone Blackwell attended the meeting of the Grand Federation of Women's Clubs in order to report back in *The Woman's Column*. Her summary and select quotations from the speech provide a good sense of what Brown ultimately decided to share with the crowd. See Alice Stone Blackwell, "The First Girls' Debating Club," *The Woman's Column*, May 29, 1892. In preparing for the speech, Brown admitted that her remarks would likely be off the cuff, confiding to Stone that "Even Mrs.

Brown does not know at all what I am to say; but it will come in part to the subject and at just the right place." Brown Blackwell to Stone, April 20, 1892, quoted in Lasser and Merrill, *Friends and Sisters*, 262.

79. Quoted in "The Barrier Seemed Impassable," *Oberlin Today*, 1963, 10–11. Antoinette Brown Blackwell's obituary notes: "while at Oberlin, she and Lucy Stone, when forbidden to participate with the young men in the debating societies, organized the first debating society ever formed among college girls." See "Antoinette L. Brown Blackwell," *The Christian Register*, November 24, 1921, 19.

80. Joan Wallach Scott, *The Fantasy of Feminist History* (Durham, NC: Duke University Press, 2011), 51. The chapter originally appeared as "Fantasy Echo: History and the Construction of Identity," *Critical Inquiry* 27, no. 2 (2001): 284–304.

81. Scott, *The Fantasy*, 52.

82. Scott, *The Fantasy*, 48–49.

83. Daphne Spain, *Gendered Spaces* (Chapel Hill: University of North Carolina Press, 1992), 4. Spain is drawing from Helen Lefkowitz Horowitz's *Alma Mater: Design and Experience in the Women's Colleges from Their Nineteenth Century Beginnings to the 1930s*, 2nd ed. (Amherst: University of Massachusetts Press, 1992), 4.

84. Spain, *Gendered Spaces*, 158–59. See also Spain's discussion of Oberlin in her book (155–57). My undergraduate alma mater, Mary Washington, is a good example of a "sister college." It was founded as the State Normal and Industrial School for Women in Fredericksburg, Virginia; was subsequently a women's college, a counterpart to the University of Virginia in Charlottesville; and is now a coeducational institution.

85. Brown Blackwell and Gilson MS., sequence 57. Despite these seemingly draconian rules, it is clear that Stone's movement around the village always pushed the boundaries of acceptability. Though Oberlin women were not supposed to walk with men for leisure, she reportedly walked to Liberty School classes with Robert, one of her African American students (Morris, *Oberlin*, 85–86).

86. Fletcher, *A History of Oberlin College*, vol. 2, 819.

87. Pierre Bourdieu, *Language and Symbolic Power*, translated by Gino Raymond and Matthew Adamson (Cambridge: Polity Press, 1991), 70.

88. In her 1918 "Reminiscences of Early Oberlin," Brown wrote about the gatherings in the woods, noting that Helen Cook and Lettice Smith attended (although

Smith, she noted, was usually a listener rather than a speaker at such meetings).
Here, she also gives a slightly different sense of Thome's role, suggesting that the
creation of the secret society predated the controversy in the rhetoric class. In
this telling, Thome opposed having women take part in the debates, but excused
them from having to be an audience for the men and offered to provide them with
a separate class. Brown and Stone declined, stating, "we preferred our debating
class in the woods, considering his offer unfair to us and to him" (seq. 25). This
version of events inverts the chronology in Alice Stone Blackwell's account, which
held that the incident in the rhetoric class hastened the creation of the secret
club. Which of these versions is ultimately correct? It is difficult to say, although
we can infer that Thome's classroom served distinctly as a counterpart to the
skills learned in the secret society.

89. Nan Johnson, *Gender and Rhetorical Space in American Life, 1866–1910*
(Carbondale: Southern Illinois University Press, 2002), 14.

90. Cazden, *Antoinette Brown Blackwell*, 22.

91. Scott, *The Fantasy*, 54, 57.

92. Scott, *The Fantasy*, 55.

93. Fletcher describes the space as "one sylvan retreat where the student nymph
might wander" in *A History of Oberlin College*, vol. 2, 819.

94. On argument as self-risk, see Maurice Natanson, "The Claims of Immediacy," in
Philosophy, Rhetoric, and Argumentation, ed. Maurice Natanson and Henry W.
Johnstone Jr. (University Park: Pennsylvania State University Press, 1962), 10–18;
Douglas Ehninger, "Argument as Method: Its Nature, Its Limitations, and Its
Uses," *Speech Monographs* 37, no. 2 (1970): 101–10.

95. Ehninger, "Argument as Method," 109. My paraphrase avoids the gendered
language in the original article.

96. Blackwell, *Lucy Stone*, 60–61.

97. Jasmine Nichole Cobb, *Picture Freedom: Remaking Black Visuality in the Early
Nineteenth Century* (New York: New York University Press, 2015), 16.

98. Cobb, *Picture Freedom*, 17. In Cobb's study, the parlor is both a place of fantasy
and nightmare, a case she compellingly makes through an analysis of the visual
practices and material objects found there. Significantly, she contrasts "the mobility
symbolized in the slave ship" with the "stagnant (but not static) parlor" (17).

99. Lawson, "Observations on an Antebellum," 3–4.

100. Cheek and Cheek, *John Mercer Langston*, 287.

101. Cobb, *Picture Freedom*, 15. For work on the communicative elements of the

contact space, see Jake Harwood, "The Contact Space: A Novel Framework for Intergroup Contact Research," *Journal of Language and Social Psychology* 29, no. 2 (2010): 144–77.

102. Phyllis M. Belt-Beyan, *The Emergence of African American Literacy Traditions: Family and Community Efforts in the Nineteenth Century* (Westport, CT: Praeger, 2004), 115–16.

103. The students listed as "females" and "colored students" during this period are Lucy A. Stanton (1846–1850), Mahala McGuire (1846–1847), Charlotte Henson (1846–1847), Josephine Miner (1846–1857), Elizabeth P. Taylor (1846–1847), Abigail A. Lyon (1846–1847), and Louisa Holman (1847–1851). Oberlin College Archives, "Catalogue and Record of Colored Students," RG 5/4/3, Minority Student Records, 1835–1862, Oberlin College Archives. I cannot say whether all of these students were present at Oberlin and/or could have even been invited to participate since the precise dates and meeting times of the secret debating society are unknown. However, Stanton was clearly a member (and eventually, president) of the LLS.

104. Minutes of the LLS, September 19, 1849.

105. While her name is usually spelled "Lucy," in official documents, Stanton sometimes wrote her name as "Lucie."

106. Case Western Reserve University and the Western Reserve Historical Society, "Brown, John," *Encyclopedia of Cleveland History*, http://ech.case.edu/cgi/article.pl?id=BJ9.

107. Minutes of the LLS, August 18, 1847; March 29, 1848. Stanton is first mentioned in the LLS minutes in August of 1847, which would have been the same time that Brown and Stone were graduating. While her time at Oberlin certainly overlapped with Stone and Brown, it is not clear whether they attended LLS meetings together.

108. John White Chadwick, ed., *A Life For Liberty: Anti-Slavery and Other Letters of Sallie Holley* (New York: G.P. Putnam's Sons, 1899), 61.

109. According to a new constitution adopted April 10, 1850.

110. "Oberlin Commencement Exercises," *Oberlin Evangelist*, September 11, 1850, 149.

111. The speech text, "A Plea for the Oppressed," is reproduced in full in the *Oberlin Evangelist*, December 17, 1850, 208.

112. "Commencement Exercises," *Oberlin Evangelist*, November 6, 1850, 180.

113. "Commencement Exercises," *Oberlin Evangelist*, November 6, 1850, 180.

114. There is much more to the story of Lucy Stanton Day Sessions. For a more

complete biographical sketch, see Ellen NicKenzie Lawson, *The Three Sarahs: Documents of Antebellum Black College Women* (New York: Edwin Mellen Press, 1984), chapter 4.

115. Minutes of the LLS, May 1, 1850.

116. Minutes of the LLS, March 31, 1852; April 9, 1952, April 21, 1852.

117. Minutes of the Aeolioian Literary Society, 1855–1860, RG 19/3/4, Box 1, Subgroup II. Aeolioian Literary Society Series 1. Oberlin College Archives. Hereafter cited as Minutes of the Aeolioian. Topics referenced here took place in the Minutes of Aeolioian, November 3, 1857; July 7, 1857; and May 19, 1857, respectively.

118. Comings, "Pioneer Woman's Club," 87.

119. Minutes of the LLS, April 16, 1873; May 29, 1872; July 18, 1866.

120. Little, "Oberlin and the Education of Women," 151.

121. Marlene Deahl Merrill, "Justice, Simple Justice: Women at Oberlin 1837–1987," *Oberlin Alumni Magazine*, Fall 1987, 13.

122. Mary Church Terrell tells of the vibrancy of this period at Oberlin in her book, *A Colored Woman in a White World* (Washington, DC: Ransdell Publishers, 1940; New York: G. K. Hall & Co., 1996), 44–45. Citations refer to the GK Hall & Co. edition. For a discussion of the lyceum as a person-shaping and culture-creating practice, see Angela G. Ray, *The Lyceum and Public Culture in the Nineteenth-Century United States* (East Lansing: Michigan State University Press, 2005), 8–9.

123. Church Terrell, *A Colored Woman*, 45.

124. Church Terrell, *A Colored Woman*, 44.

125. Helen Martin Rood, speech before the LLS entitled "A Great Heritage," Ladies' Literary Society, Subgroup 1: Ladies' Literary Society, Series 6. Alumnae Association, 1904–1953, 19/3/4, Box 1, Folder 3: LLS Alumnae, Oberlin College Archives.

126. Comings, "Pioneer Woman's Club," 84.

127. Hosford, *Father Shipherd's*, 47.

128. Minutes of the LLS, April 8, 1856.

129. Minutes of the Aeolioian, October 19, 1858. It is not clear from the minutes whether they were debating about the LLS, *their* literary society, or women's literary societies in general. They may have been referring to the LLS and the Aeolioian as one ladies' literary society because they shared the room.

130. Comings, "Pioneer Woman's Club," 84–85. An image of the room is included on page 85 of this publication.

131. *General Catalogue of Oberlin College, 1833–1909* (Oberlin: Oberlin College, 1909),

90.

132. Comings, "Pioneer Woman's Club," 85. A photograph of the room is included on page 85 of this publication.

133. Hosford, *Father Shipherd's*, 48–49.

134. A love feast is a gathering that is organized around a meal and aimed at Christian fellowship.

135. Centennial Celebration of the LLS, document, June 17, 1935, RG 19/3/4, Ladies' Literary Society, Box 1, Series 5, Historical file, 1850–1950, Folder 4, Oberlin College Archives. Underlining (shown here as italics) in original document (skit script).

136. Centennial Celebration of the LLS, document, June 17, 1935.

137. Scott, *The Fantasy*, 54.

138. Ella C. Parmenter, speech to the LLS and Aeolioan Women's Literary Society Tea, June 7, 1952, RG 19/3/4, Ladies' Literary Society, Box 1, Series 6, Folder: Ladies' Literary Society—LLS–Aeolioian Alumnae Association, 1949–1953, Oberlin College Archives.

139. Lisa Tetrault, *The Myth of Seneca Falls: Memory and the Women's Suffrage Movement, 1848–1898* (Chapel Hill: University of North Carolina Press, 2014), 3.

140. Tetrault, *Myth of Seneca Falls*, 5.

CHAPTER 2. "WOMEN OF INFINITE VARIETY":
THE LADIES' EDINBURGH DEBATING SOCIETY AS AN
INTERGENERATIONAL ARGUMENT CULTURE, 1865–1935

1. Barbara Warnick, *The Sixth Canon: Belletristic Rhetorical Theory and Its French Antecedents* (Columbia: University of South Carolina Press, 1993), 4.

2. Blair, Campbell, and Richard Whately's writings served as primary textbooks in rhetorical education for early American university students (see Nan Johnson, *Nineteenth-Century Rhetorical Education in North America* [Carbondale: Southern Illinois University Press, 1991], 19). Martin J. Medhurst argues that the 1783 publication of Blair's *Lectures on Rhetoric and Belles Lettres* was responsible for a move away from rhetoric and oratory in favor of written rhetoric in the late-eighteenth- and early-nineteenth-century United States. See Martin J. Medhurst, "The History of Public Address as an Academic Study," in *The Handbook of Rhetoric and Public Address*, ed. Shawn J. Parry-Giles and J. Michael Hogan (Oxford: Wiley-Blackwell, 2010), 19–20. Herman Cohen suggests that the Morrill

Act of 1863, which allowed for the establishments of land-grant colleges, caused a shift toward mass education in the United States that called for an alternative to the rhetorical masterworks of theorists like Blair and Whately. He traces the creation of new instructional textbooks, including the English composition text and argumentation and debate handbooks, as attempts by faculty members to better meet the needs of the American student (Cohen, *The History of Speech Communication: The Emergence of a Discipline, 1915–1945* [Washington, DC: Speech Communication Association, 1994], 13–15). For a discussion of the effect of Blair's work in Europe, see Don Abbott, "Blair 'Abroad': The European Reception of the *Lectures on Rhetoric and Belles Lettres*," in *Scottish Rhetoric and Its Influences*, ed. Lynée Lewis Gaillet (Mahwah, NJ: Lawrence Erlbaum Associates, 1998), 67–78.

3. Winifred Bryan Horner identifies this period as "the missing link" in the history of Western rhetoric and education. She works to improve the accessibility of Scottish archives in her book, *Nineteenth-Century Scottish Rhetoric: The American Connection* (Carbondale: Southern Illinois University Press, 1993), 1–15.

4. Kate Kelman's work has focused on the reading and writing practices of the LEDS, including the publication on *The Attempt*. See Kate Kelman, "'Self-Culture': The Educative Reading Pursuits of the Ladies of Edinburgh, 1865–1885," *Victorian Periodicals Review* 36, no. 1 (2003): 59–75. The LEDS is cited in other feminist histories of Scotland, primarily because its members were also active in other associations and movements, but Kelman's work is the only other scholarly publication I am aware of that does an in-depth study of the society.

5. "Letter from the Editors," *Ladies' Edinburgh Magazine* 6, 1880, 570.

6. On December 2, 1882, a motion requesting "the minutes include a short account of the debate" was formally adopted by the LEDS.

7. Lettice Milne Rae, ed., *Ladies in Debate: Being a History of the Ladies' Edinburgh Debating Society, 1865–1935* (Edinburgh: Oliver and Boyd, 1936).

8. See Jürgen Habermas, "The Model Case of British Development," in *The Structural Transformation of the Public Sphere: An Inquiry into a Category of Bourgeois Society*, trans. Thomas Burger (Cambridge: MIT Press, 1991), 57–66.

9. R. J. Morris, "Clubs, Societies, and Associations," in *The Cambridge Social History of Britain 1750–1950*, vol. 3, *Social Agencies and Institutions*, ed. F. M. L. Thompson (Cambridge: Cambridge University, 1990), 400.

10. Morris, "Clubs, Societies, and Associations," 395. Morris notes that prior to 1780, "there was a brief glimpse of collective female action in the public sphere before

the flood tide of evangelicalism swept the gender frontier back into the private and the domestic" ("Clubs, Societies, and Associations," 397). For example, The Original Female Society held a festival in 1775 in Litchfield, England. See also John Money, "Taverns, Coffee Houses, and Clubs: Local Politics and Popular Articulacy in the Birmingham Area, in the Age of the American Revolution," *The Historical Journal* 14, no. 1 (1971): 15–47; Brian Cowan, "What Was Masculine about the Public Sphere? Gender and the Coffeehouse Milieu in Post-Restoration England," *History Workshop Journal* 51 (2001): 127–57, DOI: 10.1093/hwj/2001.51.127.

11. Mary Thale, "Women in London Debating Societies in 1780," *Gender & History* 7, no. 1 (1995): 5.

12. Mary Thale, "The Case of the British Inquisition: Money and Women in Mid-Eighteenth Century London Debating Societies," *Albion: A Quarterly Journal Concerned with British Studies* 31, no. 1 (1999): 32.

13. Trevor Fawcett, "Eighteenth-Century Debating Societies," *Journal for Eighteenth-Century Studies* 3, no. 3 (1980): 216–29. For an additional account of the Robin Hood Society, see Mary Thale, "The Robin Hood Society: Debating in Eighteenth-Century London," *London Journal* 22, no. 1 (1997): 33–50, DOI: 10.1179/ldn.1997.22.1.33. In a short-lived venture in 1752, Robin Hood Society entrepreneurs attempted to create space appropriate for high class and high paying women audience members: "an attempt towards the Introduction of a new rational Entertainment [consisting of] an occasional Prologue . . . a Pangyrick . . . Propositions . . . to be debated, to conclude with an Occasional epilogue; the whole interspersed with several grand Concertos, Overtures, and Full Pieces of Music." Advertisement for an event held on February 20, 1752, in the *General Advertiser*, quoted by Thale, "The Case," 34–35.

14. For more on these societies, and a discussion of the reaction to women's attendance at debates, see Davis J. McElroy's study, *Scotland's Age of Improvement: A Survey of Eighteenth-Century Literary Clubs and Societies* (Pullman: Washington State University Press, 1969), 91–92.

15. Historians Donna T. Andrew and Mary Thale have been at the forefront of recovering this aspect of gender history in England. See Andrew's "'The Passion for Public Speaking': Women's Debating Societies," in *Women & History: Voices of Early Modern England*, ed. Valerie Frith (Toronto: Coach House Press, 1995), 165–88; and Thale's "Women in London," 5–24.

16. Hugh Blair, "Means of Improving Eloquence," in *Lectures on Rhetoric and Belles*

Lettres (New York: James and John Harper, 1826), 344.

17. Blair, "Means of Improving Eloquence," 344.

18. Susan Zaeske, "The 'Promiscuous Audience' Controversy and the Emergence of the Early Women's Rights Movement," *Quarterly Journal of Speech* 81, no. 2 (1995): 192–93.

19. Blair, "Means of Improving," 344.

20. Stephen H. Browne, "Satirizing the Debating Society in Eighteenth-Century England," *Argumentation and Advocacy* 26, no. 1 (1989): 4, 10. See also Stephen H. Browne, "Satirizing Women's Speech in Eighteenth-Century England," *Rhetoric Society Quarterly* 22, no. 3 (1992): 20–29.

21. Gerald Kahan, *George Alexander Stevens & The Lecture on Heads* (Athens: University of Georgia Press, 1984), 29.

22. George Alexander Stevens, *A Lecture on Heads* (London: W. Wilson, 1812), 33–34. Spelling in original text. By comparison, Stevens also discusses a "Male moderator, and president of eloquence" at a school dedicated to oratory that "can convert a cobler into a Demosthenes; make him thunder over porter, and lighten over gin, and qualify him to speak on either side of the question in the house of commons, who has not so much as a single vote for a member of parliament" (*Lecture on Heads*, 35). He imagines the male moderator interacting with the female moderator when she takes over a debate. See Stevens, *Lecture on Heads*, 36–37.

23. Similarly, Lewis Goldsmith Stewarton recounts the tale of a women's debating club in Paris that dramatically claims that women are integral to republican government in "Female Clubs," in *The Female Revolutionary Plutarch*, vol. 1 (London: J&W Smith, 1908), 251–71.

24. For more on these societies, see Sarah Wiggins, "Gendered Spaces and Political Identity: Debating Societies in English Women's Colleges, 1890–1914," *Women's History Review* 18, no. 5 (2009): 737–52; and L. Jill Lamberton, "Claiming an Education: The Transatlantic Performance and Circulation of Individual Identities in College Women's Writing" (PhD diss., University of Michigan, 2007), especially chapter 4.

25. "Notes at a Ladies' Debating Society," *The Graphic*, October 13, 1888, 400. British Newspaper Archive. Unfortunately, the issue does not name the artist, nor does it provide information about which ladies' debating society the caricature represents. However, "Notes at a Ladies' Debating Society" showcases the vibrancy of their meetings.

26. Eugene Chenoweth and Uvieja Good, "The Rise of Women and the Fall of Tradition in Union Debating at Oxford and Cambridge," *Speaker & Gavel* 9, no. 2 (1972): 31–32.

27. J. W. Thompson to Lord Belper, November 25, 1878, University College London: Debating Society Minute Books, MS ADD 78, A.1, Special Collections, University College London. Carol Dyhouse reviews other developments in the Women's Debating Society at University College London in *No Distinction of Sex? Women in British Universities, 1870–1939* (London: University College London Press, 1995), 206–8.

28. Nigel Shepley, *Women of Independent Mind: St. George's School, Edinburgh, and the Campaign for Women's Education, 1888–1988* (Edinburgh: St. George's School for Girls, 1988), 2.

29. Shepley, *Women of Independent Mind*, 2.

30. Jane McDermid, *The Schooling of Working-Class Girls in Victorian Scotland: Gender, Education, and Identity* (London: Routledge, 2005), 2.

31. Rosalind K. Marshall, *Virgins and Viragos: A History of Women in Scotland from 1080 to 1980* (Chicago: Academy Chicago, 1983), 254.

32. Shepley, *Women of Independent Mind*, 2.

33. Beatrice W. Welsh, *After the Dawn: A Record of the Pioneer Work in Edinburgh for the Higher Education of Women* (Edinburgh: Oliver and Boyd, 1939), 1.

34. Lettice Milne Rae, "From Beginning to End," in Rae, *Ladies in Debate*, 16.

35. Sarah Mair, "Foreword," in Rae, *Ladies in Debate*, 9.

36. Rae, "From Beginning to End," 17.

37. Lindal Buchanan, "Sarah Siddons and Her Place in Rhetorical History," *Rhetorica* 25, no. 4 (2007): 413–34. For more on Sarah Siddons, see Judith Pascoe's thoroughly enjoyable book, *The Sarah Siddons Audio Files: Romanticism and the Lost Voice* (Ann Arbor: University of Michigan Press, 2013).

38. Rae, "From Beginning to End," 15. This was presumably during the Railway Mania of the 1840s, when many families invested large sums of money before railway speculation collapsed.

39. Rae, "From Beginning to End," 17.

40. Vanessa D. Dickerson, "Introduction: Housekeeping and Housekept Angels," in *Keeping the Victorian House: A Collection of Essays*, ed. Vanessa D. Dickerson, 2nd ed. (New York: Routledge, 2016), xii.

41. Dickerson, "Introduction: Housekeeping and Housekept Angels," xii–xiv.

42. Inga Bryden and Janet Floyd, "Introduction," in *Domestic Space: Reading the*

Nineteenth-Century Interior, ed. Inga Bryden and Janet Floyd (Manchester: Manchester University Press, 1999), 2.

43. Marshall, *Virgins and Viragos*, 247.

44. Number 29 Abercromby Place has since been combined with 30 Abercromby Place and now houses the Royal Scots Club, a lavish meeting space, hotel, and restaurant.

45. Helen Neaves, "Down the Vista of Years," in Rae, *Ladies in Debate*, 51.

46. Mair quoted Rae, "From Beginning to End," 16–17.

47. Mair quoted in Rae, "From Beginning to End," 18.

48. Mair quoted in Rae, "From Beginning to End," 19.

49. Mair quoted in Rae, "From Beginning to End," 20.

50. Mair quoted Rae, "From Beginning to End," 20–21.

51. Duke Wellington's celebration of the Battle of Waterloo, to be precise. The print is William Salter's 1836 rendering of the Waterloo Banquet at Apsley House.

52. Rae, "From Beginning to End," 22.

53. Kelman, "Self-Culture," 59–75.

54. Charlotte Carmichael Stopes, "Literary Societies for Women," in *Feminism and the Periodical Press, 1900–1918*, vol. 3, ed. Lucy Delap, Maria DiCenzo, and Leila Ryan (New York: Routledge, 2006). The article was originally printed in *The Englishwoman's Review*, July 15, 1902, 158–65.

55. Mair, "Foreword," 7–8.

56. Siân Reynolds, *Paris–Edinburgh: Cultural Connections in the Belle Époque* (Burlington, VT: Ashgate Publishing, 2007), 167.

57. Minutes of the Ladies' Edinburgh Debating Society, June 3, 1899, MS 1727, National Library of Scotland Manuscript Collections, Edinburgh, Scotland (1865–1935 minutes available as NLS MS.1723–1733, ff.x-z, hereafter cited as Minutes of the LEDS).

58. Rae, "From Beginning to End," 13.

59. Mrs. Arnott, "Memories of the Crowded Years," in Rae, *Ladies in Debate*, 62.

60. Rae, "From Beginning to End," 15.

61. See, for example, Elizabeth Crawford, "Sarah Elizabeth Siddons Mair," in *The Women's Suffrage Movement: A Reference Guide, 1866–1928* (London: University College London Press, 1999), 365–66; Dyhouse, *No Distinction of Sex?* 209.

62. See Welsh's *After the Dawn* and Shepley's *Women of Independent Mind* for more detailed histories of the educational campaign.

63. Rae, *Ladies in Debate*, 32.

64. Minutes of the LEDS, May 7, 1887, NLS MS 1726. Adela Dundas came from a prominent Edinburgh family and was a talented artist.

65. Lettice Milne Rae, "Satellites Around the Planet," in Rae, *Ladies in Debate*, 42.

66. B. Evelyn Westbrook, "Debating Both Sides: What Nineteenth-Century College Literary Societies Can Teach Us about Critical Pedagogies," *Rhetoric Review* 21, no. 4 (2002): 353, DOI:10.1207/S15327981RR2104_2.

67. Neaves, "Down the Vista of Years," 51.

68. Such a claim obviously begs for comparison to Oberlin's LLS. My sense is that Oberlin's LLS was likely susceptible to at least some of Neaves's critique, as its members were less diverse in age and background than the LEDS debaters. However, the minutes do not reflect the quality of argumentation when Oberlin women debated about controversial topics, and the LLS had its distinct merits. The monthly meeting schedule of the LEDS may have helped to hedge against some of the difficulties encountered by societies that met more frequently.

69. Minutes of the LEDS, October 19, 1877. NLS MS 1725.

70. Rae, "From Beginning to End," 19. I refer to the debaters by first and last name when they are available. However, the meeting minutes and membership rolls often do not include their first names (only Mrs. or Miss and their last names).

71. G. Thomas Goodnight, "Generational Argument," in *Argumentation: Across the Lines of Discipline, Proceedings of the Conference on Argumentation 1986*, ed. Frans H. van Eemeren, Rob Grootendorst, J. Anthony Blair, and Charles A. Willard (Dordrecht, Netherlands: Foris Publications, 1987), 140.

72. Here, Goodnight draws from Mannheim's notion of "generational units" where people occupying the same spatiotemporal location are marked by opposition. Goodnight says such arguments "define the domain of disagreement to be taken seriously" ("Generational Argument," 138).

73. These axes of generational thinking (life experience and argument experience) emerged as a theme in the LEDS minutes. The term *generational* usually connotes age-based attitudes, and this can be problematic. Lisa Maria Hogeland points out this problem in the context of feminist waves—attitudes toward feminism are often cross-cutting across age groups, and it is frustrating to be grouped into second- or third-wave feminism based solely on when a person was born ("Against Generational Thinking, or, Some Things Third Wave Feminism Isn't," *Women's Studies in Communication* 24, no. 1 [2001]: 107–21). Goodnight's approach also works against an overly simplistic grouping of people by age.

74. Mary Paterson, "Impressions of Two Late-Comers," in Rae, *Ladies in Debate*,

66–67.

75. This is one salient feature of an argument culture identified by David Zarefsky in "What Does an Argument Culture Look Like?," *Informal Logic* 29, no. 3 (2009): 296–308, http://ojs.uwindsor.ca/ojs/leddy/index.php/informal_logic/article/view/2845/2277.

76. Excepting the summer months, when the Mair family traveled abroad.

77. Paterson, "Impressions of Two Late-Comers," 66–67.

78. Minutes of the LEDS, March 1, 1879, April 6, 1879, and May 5, 1877, NLS MS 1725.

79. Mair, quoted in Rae, *Ladies in Debate*, 19.

80. Minutes of the LEDS, December 7, 1867, NLS MS 1723. Lettice Milne Rae's creative rationalization of this name change is reflective of the times: "surely singularly appropriate for the Society—not so much on account of their sex, but rather because of the origin of the word—Lord is a contraction of the Saxon *hlaford*—the loaf author or bread-earner, Lady is the Saxon *hlaf-dig*—the bread-dispenser. In the Society, did she not dispense to her sisters ethical bread, food for the mind, first earned for her by the Lords of Creation, otherwise Man, in the form of ideas and government, public opinion and knowledge of all kinds?" (*Ladies in Debate*, 19).

81. Minutes of the LEDS, March 2, 1872, NLS MS 1723. Kelman explores the group's venture into print culture in more detail ("'Self-Culture'"). The society discussed several options for its decision to change the name of the journal, and even considered calling it *Margaret's Magazine* before settling on the *Ladies' Edinburgh Magazine* (Minutes of the LEDS, November 7, 1874, MS 1724).

82. Minutes of the LEDS, January 3, 1880, NLS MS 1726.

83. Minutes of the LEDS, December 4, 1880, NLS MS 1726.

84. Minutes of the LEDS, February 5, 1881, NLS MS 1726.

85. Minutes of the LEDS, February 5, 1881, NLS MS 1726.

86. Minutes of the LEDS, January 4, 1889, NLS MS 1726.

87. Speech times were decided at the November 2, 1895, meeting.

88. Minutes of the LEDS, April 3, 1886, NLS MS 1726.

89. Ex Cathedra (pen name), "Debates of the Ladies' Edinburgh Literary Society," *Ladies' Edinburgh Magazine*, January–December 1878, 45.

90. Minutes of the LEDS, January 6, 1888, NLS MS 1726.

91. Minutes of the LEDS, March 2, 1888, NLS MS 1726.

92. Minutes of LEDS, May 5, 1934, NLS MS 1733.

93. Sarah Mair, "Stray Notes," *Ladies' Edinburgh Magazine*, January–December 1877, 384.

94. Minutes of the LEDS, June 5, 1886, NLS MS 1726.

95. Minutes of the LEDS, November 6, 1886, NLS MS 1726.

96. Minutes of the LEDS, May 7, 1892, NLS MS 1726.

97. Minutes of the LEDS, November 5, 1892, NLS MS 1726.

98. Minutes of the LEDS, February 4, 1871, NLS MS 1723.

99. Minutes of the LEDS, February 7, 1903, NLS MS 1728.

100. This proposition articulates an enduring issue for those involved in debate. As detailed earlier in this volume, mid-twentieth century debate scholars and practitioners in the United States dealt with some of these very issues as they turned their attention to the question of whether collegiate debaters should switch sides and debate against their convictions.

101. This was Mrs. Bartholomew's phrasing in response to the proposition.

102. Minutes of the LEDS, May 2, 1925, NLS MS 1732.

103. A. D. (Adela Dundas), "Debates of the Ladies' Edinburgh Literary Society," *Ladies' Edinburgh Magazine* 2, 1876, 20.

104. Goodnight and Mitchell suggest that debating societies engage in Henry Jenkins's notion of a "participatory culture" in which members are encouraged to participate, and where more experienced members informally mentor novice participants. See their "Forensics as Scholarship: Testing Zarefsky's Bold Hypothesis in a Digital Age," *Argumentation and Advocacy* 45, no. 2 (2008): 81.

105. Zarefsky, "What Does an Argument Culture Look Like?," 301.

106. Rae, *Ladies in Debate*, 22.

107. Neaves, "Down the Vista," 51.

108. Minutes of the LEDS, April 1, 1871, NLS MS 1723.

109. Minutes of the LEDS, May 4, 1889, NLS MS 1726.

110. Stitt, "Impressions of Two Late-Comers," 68.

111. Zarefsky, "What Does an Argument Culture Look Like?," 301.

112. Stitt, "Impressions of Two Late-Comers," 68–69.

113. Minutes of the LEDS, January 8, 1870, February 5, 1870, NLS MS 1723.

114. Minutes of the LEDS, June 4, 1870, NLS MS 1723.

115. "Debates of the Ladies' Edinburgh Literary Society," *Ladies' Edinburgh Magazine* 3, 1877, 33.

116. Minutes of the LEDS, March 6, 1880, NLS MS 1726.

117. Minutes of the LEDS, March 3, 1883, NLS MS 1726.

118. Transcribed directly from the society's minutes. The society does not seem to have decided on a reasonable fine, or if it did, this was not recorded in the meeting minutes.

119. Minutes of the LEDS, April 27, 1883, NLS MS 1726.

120. Minutes of the LEDS, May 5, 1883, NLS MS 1726.

121. Minutes of the LEDS, November 7, 1925, NLS MS 1732.

122. Minutes of the LEDS, November 1, 1930, NLS MS 1733. Neaves remarks that the team debate format worked well in the late years of the society (in Rae, *Ladies in Debate*, 55).

123. Lorraine Code, *What Can She Know? Feminist Theory and the Construction of Knowledge* (Ithaca, NY: Cornell University Press, 1991). While the entire book ruminates on this question, Code lays out past theorizing and the stakes of the issue in chapter 1.

124. Goodnight, "Generational Argument," 141. Here, Goodnight is talking about a public realm of meaning. While the LEDS has some qualities that match up with this description, it is not an exact match. More apt would be to describe the LEDS as an organizational structure that demonstrates the permeability of public and private spaces, what Rosa Eberly calls "proto-public spaces": "where individuals can engage in rhetorical praxis shielded from fully public scrutiny." See her "Rhetoric and the Anti-Logos Doughball: Teaching Deliberating Bodies the Practices of Participatory Democracy," *Rhetoric and Public Affairs* 5, no. 2 (2002): 293.

125. Bell died unexpectedly ten years later, at age forty-seven. Her sister published a book of her poems, *Songs of Two Homes* (Edinburgh: Oliphant Anderson and Ferrier, 1899), upon her death. Consider these lines from Bell's poem, "Life": "old age that comes with sudden tread, a shaken body, heavy head—and then, short struggle with the death alarms, the old earth opens mother arms—and then, content we waken in a place where Christ shall show his blessed face, to men" (1).

126. Minutes of the LEDS, April 6, 1889, NLS MS 1726.

127. Minutes of the LEDS, February 1, 1919, NLS MS 1730.

128. Mair quoted in Rae, "From Beginning to End," 27.

129. Rae, "From Beginning to End," 28.

130. See Jennifer Phegley, *Courtship and Marriage in Victorian England* (Santa Barbara: ABC-CLIO, LLC, 2012). Phegley's book opens with a useful chronology of marriage laws.

131. This refers to marriages arranged for economic or political advancement rather

than marriage for love. The minutes refer to "our system" as if the debaters identified with the "English system." However, it is worth noting that Scotland's marital laws, especially in the acknowledgment of regular (religious ceremony) and irregular (mutual agreement without a religious ceremony) marriages, differed from those of England and the rest of Europe. See Katie Barclay, *Love, Intimacy, and Power: Marriage and Patriarchy in Scotland, 1650–1850* (Manchester: Manchester University Press, 2011).

132. Minutes of the LEDS, April 2, 1881, NLS MS 1726. In 1883, the LEDS debated, "is it desirable that marriage with a deceased wife's sister should be legalised?"— giving voice to a prohibited but highly contested practice (the LEDS voted for the negative). In 1907, the Deceased Wife's Sister Marriage Act removed the prohibition.

133. Minutes of the LEDS, May 2, 1903, NLS MS 1728. The negative won nine votes, the affirmative won four votes, and one person declined to support either side.

134. Minutes of the LEDS, December 5, 1914, NLS MS 1730.

135. For a detailed exploration of the "surplus woman" issue after the war, including its implications for social change in the United Kingdom, see Virginia Nicholson, *Singled Out: How Two Million Women Survived without Men after the First World War* (Oxford: Oxford University Press, 2008).

136. The LEDS did hold a debate on the question "should a woman take her husband's nationality in marriage?" in 1933, but that debate was about national identity more than marriage. Minutes of the LEDS, April 1, 1933, NLS MS 1733.

137. Minutes of the LEDS, May 5, 1928, NLS MS 1732.

138. Mair, "Foreword," 8.

139. Harold L. Smith, *The British Woman's Suffrage Campaign, 1866–1928*, 2nd ed. (London: Routledge, 2007), 30. Although they felt a kinship with English suffragists, advocates worked to develop a campaign with a "distinct Scottish identity"—at times, they dressed in tartan sashes and reportedly campaigned with slogans such as "what's guid for John is guid for Janet" and "ye mauna tramp on the scotch thistle, laddie" (Smith, *British Woman's*, 31).

140. Following the enfranchisement of women over thirty years of age in 1918, many suffrage movement activists turned their attention toward making sure that women could have meaningful and influential engagements as voting citizens within established political institutions. LEDS members Sarah Mair and Louisa Lumsden were founding members of the Edinburgh Women's Citizens' Association, an organization founded for this purpose. See Sue Innes,

"Constructing Women's Citizenship in the Interwar Period: The Edinburgh Women's Citizens' Association," *Women's History Review* 13, no. 4 (2004): 625.

141. Arnott, "Memories of the Crowded Years," 63.

142. The claim that they were the first to debate the subject was made by Mair, "Foreword," 9. In 1928, women over twenty-one gained the right to vote.

143. Elizabeth Crawford, "Scotland," in *The Women's Suffrage Movement in Britain and Ireland: A Regional Survey* (New York: Routledge, 2006), 232–33.

144. Minutes of the LEDS, May 1, 1866, NLS MS 1726.

145. Minutes of the LEDS, June 5, 1886; February 6, 1887, NLS MS 1726. This decision set a precedent. Later surplus funds were donated to a variety of different causes, including the Women's Employment Bureau, schools in New Zealand, and to support construction on Masson Hall, a dormitory for women.

146. Mary Kelley notes the tendency for women's clubs to deliberate on such questions in her examination of extra-institutional literary societies in the nineteenth century United States. See *Learning to Stand and Speak: Women, Education, and Public Life in America's Republic* (Chapel Hill: University of North Carolina Press, 2006), 133–46, especially her discussion of Boston's Gleaning Circle.

147. Minutes of the LEDS, June 6, 1891, NLS MS 1726. The LEDS members supported the affirmative, but by a margin of only one vote. The secretary mentioned that if visitors to the meeting had been allowed to vote that day, the verdict would have been strongly negative.

148. Minutes of the LEDS, May 3, 1924, NLS MS 1731.

149. Arthur Schopenhauer, "Of Women," in *Arthur Schopenhauer: Essays and Aphorisms*, trans. R. J. Hollingsworth (New York: Penguin Books, 1970), 80–89.

150. Schopenhauer, "Of Woman," 80.

151. Benjamin Kidd, *Social Evolution* (New York: Macmillan and Co., 1894).

152. Minutes of the LEDS, March 6, 1920, NLS MS 1730.

153. Mary Walker, quoted in Welsh, *After the Dawn*, 27.

154. Minutes of the LEDS, February 2, 1878, NLS MS 1725.

155. Minutes of the LEDS, May 7, 1932, NLS MS 1733.

156. Minutes of the LEDS, June 1, 1901, NLS MS 1728.

157. Mrs. Milne Rae, for example, traveled to India and Africa during her years as a member of the LEDS. She also wrote to her husband, George, while he was abroad in India, and told him about LEDS debate topics and meetings (Rae, "From Beginning to End," 35).

158. Minutes of the LEDS, December 4, 1915, NLS MS 1730.

159. Iain Whyte, *Scotland and the Abolition of Black Slavery, 1756–1838* (Edinburgh: Edinburgh University Press, 2006), 4. See also Steven McKenzie, "Pride and Prejudice: Scotland's Complicated Black History," *BBC News*, October 8, 2013, http://www.bbc.com/news/uk-scotland-highlands-islands-24347632.

160. Sue Innes and Jane Rendall, "Women, Gender, and Politics," in *Gender in Scottish History Since 1700*, ed. Lynn Abrams, Eleanor Gordon, Deborah Simonton, and Eileen Janes Yeo (Edinburgh: Edinburgh University Press, 2006), 54–55.

161. Although she did not specify what type of tragedy she was referring to, one wonders if this is not an opaque reference to what Angela Y. Davis refers to as the myth of the black rapist, a cultural trope that serves to justify racism. See Angela Y. Davis, *Women, Race and Class* (New York: Vintage Books, 1991), 188–90.

162. Neaves started by noting that she was strongly prejudiced on the issue. Considering that she also argued that some races are intrinsically subject in the 1915 debate, we can deduce that Neaves was not willing to "switch sides" on this issue.

163. Minutes of the LEDS, February 1, 1930, NLS MS 1732.

164. For more on black communities in the United Kingdom, see Edward Scobie, *Black Britannia* (Chicago: Johnson Publishing Company, 1972); Jeffrey Green, *Black Edwardians: Black People in Britain, 1901–1914* (New York: Frank Cass Publishers, 1998). Black intellectuals such as Frederick Douglass, Charles Lenox Remond, and Sarah Parker Remond participated in the lecture circuit across the United Kingdom. See Fionnghuala Sweeney, *Frederick Douglass and the Atlantic World* (Liverpool: Liverpool University Press, 2007); Charles Lenox Remond, "The Rights of Colored Citizens in Traveling," in *Lift Every Voice: African American Oratory, 1787–1900*, ed. Philip Sheldon Foner and Robert J. Branham (Tuscaloosa: University of Alabama Press, 1997), 189–93; Sirpa Salenus, *An Abolitionist Abroad: Sarah Parker Remond in Cosmopolitan Europe* (Amherst: University of Massachusetts Press, 2016). Vanessa D. Dickerson offers a fascinating study of transatlantic encounters between African Americans and white Britons in the nineteenth and early twentieth centuries in *Dark Victorians* (Champaign: University of Illinois Press, 2008).

165. Over the years, the LEDS received a number of inquiries from other debating societies seeking advice, and in some cases of other Scottish and English societies, requests for inter-society debates. While it often responded, and sometimes even sent debaters to participate in outside events, it seemed

ultimately more concerned with cultivating its own argument culture in Edinburgh.

166. Minutes of the LEDS, March 3, 1934, NLS MS 1733.

167. Kenneth E. Collins, *Scotland's Jews: A Guide to the History and Community of the Jews in Scotland* (Glasgow: Scottish Council of Jewish Communities, 2008), 16, 30–31, http://www.scojec.org/resources/files/scotlands_jews.pdf. According to Collins, Glasgow was a major center of Jewish life in the United Kingdom, following larger populations in London, Manchester, and Leeds (*Scotland's Jews*, 31). That LEDS members had little personal experience with Jewish people may have been due to the relatively small numbers, or, as suggested by Miss Paterson's arguments, because many Jews in Scotland lived in poorer conditions after fleeing poverty and anti-Semitism in Russia and Eastern Europe.

168. Minutes of the LEDS, March 3, 1934, NLS MS 1733.

169. Minutes of the LEDS, March 3, 1934, NLS MS 1733. Lettice Milne Rae was the secretary for this time period, and recorded her own post-debate discussion contributions in the minutes.

170. Minutes of the LEDS, October 9, 1935, NLS MS 1733.

171. Minutes of the LEDS, November 2, 1935, NLS MS 1733.

172. Mair, "Foreword," 7.

173. See Michael Calvin McGee, "'Social Movement': Phenomenon or Meaning?" *Central States Speech Journal* 31 (1980): 233–44.

CHAPTER 3. "BRITAIN'S BRAINY BEAUTIES":
INTERCULTURAL ENCOUNTER ON THE 1928 BRITISH WOMEN'S
DEBATE TOUR OF THE UNITED STATES

1. I use "British" or "English" to refer to the 1928 tour debaters throughout the chapter, following the labels that were used by the debaters to self-identify. However, it is important to note that students who come from other countries of national origin and attend U.K. universities have represented the United Kingdom on exchange tours. Similarly, I use "American" to refer to debating styles originating in the United States in this chapter, as that is how they are often referenced in the literature. However, I acknowledge that the United States of America is only one of the countries in the Americas to claim this label.

2. Intercultural encounter transforms the relationship between rhetors and audiences, profoundly impacting the range and efficacy of argumentative

resources. Speakers must consider that transnational audiences make sense of messages through sensibilities that are at once gendered, raced, classed, and otherwise shaped by the politics of their locations. Feminist scholars have called for a more cosmopolitan orientation, urging a move beyond traditional notions of nation and citizenship to consider the coalitional possibilities across a range of affiliations. See, for example, Sasha Roseneil, ed., *Beyond Citizenship? Feminism and the Transformation of Belonging* (London: Palgrave Macmillan, 2013); Bo Wang, "Rethinking Feminist Rhetoric and Historiography in a Global Context: A Cross-Cultural Perspective," *Advances in the History of Rhetoric* 15, no. 1 (2012): 28–52.

3. Margaret E. Keck and Kathryn Sikkink, *Activists beyond Borders: Advocacy Networks in International Politics* (Ithaca, NY: Cornell University Press, 1998), 39–78; Huw T. David details early transnational anti-slavery advocacy his "Transnational Advocacy in the Eighteenth Century: Transatlantic Activism and the Anti-Slavery Movement," *Global Networks* 7, no. 3 (2007): 367–82, DOI: 10.1111/j.1471–0374.2007.00174.x.

4. For a sense of the range of international topics in nineteenth century institutions, see Tom F. Wright, ed., *The Cosmopolitan Lyceum: Lecture Culture and the Globe in Nineteenth-Century America* (Amherst: University of Massachusetts Press, 2013). Of particular interest is Angela G. Ray's chapter, which showcases how a selection of antebellum lyceums from Rhode Island to Illinois engaged debate questions on the political decisions of world leaders ("How Cosmopolitan Was the Lyceum, Anyway?" in Wright, *The Cosmopolitan Lyceum*, 30–32). Moreover, Ronald J. Zboray and Mary Saracino Zboray detail how New England women developed a cosmopolitan sensibility during the same period by attending public lectures. See Ronald J. Zboray and Mary Saracino Zboray, "Women Thinking: The International Popular Lecture and Its Audience in Antebellum New England," in Wright, *The Cosmopolitan Lyceum*, 42–66.

5. For example, in 1850, Oberlin's LLS debated this proposition: "Resolved, that the British were justified in banishing Napoleon." Minutes of the Young Ladies' Association of Oberlin College Institute, 1846–1850, May 22, 1850 RG 19/3/4, Series 1, Box 1, Oberlin College Archives. The Ladies' Edinburgh Debating society engaged in debates on a variety of international topics of political and literary consequence. They regularly demonstrated an awareness of current issues in the United States. Especially during World War I, they elected to debate issues of national and international importance, such as "has the establishment of the

Peace Conference at the Hague been of benefit to the world?" in 1916 and "will there be a period of commercial and industrial depression in Great Britain after the War?" in 1917. See Lettice Milne Rae, ed. *Ladies in Debate: Being a History of the Ladies' Edinburgh Debating Society, 1865–1935* (Edinburgh: Oliver and Boyd, 1936), 104–5.

6. Egbert Ray Nichols, "A Historical Sketch of Intercollegiate Debating: III," *Quarterly Journal of Speech* 23, no. 2 (1937): 259. I elaborate on this period in the next chapter.

7. Nichols, "A Historical Sketch of Intercollegiate Debating: III," 260.

8. Nichols, "A Historical Sketch of Intercollegiate Debating: III," 260–61. Nichols notes that the travel bug bit university athletic teams around this period as well.

9. Bates College claims that its involvement in international debating started much earlier, when students from Bates and Queen's University of Ontario, Canada, took part in a debate about Great Britain's free trade policy on May 12, 1908, in Lewiston, Maine. The next year, Bates reciprocated by sending a team to debate in Ontario. However, the premature death of the debate coach, A. K. Spofford, forestalled further international competition until the 1920s. See Robert James Branham, *Stanton's Elm: An Illustrated History of Debating at Bates College* (Lewiston, ME: Bates College, 1996), 25–26. According to longtime Bates coach Frank Brooks Quimby, it is generally believed that those early events in Canada did not have the international significance of the transatlantic debate exchanges with the British and did not constitute a debate tour. See Frank Brooks Quimby, "A Decade of International Debating" (Master's thesis, Harvard University, 1931), 2–3.

10. Betty Burford Grimmer, "The International Debate Program: 1921–1958" (Master's thesis, University of Alabama, 1959), 17–18.

11. Stephen P. Duggan, *Institute for International Education: First Annual Report of the Director* (New York: Institute for International Education, 1920), 1.

12. Informal academic exchanges existed in earlier years, but many credit the University of Delaware's Junior Year Abroad program, founded in 1923, with the large upswing in U.S. study abroad students in Europe. They studied in France to hone their language skills and learn about international art, business, and culture. Other universities, including the all-women's Smith College, created study abroad programs based on the Delaware model. See Mark Rennella and Whitney Walton, "Planned Serendipity: American Travellers and the Transatlantic Voyage in the Nineteenth and Twentieth Centuries," *Journal of Social History* 38, no. 2 (2004):

372–73.

13. Rennella and Walton, "Planned Serendipity," 372. Rennella and Walton note that round-trip fares in the "tourist third class" category could be purchased for as little as $110 at this time.

14. Grimmer, "The International Debate Program," 18.

15. Martha Biehle to Brooks Quimby, October 25, 1928, telegram. Brooks Quimby Debate Council Papers, Folder: International Debate 1908–1995, Edmund S. Muskie Archives & Special Collections Library, Bates College, Lewiston, ME.

16. See B. J. C. McKercher, ed., *Anglo-American Relations in the 1920s: The Struggle for Supremacy* (Edmonton: University of Alberta Press, 1990).

17. Calvin Coolidge to Clifton D. Gray, September 18, 1923, quoted in Quimby, "A Decade of International Debating," I (appendix A).

18. There were various setbacks and gains in the transatlantic relationship during Coolidge's time in office, but he still named the British Empire as one of the U.S.'s "largest foreign interests" in a speech delivered on December 4, 1928, when Lockhart, Samuel, and Sharp's debating tour was underway. See Calvin Coolidge, "Sixth Annual Message," December 4, 1928, *The American Presidency Project*, Gerhard Peters and John T. Wooley, http://www.presidency.ucsb.edu/ws/?pid=29569.

19. "International Debating," *Christian Science Monitor*, January 30, 1928.

20. Carly Woods and Takuzo Konishi, "What Has Been Exchanged? Towards a History of the Japan–US Debate Exchange," in *Proceedings of the 3rd Tokyo Conference on Argumentation*, ed. Takeshi Suzuki and Aya Kubuta (Tokyo: Japan Debate Association, 2008), 271.

21. Quimby, "A Decade of International Debating," 17.

22. Mildred Freburg Berry, "A Survey of Intercollegiate Debate in the Mid-West Debate Conference," *Quarterly Journal of Speech* 14, no. 1 (1928): 88, DOI: 10.1080/00335632809379725.

23. Berry, "A Survey," 87.

24. See David Zarefsky and Victoria Gallagher, "From 'Conflict' to 'Constitutional Question': Transformations in Early American Discourse," *Quarterly Journal of Speech* 76, no. 3 (1990): 247–61.

25. A. Craig Baird wrote about the British debating style in his "Shall American Universities Adopt the British System of Debating?" *Quarterly Journal of Speech* 9, no. 3 (1923): 215–22. American debaters Norman J. Temple and Edward P. Dunn wrote about their experience touring England and Scotland in their "British

Debating Is Parliamentary," *Quarterly Journal of Speech* 34, no. 1 (1948): 50–53. British debaters Anthony Wedgwood Benn, Edward Boyle, and Kenneth Harris published their impressions in "American and British Debating," *Quarterly Journal of Speech* 34, no. 4 (1948): 469–72. Harris also went on to publish a book, *Travelling Tongues: Debating across America* (London: Murray, 1949). For the most comprehensive history of international debate exchanges during this period, see Robert N. Hall and Jack L. Rhodes, *Fifty Years of International Debate, 1922–1972* (New York: Speech Communication Association, 1972).

26. Egbert Ray Nichols, "A Historical Sketch of Intercollegiate Debating: I," *Quarterly Journal of Speech* 22, no. 2 (1936): 215.

27. Berry, "A Survey," 90.

28. Carol Dyhouse, *Students: A Gendered History* (New York: Routledge, 2006), 124–25.

29. Dyhouse, *Students*, 125.

30. "A Varsity Governed By Men for Men," *Evening Telegraph*, May 18, 1928, 8. According to Dyhouse, the Cambridge Union Society and the Oxford Union remained "masculine strongholds," not fully admitting women to membership until 1963, after hard-fought battles at both institutions (*Students*, 132). Eugene Chenoweth and Uvieja Good note that "female discrimination in forensic affairs dissolved first at the newer, less tradition-laden schools" in the United Kingdom, including Birmingham University, London University, and Glasgow University. See Eugene Chenoweth and Uvieja Good, "The Rise of Women and the Fall of Tradition in Union Debating at Oxford and Cambridge," *Speaker & Gavel* 9, no. 2 (1972): 31.

31. Martha H. Biehle to Brooks Quimby, October 22, 1928. Brooks Quimby Debate Council Papers, Folder: International Debate 1908–1995, Edmund S. Muskie Archives & Special Collections Library. In her letter, Biehle wrote: "I have not communicated with all the small women's colleges in the east, but I do know that Wellesley, Radcliffe, Wheaton, Bryn Mawr and Barnard do not have debate teams. Vassar, Conneticutt [*sic*] College for Women, and Pembroke College in Brown University have, as you know, debating teams. Smith, Wells, Elmira, and Mount Holyoke also have women's teams, but I am not sure how much intercollegiate debating they are prepared to do." Elmira College in Elmira, New York, was a host on the tour. The all-women's Wellesley College was originally scheduled as the final stop on the tour (December 15–16), but I have not been able to locate evidence that the visit actually occurred, and the debaters refer to

Bates College as their final stop in the transcript of a debate analyzed later in this chapter.

32. Hosts confirmed by media reports include Bates College, Elmira College, Depauw University, George Washington University, Hood College, Seton Hill, University of North Carolina, University of Kentucky, and the University of Pittsburgh, Western Teachers College, and Westminster College.

33. Here, the passenger list for their October 1928 voyage is most helpful. Records indicate that Leonora Wilhelmina Lockhart was a 21-year-old single student, born in London and with a permanent address in Carluke, Scotland. Nancy Adelaide Samuel is listed a 22-year-old single person of no occupation, born and currently residing in London. Clara Margery Sharp reported she was a 22-year-old single student, born in Salisbury, England, and currently residing in London. The paperwork also has a category for "race or people" in which Lockhart is listed as Scotch, Samuel is listed as Hebrew, and Sharp is listed as English and French. Each of the debaters indicated that this was their first trip to the United States. See New York Passenger Lists, 1820–1957, RMS *Celtic*, 1928, T715, roll 4375, page 59, Ancestry.com.

34. NEA Service, "Intellectuality of U.S. College Girls Doubted by English Girl Debaters," *Abilene Morning News*, January 17, 1929.

35. Sir Herbert Samuel's political career has been detailed in Bernard Wasserstein's *Herbert Samuel: A Political Life* (Oxford: Oxford University Press, 1992). Throughout his life, he was a key figure and campaigner for the Liberal Party, and, among other political feats, was the first British politician to deliver a televised speech. See also Jaime Reynolds, "Herbert Samuel (Viscount Samuel), 1879–1963," Liberal History. http://www.liberalhistory.org.uk/history/samuel-herbert-viscount-samuel/.

36. "College Girls to Debate Psychology and Morals," *Washington Post*, October 28, 1928,

37. "Court & Personal," *Manchester Guardian*, July 13, 1928.

38. George Stade, Karen Karbiener, and Christine L. Krueger, eds., "Sharp, Margery," in *Encyclopedia of British Writers: 19th and 20th Centuries* (New York: Book Builders LLC, 2003), 337.

39. "Court and Personal," *Manchester Guardian*, October 22, 1928.

40. See a list of national intercollegiate debate propositions in Austin J. Freeley and David L. Steinberg, *Argumentation and Debate: Critical Thinking for Reasoned Decision Making* (Boston: Wadsworth, 2014), 444.

41. "Court and Personal," October 22, 1928.

42. "Women in Debate," *Aberdeen Press & Journal*, October 16, 1928.

43. "English Girl Orators Here," *Chicago Daily Tribune*, November 2, 1928; "Britain's Brainy Beauties," *Chicago Daily Tribune*, November 18, 1928.

44. See "Court and Personal," October 22, 1928. The same vessel became lodged between rocks as it approached Cobh, Ireland, in December 1928 and was scrapped on site.

45. New York Passenger Lists, 1820–1957, RMS *Celtic*, 1928, T715, roll 4375, page 59, Ancestry.com.

46. Jo Stanley, "Co-Venturing Consumers 'Travel Back': Ships' Stewardesses and Their Female Passengers, 1919–55," *Mobilities* 3, no. 3 (2008): 443.

47. Stanley, "Co-Venturing Consumers," 444.

48. "Capital Society Events," *Washington Post*, October 31, 1928.

49. "Capital Society Events."

50. "Debaters Begin to Organize with Large Attendance," *Tar Heel*, September 29, 1928.

51. "Debate Team Picked," *Tar Heel*, October 27, 1928.

52. "University Meets English Women in Co-Ed Debate," *Tar Heel*, November 3, 1928.

53. "University Meets English Women."

54. To put this number into perspective, the total registration at the University of North Carolina that year was just over 2,500 students.

55. "Heel Debaters Get Favorable Decision Over British Women," *Tar Heel*, November 8, 1928.

56. "Heel Debaters."

57. "Heel Debaters."

58. H. J. Galland, "Is That Nice, Girls?" *Tar Heel*, November 13, 1928.

59. Clifford Amyx, "Weaver the Liberal: A Memoir," *Modern Age* 32, no. 1 (1987): 102.

60. Amyx, "Weaver the Liberal," 103.

61. Quoted in Fred Douglas Young, *Richard M. Weaver, 1910–1963: A Life of the Mind* (Columbia: University of Missouri Press, 1995), 24.

62. Young, *Richard M. Weaver*, 24.

63. For example, Samuel was interviewed about the experience of debating men on the tour. She explained that American women and men debaters alike possessed the same drive to win, while British women and men love debate for the sake of debating. Samuel also forecast more international debates for women in

the future; though they were unable to draw audiences that rivaled the Oxford men's audiences in size, their audiences had been very enthusiastic. See "British Women at Bates Tonight," *Lewiston Evening Journal*, December 11, 1928.

64. Mays used his background to engage in face-to-face debates about apartheid in South Africa with Ben Marais, as well as in debates through Pittsburgh newspapers with evangelist Billy Graham about the state of racism in the American south. As the President of Morehouse College, he went on to create an environment that encouraged debate and the free flow of ideas toward social progress. See Robert James Branham, "'Emancipating Myself': Mays the Debater," in *Walking Integrity: Benjamin Elijah Mays, Mentor to Martin Luther King, Jr.*, ed. Lawrence Edward Carter Sr. (Macon, GA: Mercer University Press, 1998), 81–109.

65. Branham, *Stanton's Elm*, 17. According to Henry L. Ewbank Jr., "not a negro" was added to the list of membership qualifications in 1922. It was contested by student delegates but was not ultimately removed from the society's constitution until 1935. See Henry L. Ewbank Jr., "Henry Lee Ewbank, Sr.: Teacher of Teachers of Speech," in *Twentieth Century Roots of Rhetorical Studies*, ed. Jim A. Kuypers and Andrew King (Westport, CT: Praeger Publishers, 2001), 57–58.

66. Branham, *Stanton's Elm*, 21–23.

67. Bates was not included in the original schedule coordinated by the NSFA, but a timely correspondence between Biehle and Quimby rectified the error, and a Bates visit was added to the tail end of the tour. Biehle to Quimby, October 22, 1928, Quimby Debating Council Papers, Muskie Archives and Special Collections Library.

68. Egbert Ray Nichols, ed., *Intercollegiate Debates: Affirmative and Negative,* vol. 10 (New York: Noble and Noble, 1930), iv.

69. Brooks Quimby to Martha Biehle, November 22, 1928. Quimby Debate Council Papers, Muskie Archives & Special Collections Library.

70. Iris Marion Young, *Inclusion and Democracy* (Oxford: Oxford University Press, 2001), 60.

71. Samuel in Nichols, *Intercollegiate Debates*, 372.

72. Samuel in Nichols, *Intercollegiate Debates*, 374.

73. Frank Darvall to Brooks Quimby, January 8, 1929, quoted in Grimmer, "The International Debate Program," 29–30.

74. Miriam McMichael in Nichols, *Intercollegiate Debates*, 381.

75. Leonora Lockhart in Nichols, *Intercollegiate Debates*, 382.

76. Lockhart in Nichols, *Intercollegiate Debates*, 384.

77. Lockhart in Nichols, *Intercollegiate Debates*, 385.

78. Lockhart in Nichols, *Intercollegiate Debates*, 386.

79. Yvonne Langlois in Nichols, *Intercollegiate Debates*, 387.

80. Langlois in Nichols, *Intercollegiate Debates*, 391. The Oxford debater she mentions is Alan Tindal Lennox-Boyd, 1st Viscount Boyd of Merton. At the time, Lennox-Boyd was president of the Oxford Debating Union, and he went on to become a well-known British MP and Colonial Secretary.

81. Langlois in Nichols, *Intercollegiate Debates*, 393.

82. Margery Sharp in Nichols, *Intercollegiate Debates*, 396.

83. Sharp in Nichols, *Intercollegiate Debates*, 396–97.

84. "Bates Women Triumph," *Bates Student*, December 14, 1928.

85. Eugenia Southard in Nichols, *Intercollegiate Debates*, 398.

86. Southard in Nichols, *Intercollegiate Debates*, 398.

87. Southard in Nichols, *Intercollegiate Debates*, 399.

88. Southard in Nichols, *Intercollegiate Debates*, 399.

89. Southard in Nichols, *Intercollegiate Debates*, 401.

90. Southard in Nichols, *Intercollegiate Debates*, 402.

91. "English and American Girl Debaters Meet," *Christian Science Monitor*, December 14, 1928. Clarification about the audience vote comes from the program for the event. "International Debate: British Universities' Women vs. Bates College Women, December 13, 1928," program, Quimby Debate Council Papers, Folder: International Debate 1908–1995, Muskie Archives & Special Collections Library.

92. "Bates Women Triumph."

93. This comment presumes that Samuel, a Jewish person, was read by audiences as white, although historian Karen Brodkin explains that the historical relationship between Jews and whiteness in the United States is much more complicated. As she notes, the 1920s and 1930s were a time in which scientific racism took hold and racism and anti-Semitism were pervasive in U.S. colleges and universities. See Karen Brodkin, *How Jews Became White Folks and What That Says about Race in America* (New Brunswick: Rutgers University Press, 2002), 30. Readers will recall that some members of the Ladies' Edinburgh Debating Society were airing extremely anti-Semitic views in their debates just a short time after Samuel represented Great Britain on this tour. However, I did not find evidence of U.S. or U.K. news coverage of the tour that explicitly named Samuel as a Jewish person,

although there are many accounts of the anti-Semitism her father, Sir Herbert Samuel, experienced in his political career.

94. Iris Marion Young, *Intersecting Voices: Dilemmas of Gender, Political Philosophy, and Philosophy* (Princeton: Princeton University Press, 1997), 64.

95. Young, *Inclusion and Democracy*, 56.

96. In one interview, the debaters even offered their opinions on the different regions of the United States, suggesting that the West was "highly standardized" with wealth and a desire to foster the arts, while the East had more of a real appreciation for the arts. "England at Christmas Time: British Women Debaters Find Snow Unusual Feature at This Season," *Lewiston Daily Sun*, December 14, 1928.

97. NEA Service, "Intellectuality of U.S. College Girls," 5.

98. "English Girl Finds Sorority Artificial," *New York Times*, December 29, 1928.

99. She reiterated her well-rehearsed argument that the comparatively large numbers of students seeking higher education in the United States led to a focus on social clubs instead of intellectual pursuits, to looks instead of books. In an argument not articulated in the Bates debate, Samuel suggested that a tutorial system, in which students had more individualized attention through private meetings with professors in addition to regular class time, might go some length to increase the seriousness with which American women approached their studies. See Rebecca Hooper Eastman, "Some Dangers of Co-Education," *The Woman's Journal* 14 (January 1929): 43.

100. Leonora W. Lockhart, "Women's Colleges: A Striking Contrast," *New York Times*, May 5, 1929.

101. Lockhart, "Women's Colleges," 13.

102. Leonora W. Lockhart, "An English College Girl Studies Ours," *New York Times*, May 19, 1929.

103. Lockhart, "English College Girl," 12.

104. Leonora W. Lockhart, "The Professional Woman: A Contrast," *New York Times*, June 2, 1929.

105. Lockhart, "The Professional Woman," 1.

106. Lockhart, "The Professional Woman," 9–10.

107. Lockhart, "The Professional Woman," 10.

108. John Durham Peters notes that Ogden and I. A. Richards sought to purify language, convinced that words themselves inhibit communication. Odgen proposed a universal language of 850 words. See *Speaking into the Air* (Chicago:

University of Chicago Press, 1999), 12–14.

109. Christine M. Gibson, "Women Pioneers of Basic English," *Christian Science Monitor*, January 22, 1944.

110. Leonora W. Lockhart, "American Ideas that Assail the Briton," *New York Times*, May 11, 1930.

111. Lockhart, "American Ideas," 11, 20.

112. Lockhart, "American Ideas," 11.

113. Mica Nava, *Visceral Cosmopolitanism: Gender, Culture, and the Normalisation of Difference* (Oxford: Berg, 2007), 59.

114. "Society Girl as Shop Assistant," *Evening Telegraph*, February 14, 1929.

115. "Society Girl as Shop Assistant."

116. Lockhart, "The Professional Woman," 9.

117. "Society Girl as Shop Assistant."

118. "Miss Nancy Samuel as a Shop Girl," *Manchester Guardian*, April 9, 1929.

119. "Biscuit" is the term Samuel used in an interview with an English newspaper. This likely means that she was employed packing what the British call "biscuits," better known in the United States as "cookies."

120. "Miss Nancy Samuel."

121. See, for example, "Miss Samuel as Packer," *Derby Daily Telegraph*, April 8, 1929; "Knight's Daughter as Shop Girl," *Nottingham Evening Post*, April 8, 1929; "American Shops: Miss Samuel's Illusion of the Hustle Dispelled," *Yorkshire Post*, April 12, 1929.

122. Herbert Samuel won two election campaigns at Darwen in 1929 and 1931.

123. See "Court & Personal," *Manchester Guardian*, April 12, 1929; "Shop Assistants Thank Jix," *Courier and Advertiser*, April 12, 1929.

124. Quote transcribed verbatim. "64 Women Running in British Election," *New York Times*, May 4, 1929.

125. "Miss Nancy Samuel to be Doctor's Bride," *New York Times*, April 2, 1935.

126. Gordon R. Mitchell, "Pedagogical Possibilities for Argumentative Agency in Academic Debate," *Argumentation and Advocacy* 35, no. 2 (1998): 41–60.

127. Gordon R. Mitchell and Takeshi Suzuki, "Beyond the 'Daily Me': Argumentation in an Age of Enclave Deliberation," in *Argumentation and Social Cognition*, ed. Takeshi Suzuki, Yoshiro Yano, and Takayuki Kato (Tokyo: Japan Debate Association, 2004), 163–64. They, of course, are talking about moving from a tournament setting to an audience-centered, public event or genre in the context of twenty-first-century debating. Still, Lockhart and Samuel made use of each of

these skills, and the first two seem most applicable to the style of public debate they engaged in on the 1928 tour. The move from tour debates to commentary in newspapers is another act of adaptation requiring flexibility on the part of the participants.

128. The potential here is ripe not only with study of longstanding exchanges between the United States, United Kingdom, and Japan but also with a number of inter- and transnational argument cultures. See Woods and Konishi, "What Has Been Exchanged?"; Brian Lain, "Rethinking the History of the Japanese–U.S. Exchange Tour: Early Tours, Early Topics, and Early Traffic," in *Disturbing Arguments: Selected Works from the 18th NCA/AFA Conference on Argumentation*, ed. Catherine H. Palczewski (New York: Routledge, 2015), 426–31; Satoru Aonuma, Junya Mooroka, and Kakuhiko Seno, "Revisiting the U.S. Footprints: A Critical Exploration of Interscholastic/Intercollegiate Policy Debate in Post-World War II Japan," in Palczewski, *Disturbing Arguments*, 432–37; Tomohiro Kanke and Junya Morooka, "In Search of an Alternative History of Debate in Early Modern Japan: The Case of Youth Club Debates in the Late Nineteenth and Early Twentieth Centuries," *Journal of Argumentation in Context* 1, no. 2 (2012): 168–93; Allison Hahn, "The World Schools Debate Championship and Intercultural Argumentation," *International Society for the Study of Argumentation Proceedings* (2010), http://rozenbergquarterly.com/issa-proceedings-2010-the-world-schools-debate-championship-and-intercultural-argumentation.

Chapter 4. "Your Gown Is Lovely, But . . .":
Negotiating Citizenship at Pennsylvania State Colleges, 1928–1945

1. Ronald Walter Greene and Darrin Hicks, "Lost Convictions: Debating Both Sides and the Ethical Fashioning of Liberal Citizens," *Cultural Studies* 19, no. 1 (2005): 102.

2. Mildred Freburg Berry, "A Survey of Intercollegiate Debate in the Mid-West Debate Conference," *Quarterly Journal of Speech* 14, no. 1 (1928): 87, DOI: 10.1080/00335632809379725. This is true of predominantly white institutions and historically black colleges, where some women debated in mixed-gender, intercollegiate competitions.

3. Barbara Miller Solomon, *In the Company of Educated Women: A History of Women and Higher Education in America* (New Haven: Yale University Press, 1985), 142.

4. See Susan Levine's discussion of the period in her *Degrees of Equality: The American Association of University Women and the Challenge of Twentieth-Century Feminism* (Philadelphia: Temple University Press, 1995), 23–66.

5. The Pennsylvania State College became known as the Pennsylvania State University in 1953. I refer to the institution as Pennsylvania State College or Penn State throughout the chapter.

6. Margaret A. Nash and Lisa S. Romero, "'Citizenship for the College Girl': Challenges and Opportunities in Higher Education for Women in the United States in the 1930s," *Teachers College Record* 114, no. 2 (2012): 6–8.

7. Nash and Romero, "'Citizenship for the College Girl,'" 7–8. Historian Susan Ware argues that multiple aspects of the New Deal led to expanded opportunities for women in public life, including the administration of social welfare and political roles in the Democratic Party in *Beyond Suffrage: Women in the New Deal* (Cambridge: Harvard University Press, 1981), 7. Susan Levine details tensions between these expanded opportunities for some and compressed opportunities for others in professional roles in *Degrees of Equality*, 25.

8. Nash and Romero, "'Citizenship for the College Girl,'" 8.

9. Eudora Ramsay Richardson, *The Woman Speaker: A Handbook and Study Course on Public Speaking* (Richmond, VA: Whittet & Shepperson, 1936), 18.

10. Jasper Vanderbilt Garland, *Public Speaking for Women* (New York: Harper and Brothers, 1938), xi.

11. I first became aware of Garland's public speaking text through Marie Hochmuth's reference to it in "Your Gown is Lovely, but"—an article that I analyze later in this chapter. Jane Sutton provides a helpful survey of public speaking texts—including Richardson's and Garland's—that were written for women from the 1930s to 2000. See her *House of My Sojourn: Rhetoric, Women, and the Question of Authority* (Tuscaloosa: University of Alabama Press, 2010), 21–25.

12. Doris G. Yoakam, "Pioneer Women Orators of America," *Quarterly Journal of Speech* 23, no. 2 (1937): 251–59; see also Karen A. Foss and Sonja K. Foss, "The Status of Research on Women and Communication," *Communication Quarterly* 31, no. 3 (1983): 195–204.

13. Egbert Ray Nichols, "A Historical Sketch of Intercollegiate Debating: III," *Quarterly Journal of Speech* 23, no. 2 (1937): 259–78.

14. Nash and Romero, "'Citizenship for the College Girl,'" 4.

15. Nash and Romero, "'Citizenship for the College Girl,'" 4.

16. Nash and Romero, "'Citizenship for the College Girl,'" 9.

17. Solomon, *In the Company*, 173.

18. Mary Weaks-Baxter, Christine Bruun, and Catherine Forslund, *We Are a College at War: Women Working for Victory in World War II* (Carbondale: Southern Illinois University Press, 2010), 3.

19. "Varsity Debaters (Did They Ever Look Like This, Boys?)," *Penn State Alumni Magazine*, April 1945, 3.

20. I found the pamphlet for this debate both in the William Pitt Debating Union Papers in the University of Pittsburgh archives and in the Eberly Family Special Collections Library at Penn State. See "Intercollegiate Debate between Pennsylvania State College and the University of Pittsburgh, March 9, 1928," program, 90/8/36/5, Box 1, Folder 8, William Pitt Debating Union, University of Pittsburgh Archives Information Files, University of Pittsburgh Library System, Pittsburgh, PA; "Intercollegiate Debate between Pennsylvania State College and the University of Pittsburgh," March 9, 1928, program, AX/CATO/PSUA/M/08.23, A Scrapbook of Intercollegiate Debate, 1926–1934, Eberly Family Special Collections Library, Pennsylvania State University Archives, State College, PA.

21. Pitt and Penn State are predominantly white institutions, and team photos in the period covered in this chapter reflect a primarily white student body. However, there are exceptions; see Ervin Dyer, "The Great Debater," *Pitt Magazine*, Summer 2008, 26–30.

22. True to the often circuitous unfolding of archival research, my exploration into the holdings in the Pitt archives led me to the personal papers of Marie Hochmuth Nichols at the University of Illinois, where I found a copy of a centennial celebration document for Penn State's Department of Speech that described women's debating activities. Thus, my travels led me back to Pennsylvania—to the special collections holdings at Penn State.

23. *The Owl* (Pittsburgh: Western University of Pennsylvania, 1907), 242. *The Owl* was the name of the Western University of Pennsylvania's yearbook, which was published annually from 1907 to 1981. The University of Pittsburgh's digital collection of university publications and images, *Documenting Pitt*, contains scans of all issues. Ensuing references to *The Owl* cite years and page numbers based on hard copies of the yearbooks, and can be accessed at http://digital.library.pitt.edu/d/documentingpitt/yearbooks.html.

24. Christine D. Meyers, *University Coeducation in the Victorian Era: Inclusion in the United States and the United Kingdom* (New York: Palgrave Macmillan, 2010), 15.

25. Agnes Lynch Starrett, *Through One Hundred and Fifty Years: The University of*

Pittsburgh (Pittsburgh: University of Pittsburgh Press, 1937), 515–16.

26. *The Owl*, 1915–1916, 399. This photograph includes seventeen debaters, including four women (beyond the visual cues, the women's first names are written out while the men's are abbreviated). Featured in the second row is Charles W. Florence, an African American student who would become the captain of the debate team in 1917. For more on Florence, see Dyer, "The Great Debater," 26–30. Throughout the nineteen teens, women students appeared in the yearbook with "girl's debate team/club" in their list of activities, and there is evidence that they appeared in public debates with Penn State. A digital history project hosted by the University of Pittsburgh's Office of the Provost claims that the team was coed until 1921. See Carolyn Sutcher Schumacher, "The History of Women at Pitt: Reflections of a Changing Society, 1895–1972," Office of the Provost, University of Pittsburgh, http://www.provost.pitt.edu.

27. *The Owl*, 1930–31, 146–47.

28. Schumacher, "The History of Women at Pitt.'"

29. I refer to Theresa Kahn Murphy by her maiden name, Kahn, throughout the chapter because that was her name at the time and to avoid confusion with Richard Murphy. However, bibliographic entries appear under the last name she used at the time of publication.

30. Mary Murphy Schroeder (a federal judge on the United States Court of Appeals for the Ninth Circuit) spoke about her parents, Richard Murphy and Theresa Kahn Murphy, in an oral history for the American Bar Association Commission on Women in the Profession's Women Trailblazers in the Law Project. Mary Murphy Schroeder, "Oral History of Mary Murphy Schroeder," Interview by Patricia Lee Refo, Women Trailblazers Project, American Bar Association, August 30, 2006, http://www.americanbar.org/content/dam/aba/directories/women_trailblazers/ schroeder_interview_1.authcheckdam.pdf. Additional references refer to pagination in the website's document.

31. Schroeder, interview, 3–4. Anti-nepotism laws prevented Murphy and Kahn from marrying while they worked at Pitt in the 1930s, as both relied on income from the university to support their families (Schroeder, 2). As it turned out, many of the major figures involved with debate at the University of Pittsburgh in the 1930s would eventually end up at the University of Illinois: Wayland Parrish, Richard Murphy, and Marie Hochmuth Nichols were all members of the Department of Speech Communication's faculty. Murphy, who had been hired at the University of Colorado in the interim, was a scholar of American

and British rhetoric, specializing in free speech topics. He continued to publish about forensics long into his career, including taking part in a heated scholarly debate about the ethics of debating both sides of a topic, in which he continued to support the perspective that debaters should defend their convictions, as laid out in "The Pittsburgh Policy" during the 1920s and 30s; see his "The Ethics of Debating Both Sides," *Speech Teacher* 6, no. 1 (1957): 1–9; and "The Ethics of Debating Both Sides II," *Speech Teacher* 7, no. 3 (1963): 242–47. Theresa (Kahn) Murphy was a Dickens scholar who published in the *Quarterly Journal of Speech*; see Theresa Murphy and Richard Murphy, "Charles Dickens as Professional Reader," *Quarterly Journal of Speech* 33, no. 3 (1947): 299–308; Theresa Murphy, "Interpretation in the Dickens Period," *Quarterly Journal of Speech* 41, no. 3 (1955): 243–50. In fact, when she published "Interpretation in the Dickens Period," the bio at the bottom of the article made note of her marital relationship (perhaps because she lacked a formal university affiliation): "Theresa Murphy, wife of Professor Richard Murphy of the University of Illinois, has taught Interpretation at the University of Pittsburgh and the University of Colorado." Although Theresa Kahn Murphy did not hold a faculty position at Illinois, she traveled to academic conventions and regularly chatted with students, especially women graduate students, who saw her not only as a "motherly figure" whom they could talk to about issues that they couldn't talk about with their professors, but an "intellectually interesting" person who knew a lot about rhetoric—as related by Jane Blankenship in an interview by author, Chicago, IL, November 14, 2009.

32. "The Pittsburgh Policy," 1929–1930, pamphlet, 90/8/36/5, Box 1, Folder 3, William Pitt Debating Union, University of Pittsburgh Archives Information Files, University of Pittsburgh Library System.

33. "Intercollegiate Debate between Pennsylvania State College and the University of Pittsburgh." An example of an audience shift ballot from a University of Pittsburgh public debate is featured in Gordon R. Mitchell, "Public Opinion, Thinly Sliced and Served Hot," *International Journal of Communication* 9 (2015): 23.

34. "The Pittsburgh Policy." Though this quote uses masculine pronouns, the Pittsburgh Program governed the men's and the women's teams.

35. Theresa Kahn, "Analyzing the Proposition: Broadcast from the University of Pittsburgh Studio on December 5, 1929," in *Debating: A Series of Six Radio Talks*, ed. Theresa Kahn and Richard Murphy (Pittsburgh: University of Pittsburgh Radio Publication, 1929), 37.

36. Richard Murphy, "The Etiquette of Argument: Rules and Ethics of Debating: Broadcast from the University of Pittsburgh Studio on November 14, 1929," in Kahn and Murphy, *Debating*, 23. Murphy is using masculine pronouns here, but the sentiment presumably applied to women debaters, who operated under the same Pittsburgh Policy.

37. "Debaters Will Start Season with Smoker," *Pitt Weekly*, September 26, 1930. Issues of *Pitt Weekly* were accessed via microfilm at the University of Pittsburgh's Hillman Library.

38. "Debate Season Opens Oct. 16 for Coeds," *Pitt Weekly*, October 10, 1930.

39. Theresa Kahn, "Organizing Debating Activities within the School: Broadcast from the University of Pittsburgh Studio on December 19, 1929," in Kahn and Murphy, *Debating*, 52–53.

40. Schroeder, interview, 3.

41. "Debating Associations Annual Banquet," May 8, 1930, program, Box 1, Folder 8, William Pitt Debating Union, University of Pittsburgh Archives Information Files, University of Pittsburgh Library System.

42. *The Owl*, 1931, 147.

43. "Women's Final Debate to Be Broadcast over KDKA," *Pitt Weekly*, April 4, 1930.

44. "Former Coed in Many Activities Tells Why She Likes Debating," *Pitt Weekly*, November 14, 1930.

45. *The Owl*, 1937, 136.

46. *The Owl*, 1937, 136.

47. "Former Coed."

48. "Annual Banquet of the University of Pittsburgh Debating Associations," May 9, 1931, program, Box 1, Folder 7, William Pitt Debating Union, University of Pittsburgh Archives Information Files, University of Pittsburgh Library System.

49. "Install Coed Debate Head," *Pitt Weekly*, October 31, 1930. Hochmuth did debate the married women proposition once during the year, on the negative side of the proposition.

50. Quoted in Valerie Markess, "Debaters Past and Present—Driven to Succeed," *Pitt*, November 1981, 23. *Pitt* is an alumni publication published between 1939 and 1986. This issue and all subsequent issues cited in this chapter are available through the University of Pittsburgh's Documenting Pitt digital collection, http://digital.library.pitt.edu/d/documentingpitt/alumni.

51. "Coeds Debate Job Question," *Pitt Weekly*, November 21, 1930. The issue of dwindling audiences was not unique to the Depression. With the exception of

international debates, there was a noticeable decline in audience numbers in
the 1920s. Raymond F. Howes, a member of Pitt's Public Speaking faculty who
coached debate alongside Parrish for a brief time, discussed this issue in 1925.
Howes noted that even in larger cities like Pittsburgh, large crowds were rare for
debates. He estimated that average audience size during this time was between
60 and 200. See his "Finding Debate Audiences," *Quarterly Journal of Speech* 11,
no. 4 (1925): 364–68, DOI: 10.1080/00335632509379586. As my later discussion
of Penn State women's debate indicates, some extension debates did yield larger
audiences of up to 1000 in the 1930s.

52. "Coed Debaters Turn Lawyers," *Pitt Weekly*, January 17, 1930. See also John
    Stanley Gray, "The Oregon Plan of Debating," *Quarterly Journal of Speech* 12, no.
    2 (1926): 175–80.

53. A note on nomenclature: Marie Hochmuth married Alan Nichols, faculty
    member and longtime director of the University of Southern California debate
    team, in 1961. Citations of her work elsewhere sometimes refer to her as Marie
    Hochmuth, Marie Hochmuth Nichols, Marie H. Nichols, and Marie Hochmuth
    (Nichols). Names like Hochmuth also provide researchers with a practical
    challenge: to think of all of the possible ways that the last name could be
    misspelled. In scholarly publications, as well as in university materials such as
    yearbooks and news articles, I found Hochmuth spelled variously as *Hockmuth,
    Hochmeth, Hockmeth*. A Web search alone might have missed these valuable
    documents. I refer to her as Hochmuth throughout this chapter, because that was
    her name during the historical period studied. Bibliographic entries will appear
    under her last name at the time of publication.

54. See Dunbar Historical Society, http://www.dunbarhistoricalsociety.com.

55. Jane Blankenship, "Marie Hochmuth Nichols: President of the National
    Communication Association, 1969," National Communication Association, http://
    www.natcom.org.

56. Marie Hochmuth, "Great Teachers of Speech: III. Wayland Maxfield Parrish,
    Teacher and Colleague," *Speech Teacher* 4, no. 3 (1955): 159.

57. Hochmuth's election followed teammate Edith Hirsch's resignation due to "excess
    activities points." "Install Coed Debate Head," *Pitt Weekly*, October 31, 1930.

58. "Coeds to Debate in Intercollegiate Tilt," *Pitt Weekly*, February 6, 1931.

59. "Genevieve Blatt Papers," Pennsylvania State Archives, http://www.phmc.state.
    pa.us/bah/dam/mg/mg283.htm.

60. On the theme of travel, it is interesting to note that at his retirement ceremony,

Wayland Parrish was remembered by both Hochmuth and Harold Ruttenberg (Pitt, Class of '35) for often reciting his favorite poem, "The Listeners" by Walter De la Mare, which features a character called "the Traveller." See Hochmuth, "Great Teachers of Speech," 159; and Harold J. Ruttenberg, "Public Speaking and Public Affairs" (Remarks in honor of Wayland Maxfield Parrish at the Annual Convention of the Speech Association of America, Chicago, IL, December 28, 1954).

61. Blankenship, "Marie Hochmuth Nichols."

62. For example, during Hochmuth's tenure at Pitt, two members of the Men's Debating Association, C. J. Phillips and Elliott Finkel, traveled with Parrish on a three-week tour of the south. Phillips was an editor of the University of Pittsburgh student newspaper, the *Pitt Weekly*, and reports from the tour were documented there in a three-part feature. In each installment, the adventures of the tour were dramatized with reports from "the cast": Prof. W. M. Parrish as "The Kernel," Elliott Finkel as "The Pistol City Flash," and C. J. Phillips as "Ten Yards Johnny." Their reports provided details about their travels, the debates, and their encounters with "fair southern lassies" to whom they suffered their only competitive losses on the tour. See C. J. Phillips, "Pitt Debaters Shake Kentucky Cornfields for Georgia Peaches on Whirlwind Southern Trip," *Pitt Weekly*, February 5, 1930; C. J. Phillips, "Adventurous Debating Trio Reports Actions in Land of Caballeros by Airmail Message," *Pitt Weekly* February 14, 1930; C. J. Phillips, "Debaters Bring Home Many Victories; Losses Sustained Only to Fair Southern Lassies," *Pitt Weekly*, February 21, 1930.

63. Gladys Pyle, "Coeds Praise Debate Trips," *Pitt Weekly*, March 27, 1931.

64. "Combined Men's and Women's Forensics Show," 1931, program, Box 1, Folder 7, William Pitt Debating Union, University of Pittsburgh Archives Information Files, University of Pittsburgh Library System.

65. "Combined Men's and Women's Forensics Show."

66. *Pitt Weekly*, May 15, 1931. Spirer went on to become a distinguished clinical psychologist, and Crowder worked as a statistical officer at the United States Bureau of the Budget.

67. Blankenship, "Marie Hochmuth Nichols."

68. See, for example, McCann's Garden Shops advertisement, "Pittsburgh . . . This Is Your Chance to Help the Unemployed," *Pittsburgh Post-Gazette*, April 1, 1931. For more on the Allegheny County Emergency Relief Association, see Dorothy M. Brown and Elizabeth McKeown, *The Poor Belong to Us: Catholic Charities and*

American Welfare (Cambridge, MA: Harvard University Press, 1997), 166.

69. *The Owl*, 1935–36, 130.

70. Marie Hochmuth, "Richard Whately's *Elements of Rhetoric*, Part III, a Critical Edition" (Master's thesis, University of Pittsburgh, 1936), Marie Hochmuth Nichols Papers, Series 15/23/25–1, Box 1, Folder 7: Master's Thesis on Whately, University of Illinois Archives.

71. Hochmuth, "Great Teachers of Speech," 160.

72. "Offer New Course at Mount Mercy," *Pittsburgh Post-Gazette*, January 16, 1939.

73. "Miss Hochmuth Convention Speaker," *The McAuleyan*, April 1938, 2.

74. Marie Hochmuth quoted in Mary Thompson, "Educator Sees Lack of Good Judgment in Choice of Student Debate Subjects," *Pittsburgh Press*, April 25, 1938, 20.

75. "Pitt Men Defy Girl Debaters," *Pittsburgh Press*, April 27, 1939. Note the inequity built into the title of this newspaper article. The article also misquotes Hochmuth' original quote from the earlier *Pittsburgh Press* article, substituting "girls" for "women."

76. Marie Hochmuth, "Your Gown Is Lovely, But . . ." *Bulletin of the Debating Association of Pennsylvania Colleges* 12 (January 16, 1939): 1–4. Despite an extensive search, I have not been able to locate a copy of this issue of the publication. References hereafter are from the five-page typewritten manuscript of the article found in the Marie Hochmuth Nichols Papers, 15/23/25–1, Box 1, File 1, University of Illinois Archives.

77. Hochmuth, "Your Gown," 1.

78. Hochmuth, "Your Gown," 2.

79. Hochmuth, "Your Gown," 2.

80. Hochmuth, "Your Gown," 2.

81. Hochmuth, "Your Gown," 3. She may have inherited her view from Richard Murphy, who professed "a glee club singing 'Who is Sylvia?' raises questions which are irrelevant to discussion" in his "The Etiquette of Argument," 20.

82. Hochmuth, "Your Gown," 3.

83. Hochmuth, "Your Gown," 3; Kahn, "Analyzing the Proposition," 43.

84. Hochmuth, "Your Gown," 4.

85. Hochmuth, "Your Gown," 4–5.

86. Hannah Arendt, *The Human Condition* (Chicago: University of Chicago Press, 1958), 48–49; Hochmuth, "Your Gown," 5.

87. This is an angle I develop in Carly S. Woods, "Women Debating Society:

Negotiating Difference in Historical Argument Cultures" (PhD dissertation, University of Pittsburgh, 2010), 130–55.

88. "Miss Hochmuth Directs Plans for Reunion," *McAuleyan*, May–June 1938, 8.

89. Marie Hochmuth, "Henry Lee Ewbank: Scholar and Teacher," (eulogy, 1961): 1, in Nichols Papers, Box 1, Folder 35: Ewbank Eulogy and correspondence, 1961–62, University of Illinois Archives. Hochmuth received her PhD from Wisconsin in 1945. From 1930 to 1945, the three leading universities for public address scholarship were Wisconsin, Cornell, and Iowa, though Martin J. Medhurst notes that studies in public address made up only a small portion of the theses and dissertations at these universities. See Martin J. Medhurst, "The History of Public Address as an Academic Study," in *The Handbook of Rhetoric and Public Address*, ed. Shawn J. Parry-Giles and J. Michael Hogan (Oxford: Wiley-Blackwell, 2010), 36–37.

90. Richard Murphy, "Colleague and Counselor," *Speech Teacher* 4, no. 3 (1955): 163.

91. *The Owl*, 1939, 180.

92. *The Owl*, 1940, 122.

93. Charles W. Lomas, "Debating, a Live Activity," *Pitt*, January 1940, 45–46.

94. *The Owl*, 1942, 152.

95. Robert C. Alberts, *Pitt: The Story of the University of Pittsburgh, 1787–1987* (Pittsburgh: University of Pittsburgh Press, 1986), 186.

96. Alberts, *Pitt*, 187.

97. Charles W. Lomas, "War Information and Training," *Pitt*, Autumn 1942, 22.

98. Helen Pool Rush, "Women Students and the War," *Pitt*, Autumn 1942, 26. Helen Pool Rush was a longtime member of the Pitt faculty who took over when Thrysa Amos passed away in 1941. As Rush points out, many women's organizations reoriented their efforts during the war. For example, the Style Committee was integrated into the War Activities Committee, and nursing classes were offered. See Rush, "Women Students," 26. Amos's and Rush's visions for Pitt students confirm what historian Susan Levine has observed about "equality with a difference" as a dominant belief that characterized women's conflicting professional and gender identities—and so the focus of women's education shifted to leadership and social graces. See Levine, *Degrees of Equality*, 33.

99. Lomas, "War Information and Training."

100. *The Owl*, 1943, 47.

101. *The Owl*, 1943, 48.

102. *The Owl*, 1943, 48.

103. *The Owl*, 1943, 49.

104. Ruth R. Haun, "The Speech Program for 1944," *Pitt*, Autumn 1944, 48.

105. This conclusion can be considered in light of Greene and Hicks's argument in "Lost Convictions" that "the debating both sides controversy articulates debate to Cold War liberal discourses of 'American exceptionalism' by folding the norm of free and full expression onto the soul of the debater" (102). This chapter is not in direct conversation with "Lost Convictions" because of the historical period and because the women debaters did not regularly debate both sides of propositions. However, it does provide additional and explicit historical evidence, predating the discourses of Cold War liberalism that came to a head in the switch-sides debate controversy of 1954, of the ways that debate was enlisted in the service of patriotism.

106. Carol Sonenklar, *We Are a Strong, Articulate Voice: A History of Women at Penn State* (University Park: Pennsylvania State University Press, 2006), 5–6. See also Meyers, *University Coeducation*, 14–15.

107. John H. Frizzell, "Notes on the History of Intercollegiate Debating, 1898–1927," 1939, document, AX/PSUA/O5234, Speech Department Notebooks, Folder: Department History #1, Penn State University Archives.

108. "Penn State University Department of Speech Centennial History," 1955, pamphlet, Marie Hochmuth Nichols Papers, 15/23/025, Folder 13: Boeckh, Penn State Centennial History (1955), University of Illinois Archives.

109. Quoted in Frizzell, "Notes on the History."

110. "Penn State University Centennial."

111. Frizzell, "Notes on the History." For more on Frizzell's efforts to forge different debate formats, see "New Debate Form Gains Popularity: Parliamentary Session Developed at Penn State Spreads to Other Colleges," *New York Times*, January 9, 1937.

112. "Clayton H. Schug Papers, 1903–1971," Penn State University Archives, http://www.libraries.psu.edu/findingaids/1325.htm. I write more extensively about Schug's role as a faculty advisor to the women's debate team, and the way he was remembered by debaters who attended Penn State in the 1930s and 1940s, in Carly S. Woods, "Taking Women Seriously: Debaters, Faculty Allies, and the Feminist Work of Debating in the 1930s and 1940s," in *Speech and Debate as Civic Education*, ed. J. Michael Hogan, Jessica A. Kurr, Michael J. Bergmaier, and Jeremy D. Johnson (University Park: Penn State University Press, 2017), 53–63.

113. Carol Sonenklar points out that the number of women enrolled at Penn State

doubled during the Depression, with women students comprising approximately 16% of the total student body in 1930, and 20–25% by 1935, in her *We Are a Strong, Articulate Voice*, 56. Despite its title, Sonenklar's history mentions Penn State women's debate only once, and in passing (64).

114. "A Summary Report Showing the Growth of Women's Debate at the Pennsylvania State College, 1931 to 1937," 1937, document, Paterno/GST/A001.21, Group #282, Box 1, Folder: Women's Debate Annual Report, 1931–1947, Clayton Schug Papers, Penn State University Archives. There is a discrepancy in the number of debaters reported in this document and the number in the Penn State University Centennial document, which states "in 1931, only three persons made an appearance at an organizational meeting" (16). While it is not clear why this discrepancy exists, these statistics are nevertheless quite illustrative of the considerable expansion of the women's team in the 1930s.

115. "He-She Debate," May 5, 1932, flyer in scrapbook, AX/CATO/PSUA/M/08.23, Box: Intercollegiate Debate, 1926–1934, Penn State University Archives. Seth Low Junior College was a short-lived two-year college associated with Columbia University that enrolled mostly Jewish immigrants. See Herbert Aptheker's description in "Vindication in Speaking Truth to Power," in *Against the Odds: Scholars Who Challenged Racism in the Twentieth Century*, ed. Benjamin Bowser and Louis Kushnick (Amherst: University of Massachusetts Press, 2004), 194.

116. "Penn State Debate Teams Here Yesterday," newspaper clipping, *Daily Record* (Renovo, PA), March 24, 1933, in AX/PSUA/05234, Box: Speech Department Notebooks, Speech Notebook #3: History of Penn State Debating, Penn State University Archives.

117. "Penn State Women's Varsity Debate, 1934–35," 1935, pamphlet, Paterno/GST/A001.21, Group #282, Box 1, Folder: Women's Debate Annual Report, 1931–1947, Clayton Schug papers, Penn State University Archives.

118. "Penn State University Centennial."

119. "The Forensic Counsel presents the University of Pittsburgh and the Pennsylvania State College in an intercollegiate debate," February 28, 1935, pamphlet, AX/PSUA/05234, Box: Speech Department Notebooks, Speech Notebook #6: Debate Pictures and Memorabilia, Penn State University Archives.

120. Nash and Romero, "'Citizenship for the College Girl,'" 8.

121. "Constitution of Delta Alpha Delta," (revised 1934), document, Paterno/GST/A001.21, Clayton Schug Papers, Group #282, Box 1, Folder: Delta Alpha Delta, Penn State University Archives.

122. Minutes of the Forensic Council, February 23, 1933, AX/PSUA/05234, Box: Speech Department Notebooks, Speech Notebook #4: The Forensic Council Minutes, 1926–1939, Penn State University Archives.

123. "Penn State University Centennial."

124. Clayton H. Schug, "The Secret Ritual of Delta Alpha Delta," document. Paterno/ GST/A001.21, Clayton Schug Papers, Group #282, Box 1, Folder: Delta Alpha Delta, Penn State University Archives.

125. Florence Watkins Patrick, '39, to Clayton Schug, November 8, 1971. Paterno/ GST/A001.20, Clayton Schug Papers, Group #282, Box 3, Penn State University Archives. This letter and others from women's debate alumni were pasted into a book honoring Schug upon his retirement from Penn State in 1971.

126. Minutes of the Forensic Council, September 15, 1927, AX/PSUA/05234, Box: Speech Department Notebooks, Speech Notebook #4: The Forensic Council Minutes, 1926–1939, Penn State University Archives.

127. "Statement of Principles for the Coordination of Men's and Women's Debate at the Pennsylvania State College," 1936–1937, document, AX/PSUA/05234, Box: Speech Department Notebooks, Speech Notebook #3: History of Penn State Debating, Penn State University Archives.

128. "Sound, Mere Sound: The Forensic Follies of 1935," 1935, program, AX/ PSUA/05234, Box: Speech Department Notebooks, Speech Notebook #6: Debate Pictures and Memorabilia, Penn State University Archives.

129. "Action! Action! Action! Forensics Follies of 1936," 1936, program, AX/ PSUA/05234, Box: Speech Department Notebooks, Speech Notebook #3: History of Penn State Debating, Penn State University Archives.

130. Marjorie Witsil Gemmill to Clayton Schug, November 10, 1971, Clayton Schug Papers, Group #282, Box 3, Penn State University Archives.

131. Joan Huber to William W. Hamilton, October 23, 1971, Clayton Schug Papers, Group #282, Box 3, Penn State University Archives. The letter appears pasted in a book honoring Clayton Schug upon his retirement from Penn State.

132. Clayton H. Schug to Dean Charlotte E. Ray, November 15, 1938, Clayton Schug Papers, Group #282, Folder: Job offers (Schug), Penn State University Archives.

133. Charlotte E. Ray to Clayton Schug, November 18, 1938, Clayton Schug Papers, Group #282, Folder: Job offers (Schug), Penn State University Archives.

134. Michael Bezilla, *Penn State: An Illustrated History* (University Park: Pennsylvania State University Press, 1985), chap. 7, https://libraries.psu.edu/about/collections/ penn-state-university-park-campus-history-collection/penn-state-illustrated.

135. Bezilla, *Penn State*, chap. 7.

136. Bezilla, *Penn State*, chap. 7.

137. This estimate is based on numbers quoted in Frizzell's speech at a 1946 banquet to the Pennsylvania Speech Association, which stated, "now we have two debate squads averaging, even in the war years, twenty-five to thirty men and nearly twice that many women" (5). See John H. Frizzell, "A Half Century of Speech in Pennsylvania," October 11, 1946, speech, AX/PSUA/05234, Box: Speech Department Notebooks, Folder: Misc. Dept. of Speech Documents, Penn State University Archives.

138. Huber to Hamilton, October 23, 1971. I had the good fortune of corresponding with Huber, and she recalled the 1944 clash over funding as a turning point when she realized the disadvantage of being a woman debater, one that tainted her experience in the activity (email message to the author, October 30, 2014).

139. Charlotte E. Ray quoted in Sonensklar, *We Are a Strong, Articulate Voice*, 68.

140. Charlotte E. Ray to Clayton Schug, August 20, 1945, Clayton Schug Papers, Group #282, Folder: Letters of Appreciation to Schug, Penn State University Archives.

141. Hochmuth, "Your Gown," 3.

142. "Varsity Debaters," 4.

143. Schug quoted in "Varsity Debaters," 4.

144. Ruth Zang Potts to Clayton Schug, November 5, 1971, Clayton Schug Papers, Group #282, Box 3, Penn State University Archives.

145. Schug quoted in "Varsity Debaters," 4.

146. Schug quoted in "Varsity Debaters," 4.

147. Nash and Romero, "'Citizenship for the College Girl,'" 12.

148. Ana M. Martinez Aleman and Kristen Renn, *Women in Higher Education: An Encyclopedia* (Santa Barbara: ABC-CLIO Press, 2002), 251–52.

149. Huber to Hamilton, October 23, 1971. Huber eventually went on to earn a PhD in sociology. Her many accomplishments include becoming a member of the faculty, vice president of Academic Affairs, and university provost at Ohio State University, as well as serving as the president of the American Sociological Association.

150. "They Have the Last Word," *Pittsburgh Press*, May 6, 1945, Clayton Schug Papers, Group #282, Box 2, Folder: Press Releases on Debate Members, Penn State University Archives.

151. Although this caption states that the debaters called Schug "Sugar," when the

article came out this claim reportedly irritated the debaters, who denied that anyone on the team at the time actually used the nickname (Huber, email message to the author, October 30, 2014).

152. "2 College Men Among 651 Pa. Prisoners," *Afro-American*, March 25, 1933.

153. Robert Branham, "'I Was Gone on Debating': Malcolm X's Prison Debates and Public Confrontations," *Argumentation and Advocacy* 31 (1995): 117–37.

154. C. F. Lauer to John H. Frizzell, March 10, 1941, Clayton Schug Papers, Group #282, Box 1, Folder: Letters of Appreciation to Schug, Penn State University Archives. Lauer used this same language in a letter to the Princeton debate team after the event. See Frederick B. Haberman, "NO Whispering Gallery," *Princeton Alumni Weekly*, May 19, 1941. According to that report, the Princeton debate team had also participated in a debate at the U.S. penitentiary in Lewisburg, PA earlier that day.

155. Lauer to Frizzell, March 10, 1941.

156. Joseph S. Roucek, "Experiment in Adult Education at Rockview Farm Prison," *School and Society* 42 (1935): 200. In 1933, it was reported that the vast majority of inmates at the Western Pennsylvania and Rockview penitentiaries did not graduate from high school; the "average mental age" was fifth grade. At that time, 30% of the population was African American, even though they only made up one-tenth of the population in that part of the state. See "2 College Men." Later, classes were established in order to aid inmates who needed to pass educational requirements in order to be eligible for parole. Courses were offered on radio maintenance, farming, and diesel motors, in addition to advanced grades and college courses. See "School Is Reopening at Wall-Less Prison," *New York Times*, September 5, 1937. Penn State participated by offering extension courses in reading and writing in the 1940s, and there is evidence that some other Penn State student groups went to Rockview to play intramural sports or went to talk to the prisoners about religion in the 1940s and 1950s.

157. Although it was a medium security prison at the time, the prison would have been regarded with considerable caution, especially by young women, due to several crimes or alleged crimes committed by escaped inmates during this period. I was able to locate evidence that the debates continued until at least 1951, when the *Daily Collegian* reported that nine PSU women went to the prison to debate against SUNY-Oswego men in a non-decision debate. The most dramatic thing that happened in that debate was that a mouse appeared on the stage during the debate, though the women students confessed that they were on edge. See

Moylan Mills, "Debaters Capture Prisoners," *Daily Collegian*, April 19, 1951, 2. In 1953, Rockview made national headlines when 400 of its 800 inmates took part in a revolt. See "Half of Convicts End Prison Revolt," *New York Times*, January 21, 1953.

158. C. F. Lauer to John H. Frizzell, April 17, 1946, Clayton Schug Papers, Group #282, Box 1, Folder: Letters of Appreciation to Schug, Penn State University Archives.

159. Berry, "A Survey," 87.

160. Thorrel B. Fest, "A Survey of College Forensics," *Quarterly Journal of Speech* 34, no. 2 (1948): 168.

161. Emogene Emery, "Rehabilitating Women's Debate," *Southern Speech Journal* 17, no. 3 (1952): 186, DOI:10.1080/10417945209371221.

CONCLUSION

1. See Daphne Spain, *Gendered Spaces* (Chapel Hill: University of North Carolina Press, 1992); Helen Lefkowitz Horowitz, *Alma Mater: Design and Experience in the Women's Colleges from Their Nineteenth Century Beginnings to the 1930s*, 2nd ed. (Amherst: University of Massachusetts Press, 1992).

2. Here, I am returning to Lorraine Code's definition of rhetorical space. See Lorraine Code, *Rhetorical Spaces: Essays on Gendered Locations* (New York: Routledge, 1995), x.

3. Hannah Arendt, *Lectures on Kant's Political Philosophy*, ed. Ronald Beiner (Chicago: University of Chicago Press, 1992), 43. Michele Kennerly argues that rhetoric itself has the ability to transport bodies and minds, where "words launch us on journeys of judgment," in "Getting Carried Away: How Rhetorical Transport Gets Judgment Going," *Rhetoric Society Quarterly* 40, no. 3 (2010): 288. In feminist history and rhetoric, the language of mobility and travel is often used to explain the negotiation of public and private spheres. For example, the ongoing appeal of the woman orator, as Joan Wallach Scott explains, is in movement, in that it "projects women into masculine space, where they experience the pleasures and danger of transgressing social and sexual boundaries." See Joan Wallach Scott, *The Fantasy of Feminist History* (Durham, NC: Duke University Press, 2011), 54. Mary P. Ryan uses the language of "circuitous routes" to describe the sometimes unorthodox ways that women found avenues to enter the public sphere in the nineteenth century in her "Gender and Public Access: Women's Politics in Nineteenth-Century America," in *Feminism, the Public and the Private*,

ed. Joan B. Landes (Oxford: Oxford University Press, 1998), 218.

4. Arendt, *Lectures on Kant's*, 43.

5. Minutes of the LEDS, June 2, 1877, MS 1725.

6. George Lakoff and Mark Johnson identify argument-as-war as a central conceptual metaphor in *Metaphors We Live By* (Chicago: University of Chicago Press, 1980), 4. This view of debate undergirds Deborah Tannen's critique in her book *The Argument Culture: Moving from Debate to Dialogue* (New York: Random House, 1998). In fact, the hardback cover of Tannen's book shows an image of a bomb about to detonate.

7. Phyllis Rooney, "Philosophy, Adversarial Argumentation, and Embattled Reason," *Informal Logic* 30, no. 3 (2001): 211. Moreover, as Sylvia Burrow explains, women who adopt aggressive styles of speech must contend with gendered stereotypes or double binds facing women in power. See Sylvia Burrow, "Verbal Sparring and Apologetic Points: Politeness in Gendered Argumentation Contexts," *Informal Logic* 30, no. 3 (2010): 239.

8. Richard Murphy, "The Etiquette of Argument: Rules and Ethics of Debating: Broadcast from the University of Pittsburgh Studio on November 14, 1929," in *Debating: A Series of Six Radio Talks*, ed. Theresa G. Kahn and Richard Murphy (Pittsburgh: University of Pittsburgh Radio Publication, 1929), 21–22.

9. Sarah Mair, quoted in Lettice Milne Rae, "From Beginning to End," in *Ladies in Debate: Being a History of the Ladies' Edinburgh Debating Society, 1865–1935*, ed. Lettice Milne Rae (Edinburgh: Oliver and Boyd, 1936), 21.

10. Sarah Mair, "Foreword," in Rae, *Ladies in Debate*, 11.

11. See Wayne Brockriede, "Arguers as Lovers," *Philosophy & Rhetoric* 5, no.1 (Winter 1972): 1–11. In the article, Brockriede suggests that the ideal arguer will treat their interlocutor as a lover: they share risk in a symbiotic relationship geared toward cooperative knowledge production. Instead, what happens most of the time is that arguers treat their interlocutors as competitors that they seek to seduce or rape. Although he is critiquing these orientations, Brockriede's language here is distasteful, risking the trivialization of sexual violence by comparing it to meta-communication about an intercollegiate debate. This says something about not only intercollegiate debate but also the academic culture of the 1970s, that a metaphor steeped in jarring sexual violence was so easily used as a schema for talking about argumentation. However, I include it here because it is representative of the problematic excesses of violent metaphors running throughout argumentation theory (even theory that explicitly tries to

move away from such associations). More importantly, the problematic nature of this metaphor is indicative of the need for scholarly feminist intervention. Based on a particular kind of feminist critique, Brockriede's observations about the dominating arguer can be extended to the whole enterprise of persuasion, especially Sally Miller Gearhart's "The Womanization of Rhetoric," *Women's Studies International Quarterly* 2 (1979): 197. A special issue of *Argumentation and Advocacy* was dedicated to the issue: vol. 32, no. 4 (1996). For extensions and critiques, see especially Nina M. Lozano-Reich and Dana L. Cloud, "The Uncivil Tongue: Invitational Rhetoric and the Problem of Inequality," *Western Journal of Communication* 73, no. 2 (2009): 220–26; Jennifer Emerling Bone, Cindy L. Griffin, and T. M. Linda Scholz, "Beyond Traditional Conceptualizations of Rhetoric: Invitational Rhetoric and a Move toward Civility," *Western Journal of Communication* 72, no. 4 (2008): 434–62; Trudy Govier, *The Philosophy of Argument* (Newport News, VA: Vale Press, 1999), 45–68; Richard Fulkerson, "Transcending Our Conception of Argument in Light of Feminist Critiques," *Argumentation and Advocacy* 32, no. 4 (1996): 199–218; and M. Lane Bruner, "Producing Identities: Gender Problematization and Feminist Argumentation," *Argumentation and Advocacy* 32, no. 4 (1996): 185–98.

12. This is especially unfortunate given the sheer number of contemporary U.S. scholars who entered to the discipline of communication through debate participation. Jarrod Atchison and Edward Panetta note that "intercollegiate debating brought some of the leading rhetorical critics of the 20th century to the discipline through their participation in debate. A. Craig Baird, Edwin Black, Celeste Condit, Douglas Ehninger, Thomas Goodnight, Michael McGee, Robert Newman, Marie Nichols, David Zarefsky, and many more of our critics came to the field through participation in debate." See Jarrod Atchison and Edward Panetta, "Intercollegiate Debate and Speech Communication: Historical Developments and Issues for the Future," in *The Sage Handbook of Rhetorical Studies*, ed. Andrea A. Lunsford, Kirt H. Wilson, and Rosa A. Eberly (Thousand Oaks, CA: Sage Publications, 2009), 322. For a sense of the centrality of forensics to the early history of speech communication, and possibilities for its future, see Matthew P. Brigham, "Nostalgia or Hope: On the Relationship Between Competitive Debate and Speech Communication Departments—Past, Present, and Future" (paper presented at the National Communication Association convention, San Diego, CA, November 23, 2008).

13. I have endeavored to be specific and attentive to the intersections of gender

and race, but there is much more work to be done concerning the historical experiences of debaters of color. For example, this study is limited by its focus on predominantly white institutions (PWIs), and there is a rich history of debate to be explored at historically black institutions (HBCUs, historically black colleges and universities). Past work focused on HBCU debating societies includes David Gold, *Rhetoric at the Margins: Revising the History of Writing Instruction in American Colleges, 1873–1947* (Carbondale: Southern Illinois University, 2008); Marcus H. Boulware, "Speech Training in the Negro College," *Journal of Negro Education* 16, no.1 (Winter 1947): 115–20; Timothy M. O'Donnell, "'The Great Debaters': A Challenge to Higher Education," *Inside Higher Education*, January 7, 2008, https://www.insidehighered.com/views/2008/01/07/odonnell; *The Great Debaters*, DVD, directed by Denzel Washington (Chicago: Harpo Films, 2007); Brittany Cooper, "Take No Prisoners: The Role of Debate in a Liberatory Education," in *Using Debate in the Classroom: Encouraging Critical Thinking, Communication, and Collaboration*, ed. Karyl A. Davis et al. (New York: Routledge, 2017), 11–21.

14. Mimi Barash Coppersmith, interview with the author, August 13, 2013.

15. There are countless testimonies that confirm the importance of contemporary debate. In 2015, Pennsylvania State University's Center for Democratic Deliberation and Department of Communication Arts and Sciences hosted a conference on Speech and Debate as Civic Education, co-sponsored by the National Endowment for the Humanities and the National Communication Association, that featured research presentations on debate in a range of contexts: contemporary and historical, domestic and international. See also New York City middle school educator Paul Deard's article, "Making the Case for Teaching Students Debate," *Education Week*, August 12, 2014, http://www.edweek.org/ew/articles/2014/08/12/01deards.h34.html, and numerous research studies about the impact of debate participation on academic achievement from the National Association of Urban Debate Leagues, "Our Results," http://urbandebate.org/Our-Results.

16. For example, eleven of the top twenty (including the top three) speakers at the 2015 Urban Debate National Championship were women. Such participation is encouraged through efforts such as emphasizing novice debate, urban debate leagues, and the Women's Debate Institute. Joe Miller's *Cross-X: The Amazing True Story of How the Most Unlikely Team from the Most Unlikely of Places Overcame Staggering Obstacles at Home and at School to Challenge the Debate*

Community on Race, Power and Education (New York: Picador, 2006) showcases how debate allowed African American high school students in Kansas City to achieve success and overcome barriers in their education and home lives. A 1998 forum in *Contemporary Argumentation & Debate* demonstrates the potential benefits of urban debate leagues. See especially Melissa Maxcy Wade, "The Case for Urban Debate Leagues," *Contemporary Argumentation & Debate* 19 (1998): 60–65. See also Richard Pineda and Chris Salinas, "Model Proposal: Increasing Latina/o Involvement in Policy Debate through Summer Debate Workshops," *Contemporary Argumentation & Debate* 30 (September 2009): 114–29. Shanara Rose Reid-Brinkley's work demonstrates how despite their benefits, media representations of urban debate leagues operate within a narrow framework of racial stereotypes in which African American students are headed for disaster and are "saved" by debate. See her "The Harsh Realities of 'Acting Black': How African American Policy Debaters Negotiate Representation through Racial Performance and Style," (PhD dissertation, University of Georgia, 2008) and "Ghetto Kids Gone Good: Race, Representation, and Authority in the Scripting of Inner City Youths in the Urban Debate League," *Argumentation and Advocacy* 49, no. 1 (2012): 77–99.

17. Examples of publications that engage issues of diversity in debate include Michael D. Bartanen and Robert Littlefield, *Forensics in America: A History* (Lanham, MD: Rowman and Littlefield, 2014); Joseph P. Zompetti, "Personalizing Debating: Diversity and Tolerance in the Debate Community," *Contemporary Argumentation & Debate* 25 (September 2004): 26–39; Jon Bruschke, "Debate Factions and Affirmative Actions," *Contemporary Argumentation & Debate* 25 (September 2004): 78–88; Mike Allen et al., "Diversity in United States Forensics: A Report on Research Conducted for the American Forensic Association," *Argumentation and Advocacy* 40, no. 3 (2004): 173–84; Pamela L. Stepp and Beth Gardner, "Ten Years of Demographics: Who Debates in America?" *Argumentation and Advocacy* 38, no. 2 (2001): 69–83. See also a special issue of the *Monash Debating Review* dedicated to gender, linguistic, and religious diversity in debate (vol. 11, 2013).

18. See Emma Pierson, "Men Outspeak Women: Analysing the Gender Gap in Competitive Debate," *Monash Debating Review* 11 (2013). In 2013, two debaters were booed and subjected to sexist jeers as they spoke at a debate competition hosted by the Glasgow University Union. The incident made national and international news, and sparked follow-on conversations about sexism in debate

and university campuses in a broader sense. See Laura Bates, "The Sexist Laddism Emanating from Our Universities," *The Guardian*, March 8, 2013. And when two Towson University students, Ameena Ruffin and Korey Johnson, became the first African American women to win the Cross-Examination Debate Association's national tournament in 2014, those inside and outside the debate circuit diminished their accomplishment. Brittney Cooper, "'I Was Hurt': How White Elite Racism Invaded a College Debate Championship," *Salon*, May 13, 2014. Hicks and Greene review this controversy under the heading of "The Politics of Performance," in "Managed Convictions: Debate and the Limits of Electoral Politics," *Quarterly Journal of Speech* 101, no. 1 (2015): 102–4. They note that much media attention and criticism surrounded their choice to make "debate performance and style a topic of debate" (103).

19. Kathryn T. Flannery, "Shifting the Center of Gravity: The Rhetorics of Radical Feminist Pedagogy," in *Teaching Rhetorica: Theory, Pedagogy, Practice*, ed. Kate Ronald and Joy Ritchie (Portsmouth, NH: Boyton-Cook Publishers, 2006), 49.

20. Catherine H. Palczewski discusses the work of the Women's Debate Institute in her "Beyond Peitho: The Women's Debate Institute as Civic Education," in *Speech and Debate as Civic Education*, ed. J. Michael Hogan et al. (University Park: Penn State University Press, 2017). See also Jackie Poapst and Allison Harper, "Reflections on the 2014 Celebration of Women in Debate Tournament at George Mason University," *Argumentation and Advocacy* 53, no. 2 (2017): 127–37.

21. J. Michael Hogan et al., "Speech and Debate as Civic Education," *Communication Education* 65, no. 4 (2016): 377.

22. Louisa Peacock, "Sarah Wollaston: Female MPs Fear Being Derided in Commons Due to Their High-Pitched Voices," *The Telegraph*, November 21, 2013.

23. Guy Hedgecoe, "Sexism Rears Ugly Head in Spanish Election Debate," *The Irish Times*, May 20, 2014.

24. Charlotte Alter, "The Presidential Debate was a Battle of the Sexes," *Time*, September 6, 2016.

25. While I am not suggesting a seamless parallel to the gender politics of contemporary political debates, contemporary political debates are a dynamic research area in rhetoric and public address. The centennial of the National Communication Association prompted a generative moment of reflection on this relationship in the *Quarterly Journal of Speech*. Jamieson's essay, "The Discipline's Debate Contributions: Then, Now, Next," made the initial connection between the discipline's debate history and contemporary analysis of electoral debates

(*Quarterly Journal of Speech* 101, no. 1 [2015]: 85–97, DOI:10.1080/00335630.2 015.994905). She states: "Over the past 100 years, our discipline's researchers and teachers have nurtured inter-collegiate debate on their campuses and contributed both to the evolution of presidential debates and to scholarship making sense of them" (86). Trevor Parry-Giles and Shawn J. Parry-Giles's response essay ("Expanding the Discipline's Debate Contributions: New Potentials, Beyond Effects," *Quarterly Journal of Speech* 101, no. 1 [2015]: 113–26, DOI: 10.1080/00335630.2015.994902) draws upon different research trajectories to build the case for the rhetorical analysis of political debates. Hicks and Greene's response essay, "Managed Convictions," urges an ongoing examination of competitive debate's public controversies in order to probe electoral debate as a cultural technology for managing convictions.

26. See Mary Beard, "Women in Power," *London Review of Books* 39, no. 6 (2017): 9–14; Michele Kennerly and Carly S. Woods, "Moving Rhetorica," *Rhetoric Society Quarterly* 48, no. 1 (2018): 3–27, DOI: 10.1080/02773945.2017.1315445.

Bibliography

——————◆·——————

Abbott, Don. "Blair 'Abroad': The European Reception of the *Lectures on Rhetoric and Belles Lettres*." In *Scottish Rhetoric and Its Influences*, edited by Lynée Lewis Gaillet, 67–78. Mahwah, NJ: Lawrence Erlbaum Associates, 1998.

Alberts, Robert C. *Pitt: The Story of the University of Pittsburgh, 1787–1987*. Pittsburgh: University of Pittsburgh Press, 1986.

Aleman, Ana M. Martinez, and Kristen Renn. *Women in Higher Education: An Encyclopedia*. Santa Barbara: ABC-CLIO Press, 2002.

Allen, Mike, Mary Trejo, Michael Bartanen, Anthony Schroeder, and Tammie Ulrich. "Diversity in United States Forensics: A Report on Research Conducted for the American Forensic Association." *Argumentation and Advocacy* 40, no. 3 (2004): 173–84.

Amyx, Clifford. "Weaver the Liberal: A Memoir." *Modern Age* 32, no. 1 (1987): 101–6.

Andrew, Donna T. "Popular Culture and Public Debate: London 1780's." *The Historical Journal* 39, no. 2 (1996): 405–23.

———. "'The Passion for Public Speaking': Women's Debating Societies." In *Women &*

History: Voices of Early Modern England, edited by Valerie Frith, 165–88. Toronto: Coach House Press, 1995.

Aonuma, Satoru, Junya Mooroka, and Kakuhiko Seno. "Revisiting the U.S. Footprints: A Critical Exploration of Interscholastic/Intercollegiate Policy Debate in Post-World War II Japan." In Palczewski, *Disturbing Arguments*, 432–37.

Aptheker, Herbert. "Vindication in Speaking Truth to Power." In *Against the Odds: Scholars Who Challenged Racism in the Twentieth Century*, edited by Benjamin Bowser and Louis Kushnick, 193–226. Amherst: University of Massachusetts Press, 2004.

Arendt, Hannah. *Lectures on Kant's Political Philosophy*. Edited by Ronald Beiner. Chicago: University of Chicago Press, 1992.

———. *The Human Condition*. Chicago: University of Chicago Press, 1958.

Asen, Robert, and Daniel C. Brouwer, eds. *Counterpublics and the State*. Albany: State University of New York Press, 2001.

Atchison, Jarrod, and Edward Panetta. "Intercollegiate Debate and Speech Communication: Historical Developments and Issues for the Future." In Lunsford, Wilson, and Eberly, *The Sage Handbook of Rhetorical Studies*, 317–33.

Axford, Robert. "The Background of the Adult Education Movement." In *Transactions of the Wisconsin Academy of Sciences, Arts, and Letters*, vol. 1, edited by Stanley D. Beck, 345–51. Madison: Wisconsin Academy of Sciences, Arts, and Letters, 1961. Http://digital.library.wisc.edu/1711.dl/WI.WT1961.

Bacon, Jacqueline, and Glen McClish. "Reinventing the Master's Tools: Nineteenth Century African-American Literary Societies of Philadelphia and Rhetorical Education." *Rhetoric Society Quarterly* 30, no. 4 (2000): 19–47.

Baird, A. Craig. "Shall American Universities Adopt the British System of Debating?" *Quarterly Journal of Speech Education* 9, no. 3 (1923): 215–22.

Ballantine, W. G., ed. *The Oberlin Jubilee, 1833–1883*. Oberlin, OH: E.J. Goodrich, 1883.

Barclay, Katie. *Love, Intimacy, and Power: Marriage and Patriarchy in Scotland, 1650–1850*. Manchester: Manchester University Press, 2011.

Bartanen, Michael D., and Robert Littlefield. *Forensics in America: A History*. Lanham, MD: Rowman and Littlefield, 2014.

Bauer, Otto F. "The Harvard–Yale Myth." *The AFA Register* 11 (1963): 20.

———. "A Century of Debating at Northwestern University: 1855–1955." Master's thesis, Northwestern University, 1955.

Baumann, Roland M. *Constructing Black Education at Oberlin College: A Documentary History*. Athens: Ohio University Press, 2010.

Beard, Mary. "Women in Power." *London Review of Books* 39, no. 6 (2017): 9–14.

———. "The Public Voice of Women." *Women's History Review* 24, no. 5 (2015): 809–18.

Bell, Maria. *Songs of Two Homes*. Edinburgh: Oliphant Anderson and Ferrier, 1899.

Belt-Beyan, Phyllis M. *The Emergence of African American Literacy Traditions: Family and Community Efforts in the Nineteenth Century*. Westport, CT: Praeger, 2004.

Benhabib, Seyla. "Models of Public Space: Hannah Arendt, the Liberal Tradition, and Jürgen Habermas." In Landes, *Feminism*, 85–92.

Benn, Anthony Wedgwood, Edward Boyle, and Kenneth Harris. "American and British Debating." *Quarterly Journal of Speech* 34, no. 4 (1948): 469–72.

Benoit, William L., Dale Hample, and Pamela J. Benoit, ed. *Readings in Argumentation*. Berlin: Foris Publications, 1992.

Berry, Mildred Freburg. "A Survey of Intercollegiate Debate in the Mid-West Debate Conference." *Quarterly Journal of Speech* 14, no. 1 (1928): 86–94. DOI: 10.1080/00335632809379725.

Bezilla, Michael. *Penn State: An Illustrated History*. University Park: Pennsylvania State University Press, 1985.

Biesecker, Barbara. "Negotiating with Our Tradition: Reflecting Again (without Apologies) on the Feminization of Rhetoric." *Philosophy & Rhetoric* 26, no. 3 (1993): 236–41.

———. "Coming to Terms with Attempts to Write Women into the History of Rhetoric." *Philosophy & Rhetoric* 25, no. 2 (1992): 140–61.

Blackwell, Alice Stone. *Lucy Stone: Pioneer of Women's Rights*. Charlottesville: University Press of Virginia, 1930.

Blackwell, Antoinette Brown, and Sarah [Mrs. Claude U.] Gilson. "Antoinette Brown Blackwell: The First Woman Minister." Manuscript. Blackwell Family Papers, Schlesinger Library, Radcliffe Institute, Harvard University, Cambridge, MA.

Blair, Hugh. *Lectures on Rhetoric and Belles Lettres*. New York: James and John Harper, 1826.

Blankenship, Jane. "Marie Hochmuth Nichols: President of the National Communication Association, 1969." National Communication Association, http://www.natcom.org/index.asp?bid=1212.

Bone, Jennifer Emerling, Cindy L. Griffin, and T. M. Linda Scholz. "Beyond Traditional Conceptualizations of Rhetoric: Invitational Rhetoric and a Move toward Civility." *Western Journal of Communication* 72, no. 4 (2008): 434–62.

Bordelon, Suzanne. "'Resolved That the Mind of Woman Is Not Inferior to That of Man': Women's Oratorical Preparation in California State Normal School

Coeducation Literary Societies in the Late Nineteenth Century." *Advances in the History of Rhetoric* 15 (2012): 159–84. DOI: 10.1080/15362426.2012.697679.

———. "Contradicting and Complicating Feminization of Rhetoric Narratives: Mary Yost and Argument from a Sociological Perspective." *Rhetoric Society Quarterly* 35, no. 3 (2005): 101–24.

Bordogna, Francesca. *William James at the Boundaries: Philosophy, Science, and the Geography of Knowledge*. Chicago: University of Chicago Press, 2008.

Boulware, Marcus H. "Speech Training in the Negro College." *Journal of Negro Education* 16, no. 1 (1947): 115–20.

Bourdieu, Pierre. *Language and Symbolic Power*. Translated by Gino Raymond and Matthew Adamson. Cambridge: Polity Press, 1991.

Bowden, A. O. "The Woman's Club Movement: Appraisal and Prophecy." *Journal of Education* 111, no. 9 (1930): 257–60.

Branham, Robert James. "'Emancipating Myself': Mays the Debater." In *Walking Integrity: Benjamin Elijah Mays, Mentor to Martin Luther King, Jr.*, edited by Lawrence Edward Carter Sr., 81–109. Macon, GA: Mercer University Press, 1998.

———. *Stanton's Elm: An Illustrated History of Debating at Bates College*. Lewiston, ME: Bates College, 1996.

———. "'I Was Gone on Debating': Malcolm X's Prison Debates and Public Confrontations." *Argumentation & Advocacy* 31, no. 3 (1995): 117–37.

———. "Debate and Dissent in Late Tokugawa and Meiji Japan." *Argumentation and Advocacy* 30, no. 3 (1994): 131–49.

———. *Debate and Critical Analysis: A Harmony of Conflict*. Hillsdale, NJ: Lawrence Erlbaum Associates, 1991.

Brigham, Matthew P. "Nostalgia or Hope: On the Relationship Between Competitive Debate and Speech Communication Departments—Past, Present, and Future." Paper presented at the National Communication Association convention, San Diego, CA, November 23, 2008.

Brockmeier, Jens. *Beyond the Archive: Memory, Narrative, and the Autobiographical Process*. Oxford: Oxford University Press, 2015.

Brockriede, Wayne. "Where Is Argument?" In Benoit, Hample, and Benoit, *Readings in Argumentation*, 73–78.

———. "Arguers as Lovers." *Philosophy & Rhetoric* 5, no. 1 (1972): 1–11.

Broda-Bahm, Kenneth T., Daniela Kempf, and William J. Driscoll. *Argument and Audience: Presenting Public Debates in Public Settings*. New York: International Debate Education Association, 2004.

Brodkin, Karen. *How Jews Became White Folks and What That Says about Race in America*. New Brunswick: Rutgers University Press, 2002.

Brouwer, Daniel C. "ACT-ing UP in Congressional Hearings." In Asen and Brouwer, *Counterpublics and the State*, 87–110.

Brouwer, Daniel C., and Robert Asen, eds. *Public Modalities*. Tuscaloosa: University of Alabama Press, 2010.

Brown, Dorothy M., and Elizabeth McKeown. *The Poor Belong to Us: Catholic Charities and American Welfare*. Cambridge, MA: Harvard University Press, 1997.

Brown, Hildegard Gordon. *Conclusions of an Everyday Woman*. London: John Lane, The Bodley Head, 1908.

Browne, Stephen H. *Angelina Grimké: Rhetoric, Identity, and the Radical Imagination*. East Lansing: Michigan State University Press, 1999.

———. "Satirizing the Debating Society in Eighteenth-Century England." *Argumentation and Advocacy* 26, no. 1 (1989): 1–10.

———. "Satirizing Women's Speech in Eighteenth-Century England." *Rhetoric Society Quarterly* 22, no. 3 (1992): 20–29.

Bruner, M. Lane. "Producing Identities: Gender Problematization and Feminist Argumentation." *Argumentation and Advocacy* 32, no. 4 (1996): 185–98.

Bruschske, Jon. "Debate Factions and Affirmative Actions." *Contemporary Argumentation & Debate* 25 (September 2004): 78–88.

Bryden, Inga, and Janet Floyd. "Introduction." In *Domestic Space: Reading the Nineteenth-Century Interior*, edited by Inga Bryden and Janet Floyd, 1–17. Manchester: Manchester University Press, 1999.

Buchanan, Lindal. "Sarah Siddons and Her Place in Rhetorical History." *Rhetorica* 25, no. 4 (2007): 413–34.

———. *Regendering Delivery: The Fifth Canon and Antebellum Women Rhetors*. Carbondale: Southern Illinois University Press, 2005.

Buchanan, Lindal, and Kathleen J. Ryan, eds. *Walking and Talking Feminist Rhetorics: Landmark Essays and Controversies*. West Lafayette, IN: Parlor Press, 2010.

Burke, Kenneth. *A Grammar of Motives*. 3rd ed. Berkeley: University of California Press, 1969.

Burrow, Sylvia. "Verbal Sparring and Apologetic Points: Politeness in Gendered Argumentation Contexts." *Informal Logic* 30, no. 3 (2010): 235–62.

Calhoun, Craig J., ed. *Habermas and the Public Sphere*. Cambridge: MIT Press, 1992.

Campbell, Karlyn Kohrs. *Women Public Speakers in the United States, 1800–1925: A Bio-Critical Sourcebook*. Westport, CT: Greenwood Publishing Group, 1993.

———. "Biesecker Cannot Speak for Her Either." *Philosophy & Rhetoric* 26, no. 3 (1993): 153–59.

———. *Man Cannot Speak for Her: A Critical Study of Early Feminist Rhetoric.* Vol. 1. New York: Praeger, 1989.

Carter, Phillip. *Men and the Emergence of Polite Society, 1660–1800.* New York: Routledge, 2014.

Cazden, Elizabeth. *Antoinette Brown Blackwell: A Biography.* Old Westbury, NY: The Feminist Press, 1983.

Chadwick, John White, ed. *A Life for Liberty: Anti-Slavery and Other Letters of Sallie Holley.* New York: G.P. Putnam's Sons, 1899.

Cheek, William F., and Aimee Lee Cheek. *John Mercer Langston and the Fight for Black Freedom, 1829–1865.* Urbana: University of Illinois Press, 1989.

Chenoweth, Eugene, and Uvieja Good. "The Rise of Women and the Fall of Tradition in Union Debating at Oxford and Cambridge." *Speaker & Gavel* 9, no. 2 (1972): 31–34.

Clary-Lemon, Jennifer. "Archival Research Processes: The Case for Material Methods." *Rhetoric Review* 33, no. 4 (2014): 381–402.

Cobb, Jasmine Nichole. *Picture Freedom: Remaking Black Visuality in the Early Nineteenth Century.* New York: New York University Press, 2015.

Code, Lorraine. *Rhetorical Spaces: Essays on Gendered Locations.* New York: Routledge, 1995.

———. *What Can She Know? Feminist Theory and the Construction of Knowledge.* Ithaca, NY: Cornell University Press, 1991.

Cohen, Herman. *The History of Speech Communication: The Emergence of a Discipline, 1915–1945.* Washington, DC: Speech Communication Association, 1994.

Collins, Kenneth E. *Scotland's Jews: A Guide to the History and Community of the Jews in Scotland.* Glasgow: Scottish Council of Jewish Communities, 2008. Http://www. scojec.org/resources/files/scotlands_jews.pdf.

Collins, Laurel. *The Firebrand.* New York: Kensington Publication Corp., 1997.

Collins, Vickie Tolar. "The Speaker Respoken: Material Rhetoric as Feminist Methodology." *College English* 61, no. 5 (1999): 545–73. DOI: 10.2307/378973.

Comings, Emilie Royce. "The Pioneer Woman's Club." *Club Notes for Women* 8, no. 111 (1907): 83–90.

Comings, Emilie Royce, and Francis J. Hosford. "The Pioneer Women of Oberlin College." *The Oberlin Alumni Magazine*, March 1927, 10–13.

Connors, Robert J. *Composition-Rhetoric: Backgrounds, Theory and Pedagogy.* Pittsburgh:

University of Pittsburgh Press, 1997.

Conway, Kathryn M. "Woman Suffrage and the History of Rhetoric at the Seven Sisters Colleges, 1865–1919." In Lunsford, *Reclaiming Rhetorica: Women in the Rhetorical Tradition*, 203–26.

Coolidge, Calvin. "Sixth Annual Message." December 4, 1928. *The American Presidency Project*, Gerhard Peters and John T. Wooley. Http://www.presidency.ucsb.edu/ws/?pid=29569.

Cooper, Brittany. "Take No Prisoners: The Role of Debate in a Liberatory Education." In *Using Debate in the Classroom: Encouraging Critical Thinking, Communication, and Collaboration*, edited by Karyl A. Davis, M. Leslie Wade Zorwick, James Roland, and Melissa Maxcy Wade, 11–21. New York: Routledge, 2017.

———. "'I Was Hurt': How White Elite Racism Invaded a College Debate Championship." *Salon*, May 13, 2014.

Cowan, Brian. "What Was Masculine about the Public Sphere? Gender and the Coffeehouse Milieu in Post-Restoration England." *History Workshop Journal* 51 (2001): 127–57. DOI: 10.1093/hwj/2001.51.127.

Cowperthwaite, L. Leroy, and A. Craig Baird. "Intercollegiate Debating." In Wallace, *History of Speech Education*, 259–76.

Crawford, Elizabeth. *The Women's Suffrage Movement in Britain and Ireland: A Regional Survey*. New York: Routledge, 2006.

———. "Sarah Elizabeth Siddons Mair." In *The Women's Suffrage Movement: A Reference Guide, 1866–1928*, 365–66. London: University College London Press, 1999.

Cresswell, Tim. *On the Move: Mobility in the Modern Western World*. New York: Routledge, 2006.

———. *In Place/Out of Place: Geography, Ideology and Transgression*. Minneapolis: University of Minnesota Press, 1996.

Daniels, Roger. *Asian America: Chinese and Japanese in the United States Since 1850*. Seattle: University of Washington Press, 1988.

David, Huw T. "Transnational Advocacy in the Eighteenth Century: Transatlantic Activism and the Anti-Slavery Movement." *Global Networks* 7, no. 3 (2007): 367–82. DOI: 10.1111/j.1471–0374.2007.00174.x.

Davidoff, Leonore. "Regarding Some 'Old Husbands' Tales': Public and Private in Feminist History." In Landes, *Feminism*, 164–94.

Davis, William Hawley. "Is Debating Primarily a Game?" *Quarterly Journal of Public Speaking* 2, no. 2 (1916): 171–79.

Davis, Angela Y. *Women, Race and Class*. New York: Vintage Books, 1991.

Deard, Paul. "Making the Case for Teaching Students Debate." *Education Week*, August 12, 2014.

"Debates of the Ladies' Edinburgh Literary Society." *Ladies' Edinburgh Magazine* 3, 1877, 33.

DeCerteau, Michel. *The Practice of Everyday Life*. Vol. 1. Berkeley: University of California Press, 1984.

Dickerson, Vanessa D. "Introduction: Housekeeping and Housekept Angels." In *Keeping the Victorian House: A Collection of Essays*, edited by Vanessa D. Dickerson, 2nd ed., xiii–xxxi. New York: Routledge, 2016.

———. *Dark Victorians*. Champaign: University of Illinois Press, 2008.

Diem, William Roy, and Rollin Clarence Hunter. *The Story of Speech at Ohio Wesleyan*. Columbus, OH: F.J. Heer Printing Company, 1964.

Donawerth, Jane. "Conduct Book Rhetoric: Constructing a Theory of Feminine Discourse." In *Conversational Rhetoric: The Rise and Fall of a Women's Tradition, 1600–1900*, 41–72. Carbondale: Southern Illinois University Press, 2012.

Duffy, Bernard K., and Halford Ryan Ross. *American Orators before 1900: Critical Studies and Sources*. Westport, CT: Greenwood Press, 1987.

Duggan, Stephen P. *Institute for International Education: First Annual Report of the Director*. New York: Institute for International Education, 1920.

[Dundas, Adela]. "Debates of the Ladies' Edinburgh Literary Society." *Ladies' Edinburgh Magazine* 2, 1876, 16–20.

Dyer, Ervin. "The Great Debater." *Pitt Magazine*, Summer 2008, 26–30.

Dyhouse, Carol. *Students: A Gendered History*. New York: Routledge, 2006.

———. *No Distinction of Sex? Women in British Universities, 1870–1939*. London: University College London Press, 1995.

Eastman, Carolyn. *A Nation of Speechifiers: Making an American Public after the Revolution*. Chicago: University of Chicago Press, 2009.

Eastman, Rebecca Hooper. "Some Dangers of Co-Education." *The Woman's Journal* 14 (January 1929): 10+.

Eberly, Rosa A. "Rhetoric and the Anti-Logos Doughball: Teaching Deliberating Bodies the Practices of Participatory Democracy." *Rhetoric and Public Affairs* 5, no. 2 (2002): 287–300.

Ede, Lisa, Cheryl Glenn, and Andrea Lunsford. "Border Crossings: Intersections of Rhetoric and Feminism." *Rhetorica* 12, no. 4 (1995): 401–41.

Ehninger, Douglas. "Argument as Method: Its Nature, Its Limitations, and Its Uses."

Speech Monographs 37, no. 2 (1970): 101–10.

Ehninger, Douglas, and Wayne Brockriede. *Decision by Debate*. New York: Dodd, Mead, and Company, 1963.

Emerson, James Gordon. "The Old Debating Society." *Quarterly Journal of Speech* 17, no. 3 (1931): 362–75.

Emery, Emogene. "Rehabilitating Women's Debate." *Southern Speech Journal* 17, no. 3 (1952): 186–91. DOI:10.1080/10417945209371221.

English, Eric, Steven Llano, Gordon R. Mitchell, Catherine E. Morrison, John Rief, and Carly Woods. "Debate as a Weapon of Mass Destruction." *Communication and Critical/Cultural Studies* 4, no. 2 (2007): 221–25.

Enoch, Jessica. "Releasing Hold: Feminist Historiography without the Tradition." In *Theorizing Histories of Rhetoric*, edited by Michelle Ballif, 58–73. Carbondale: Southern Illinois University Press, 2013.

———. *Refiguring Rhetorical Education: Women Teaching African American, Native American, and Chicano/a Students, 1865–1911*. Carbondale: Southern Illinois University Press, 2008.

———. "A Woman's Place Is in the School: Rhetorics of Gendered Space in Nineteenth-Century America." *College English* 70, no. 3 (2008): 275–95.

Enos, Richard Leo. "The Archaeology of Women in Rhetoric: Rhetorical Sequencing as a Research Method for Historical Scholarship." *Rhetoric Society Quarterly* 32, no. 1 (2002): 65–79.

Ex Cathedra. "Debates of the Ladies' Edinburgh Literary Society." *Ladies' Edinburgh Magazine* 4, 1878, 44.

Ewalt, Joshua P. "Rhetorical Constellations: On the Materiality and Mobility of Arrangement and Invention." PhD diss., University of Nebraska–Lincoln, 2015.

Ewbank, Henry Lee, Jr. "Henry Lee Ewbank, Sr.: Teacher of Teachers of Speech." In Kuypers and King, *Twentieth Century Roots of Rhetorical Studies*, 31–70.

Farrell, Thomas B. *Norms of Rhetorical Culture*. New Haven: Yale University Press, 1995.

Fawcett, Trevor. "Eighteenth-Century Debating Societies." *Journal for Eighteenth-Century Studies* 3, no. 3 (1980): 216–29.

Felski, Rita. *Beyond Feminist Aesthetics: Feminist Literature and Social Change*. Cambridge, MA: Harvard University Press, 1989.

Fest, Thorrel B. "A Survey of College Forensics." *Quarterly Journal of Speech* 34, no. 2 (1948): 168–73.

Flannery, Kathryn T. "Shifting the Center of Gravity: The Rhetorics of Radical Feminist Pedagogy." In *Teaching Rhetorica: Theory, Pedagogy, Practice*, edited by Kate

Ronald and Joy Ritchie, 48–65. Portsmouth, NH: Boyton-Cook Publishers, 2006.

Fletcher, Robert Samuel. *A History of Oberlin College: From Its Foundation through the Civil War.* 2 vols. Oberlin: Oberlin College, 1943.

Flores, Lisa A. "Creating Discursive Space through a Rhetoric of Difference: Chicana Feminists Craft a Homeland." *Quarterly Journal of Speech* 82, no. 2 (1996): 142–56.

Foss, Karen A., and Sonja K. Foss. "The Status of Research on Women and Communication." *Communication Quarterly* 31, no. 3 (1983): 195–204.

Foss, Sonja K. "Response." *Contemporary Argumentation & Debate* 21 (2000): 95–98.

Foss, Sonja K., and Cindy L. Griffin. "Beyond Persuasion: A Proposal for an Invitational Rhetoric." *Communication Monographs* 62 (March 1995): 2–18.

Fraser, Nancy. *Fortunes of Feminism: From State-Managed Capitalism to Neoliberal Crisis.* London: Verso Books, 2013.

———. "Rethinking the Public Sphere: A Contribution to the Critique of Actually Existing Democracy." In Calhoun, *Habermas and the Public Sphere*, 109–43.

Freeley, Austin J., and David L. Steinberg. *Argumentation and Debate: Critical Thinking for Reasoned Decision Making.* Boston: Wadsworth, 2014.

Fulkerson, Richard. "Transcending Our Conception of Argument in Light of Feminist Critiques." *Argumentation & Advocacy* 32, no. 4 (1996): 199–21.

Gaillet, Lynée Lewis. "Archival Survival: Navigating Historical Research." In *Working in the Archives: Practical Research Methods for Rhetoric and Composition*, edited by Alexis E. Ramsey, Wendy B. Sharer, and Barbara L'Eplattenier, 28–39. Carbondale: Southern Illinois University Press, 2009.

———. ed. *Scottish Rhetoric and Its Influences.* Mahwah, NJ: Lawrence Erlbaum Associates, 1998.

Garland, Jasper Vanderbilt. *Public Speaking for Women.* New York: Harper and Brothers Publishers, 1938.

Gearhart, Sally Miller. "The Womanization of Rhetoric." *Women's Studies International Quarterly* 2 (1979): 195–201.

General Catalogue of Oberlin College, 1833–1909. Oberlin: Oberlin College, 1909.

Gere, Anne Ruggles. *Intimate Practices: Literacy and Cultural Work in U.S. Women's Clubs, 1880–1920.* Urbana: University of Illinois Press, 1997.

Gehrke, Pat J. *The Ethics and Politics of Speech.* Carbondale: Southern Illinois University Press, 2009.

Gehrke, Pat J., and William M. Keith, eds. *A Century of Communication Studies: The Unfinished Conversation.* New York: Routledge, 2015.

Ginzberg, Lori D. "The 'Joint Education of the Sexes': Oberlin's Original Vision." In

Lasser, *Educating Men and Women Together*, 67–80.

Glenn, Cheryl, ed. *Rhetoric Retold: Regendering the Tradition from Antiquity through the Renaissance*. Carbondale: Southern Illinois University Press, 1997.

———. "Remapping Rhetorical Territory." *Rhetoric Review* 13 (1995): 287–303.

Gold, David. *Rhetoric at the Margins: Revising the History of Writing Instruction in American Colleges, 1873–1947*. Carbondale: Southern Illinois University Press, 2008.

Goodnight, G. Thomas. "The Personal, Technical, and Public Spheres: A Note on 21st Century Critical Communication Inquiry." *Argumentation and Advocacy* 48, no. 4 (2012): 258–68.

———. "Generational Argument." In *Argumentation: Across the Lines of Discipline, Proceedings of the Conference on Argumentation 1986*, edited by Frans H. van Eemeren, Rob Grootendorst, J. Anthony Blair, and Charles A. Willard, 129–44. Dordrecht, Netherlands: Foris Publications, 1987.

———. "The Personal, Technical, and Public Spheres of Argument: A Speculative Inquiry into the Act of Public Deliberation." *Journal of the American Forensic Association* 18 (1982): 214–27.

———. "The Re-Union of Argumentation and Debate Theory." In *Dimensions of Argument: Proceedings of the National Communication Association/American Forensics Association Alta Conference on Argumentation*, edited by George Ziegelmueller and Jack Rhodes, 415–32. Annandale, VA: Speech Communication Association, 1981.

Goodnight, G. Thomas, and David B. Hingstman. "Studies in the Public Sphere." *Quarterly Journal of Speech* 83, no. 3 (1997): 351–99.

Goodnight, G. Thomas, Zoltan P. Majdik, and John M. Kephart III. "Presidential Debates as Public Argument." In *Concerning Argument: Proceedings of the 2007 National Communication Association/American Forensics Association Alta Conference on Argumentation*, edited by Scott Jacobs, 267–79. Washington, DC: National Communication Association, 2009.

Goodnight, G. Thomas, and Gordon R. Mitchell. "Forensics as Scholarship: Testing Zarefsky's Bold Hypothesis in a Digital Age." *Argumentation and Advocacy* 45, no. 2 (2008): 80–97.

Gordon, Peter, and David Doughan. *Dictionary of British Women's Organizations, 1825–1960*. 2nd ed. Oxford: Routledge, 2013.

Gorman, Ron. "William Lloyd Garrison and Frederick Douglass Debate in Oberlin." *Oberlin Heritage Center* (blog). June 19, 2013. Http://www.oberlinheritagecenter.

org/blog/tag/abby-kelley-foster.

Govier, Trudy. *The Philosophy of Argument*. Newport News, VA: Vale Press, 1999.

Graff, Gerald. *Clueless in Academe: How Schooling Obscures the Life of the Mind*. New Haven: Yale University Press, 2003.

Graff, Richard, and Michael Leff. "Revisionist Historiography and Rhetorical Tradition(s)." In *The Viability of the Rhetorical Tradition*, edited by Richard Graff, Arthur E. Walzer, and Janet M. Atwill, 11–30. Albany: State University of New York Press, 2005.

Gray, John Stanley. "The Oregon Plan of Debating." *Quarterly Journal of Speech* 12, no. 2 (1926): 175–80. DOI: 10.1080/00335632609379617.

Great Debaters, The. DVD. Directed by Denzel Washington. Chicago: Harpo Films, 2007.

Green, Jeffrey. *Black Edwardians: Black People in Britain, 1901–1914*. New York: Frank Cass Publishers, 1998.

Greene, Ronald Walter, and Darrin Hicks. "Lost Convictions: Debating Both Sides and the Ethical Fashioning of Liberal Citizens." *Cultural Studies* 19, no. 1 (2005): 100–126.

Grimmer, Betty Burford. "The International Debate Program: 1921–1958." Master's thesis, University of Alabama, 1959.

Gring-Pemble, Lisa M. "Writing Themselves into Consciousness: Creating a Rhetorical Bridge between Public and Private Spheres." *Quarterly Journal of Speech* 84, no. 1 (1998): 41–61. DOI: 10.1080/00335639809384203.

Haberman, Frederick B. "NO Whispering Gallery." *Princeton Alumni Weekly*, May 19, 1941.

Habermas, Jürgen. *The Structural Transformation of the Public Sphere: An Inquiry into a Category of Bourgeois Society*. Translated by Thomas Burger. Cambridge, MA: MIT Press, 1991.

Hahn, Allison. "The World Schools Debate Championship and Intercultural Argumentation." *International Society for the Study of Argumentation Proceedings*, 2010. Http://rozenbergquarterly.com/issa-proceedings-2010-the-world-schools-debate-championship-and-intercultural-argumentation.

Hall, Robert N., and Jack L. Rhodes. *Fifty Years of International Debate, 1922–1972*. New York: Speech Communication Association, 1972.

Hample, Dale. "A Third Perspective on Argument." In Benoit, Hample, and Benoit, *Readings in Argumentation*, 91–116.

Harris, Kenneth. *Travelling Tongues: Debating across America*. London: Murray, 1949.

Harwood, Jake. "The Contact Space: A Novel Framework for Intergroup Contact Research." *Journal of Language and Social Psychology* 29, no. 2 (2010): 144–77.

Hauser, Gerard A. *Vernacular Voices: The Rhetoric of Publics and Public Spheres.* Columbia: University of South Carolina Press, 1999.

Hicks, Darrin, and Ronald Walter Greene. "Managed Convictions: Debate and the Limits of Electoral Politics." *Quarterly Journal of Speech* 101, no. 1 (2015): 99–112. DOI:10.1080/00335630.2015.994903.

Hochmuth, Marie. "Great Teachers of Speech: III. Wayland Maxfield Parrish, Teacher and Colleague." *Speech Teacher* 4, no. 3 (1955): 159.

———. "Your Gown Is Lovely, But . . ." *Bulletin of the Debating Association of Pennsylvania Colleges* 12 (January 16, 1939): 1–4.

———. "Richard Whately's *Elements of Rhetoric*, Part III, a Critical Edition." Master's thesis, University of Pittsburgh, 1936.

Hochmuth, Marie, and Richard Murphy. "Rhetorical and Elocutionary Training in Nineteenth-Century Colleges." In Wallace, *History of Speech Education*, 153–77.

Hogan, J. Michael. "Public Address and the Revival of American Civic Culture." In Parry-Giles and Hogan, *The Handbook of Rhetoric and Public Address*, 422–47.

Hogan, J. Michael, Jessica A. Kurr, Michael J. Bergmaier, and Jeremy D. Johnson, eds. *Speech and Debate as Civic Education.* University Park: Penn State University Press, 2017.

Hogan, J. Michael, Jessica A. Kurr, Jeremy D. Johnson, and Michael J. Bergmaier. "Speech and Debate as Civic Education." *Communication Education* 65, no. 4 (2016): 377–81.

Hogeland, Lisa Maria. "Against Generational Thinking, or, Some Things Third Wave Feminism Isn't." *Women's Studies in Communication* 24, no. 1 (2001): 107–21.

Horner, Winifred Bryan. *Nineteenth-Century Scottish Rhetoric: The American Connection.* Carbondale: Southern Illinois University Press, 1993.

Horowitz, Helen Lefkowitz. *Alma Mater: Design and Experience in the Women's Colleges from Their Nineteenth Century Beginnings to the 1930s.* 2nd ed. Amherst: University of Massachusetts Press, 1992.

Hosford, Frances Juliette. *Father Shipherd's Magna Charta: A Century of Coeducation in Oberlin College.* Boston: Marshall Jones Company, 1937.

Howes, Raymond F. "Herbert Wichelns and the Study of Rhetoric." *Cornell Alumni News* (January 1970): 13–14.

———. "Finding Debate Audiences." *Quarterly Journal of Speech* 11, no. 4 (1925): 364–68. DOI: 10.1080/00335632509379586.

Innes, Sue. "Constructing Women's Citizenship in the Interwar Period: The Edinburgh Women's Citizens' Association." *Women's History Review* 13, no. 4 (2004): 621–47.

Innes, Sue, and Jane Rendall. "Women, Gender, and Politics." In *Gender in Scottish History Since 1700*, edited by Lynn Abrams, Eleanor Gordon, Deborah Simonton, and Eileen Janes Yeo, 43–83. Edinburgh: Edinburgh University Press, 2006.

Jamieson, Kathleen Hall. "The Discipline's Debate Contributions: Then, Now, Next." *Quarterly Journal of Speech* 101, no. 1 (2015): 85–97. DOI:10.1080/00335630.2015.9 94905.

Jasinski, James. *Sourcebook on Rhetoric: Key Concepts in Contemporary Rhetorical Studies*. Thousand Oaks, CA: Sage Publications, 2001.

Johnson, Nan. *Gender and Rhetorical Space in American Life, 1866–1910*. Carbondale: Southern Illinois University Press, 2002.

———. *Nineteenth-Century Rhetorical Education in North America*. Carbondale: Southern Illinois University Press, 1991.

Kahan, Gerald. *George Alexander Stevens & The Lecture on Heads*. Athens: University of Georgia Press, 1984.

Kahn, Theresa, and Richard Murphy, eds. *Debating: A Series of Six Radio Talks*. Pittsburgh: University of Pittsburgh Radio Publication, 1929.

Kanke, Tomohiro, and Junya Morooka. "In Search of an Alternative History of Debate in Early Modern Japan: The Case of Youth Club Debates in the Late Nineteenth and Early Twentieth Centuries." *Journal of Argumentation in Context* 1, no. 2 (2012): 168–93.

Keck, Margaret, and Kathryn Sikkink. *Activists beyond Borders: Advocacy Networks in International Politics*. Ithaca, NY: Cornell University Press, 1998.

Keenan, Claudia J. "Intercollegiate Debate: Reflecting American Culture, 1900–1930." *Argumentation and Advocacy* 46, no. 2 (2009): 79–97.

Keith, William. "Crafting a Usable History." *Quarterly Journal of Speech* 93, no. 3 (2007): 345–48.

———. *Democracy as Discussion: Civic Education and the American Forum Movement*. Lanham, MD: Lexington Books, 2007.

Kelley, Mary. *Learning to Stand and Speak: Women, Education, and Public Life in America's Republic*. Chapel Hill: University of North Carolina Press, 2006.

Kelman, Kate. "'Self-Culture': The Educative Reading Pursuits of the Ladies of Edinburgh, 1865–1885." *Victorian Periodicals Review* 36, no. 1 (2003): 59–75.

Kennerly, Michele. "Getting Carried Away: How Rhetorical Transport Gets Judgment Going." *Rhetoric Society Quarterly* 40, no. 3 (2010): 269–91.

Kennerly, Michele, and Carly S. Woods. "Moving Rhetorica." *Rhetoric Society Quarterly* 48, no. 1 (2018): 3–27. DOI: 10.1080/02773945.2017.1315445.

Kerber, Linda. *Toward an Intellectual History of Women*. Chapel Hill: University of North Carolina Press, 1997.

Kerr, Andrea Moore. *Lucy Stone: Speaking Out for Equality*. New Brunswick, NJ: Rutgers University Press, 1995.

Kidd, Benjamin. *Social Evolution*. New York: Macmillan and Co., 1894.

Kirsch, Gesa E., and Liz Rohan, eds. *Beyond the Archives: Research as a Lived Process* Carbondale: Southern Illinois University Press, 2008.

Klein, Lawrence E. "Gender, Conversation and the Public Sphere in Early Eighteenth-Century England." In *Textuality and Sexuality: Reading Theories and Practices*, edited by Judith Sill and Michael Worton, 100–115. Manchester: Manchester University Press, 1993.

Kraus, Manfred. "Cognitive Communities and Argument Communities." In *Argumentation: Cognition and Community; Proceedings of the 9th International Conference of the Ontario Society for the Study of Argumentation*, edited by F. Zenker, 1–11. Windsor, ON: University of Windsor, 2011.

Kuypers, Jim A., and Andrew King, eds. *Twentieth Century Roots of Rhetorical Studies*. Westport, CT: Praeger Publishers, 2001.

Lain, Brian. "Rethinking the History of the Japanese–U.S. Exchange Tour: Early Tours, Early Topics, and Early Traffic." In Palczewski, *Disturbing Arguments*, 426–31.

Lakoff, George, and Mark Johnson. *Metaphors We Live By*. Chicago: University of Chicago Press, 1980.

Lamberton, L. Jill. "Claiming an Education: The Transatlantic Performance and Circulation of Individual Identities in College Women's Writing." PhD diss., University of Michigan, 2007.

Landes, Joan B., ed. *Feminism, the Public and the Private*. Oxford: Oxford University Press, 1998.

Lane, Frank Hardy. "Faculty Help in Intercollegiate Contests." *Quarterly Journal of Public Speaking* 1, no. 1 (1915): 9–16.

Lasser, Carol, ed. *Educating Men and Women Together: Coeducation in a Changing World*. Urbana: University of Illinois Press, 1987.

Lasser, Carol, and Marlene Deahl Merrill. *Friends and Sisters: Letters Between Lucy Stone and Antoinette Brown Blackwell, 1846–93*. Urbana: University of Illinois Press, 1987.

Lawson, Ellen NicKenzie. "Observations on an Antebellum Interracial Utopia." *Oberlin*

College Observer (March 4, 1982): 4.

———. *The Three Sarahs: Documents of Antebellum Black College Women*. New York: Edwin Mellen Press, 1984.

Lawson, Ellen N., and Marlene Merrill. "The Antebellum 'Talented Thousandth': Black College Students at Oberlin before the Civil War." *Journal of Negro Education* 52, no. 2 (1983): 142–55. DOI: 10.2307/2295031.

L'Eplattenier, Barbara E. "Questioning Our Methodological Metaphors." In *Calling Cards: Theory and Practice in the Study of Race, Gender, and Culture*, edited by Jacqueline Jones Royster and Ann Marie Mann Simpkins, 133–46. Albany: State University of New York Press, 2005.

"Letter from the Editors." *Ladies' Edinburgh Magazine* 6, 1880, 570.

Levine, Susan. *Degrees of Equality: The American Association of University Women and the Challenge of Twentieth-Century Feminism*. Philadelphia: Temple University Press, 1995.

Little, Sarah C. "Oberlin and the Education of Women." In Ballantine, *The Oberlin Jubilee*, 147–58.

Littlefield, Robert S. "Gaining a Broader Focus: The Benefits of Archival Research Exploring Forensic Education and Activity in the 20th Century." Paper presented at the National Communication Association Annual Convention, Chicago, IL, November 16, 2007.

Livingstone, David N. "The Spaces of Knowledge: Contributions toward a Historical Geography of Science." *Environment and Planning D: Society and Space* 13, no. 1 (1995): 5–34.

Logan, Shirley Wilson. *Liberating Language: Sites of Rhetorical Education in Nineteenth-Century Black America*. Carbondale: Southern Illinois University Press, 2008.

———. *We Are Coming: The Persuasive Discourse of Nineteenth Century Black Women*. Carbondale: Southern Illinois University Press, 1999.

Lomas, Charles W. "War Information and Training." *Pitt Magazine*, Autumn 1942.

———. "Debating, a Live Activity." *Pitt Magazine*, January 1940.

Lozano-Reich, Nina M., and Dana L. Cloud. "The Uncivil Tongue: Invitational Rhetoric and the Problem of Inequality." *Western Journal of Communication* 73, no. 2 (2009): 220–26.

Lunsford, Andrea A., ed. *Reclaiming Rhetorica: Women in the Rhetorical Tradition*. Pittsburgh: University of Pittsburgh Press, 1995.

Lunsford, Andrea A., Kirt H. Wilson, and Rosa A. Eberly, eds. *The Sage Handbook of Rhetorical Studies*. Thousand Oaks, CA: Sage Publications, 2009.

Mair, Sarah. "Stray Notes." *Ladies' Edinburgh Magazine* 3, 1877, 383–84.

Markess, Valerie. "Debaters Past and Present—Driven to Succeed." *Pitt Magazine*, November 1981.

Marshall, Rosalind K. *Virgins and Viragos: A History of Women in Scotland from 1080 to 1980*. Chicago: Academy Chicago, 1983.

Massey, Doreen. *Space, Place, and Gender*. Minneapolis: University of Minnesota Press, 2004.

Mastrangelo, Lisa. "They Argued in White Shirtwaists and Black Skirts': Women's Participation in Debate Competitions." In *Contest(ed) Writing: Reconceptualizing Literacy Competitions*, edited by Mary Lamb, 115–38. Newcastle: Cambridge Scholars Publishing, 2013.

———. "Learning from the Past: Rhetoric, Composition, and Debate at Mount Holyoke College." *Rhetoric Review* 18 (1999): 46–64.

Mattingly, Carol. *Appropriate[ing] Dress: Women's Rhetorical Style in Nineteenth Century America*. Carbondale: Southern Illinois University Press, 2002.

———. "Telling Evidence: Rethinking What Counts in Rhetoric." *Rhetoric Society Quarterly* 32, no. 1 (2002): 99–108.

McAlister, Joan Faber. "Ten Propositions for Communication Scholars Studying Space and Place." *Women's Studies in Communication* 39, no. 2 (2016): 113–21.

McDermid, Jane. *The Schooling of Working-Class Girls in Victorian Scotland: Gender, Education, and Identity*. London: Routledge, 2005.

McDowell, Linda. *Gender, Identity, and Place: Understanding Feminist Geographies*. Minneapolis: University of Minnesota Press, 1999.

McElroy, Davis J. *Scotland's Age of Improvement: A Survey of Eighteenth-Century Literary Clubs and Societies*. Pullman: Washington State University Press, 1969.

McGee, Michael Calvin. "'Social Movement': Phenomenon or Meaning?" *Central States Speech Journal* 31 (1980): 233–44.

McHenry, Elizabeth. *Forgotten Readers: Recovering the Lost History of African American Literary Societies*. Durham, NC: Duke University Press, 2002.

McKercher, B. J. C., ed. *Anglo-American Relations in the 1920s: The Struggle for Supremacy*. Edmonton: University of Alberta Press, 1990.

McKittrick, Katherine. *Demonic Grounds: Black Women and the Cartographies of Struggle*. Minneapolis: University of Minnesota Press, 2006.

McKittrick, Katherine, and Clyde Woods, eds. *Black Geographies and the Politics of Place*. Cambridge, MA: South End Press, 2007.

McKown, Jamie. "Renewing a 'Very Old Means of Education': Civic Engagement and the Birth of Intercollegiate Debate in the United States." In Hogan, Kurr, Bergmaier, and Johnson, *Speech and Debate as Civic Education*, 36–52.

McMillen, Sally G. *Lucy Stone: An Unapologetic Life*. Oxford: Oxford University Press, 2015.

Medhurst, Martin J. "The History of Public Address as an Academic Study." In Parry-Giles and Hogan, *The Handbook of Rhetoric and Public Address*, 19–66.

Merrill, Marlene Deahl. "Justice, Simple Justice: Women at Oberlin 1837–1987." *Oberlin Alumni Magazine*, Fall 1987, 11–16.

Meyers, Christine D. *University Coeducation in the Victorian Era: Inclusion in the United States and the United Kingdom*. New York: Palgrave Macmillan, 2010.

Miller, Joe. *Cross-X: The Amazing True Story of How the Most Unlikely Team from the Most Unlikely of Places Overcame Staggering Obstacles at Home and at School to Challenge the Debate Community on Race, Power and Education*. New York: Picador, 2006.

Mitchell, Gordon R. "Public Opinion, Thinly Sliced and Served Hot." *International Journal of Communication* 9 (2015): 21–45.

———. *Strategic Deception: Rhetoric, Science and Politics in Missile Defense Advocacy*. East Lansing: Michigan State University Press, 2000.

———. "Simulated Public Argument as Pedagogical Play on Worlds." *Argumentation and Advocacy* 36, no. 3 (2000): 134–51.

———. "Pedagogical Possibilities for Argumentative Agency in Academic Debate." *Argumentation and Advocacy* 35, no. 2 (1998): 41–60.

Mitchell, Gordon R., and Takeshi Suzuki. "Beyond the 'Daily Me': Argumentation in an Age of Enclave Deliberation." In *Argumentation and Social Cognition*, edited by Takeshi Suzuki, Yoshiro Yano, and Takayuki Kato, 160–66. Tokyo: Japan Debate Association, 2004.

Mitchell, Gordon R., Carly S. Woods, Matthew Brigham, Eric English, Catherine E. Morrison, and John Rief. "The Debate Authors Working Group Model for Collaborative Knowledge Production in Forensics Scholarship." *Argumentation and Advocacy* 47, no. 1 (2010): 1–24.

Money, John. "Taverns, Coffee Houses, and Clubs: Local Politics and Popular Articulacy in the Birmingham Area, in the Age of the American Revolution." *The Historical Journal* 14, no. 1 (1971): 15–47.

Morris, J. Brent. *Oberlin, Hotbed of Abolitionism: College, Community, and the Fight for Freedom and Equality in Antebellum America*. Chapel Hill: University of North Carolina Press, 2014.

Morris, R. J. "Clubs, Societies, and Associations." In *The Cambridge Social History of Britain, 1750–1950*, vol. 3, *Social Agencies and Institutions*, edited by F. M. L. Thompson, 395–443. Cambridge: Cambridge University Press, 1990.

Mountford, Roxanne. *The Gendered Pulpit: Preaching in American Protestant Spaces.* Carbondale: Southern Illinois University Press, 2003.

———. "The Feminization of Rhetoric?" *JAC* 19 no. 3 (1999): 485–92.

Murphy, Richard. "The Ethics of Debating Both Sides II." *Speech Teacher* 7, no. 3 (1963): 242–47.

———. "The Ethics of Debating Both Sides." *Speech Teacher* 6, no. 1 (1957): 1–9.

———. "Colleague and Counselor." *Speech Teacher* 4, no. 3 (1955): 161–63.

Murphy, Theresa. "Interpretation in the Dickens Period." *Quarterly Journal of Speech* 41, no. 3 (1955): 243–50.

Murphy, Theresa, and Richard Murphy. "Charles Dickens as Professional Reader." *Quarterly Journal of Speech* 33, no. 3 (1947): 299–308.

Nash, Margaret A. *Women's Education in the United States, 1780–1840*. New York: Palgrave MacMillan, 2005.

Nash, Margaret A., and Lisa S. Romero. "'Citizenship for the College Girl': Challenges and Opportunities in Higher Education for Women in the United States in the 1930s." *Teachers College Record* 114, no. 2 (2012): 1–35.

Natanson, Maurice. "The Claims of Immediacy." In *Philosophy, Rhetoric, and Argumentation*, edited by Maurice Natanson and Henry W. Johnstone Jr., 10–18. University Park: Pennsylvania State University Press, 1962.

Nava, Mica. *Visceral Cosmopolitanism: Gender, Culture, and the Normalisation of Difference*. Oxford: Berg, 2007.

Nichols, Egbert Ray. "A Historical Sketch of Intercollegiate Debating: I." *Quarterly Journal of Speech* 22, no. 2 (1936): 213–20.

———. "A Historical Sketch of Intercollegiate Debating: II." *Quarterly Journal of Speech* 22, no. 4 (1936): 591–603.

———. "A Historical Sketch of Intercollegiate Debating: III." *Quarterly Journal of Speech* 23, no. 2 (1937): 259–78.

———. ed. *Intercollegiate Debates: Affirmative and Negative*. Vol. 10. New York: Noble and Noble, 1930.

Nicholson, Victoria. *Singled Out: How Two Million Women Survived without Men after the First World War*. Oxford: Oxford University Press, 2008.

Nora, Pierre. "Between Memory and History: *Les Lieux de Mémoire*." *Representations* 26 (1989): 7–24.

O'Connor, Lillian. *Pioneer Women Orators: Rhetoric in the Ante-bellum Reform Movement*. New York: Columbia University Press, 1954.

O'Donnell, Timothy M. "'The Great Debaters': A Challenge to Higher Education." *Inside Higher Education*, January 7, 2008.

O'Keefe, Daniel J. "Two Conceptions of Argument." In Benoit, Hample, and Benoit, *Readings in Argumentation*, 79–90.

Olson, Donald Orrin. "Debating at the University of Nebraska." Master's thesis, University of Wisconsin, 1947.

Olson, Lester C. "Rhetorical Criticism and Theory: Rhetorical Questions, Theoretical Fundamentalism, and the Dissolution of Judgment." In *A Century of Transformation: Studies in Honor of the 100th Anniversary of the Eastern Communication Association*, edited by James W. Chesebro, 37–71. New York: Oxford University Press, 2010.

O'Neill, J. M. "Game or Counterfeit Presentment." *Quarterly Journal of Public Speaking* 2, no. 2 (1916): 193–97.

Owl: The Annual of the University of Pittsburgh. Pittsburgh: University of Pittsburgh. Published annually between 1907 and 1981. Http://digital.library.pitt.edu/d/documentingpitt/yearbooks.html.

Palczewski, Catherine H. "Beyond Peitho: The Women's Debate Institute as Civic Education." In Hogan, Kurr, Bergmaier, and Johnson, *Speech and Debate as Civic Education*, 136–48.

———, ed. *Disturbing Arguments: Selected Works from the 18th NCA/AFA Conference on Argumentation*. New York: Routledge, 2015.

———. "Argumentation and Feminism: An Introduction." *Argumentation and Advocacy* 32, no. 4 (1996): 161–70.

Park, Maud Wood. *Lucy Stone: A Chronicle Play*. Boston: Walter H. Baker Company, 1938.

Parry-Giles, Shawn J., and J. Michael Hogan, eds. *The Handbook of Rhetoric and Public Address*. Oxford: Wiley-Blackwell, 2010.

———. "The Study of Rhetoric and Public Address." In Parry-Giles and Hogan, *The Handbook of Rhetoric and Public Address*, 1–16.

Parry-Giles, Trevor, and Shawn J. Parry-Giles. "Expanding the Discipline's Debate Contributions: New Potentials, Beyond Effects." *Quarterly Journal of Speech* 101, no. 1 (2015): 113–26. DOI: 10.1080/00335630.2015.994902.

Pascoe, Judith. *The Sarah Siddons Audio Files: Romanticism and the Lost Voice*. Ann Arbor: University of Michigan Press, 2013.

Patton, John H. "Marie Hochmuth Nichols: Voice of Rationality in the Humane Tradition of Rhetoric and Criticism." In Kuypers and King, *Twentieth Century Roots of Rhetorical Studies*, 123–42.

Peters, John Durham. *Speaking into the Air*. Chicago: University of Chicago Press, 1999.

Phegley, Jennifer. *Courtship and Marriage in Victorian England*. Santa Barbara: ABC-CLIO, LLC, 2012.

Pierson, Emma. "Men Outspeak Women: Analysing the Gender Gap in Competitive Debate." *Monash Debating Review* 11 (2013).

Pineda, Richard, and Chris Salinas. "Model Proposal: Increasing Latina/o Involvement in Policy Debate through Summer Debate Workshops." *Contemporary Argumentation & Debate* 30 (September 2009): 114–29.

Pinto, Robert C. "Argumentation and the Force of Reasons." *Informal Logic* 29, no. 3 (2009): 268–95. DOI: 10.22329/il.v29i3.2844.

Poapst, Jackie, and Allison Harper. "Reflections on the 2014 Celebration of Women in Debate Tournament at George Mason University." *Argumentation and Advocacy* 53, no. 2 (2017): 127–37.

Portnoy, Alisse. *Their Right to Speak: Women's Activism in the Indian and Slave Debates*. Cambridge, MA: Harvard University Press, 2005.

Potter, David. "The Literary Society." In Wallace, *A History of Speech Education*, 238–58.

Prospectus of the Vassar Female College, Poughkeepsie, N.Y. New York: C.A. Alvord, 1865.

Quimby, Frank Brooks. "A Decade of International Debating." Master's thesis, Harvard University, 1931.

Radke-Moss, Andrea G. *Bright Epoch: Women and Coeducation in the American West*. Lincoln: University of Nebraska Press, 2008.

Rae, Lettice Milne, ed. *Ladies in Debate: Being a History of the Ladies' Edinburgh Debating Society, 1865–1935*. Edinburgh: Oliver and Boyd, 1936.

Rakow, Lana F., and Laura A. Wackwitz. *Feminist Communication Theory: Selections in Context*. Thousand Oaks, CA: Sage Publications, 2004.

Ray, Angela G. "Rhetoric and Feminism in the Nineteenth-Century United States." In *The Oxford Handbook of Rhetorical Studies*, edited by Michael J. MacDonald. Oxford: Oxford University Press, 2017. DOI: 10.1093/oxfordhb/9780199731596.013.046.

———. "Warriors and Statesmen: Debate Education among Free African American Men in Antebellum Charleston." In Hogan, Kurr, Bergmaier, and Johnson, *Speech and Debate as Civic Education*, 25–35.

———. "How Cosmopolitan Was the Lyceum, Anyway?" In Wright, *The Cosmopolitan*

Lyceum, 23–41.

———. "'A Green Oasis in the History of My Life': Race and the Culture of Debating in Antebellum Charleston, South Carolina." Lecture given at the Twenty-eighth Annual B. Aubrey Fisher Memorial Lecture, University of Utah, Salt Lake City 2014.

———. "The Rhetorical Ritual of Citizenship: Women's Voting as Public Performance, 1868–1875." *Quarterly Journal of Speech* 93, no. 1 (2007): 1–26.

———. *The Lyceum and Public Culture in the Nineteenth-Century United States*. East Lansing: Michigan State University Press, 2005.

———. "The Permeable Public: Rituals of Citizenship in Men's Antebellum Debating Clubs." *Argumentation and Advocacy* 41, no. 1 (2004): 1–16.

Reid-Brinkley, Shanara Rose. "Ghetto Kids Gone Good: Race, Representation, and Authority in the Scripting of Inner City Youths in the Urban Debate League." *Argumentation and Advocacy* 49, no. 1 (2012): 77–99.

———. "The Harsh Realities of 'Acting Black': How African American Policy Debaters Negotiate Representation through Racial Performance and Style." PhD diss., University of Georgia, 2008.

Remond, Charles. "The Rights of Colored Citizens in Traveling." In *Lift Every Voice: African American Oratory, 1787–1900*, edited Philip Sheldon Foner and Robert J. Branham, 189–93. Tuscaloosa: University of Alabama Press, 1997.

Rennella, Mark, and Whitney Walton. "Planned Serendipity: American Travellers and the Transatlantic Voyage in the Nineteenth and Twentieth Centuries." *Journal of Social History* 38, no. 2 (2004): 365–83.

Reynolds, Jaime. "Herbert Samuel (Viscount Samuel), 1879–1963." Liberal History. http://www.liberalhistory.org.uk/history/samuel-herbert-viscount-samuel/.

Reynolds, Siân. *Paris–Edinburgh: Cultural Connections in the Belle Époque*. Burlington, VT: Ashgate Publishing, 2007.

Rice, Jenny. "From Architechtonic to Tectonics: Introducing Regional Rhetorics." *Rhetoric Society Quarterly* 42, no. 3 (2012): 201–13.

Richardson, Eudora Ramsay. *The Woman Speaker: A Handbook and Study Course on Public Speaking*. Richmond, VA: Whittet & Shepperson, 1936.

Ricker, Lisa Reid. "'Ars Stripped of Practice': Robert J. Connors and the Demise of Agonistic Rhetoric." *Rhetoric Review* 23, no. 3 (2004): 235–52.

Roberts-Miller, Patricia. *Deliberate Conflict: Argument, Political Theory, and Composition Classes*. Carbondale: Southern Illinois University Press, 2004.

Rohrer, Daniel Morgan. "Young Ladies Literary Society of Oberlin College, 1835–1860."

Master's thesis, University of Wisconsin, 1969.

Ronald, Kate. "Feminist Approaches to the History of Rhetoric." In Lunsford, Wilson, and Eberly, *Sage Handbook for Rhetorical Studies*, 139–52.

Rooney, Phyllis. "Philosophy, Adversarial Argumentation, and Embattled Reason." *Informal Logic* 30, no. 3 (2010): 203–34.

Rose, Gillian. *Feminism and Geography: The Limits of Geographical Knowledge.* Minneapolis: University of Minnesota Press, 1993.

Roseneil, Sasha, ed. *Beyond Citizenship? Feminism and the Transformation of Belonging.* London: Palgrave Macmillan, 2013.

Rossi, Alice S., ed. *The Feminist Papers: From Adams to de Beauvoir.* Lebanon, NH: Northeastern University Press, 1973.

Rothermel, Beth Ann. "A Sphere of Nobel Action: Gender, Rhetoric, and Influence at a Nineteenth-Century Massachusetts State Normal School." *Rhetoric Society Quarterly* 33, no. 1 (2003): 35–64.

Roucek, Joseph S. "Experiment in Adult Education at Rockview Farm Prison." *School and Society* 42 (1935): 199–200.

Rowe, Aimee Marie Carillo. "Be Longing: Toward a Feminist Politics of Relation." *NWSA Journal* 17, no. 2 (2005): 15–46.

Royster, Jacqueline Jones. *Traces of a Stream: Literacy and Social Change among African American Women.* Pittsburgh: University of Pittsburgh Press, 2000.

Royster, Jacqueline Jones, Gesa E. Kirsch, and Patricia Bizzell. "Documenting a Need for Change in Rhetorical Studies." In *Feminist Rhetorical Practices: New Horizons for Rhetoric, Composition, and Literacy Studies*, 13–25. Carbondale: Southern Illinois University Press, 2012.

Ruttenberg, Harold J. "Public Speaking and Public Affairs." Remarks in Honor of Wayland Maxfield Parrish at the Annual Convention of the Speech Association of America, Chicago, IL, December 28, 1954.

Ryan, Mary P. "Gender and Public Access: Women's Politics in Nineteenth-Century America." In Landes, *Feminism*, 195–222.

———. *Women in Public: Between Banners and Ballots, 1825–1800.* Baltimore: Johns Hopkins University Press, 1990.

Salenus, Sirpa. *An Abolitionist Abroad: Sarah Parker Remond in Cosmopolitan Europe.* Amherst: University of Massachusetts Press, 2016.

Samek, Alyssa A. "Mobility, Citizenship, and 'American Women on the Move' in the 1977 International Women's Year Torch Relay." *Quarterly Journal of Speech* 103, no. 3 (2017): 207–29. DOI: 10.1080/00335630.2017.1321134.

Schopenhauer, Arthur. "Of Women." In *Arthur Schopenhauer: Essays and Aphorisms*, translated by R. J. Hollingsworth, 80–89. New York: Penguin Books, 1970.

Schroeder, Mary Murphy. "Oral History of Mary Murphy Schroeder." By Patricia Lee Refo. Women Trailblazers Project, American Bar Association, August 30, 2006. Http://www.americanbar.org/content/dam/aba/directories/women_trailblazers/ schroeder_interview_1.authcheckdam.pdf.

Schudson, Michael. "Was There Ever a Public Sphere? If So, When? Reflections on the American Case." In Calhoun, *Habermas and the Public Sphere*, 143–63.

Schumacher, Carolyn Sutcher. "The History of Women at Pitt: Reflections of a Changing Society, 1895–1972." Office of the Provost, University of Pittsburgh. Http://www.provost.pitt.edu.

Scobie, Edward. *Black Britannia*. Chicago: Johnson Publishing Company, 1972.

Scott, Joan Wallach. *The Fantasy of Feminist History*. Durham, NC: Duke University Press, 2011.

Seidman, Rachel F. "The Ladies' Literary Society: Oberlin's Early Feminists." *Oberlin Alumni Magazine* 83, no. 4, Fall 1987, 14.

Sharer, Wendy B. *Vote and Voice: Women's Organizations and Political Literacy, 1915–1930*. Carbondale: Southern Illinois University Press, 2004.

Shepley, Nigel. *Women of Independent Mind: St. George's School, Edinburgh, and the Campaign for Women's Education, 1888–1988*. Edinburgh: St. George's School for Girls, 1988.

Solomon, Barbara Miller. *In the Company of Educated Women: A History of Women and Higher Education in America*. New Haven: Yale University Press, 1985.

Sonenklar, Carol. *We Are a Strong, Articulate Voice: A History of Women at Penn State*. University Park: Pennsylvania State University Press, 2006.

Smith, Harold L. *The British Woman's Suffrage Campaign, 1866–1928*. 2nd ed. London: Routledge, 2007.

Spain, Daphne. *Gendered Spaces*. Chapel Hill: University of North Carolina Press, 1992.

Squires, Catherine R. "Rethinking the Black Public Sphere: An Alternative Vocabulary for Multiple Public Spheres." *Communication Theory* 12, no. 3 (2002): 446–68.

Stade, George, Karen Karbiener, and Christine L. Krueger, eds. *Encyclopedia of British Writers: 19th and 20th Centuries*. New York: Book Builders LLC, 2003.

Stanley, Jo. "CoⓍVenturing Consumers 'Travel Back': Ships' Stewardesses and Their Female Passengers, 1919–55." *Mobilities* 3, no. 3 (2008): 437–54.

Starrett, Agnes Lynch. *Through One Hundred and Fifty Years: The University of Pittsburgh*. Pittsburgh: University of Pittsburgh Press, 1937.

Stepp, Pamela L., and Beth Gardner. "Ten Years of Demographics: Who Debates in America?" *Argumentation and Advocacy* 38, no. 2 (2001): 69–83.

Stevens, George Alexander. *A Lecture on Heads*. London: W. Wilson, 1812.

Stewarton, Lewis Goldsmith. *The Female Revolutionary Plutarch*. Vol. 1. London: J&W Smith, 1908.

Stob, Paul. *William James and the Art of Popular Statement*. East Lansing: Michigan State University Press, 2013.

Stone, Lucy. "Oberlin and Woman." In Ballantine, *The Oberlin Jubilee*, 311–21.

Stopes, Charlotte Carmichael. "Literary Societies for Women." In *Feminism and the Periodical Press, 1900–1918*, vol. 3, edited by Lucy Delap, Maria DiCenzo, and Leila Ryan. New York: Routledge, 2006.

Sutton, Jane. *House of My Sojourn: Rhetoric, Women, and the Question of Authority*. Tuscaloosa: University of Alabama Press, 2010.

Sweeney, Fionnghuala. *Frederick Douglass and the Atlantic World*. Liverpool: Liverpool University Press, 2007.

Tague, Ingrid H. *Women of Quality: Accepting and Contesting Ideals of Femininity in England, 1690–1760*. Suffolk: Boydell Press, 2002.

Tannen, Deborah. *The Argument Culture: Moving from Debate to Dialogue*. New York: Random House, 1998.

Temple, Norman J., and Edward P. Dunn. "British Debating Is Parliamentary." *Quarterly Journal of Speech* 34, no. 1 (1948): 50–53.

Terrell, Mary Church. *A Colored Woman in a White World*. New York: G. K. Hall & Co., 1996.

Tetrault, Lisa. *The Myth of Seneca Falls: Memory and the Women's Suffrage Movement, 1848–1898*. Chapel Hill: University of North Carolina Press, 2014.

Thale, Mary. "The Case of the British Inquisition: Money and Women in Mid-Eighteenth Century London Debating Societies." *Albion: A Quarterly Journal Concerned with British Studies* 31, no. 1 (1999): 31–48.

———. "The Robin Hood Society: Debating in Eighteenth-Century London." *London Journal* 22, no. 1 (1997): 33–50. DOI: 10.1179/ldn.1997.22.1.33.

———. "Women in London Debating Societies in 1780." *Gender & History* 7, no. 1 (1995): 5–24.

Turner, Kathleen J., ed. *Doing Rhetorical History: Concepts and Cases*. Tuscaloosa: University of Alabama Press, 1998.

Von Burg, Alessandra Beasley. "Mobility: The New Blue." *Quarterly Journal of Speech* 100, no. 2 (2014): 241–57.

Wade, Melissa Maxcy. "The Case for Urban Debate Leagues." *Contemporary Argumentation & Debate* 19 (1998): 60–65.

Waggenspack, Beth. "Women Emerge as Speakers: Nineteenth-Century Transformations of Women's Role in Public Arenas." In *The Rhetoric of Western Thought,* edited by James L. Golden, Goodwin F. Berquist, William E. Coleman, and J. Michael Sproule, 218–36. Dubuque, IA: Kendall-Hunt Publishing Company, 2004.

Wallace, Karl R., ed. *History of Speech Education in America: Background Studies.* New York: Appleton-Century-Crofts, 1954.

Wang, Bo. "Rethinking Feminist Rhetoric and Historiography in a Global Context: A Cross-Cultural Perspective." *Advances in the History of Rhetoric* 15, no. 1 (2012): 28–52.

Ware, Susan. *Beyond Suffrage: Women in the New Deal.* Cambridge, MA: Harvard University Press, 1981.

Warnick, Barbara. *The Sixth Canon: Belletristic Rhetorical Theory and Its French Antecedents.* Columbia: University of South Carolina Press, 1993.

Wasserstein, Bernard. *Herbert Samuel: A Political Life.* Oxford: Oxford University Press, 1992.

Waters, Robert. *Intellectual Pursuits, or, Culture by Self-Help.* New York: Worthington Company, 1892.

Weaks-Baxter, Mary, Christine Bruun, and Catherine Forslund. *We Are a College at War: Women Working for Victory in World War II.* Carbondale: Southern Illinois University Press, 2010.

Welsh, Beatrice W. *After the Dawn: A Record of the Pioneer Work in Edinburgh for the Higher Education of Women.* Edinburgh: Oliver and Boyd, 1939.

Welter, Barbara. "The Cult of True Womanhood: 1820–1860." *American Quarterly* 18, no. 2 (1966): 151–74.

West, Helen C. "The History of Debating." *The Vassar Miscellany: Fiftieth Anniversary Number* (October 1915): 144–61.

Westbrook, B. Evelyn. "Debating Both Sides: What Nineteenth-Century College Literary Societies Can Teach Us about Critical Pedagogies." *Rhetoric Review* 21, no. 4 (2002): 339–56. DOI:10.1207/S15327981RR2104_2.

Whyte, Iain. *Scotland and the Abolition of Black Slavery, 1756–1838.* Edinburgh: Edinburgh University Press, 2006.

Wichelns, Herbert A. "Colleague and Scholar." *Speech Teacher* 4, no. 3 (1955): 163–64.

Wiggins, Sarah. "Gendered Spaces and Political Identity: Debating Societies in English

Women's Colleges, 1890–1914." *Women's History Review* 18, no. 5 (2009): 737–52.

Williams, Raymond. *Keywords: A Vocabulary of Culture and Society*. 2nd ed. New York: Oxford University Press, 1985.

Wolf, Naomi. *Fire with Fire: The New Female Power and How to Use It*. New York: Vintage, 1994.

Woods, Carly S. "Taking Women Seriously: Debaters, Faculty Allies, and the Feminist Work of Debating in the 1930s and 1940s." In Hogan, Kurr, Bergmaier, and Johnson, *Speech and Debate as Civic Education*, 53–63.

———. "(Im)Mobile Metaphors: Toward an Intersectional Rhetorical History." In *Standing in the Intersection: Feminist Voices, Feminist Practices in Communication Studies*, edited by Karma Chávez and Cindy Griffin, 78–96. Albany: State University of New York Press, 2012.

———. "Women Debating Society: Negotiating Difference in Historical Argument Cultures." PhD diss., University of Pittsburgh, 2010.

Woods, Carly S., Joshua P. Ewalt, and Sara J. Baker. "A Matter of Regionalism: Remembering Brandon Teena and Willa Cather at the Nebraska History Museum." *Quarterly Journal of Speech* 99, no. 3 (2013): 341–63.

Woods, Carly, and Takuzo Konishi. "What Has Been Exchanged? Towards a History of Japan–US Debate Exchange." In *Proceedings of the 3rd Tokyo Conference on Argumentation*, edited by Takeshi Suzuki and Aya Kubuta, 271–79. Tokyo: Japan Debate Association, 2008.

Woody, Thomas. *A History of Women's Education in the United States*. New York: Octagon Books, 1966.

Wright, Tom F., ed. *The Cosmopolitan Lyceum: Lecture Culture and the Globe in Nineteenth-Century America*. Amherst: University of Massachusetts Press, 2013.

Yoakam, Doris G. "Pioneer Women Orators of America." *Quarterly Journal of Speech* 23, no. 2 (1937): 251–59.

Young, Fred Douglas. *Richard M. Weaver, 1910–1963: A Life of the Mind*. Columbia: University of Missouri Press, 1995.

Young, Iris Marion. *Inclusion and Democracy*. Oxford: Oxford University Press, 2001.

———. *Intersecting Voices: Dilemmas of Gender, Political Philosophy, and Philosophy*. Princeton: Princeton University Press, 1997.

Zaeske, Susan. *Signatures of Citizenship: Petitioning, Antislavery, and Women's Political Identity*. Chapel Hill: University of North Carolina Press, 2003.

———. "The 'Promiscuous Audience' Controversy and the Emergence of the Early Women's Rights Movement." *Quarterly Journal of Speech* 81, no. 2 (1995): 191–207.

Zaeske, Susan, and Sarah Jedd. "From Recovering Women's Words to Documenting Gender Constructs: Archival Research in the Twenty-First Century." In Parry-Giles and Hogan, *The Handbook of Rhetoric and Public Address*, 184–202.

Zarefsky, David. "Public Address Scholarship in the New Century: Achievements and Challenges." In Parry-Giles and Hogan, *The Handbook of Rhetoric and Public Address*, 67–85.

———. "What Does an Argument Culture Look Like?" *Informal Logic* 29, no. 3 (2009): 296–308. Http://ojs.uwindsor.ca/ojs/leddy/index.php/informal_logic/article/view/2845/2277.

———. "Four Senses of Rhetorical History." In Turner, *Doing Rhetorical History*, 19–32.

———. *Lincoln, Douglas, and Slavery: In the Crucible of Public Debate*. Chicago: University of Chicago Press, 1990.

Zarefsky, David, and Victoria Gallagher. "From 'Conflict' to 'Constitutional Question': Transformations in Early American Discourse." *Quarterly Journal of Speech* 76, no. 3 (1990): 247–61.

Zboray, Ronald J., and Mary Saracino Zboray. "Women Thinking: The International Popular Lecture and Its Audience in Antebellum New England." In Wright, *The Cosmopolitan Lyceum*, 42–66.

———. *Everyday Ideas: Socioliterary Experience among Antebellum New Englanders*. Knoxville: University of Tennessee Press, 2006.

Zompetti, Joseph P. "Personalizing Debating: Diversity and Tolerance in the Debate Community." *Contemporary Argumentation & Debate* 25 (September 2004): 26–39.

Zulick, Margaret, and E. Anne Laffoon. "Enclaved Publics as Inventional Resources: An Essay on Generative Rhetoric." In *Argument in Controversy: Proceedings of the Seventh SCA/AFA Conference on Argumentation*, edited by Donn W. Parson, 249–55. Annandale, VA: Speech Communication Association, 1991.

Index